SEATTLE

Welcome to Seattle

Seattle is a city of many personalities: eclectic, urban, outdoorsy, artsy, gritty, down-to-earth, or posh—it's all here, from the quirky character of the eccentric "Republic of Fremont," to hipsters walking baby carriages past aging mansions on Capitol Hill. There's something for just about everyone within this vibrant Emerald City. Taking a stroll, browsing a bookstore, or enjoying a cup of coffee can feel different in every one of Seattle's neighborhoods. It's the adventure of exploring that will really introduce you to the character of Seattle.

TOP REASONS TO GO

★ **Fresh seafood:** Shop for local produce and seafood at the Pike Place Market, and then eat at Seattle's renowned restaurants.

★ **Craft beer:** Seattle is so obsessed with the stuff that its annual Beer Week lasts for two.

★ **Art and architecture:** Chihuly Garden and Glass is located at the base of the Space Needle.

★ **Coffee culture:** Seattle may be the birthplace of Starbucks, but you'll find cool local coffee shops on every corner.

★ **Gardens and parks:** Visit Alki Beach or stroll through the Olympic Sculpture Park.

Contents

Fodor's Features

MAPS

Chapter 1

EXPERIENCE
SEATTLE

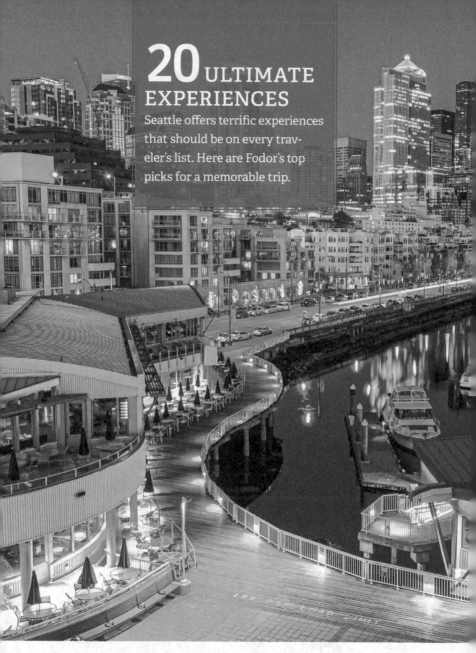

20 ULTIMATE EXPERIENCES

Seattle offers terrific experiences that should be on every traveler's list. Here are Fodor's top picks for a memorable trip.

1 Seattle waterfront

Along the waterfront, stretching down Elliott Bay from the Olympic Sculpture Park to Pioneer Square, you can walk the piers to catch the Washington State Ferry, grab a cup of chowder, check out the Seattle Aquarium, or hop on the Seattle Great Wheel. *(Ch. 3)*

2 Pike Place

A tradition since 1907, Pike Place is among the oldest continuously operated public farmers' markets in the U.S. and draws locals and tourists alike. *(Ch. 3)*

3 Burke Museum of Natural History

Founded in 1899, the Burke Museum has living exhibits on paleontology, archaeology, biology, and contemporary culture in an enormous modern facility. *(Ch. 12)*

4 The Children's Museum

Let your children wander through an immersive world of imagination in this 18,000-square-foot exhibition, updated in 2022. If they can dream it, they can be it. *(Ch. 4)*

5 The Seattle Center

Enjoy the city's cultural spoils here—five museums, performing arts spaces, a giant fountain, parks, an arena, the Space Needle, and plenty of food to try. *(Ch. 4)*

6 Sky View Observatory

Head 902 feet up to the 73rd floor of the Columbia Center downtown for incredible 360-degree views of Seattle's magnificent skyline attractions. *(Ch. 3)*

7 Olympic Sculpture Park

This 9-acre outdoor sculpture art park is filled with enormous works within a sprawling natural path weaving past Elliott Bay. *(Ch. 3)*

8 Chihuly Garden and Glass

Considered to be among the modern masters in glasswork, artist Dale Chihuly is behind Seattle's unique and vibrant technicolor sculptural garden. *(Ch. 4)*

9 Visit the Original Starbucks

Opened in 1975 across from Pike Place Market, the "Original Starbucks" is technically its second location, but it's still exciting for many to pay respects to the storefront. *(Ch. 3)*

10 Woodland Park Zoo

Come get up close and personal with more than 900 animals representing more than 250 species at this historic zoo dating back to 1899. *(Ch. 9)*

11 Space Needle

Erected for the 1962 World's Fair, this 602-foot-tall internationally renowned Space Age–era relic remains a quintessential Seattle experience. *(Ch. 4)*

12 The Seattle Public Library

This 11-story building has a distinctive design with tremendous space that can hold up to 1.45 million books, along with an innovative "Books Spiral," that winds up four stories. *(Ch. 3)*

13 Underground tours

Underneath the streets lies a whole subterranean layer of tunnels, bypasses, and secrets. See the gritty underground via a fascinating tour. *(Ch. 5)*

14 Pioneer Square

Anchored between Chinatown and SoDo District just steps away from the waterfront, Pioneer Square is considered the heart of Seattle's historic downtown. *(Ch. 5)*

15 Fremont Troll

Inspired by Scandinavian folklore, this towering mixed media statue is the work of four local artists and large enough to clutch a full-sized Volkswagen Beetle. *(Ch. 9)*

16 Volunteer Park

Seattle's largest park is 534 acres of winding woodland trails, picturesque sea-cliff views, sprawling open meadows, and other natural landscapes. *(Ch. 8)*

17 Smith Tower Observatory

Travel back in time at this scenic 35th floor historic skyscraper lounge with a Prohibition-era speakeasy and scenic views for miles from an open-air deck. *(Ch. 5)*

18 Seattle Aquarium

The ninth largest aquarium in the U.S, the big showstopper here is a 360-degree view, 400,000-gallon glass tank showcasing the life swimming around Puget Sound. *(Ch. 3)*

19 Museum of Pop Culture

Learn the stories behind the ascension of rock legends like Prince and Nirvana; see props and costumes from *A Nightmare on Elm Street* and *Buffy the Vampire Slayer*. *(Ch. 4)*

20 Museum of Flight

If it flies, then it's probably here at this 185,000 square-foot aviation museum that's home to 175 aircraft and spacecraft vehicles. *(Ch. 13)*

WHAT'S WHERE

1 Downtown and Belltown. Popular tourist spots including the waterfront, iconic Pike Place Market, and Seattle Art Museum are here. Belltown is home to the Olympic Sculpture Park.

2 South Lake Union and Queen Anne. Queen Anne rises up from Seattle Center to the Lake Washington Ship Canal. South Lake Union has the REI superstore, Museum of History and Industry, and a nice lakefront.

3 Pioneer Square. Seattle's oldest neighborhood has historic redbrick and sandstone buildings.

4 Chinatown–International District. The I.D. is a fun place to shop and eat. The stunning Wing Luke Museum anchors the neighborhood.

5 First Hill and the Central District. Nicknamed "Pill Hill", the First Hill neighborhood has the Frye Art Museum. Farther east is the Central District, with beautiful churches, street art, and a renaissance of Black business ownership.

6 Capitol Hill and Madison Park. One side is young and edgy, full

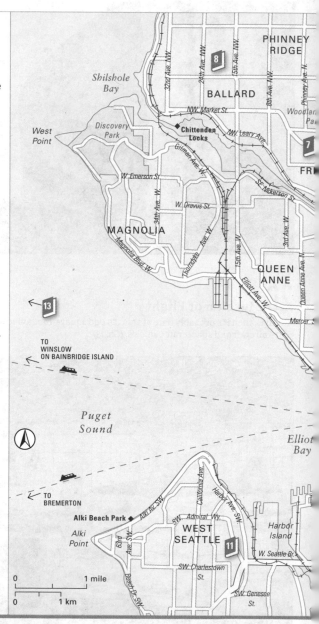

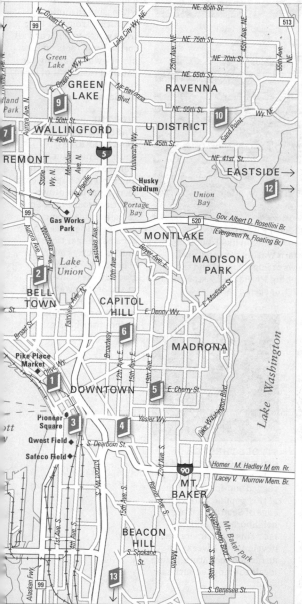

of artists, musicians, and students. The other is elegant and upscale, with 19th-century mansions.

7 Fremont, Phinney Ridge, and Greenwood. Fremont is a mix of pricey boutiques and restaurants. Phinney Ridge includes the Woodland Park Zoo.

8 Ballard. This historically Scandinavian neighborhood is now booming with new builds and trendy bars.

9 Wallingford and Green Lake. Wallingford starts at the Ship Canal with Gas Works Park. Green Lake's park has a three-mile paved path that circles the lake.

10 The University District. The University of Washington's vast campus is lovely, and the surrounding neighborhood can be both gritty and inviting.

11 West Seattle. West Seattle's California Avenue has appealing shops and restaurants.

12 Eastside. These suburbs are home to Microsoft. Bellevue has its own skyline, an art museum, and high-end shops.

13 Side Trips from Seattle. Visit the Islands, Mt. Rainier, and Olympic National Park.

Seattle's Natural Wonders

TAKE IN VIEWS FROM DISCOVERY PARK

The largest park in Seattle is a wonder in itself, but it also offers views of many of Western Washington's natural wonders. Sweeping bluff views of Puget Sound and the Olympic Mountains and stunning Mt. Rainier vistas are all visible from various points in this scenic park.

CRUISE THE LOCKS

On a nice day, the views from the Argosy Cruises Locks tour between Elliott Bay and Lake Union are magical. Aside from witnessing the unique transition from salt to fresh water, you'll learn all sorts of cool facts on local history while passing the nautical rush hour of large fishing vessels and seaplanes.

RIDE THE WASHINGTON STATE FERRIES

Tours are nice, but if you want to pack in something quick 'n' easy, hop a scenic ferry from Downtown Seattle across Puget Sound to Bainbridge Island. You can't beat the price ($9.25 for a passenger ticket), and its hourly commuter schedule from Colman Dock on the prime strip of the Seattle waterfront makes it easy to arrange an impromptu boat ride without the hassle.

HIKE MT. SI OR MT. RAINIER

If Seattle's steep streets aren't enough for you, spend an afternoon trekking the trails. Mt. Si is the most popular: the 8-mile trek goes to 3,900 feet. Mt. Rainier National Park, with over 260 miles of trails with forests, lakes, and a network of glaciers, should be on your bucket list.

STROLL THROUGH GOLDEN GARDENS PARK

Take a walk along the rugged 300-foot shoreline at this popular park at the edge of Seattle's Ballard neighborhood. Built in 1907, this historic site was developed as a weekend attraction for nature-loving locals to enjoy the surf and sand.

Mt. Si and Mt. Rainier

KAYAK OR PADDLEBOARD AT THE NORTHWEST OUTDOOR CENTER

If you'd rather navigate the water than be a passenger, head to the Northwest Outdoor Center to rent a kayak or paddleboard for an afternoon around Lake Union and Puget Sound. Kayak rentals are reasonable for budget-conscious travelers, ranging from $23 to $40 per hour, with kayak instructors and organized trips available if you'd like to join a crew. Northwest Outdoor Center offers classes in sea and river kayaking, as well as stand-up paddleboarding. The company has been around since 1980, so you can be sure you're in good hands with them.

BIKE ALONG THE WATERFRONT

For Seattle denizens, biking is more than just a mode of transportation or a leisurely pastime—it's a way of life. When visiting, expect to share the road when you hit the 8½-mile Seattle Waterfront Pathway. Smooth pavement and endless views of the Elliott Bay shoreline make this bike path a must for experiencing the best of coastal nature and city sights on wheels. The trail will wiggle a bit until construction finishes near the Pike Street Hillclimb and the Lenora Street Bridge, but eventually brings riders to the Olympic Sculpture Park and Myrtle Edwards Park, where another path continues north.

GO WHALE-WATCHING

The whale-watching in Puget Sound and the San Juan Islands is legendary—a dream that many will still travel the world for. There are many ways to have an encounter, including boat rides, seaplanes, and guided kayak tours. Peak season happens from May to October.

Seattle's Best Cafés

LIGHTHOUSE ROASTERS

The dream of the '90s is alive at this cozy coffee shop and roastery that has been keeping Fremont caffeinated with expertly curated and meticulously roasted small-batch artisan brews since 1993. Using a vintage cast-iron roaster, Lighthouse is all about the slow drip.

MR. WEST

No, it's not the famous Mr. West you're probably thinking of—though this café-bar concept is certainly cool enough to name-drop. With two locations in Downtown and University Village, this trendy all-day café serves breakfast and lunch items like toasts topped with aged cheddar, honey, and sea salt; local-market Greek yogurt topped with apple compote; and an herbed pork meatball sandwich with fontina and mornay on demi-baguette. Their sleek, plant-filled interior is inviting; you might even want to stay and wind down after coffee with some beer or wine.

VICTROLA COFFEE ROASTERS

Victrola is among Seattle's must-see destinations for coffee geeks. Named for the Victrola phonograph that was popular in the 1920s, this roaster and café pays homage to that decade through their aesthetic and vibe of their spaces. Top-notch latte art and sumptuous small batch roasted brews make this among the best places for a coffee tasting. Coffee might be taken seriously here, but the vibe is laid back with plenty of room to bring a group without worrying about a table.

ELM COFFEE ROASTERS

Modern with a touch of twee, this sunny contemporary roastery and café nestled in Pioneer Square isn't just a great place to sip a solid brew—it's a place to get educated on coffee beans from around the world. Learn to cup and brew like a certified barista or come see how beans are roasted on-site through windows that offer views into the back room. Grab a freshly baked pastry courtesy of local favorite Salmonberry Goods, and take a seat at the long marble bar where you can sip on lightly roasted brews and chat with friendly baristas. Elm Coffee Roasters showcase vibrant blends from places like Ethiopia, Rwanda, and Colombia. If you have a discerning palate, you're sure to taste the subtle notes of their unique blends. A second location in South Lake Union shares the same characteristics, minus the on-site roastery.

FULCRUM COFFEE

Though the roastery sits in SoDo, Fulcrum's café is located just north of Seattle Center, making it convenient to step into the bright, modern space and taste through its unique selection of single-origin beans from China, Myanmar, and elsewhere.

BOON BOONA COFFEE
Brewing exclusively African beans, Boon Boona takes inspiration from the Eritrean and Ethiopian coffee worlds and translates that into a community-oriented specialty coffee shop. The spacious original location is in suburban Renton, but the 12th Avenue location is in the traditional heart of the city's Ethiopian community and convenient from Downtown and Capitol Hill.

HELLO EM VIET COFFEE & ROASTERY
On the edge of the Little Saigon section of the Chinatown-International District, this little roastery and snack shop sits just inside a community center. The original twists on Vietnamese-style coffees and sandwiches go well with the history of the neighborhood printed on the walls.

MONORAIL ESPRESSO
Quick, convenient, and classic, these small counters serve excellent espresso drinks to passers-by on Downtown Seattle streets. Started as one of the city's (and country's) first coffee carts, all three locations are now stationary, but maintain that old-school streetside feeling from literal holes in the wall.

MILSTEAD AND CO.
The city's best third-wave, multiroaster cafe, this Fremont shop makes for the best place to fall in love with a bean, explore new methods of brewing, or simply learn more about coffee and what you like to drink.

ESPRESSO VIVACE
One of Seattle's pioneering coffee roasters, Vivace stays true to its roots with precise Italian-style roasting and brewing. Either of its two cafes (in South Lake Union and on Capitol Hill) offers classic Pacific Northwest coffeeshop experiences, but the sidewalk café across Broadway from the flagship location gives the truest feeling of the early '90s coffee scene Vivace helped build.

What to Eat and Drink in Seattle

SEATTLE DOG
Every city has its signature hot dog topping, and Seattle's is the surprising—and surprisingly good—squiggle of cream cheese. People tend to be dubious until they try it, so stop by any hot-dog cart, especially the late-night ones parked outside bars in Capitol Hill, Belltown, and Pioneer Square.

LOCALLY ROASTED COFFEE
Seattle's coffee reputation has long been tied to the hometown chain, Starbucks, but it's smaller independent roasters like Broadcast, Cáfe Avole, and Lighthouse that locals love, and that keep the city caffeinated.

FRESHLY SHUCKED OYSTERS
The cold, clean waters of the Pacific Northwest brim with nutrients, which produces crisp, briny oysters that are the pride of the region. The rare, native Olympia oyster, specifically, garners the most praise. The state is home to America's largest shellfish farm and you can find these flavorful delights throughout Seattle. Look for weekday-afternoon happy hours for a discounted dozen paired with a delicious beverage.

RAINIER CHERRIES
Washington's apples might make headlines, but Seattleites wait all year for Rainier cherries, the two-tone (golden and pink), ultra-sweet gems named, of course, for the nearby landmark. The eponymous delights arrive midsummer.

WILD SALMON
Seattle is undeniably a seafood town, and its most famous product might just be wild salmon, whose color is a rainbow of pink, orange, and red. The dish graces many menus and sushi bars.

GEODUCK
Less famous than the salmon and oysters, but most symbolic for locals, this giant saltwater clam (pronounced "gooey-duck") is the purest taste of local merroir (flavor of the sea). Surprisingly sweet and crunchy, you can eat it cooked or raw, though it looks most impressive when viewed whole.

PHO
If you've ever wondered how Seattle survives the damp and dark of winter here, the answer lies at the bottom of a bowl of this subtle, fragrant Vietnamese noodle soup, found every few blocks. Vietnamese food, in general, is very popular in the city, but hot noodle soup filled with beef or vegetables particularly complements rainy days.

CRAFT-BREWED IPA

Craft breweries serve as a second home for most Seattleites, and nobody dare open one without serving their version of the hoppy Northwest India pale ale. Ballard is a certified brewery destination, though excellent small-batch breweries are sprinkled across various Seattle neighborhoods.

TERIYAKI

Lesser known than some of the others on this list, Seattle-style teriyaki is a classic workday lunch here. The affordable package of grilled meat with sweet sauce, a pile of fluffy white rice, and a crisp salad sells from small strip-mall shops and corner stores.

WASHINGTON WINE

Woodinville is the destination for oenophiles in the Pacific Northwest, with many wineries to tour and vintners to learn from. If you can't make it out for a tasting in Woodinville, check menus for sips of Washington's acclaimed wines, including those from Walla Walla, which is often compared to Napa Valley in quality.

Free and Almost Free

WASHINGTON PARK ARBORETUM

Get lost in over 230 acres and 10,000 native plants at Seattle's premier oasis for flora and fauna fanatics. Explore gardens brimming with indigenous plants, shoreline marshes and wetlands, paved woodlands, flowering cherries and dogwoods, plus one of the largest Japanese maple collections in North America.

KERRY PARK

Don't judge Kerry Park by its small size—it's unanimously agreed upon that this is where you'll find the best panoramic views of Seattle. In fact, you might get a little déjà vu while up there; it's the backdrop featured in '90s pop culture classics like *Frasier* and *10 Things I Hate About You*. Located on Queen Anne Hill's south side, from here you can see the Space Needle and Elliott Bay. It's a moderately steep hike or a quick drive from Seattle Center, and more of a lookout than a park, but well worth the visit. The park also features an abstract sculpture made of steel by artist Doris Totten Chase, entitled *Changing Form*, installed in the early 1970s.

KEXP GATHERING SPACE

This big, bright indoor space takes its name from the user-powered radio station that broadcasts from here. Check out if a band is recording a live show, browse the current art exhibit, or just relax in the comfy chairs to hang out, use the free Wi-Fi, and listen to the (obviously great) tunes.

HIRAM M. CHITTENDEN LOCKS

Watch boats lowered and raised on these historic locks that separate Lake Washington, Lake Union, and Salmon Bay from the tidal waters of Puget Sound. Underground is a viewing area where salmon migrate throughout the year. Rangers give excellent free public tours.

FRYE ART MUSEUM

Soak up daring contemporary art from late-19th- and early-20th-century local and international masters at this innovative art museum located in Seattle's First Hill neighborhood. Frequently rotating exhibitions bring life to contemporary issues, where you can discover famous and emerging voices.

VOLUNTEER PARK
The influential landscape architectural firm, the Olmsted Brothers, designed this iconic urban park. It encompasses one of Seattle's first reservoirs built in 1900, along with the Volunteer Park Conservatory, the Seattle Asian Art Museum, and a seasonal wading pool during the summer. The water tower's observation deck offers one of the best views in Seattle, at no cost beyond the toll that the 107 steps to the top take on your legs.

DISCOVERY PARK
Boasting 534 acres of winding woodland trails, picturesque sea-cliff views, sprawling open meadows, and other natural landscapes all nestled right in the heart of the Magnolia neighborhood, Discovery Park is the largest park in Seattle and is considered its natural crown jewel. Two miles of protected tidal beaches with a historic lighthouse and high bluffs give it the feel of a sanctuary away from busy city life.

COAST GUARD MUSEUM
Seattle is the last frontier onto the Pacific ocean, so make time to stretch those sea legs exploring its incredible shipping history—all free of charge. Nestled within the Seattle waterfront at Pier 36, the Coast Guard Museum is where you can discover over 15,000 photographs dating from the mid-1800s, and the largest public collection of Coast Guard patches, historic memorabilia, vintage uniforms, and restored artillery.

Seattle's Best Music Venues

Burlesque, jazz, R&B, punk, grunge, indie rock, and everything in between—Seattle has no shortage of legendary musicians that have put the city on the map. Today you can catch national touring acts alongside emerging talent at these renowned venues.

THE SHOWBOX AND THE SHOWBOX SODO

The Showbox has hosted many famous names on its stage since opening in 1939. This stunning art deco theater, situated right near Pike Place, long provided a stage for stadium headliners like Pearl Jam and Prince. Its sister theater, The Showbox SoDo, opened in 2007. Formerly a warehouse, this converted concert venue has a more industrial vibe.

NEUMOS AND BARBOZA

Neumos (née Neumos Crystal Ball Reading Room), is a scrappy little mid-size club pulling in Capitol Hill's indie crowd for dance parties and live shows. In the basement is bar and club Barboza.

THE CROCODILE

This long-running indie rock club got a new location that shed its legendary grunginess while keeping its legendary status as one of the birthplaces of grunge music. The new location includes multiple venues and bars, plus an attached hotel, and keeps the reputation for headlining talent. Catch national acts, local bands, comedy shows, and Mario Kart tournaments, and grab a drink at The Society, the adjoining craft cocktail bar.

TRACTOR TAVERN

If your vibe leans more rock and country, Tractor Tavern is your down-home destination for live music. Anchoring Ballard's historic district since 1994, they host acts from reggae and bluegrass to rockabilly and folk.

SUNSET TAVERN

A former Chinese restaurant turned dive bar and club, this trendy watering hole in the Ballard neighborhood is a destination for cool up-and-coming indie shows. In the front is Betty's Room, a wood-paneled cocktail lounge inspired by a basement lounge that belonged to the owner's family friends.

BALLARD SUBSTATION

The high-quality sound system at this venue means that shows can get loud for a small crowd. Expect niche styles and up-and-coming bands, with a focus on metal, bass, and electronic styles. The main room gives intimate, living room vibes, with a full bar, while the annex has more of a warehouse feel.

THE NEPTUNE

The Neptune dates back to 1921 when it first operated as The U-Neptune Theatre playhouse screening silent films and live performances. In 2011, it got a complete remodel and restoration, keeping its classic movie-house feel but creating an excellent performing arts space for music, comedy, cinema, lectures, and more.

THE PARAMOUNT

Over its nearly century-long tenure, this French baroque-style performing arts ballroom and theater on the National Historic Register has featured a never-ending line up of epic shows including Pink Floyd and the Grateful Dead.

THE TRIPLE DOOR

The Triple Door first opened as a vaudeville house in 1926, transformed into a cinema, and eventually became the dinner-music theater of today in 2002. Chow down on food from its from sister restaurant Wild Ginger while watching a wide variety of national acts, leaning toward jazz, cabaret, and reggae.

What to Listen to by Decade

From funk to punk and everything in between, Seattle's music scene has constantly evolved. A wide variety of artists have discovered their sound in Seattle. If you're searching for musical inspiration, tune into local radio station KEXP for Seattle's latest and greatest.

THE '60S AND '70S

The Seattle funk scene, though not as prevalent today, was very much alive in the mid-'60s to early '70s, with about 20 clubs hosting live soul and funk acts on any given night (it's even how Kenny G got his start). While few of the names from that movement gained national fame, other local performers of the time did, including Quincy Jones and Ray Charles. In the rock realm, Seattle-born Jimi Hendrix has gone down in history as one of the greatest guitarists and songwriters of all time, and his legacy is still honored in Seattle today.

THE '80S

Punk was alive in the '80s in Seattle, with influence from other Pacific Northwest cities like San Francisco. Prominent bands included the Fastbacks, the Melvins, Green River, and Bam Bam, which influenced many early grunge bands. Heart rose to fame from Bellevue.

THE '90S

Seattle will always be proud of its association with Kurt Cobain, the late great golden boy of grunge. Nirvana was signed to seminal Seattle label Sub Pop, which gave rise to the grunge movement, and was also the home of bands like Mudhoney. Alice in Chains and Pearl Jam also formed in the early '90s, while Soundgarden peaked around then, too. Hole, fronted by the infamous Courtney Love, came out with *Live Through This* in 1994, their best-known and most accessible album— tracks like "Miss World" were written in Seattle. Kathleen Hanna of Bikini Kill, the Julie Ruin, and Le Tigre, is credited as being one of the most influential female punk artists, not just in the Pacific Northwest but everywhere. The birthers of the Riot Grrrl movement, Bikini Kill put out the perfectly '90s punk album *Revolution Girl Style Now!* in 1991, inspiring acts like Sleater-Kinney (also originally out of Olympia, Washington), and influencing contemporaries like Nirvana. Hip-hop was also prevalent at this time, with one of most notable PNW-based acts being Sir Mix-a-Lot.

THE 2000S

Grunge dissipated and evolved into indie pop, and the Seattle sound favored ethereal production over rawness. Joining the Sub Pop label were bands like Fleet Foxes, Sunny Day Real Estate, the Postal Service, Death Cab for Cutie, and more.

TODAY

Rapper Macklemore is probably one of the most famous contemporary artists out of Seattle, but the city continues to pump out amazing artists across a wide range of genres, including Brandi Carlile, Car Seat Headrest, the Head and the Heart, Odesza, Parisalexa, and Tacocat.

Space Needle 101

Ready for a 42-second elevator ride to the future? When it was built for the future-focused "Century 21" World's Fair in 1962, the Space Needle symbolized Seattle's innovative spirit and technological might. Today, the 605-foot spire is one of the world's most recognizable skyline landmarks and the city's most popular tourist attraction, with a revolving restaurant and an observation deck in the flying saucer-like Tophouse.

WHAT WENT INTO THE NEW-AND-IMPROVED SPACE NEEDLE?

Many years in the planning, the Century Project involved a large global team of experts and the creation of a new kind of glass before it was completed in 2019. More than 100 crew members worked around the clock during the installation phase of the renovation, which was done in sections to keep the Space Needle open to visitors. To install the floor-to-ceiling glass enclosure for the observation deck, a special crane hoisted glass panels weighing more than a ton around 520 feet in the air, where the panels were set in place using a custom robotic arm with giant suction cups. It's a true feat of engineering, as is the glass rotating floor that's the first of its kind in the world.

IS IT WORTH THE CROWDS AND THE PRICE?

The Space Needle has always been a popular tourist attraction, with crowds zipping up the elevator hundreds of times a day to take in epic 360-degree views of the city, mountains, and Puget Sound. The original observation deck design included a solid guardrail and horizontal metal safety cables that got in the way of a seamless panorama. Now there's nothing between you and the bird's-eye views but glass. Wrapping all the way around the observation deck at 520 feet, a series of 11-foot-tall, 7-foot-wide glass panels start at the floor and tilt outward. Glass benches around the perimeter follow the angle of the transparent walls, making a jaw-dropping backdrop for selfies. Even on cloudy days, you can see for what seems like forever. A striking grand staircase leads down to the 500-foot level, where floor-to-ceiling glass walls and a high-tech glass revolving floor overlook the ground below.

SHOULD I GO IF I'M AFRAID OF HEIGHTS?

That depends. Do you just get a little nervous or are we talking full-on acrophobia? Space Needle tours start in an elevator that holds 25 people and has windows so you can watch your rapid ascent. Your stomach might drop a little on the 42-second ride up. Once you've reached the Tophouse, you'll be surrounded by glass, so there's no getting around how high off the ground you are, especially inside the 500-foot level with glass floors. Looking down isn't for the faint of heart.

WHY WOULD I VISIT TWICE IN ONE DAY?

The Space Needle offers a two-visit package that's well worth it if you have the time. On a clear day, you'll enjoy sweeping views of the city, the mountains, and the glittering Puget Sound. Even when it's gray and drizzly, the city and water views are unparalleled. For your second visit, there are a couple of options. During the summer, Seattle sunsets are sublime, and there's no better perch than the needle for watching the sun go down over the sound. If you can't swing sunset, return after dark, when the city sparkles all around you. You can even glimpse ferries gliding through the inky waters of Elliott Bay on their way to the islands in the distance.

WHERE CAN I GET THE BEST SHOTS OF THE SPACE NEEDLE FROM THE GROUND?

You can spot the Space Needle from many parts of the city, but the most famous vantage point is Kerry Park on the south slope of Queen Anne. In a posh part of town, the park features a large terrace that overlooks the city and bay and offers an unobstructed view of the Space Needle. On especially clear days, snow-capped Mt. Rainier rises behind the city just to the right of the Space Needle. Alki Beach in West Seattle also boasts a panoramic view starring the famous landmark.

DO LOCALS EVER VISIT?

Most Seattleites have been to the Space Needle at least a few times, usually with out-of-town visitors in tow. On the Fourth of July and New Year's Eve, locals pour into Seattle Center to ooh and aah at fireworks above the Space Needle. World-famous local radio station KEXP, which has its HQ in Seattle Center, provides music for the elaborate explosions of light and color.

SHOULD I BUY TICKETS IN ADVANCE?

There are definitely advantages to buying tickets in advance, especially during the peak summer season. Tickets are timed so you don't have to wait in line for long. The downside? You might pick a day with lousy weather (though it's still worth going!). You can pre-purchase tickets the day of your visit, as well, to save a bit of cash and guarantee your spot.

ARE THERE ANY DISCOUNTS OR PACKAGE DEALS?

If you plan to do a lot of exploring, you'll save up to 45 percent using the popular Seattle CityPASS ticket booklet. For $115 (or $87 for kids 12 and under), the pass, which lasts for nine days from first use, includes a day/night admission (good for two visits in 24 hours) to the Space Needle, as well as tickets to the Seattle Aquarium, plus three option tickets for your choice of the Argosy Harbor Cruise, MoPOP, the Woodland Park Zoo, and Chihuly Garden and Glass.

HOW DO I GET THERE?

The Seattle Center Monorail must've seemed so futuristic when it was built for the World's Fair in 1962. Today it's a charming throwback that whisks tourists from Westlake Center—close to many of Seattle's hotels—to Seattle Center. One-way fares are $3.25 for adults and $1.50 for kids 5 to 12 (kids under 5 are free). You can also get to the Space Needle by foot, bus, or car, but riding the monorail is a classic part of the experience.

Seattle Today

Seattle doesn't stand on convention. From its well-earned reputation for quirky music and art to its laid-back population of obsessive foodies, the city defies easy categorization. You're as likely to see millionaires riding the bus as PhDs behind the counter at a coffee shop. Grizzled fishermen at Ballard bars mingle with mustachioed hipsters, techies in performance clothing, and tattooed moms. It's an international city, with a strong Asian influence and a history of innovation. This is a place that successfully rallied for the statewide legalization of marijuana, yet people still refuse to jaywalk, even during protests.

TODAY'S SEATTLE

… is influenced by its environment. The Seattleite way of life is shaped by the mountains, water, and massive evergreen trees that hang like verdant shrouds over Craftsman homes. You can see it in Seattleite fashion—for many, waterproof gear and sensible shoes take precedence over trends. You can see it in the hobbies—Seattle is thought to have the highest ownership of pleasure boats per capita in the country, and this outdoorsy, active population is constantly on a hike, bike, or paddle adventure (REI started here for a reason). With such a connection to nature, Seattleites are rabid recyclers and composters and the city has enacted a ban on Styrofoam takeout containers, plastic bags, and plastic straws. The rain makes the population introspective and dark—which they channel into wildly imaginative writing, art, and music.

… is highly educated. This is a city of nerds. Go ahead, make that obscure reference to Hessian fighters or binary code—you'll find an appreciative audience. Seattle is the most educated city in the country, and constantly vies for most literate with Minneapolis. It has always attracted educated, creative people, from the first influx of Boeing engineers and University of Washington students to today's high-tech innovators.

… is liberal, progressive, and alternative. One of the most liberal cities in the country, Seattle can be counted on to vote overwhelmingly Democrat in any given election. This progressive hotbed is also host to one of the largest LGBTQ+ populations, one of the highest mixed-race populations nationwide, and a hugely influential alternative press—including *The Stranger* and various neighborhood blogs. Which is not to say they're always tolerant, especially when it comes to politicizing treatment of marginalized and houseless people.

… is growing. Fast. With a near-constant influx of newcomers arriving, the population is growing ahead of the national average. Transplants now outweigh natives—a fact many old-timers lament. Hemmed by the geographical limits of mountains and water, the city has had no choice but to expand skyward. Density is growing, as are light rail and other forms of mass transit. And not a moment too soon, as roads and housing are bursting at the seams. Luckily, the city is walkable and bikeable, and most neighborhoods are well equipped with all the necessities within walking distance. With all this expansion, housing costs are sky-high, and Seattle is fast becoming one of the most expensive cities in the U.S. Understandably, you won't see a lot of kids—only San Francisco boasts fewer families with children. Dogs, however, are another story—the canine-to-kid ratio is decidedly in Fido's favor.

Seattle Then and Now

THE EARLY DAYS

"There is plenty of room for one thousand settlers. Come at once." Upon receiving his brother's note, Arthur Denny set out from Portland on the schooner *Exact* with two dozen settlers. It landed at Alki Point on November 13, 1851.

The Denny party wasn't the first to arrive at the wild land that would become the Emerald City, though: the Duwamish tribe had been living there for millennia, and British explorers surveyed the same spot in 1792. But Arthur Denny was the first of Seattle's many mad visionaries. He dreamed of creating a future endpoint for the transcontinental railroad, one to rival the already steadily developing Portland. The party moved to Elliot Bay's eastern shore in 1852; in 1853, the first boundaries of the city were marked on present-day Pioneer Square and Belltown, and Seattle—named after Chief Seattle (Si'ahl) of the Duwamish and Suquamish tribes—was born.

Despite a 1856 attack on the settlement by displaced Native Americans, Seattle's rise continued. Before the city was named, Denny had persuaded Henry Yesler to build a steam-powered sawmill here, which quickly turned the city into a major lumber producer. Even being snubbed by the Northern Pacific Railroad (which chose Tacoma for its western terminus) couldn't deter the founders: they built their own small rail lines from the city to outlying coal deposits and watched their city boom while Tacoma waited for its rail link.

THE GOLD RUSH

Amid all the growth came a series of disasters. In 1889, the Great Fire burned 64 acres. Then the "Panic of 1893" stock-market crash crippled the local economy. Seattle seemed down on its luck until, in 1897, a boat docked carrying gold from the Klondike, heralding the last Gold Rush.

The city quickly repositioned itself as the "Gateway to Alaska" (Alaska being the preferred point of entry into the Klondike). The assay office that journalist Erastus Brainerd convinced the federal government to open was just part of the city's Gold Rush revenue—Canada's Northwest Mounted Police required that each prospector show up with a year's worth of supplies, and Seattle merchants profited heavily from the edict.

FLOATPLANES AND POSTWAR PROSPERITY

William E. Boeing launched his first floatplane from Lake Union in 1916. This marked the start of an industry that would define the city and long outlast timber. World War I bolstered aircraft manufacturing enough that Boeing moved south to a former shipyard.

Seattle was devastated by the Great Depression, with its only growth the result of New Deal programs that built parks, housing, and roads, including the floating bridge that links Seattle and Mercer Island. Entry into World War II again buoyed shipbuilding and aircraft industries, though at a moral cost: Boeing produced the B-29 bomber, the aircraft used to drop atomic bombs on Hiroshima and Nagasaki.

Seattle's renewed prosperity, which prompted it to host the 1962 World's Fair, remained tethered to Boeing. The early '70s "Boeing Bust," when loss of federal funding caused Boeing to lay off tens of thousands of employees, sunk the city back into recession. After that, although Boeing would remain an influential employer, new industries began to take its place. In 1963, Seattle spent $100 million to upgrade its port in a successful bid to lure cargo traffic from Asia away from Portland and San Francisco. In 1970, six Japanese shipping lines started calling at Seattle.

THE TECH BOOM AND TODAY'S SEATTLE

The tech boom may have defined the '90s, but its roots in Seattle stretch back to the '70s. In 1978, Microsoft moved from Albuquerque to the Eastside suburb of Bellevue, bringing the first influx of tech money—even today "Microsoft money" is shorthand for wealthy techies (Microsoft moved to its current Redmond campus in 1986). In 1994, Amazon.com became incorporated in the State of Washington; it is now one of Seattle's largest employers and has such a significant presence in South Lake Union that many locals refer to it as Amazonia. Although the dot-com bust temporarily took the wind out of Seattle's entrepreneurial sails, the city continued to define itself as a major tech player, with companies such as Facebook, Google, and Tableau having local offices. And an increasing number of other companies are basing themselves here, including Expedia, Zillow, AllRecipes, and Redfin. Today, the metro area of almost four million holds a diverse portfolio: one part of the port is dominated by container ships while the other side welcomes Alaska-bound ships to Smith Cove Cruise Terminal. The food and beverages industries are a major part of the economy, with coffee giant Starbucks and MOD Pizza standing alongside such major seafood companies as Trident Seafoods.

Like tech, the gaming industry is huge here, with Big Fish Games, PopCap, Nintendo of America, and Wizards of the Coast based in the metro area. T-Mobile's national headquarters is here, too, as is a long list of hardware companies. The University of Washington is a national leader in medical research, and a biotech hub is rising in the city center. Retail giants Nordstrom, Tommy Bahama, REI, Costco, and, of course, Amazon, keep money flowing into the area.

IMPORTANT DATES

1851: Denny party arrives in Seattle.

1853: Washington Territory formed; Seattle loses out to Olympia as state capital.

1861: University of Washington is established.

1889: Seattle's Great Fire destroys the commercial core.

1889: Washington becomes the 42nd state.

1903: John C. Olmsted arrives; his master plan creates most of the city's parks.

1907: The city annexes Ballard, West Seattle, and Southeast Seattle, doubling its size.

1910: Washington women get the vote, 10 years before the rest of the nation; of course it would be another 50 years until women of color gained suffrage nationwide.

1911: The Port of Seattle is created, with public control of waterfront.

1919: Port workers initiate first general strike in the nation.

1941: After Pearl Harbor is attacked, 8,000 Japanese immigrants are sent to internment camps.

1951: First Seafair festival commemorates the centennial.

1962: The World's Fair (and Space Needle) opens and runs for six months.

1982: Visitors Bureau starts using nickname "Emerald City." Seattle has also been called Queen City, Jet City, Rat City, and, of course, Rain City.

1999: World Trade Organization protests occur in Seattle.

2001: Seattle's sesquicentennial coincides with a 6.8 earthquake that causes more than $1 billion in damage.

2004: The Central Library opens, the crown jewel in the city's massive "Libraries for All" project.

2009: Sound Transit completes its first light rail project, the Central Link, connecting Downtown to Sea-Tac.

2013: The 57-foot-diameter "Bertha" boring machine breaks ground on an ambitious tunnel to replace the aging Alaska Way Viaduct.

2015: The *New Yorker* publishes Pulitzer-winning "The Really Big One," which predicts a devastating PNW earthquake.

2016: The city celebrates a newly expanded light-rail system and passes a $54 billion transit bill to keep the improvements coming.

2017: Pike Place Market debuts a new expansion, and Seattle continues to develop a new, tourist-friendly waterfront.

2018: Space Needle unveils a $100 million renovation, adding the world's first revolving glass floor.

2021: Seattle's newest major league sports team, the Seattle Kraken, plays its first game as part of the National Hockey League.

Seattle with Kids

Seattle is great for kids. After all, a place where floatplanes take off a few feet from houseboats and where harbor seals might be spotted on a routine ferry ride doesn't have to try too hard to feel like a wonderland. And if the rain falls, there are plenty of great museums to keep the kids occupied. A lot of child-centric sights are easily reached via public transportation, and the piers and the Aquarium can be explored on foot from most Downtown hotels. A few spots (the Ballard Locks and Discovery and Gas Works Parks) are easier to visit by car.

MUSEUMS

Several museums cater specifically to kids, and many are conveniently clustered at the Seattle Center. The Center's winning trio, the **Pacific Science Center,** which has interactive exhibits and IMAX theaters; the **Children's Museum,** which has exhibits on Washington State and foreign cultures plus plenty of interactive art spaces catering to kids ages 10 months to 10 years; and, of course, the **Space Needle,** all underwent remodels and upgrades between 2018 and 2022. For older, hipper siblings there's a skate park; the Vera Project, a teen music and art space; and **MoPOP**.

Downtown there are miles of waterfront to explore along the piers. The **Seattle Aquarium** is here and has touch pools and adorable otters—what more could a kid want?

PARKS AND OUTDOOR ATTRACTIONS

Discovery Park has an interpretive center, a Native American cultural center, easy forest trails, and accessible beaches. **Alki Beach** in West Seattle is lively and fun; a wide paved path is the perfect surface for wheels of all kinds—you can rent bikes and scooters, or take to the water on rented paddleboats and kayaks.

Gas Works Park has great views of the skyline, floatplanes over Lake Union, and the evocative rusty remnants of the old machinery, some of which is now a climbable play structure. **Volunteer Park** and **Green Lake** have wide lawns and shallow pools made for splashing toddlers.

The **Woodland Park Zoo** has 250 different species of animals from jaguars to mountain goats, cheap paid parking, and an adjacent playground; stroller rentals are available. Watching an astonishing variety of boats navigate the ship canal at the **Ballard Locks** entertains visitors of any age.

HOTELS

Downtown, the **Hotel Monaco** offers a happy medium between sophisticated and family-friendly. The colorful, eccentric decor will appeal to kids but remind adults that they're in a boutique property. Fun amenities abound, like optional goldfish in the rooms and toys in the lobby. Surprisingly, one of the city's most high-end historic properties, the **Fairmont Olympic,** is also quite kid-friendly and unveiled a $25 million restoration and remodel in 2022. The grand staircases in the lobby will awe most little ones, and there's a great indoor pool area. In addition, the hotel offers babysitting, a kids' room-service menu, and toys and board games.

Several properties offer kitchenette suites that help families save some money on food costs. The **Silver Cloud Inn** in Lake Union has suites with kitchens. It's north of Downtown on Lake Union, but the South Lake Union streetcar is across the street and gets you into Downtown and to bus connections quickly.

Seattle's Best Parks

Mountain ranges, ocean waters, and islands surround the city, but Seattleites are often content to stay put on sunny weekends. Why? Because the incredible park system makes for fantastic outdoor adventures, offering opportunities for everything from throwing beach rocks into the ocean against the backdrop of the Olympics to hiking under canopies of old growth, and from eating ice cream next to gurgling fountains in the center of town to wandering pathways of a traditional Japanese garden.

Luckily for today's residents, more than a century ago the city's Board of Commissioners had the wisdom to hire the Olmsted Brothers (who inherited the firm from Frederick Law Olmsted, designer of New York's Central Park) of Brookline, Massachusetts, to conduct a survey of the potential for a park system. J. C. Olmsted's visionary plan not only placed a park, playground, or playing field within walking distance of most homes in Seattle, it also created a 20-mile greenway connecting many of the urban parks, starting at Seward Park on Lake Washington and traveling across the city to Woodland Park and Discovery Park. Later the architect created plans for the campus of the University of Washington and the Washington Park Arboretum.

What follows are our top picks for best parks in the city.

(See also the Neighborhood listings for more in-depth reviews of top parks.)

BEST FOR FAMILIES AND PICNICS

Cal Anderson Park. An urban park in every sense, this Capitol Hill expanse has a lovely water sculpture, a playing field, and green space. Grab an ice cream at nearby Molly Moon's (⊠ *917 E. Pine St.*) and enjoy. ⊠ *1635 11th Ave., Capitol Hill.*

Gas Works Park. Reachable by the Burke-Gilman Trail, this Wallingford park gets its name from the remains of an old gasification plant, part of which is repurposed for kids to climb on. Twenty acres of rolling green space look out over Lake Union and the city skyline, including "Kite Hill," and a large, modern playground. ⊠ *North end of Lake Union at N. Northlake Way and Meridian Ave. N, Wallingford.*

Volunteer Park. Capitol Hill's best green spot houses a plant conservatory, the Seattle Asian Art Museum (which got a $56 million remodel in 2020), a water tower, paths, and an Isamu Noguchi sculpture (along with a great view). Kids will enjoy the play structure and wading pool. ⊠ *14th Ave. E at Prospect St., Capitol Hill.*

(See also: Carkeek Park, Marymoor Park, Olympic Sculpture Park, and Warren G. Magnuson Park.)

BEST FOR SEASONAL BLOOMS

Kubota Garden. In Seattle's southern stretches, Kubota Garden's 20 acres of landscaped gardens blend Japanese and native plants and techniques. ⊠ *817 55th Ave. S, South Seattle.*

Washington Park Arboretum. This 230-acre expanse houses the University of Washington's botanical gardens, with flowering fruit trees in early spring, vibrant rhododendrons and azaleas in late spring and early summer, and brightly hued trees and shrubs in fall. ⊠ *2300 Arboretum Dr. E, Washington Park.*

(See also: Bellevue Botanical Gardens.)

BEST VIEWS

Alki Point. West Seattle comes to life in summer, and there's no better way to enjoy it than walking along this beachfront path to enjoy the sparkling views of Puget Sound, the Seattle skyline, and the Olympics. ⊠ *1702 Alki Ave. SW, West Seattle.*

Carkeek Park. North of Ballard, Carkeek has awe-inspiring views of Puget Sound and the Olympics, and sometimes even salmon swimming in Pipers Creek. Its beach, playgrounds, picnic areas, and forest trails make this a fun family spot. ⊠ *950 NW Carkeek Park Rd., Broadview.*

Discovery Park. Seattle's largest park, in Magnolia, is all about variety, with shaded forest, open meadows, pebbled beach stretches, and even sand dunes. A lighthouse, plus sweeping views of Puget Sound and the mountains make this an extremely picturesque spot, and many of the trails make good, short, kid-friendly hikes. ⊠ *3801 W. Government Way, Magnolia.*

Golden Gardens. This Ballard park, perched on Puget Sound, is the social destination of every summer day. Loads of facilities and a pretty pathway make this spot even more special. ⊠ *8498 Seaview Pl. NW, Ballard.*

Myrtle Edwards. Adjacent to the Olympic Sculpture Park, Myrtle Edwards has a bike and pedestrian path along Elliott Bay, with vistas of the sound and the mountains. ⊠ *3130 Alaskan Way W, Downtown.*

Olympic Sculpture Park. The Seattle Art Museum's nine-acre outdoor playground, located in Belltown, has fabulous views of Elliot Bay and the Olympics, complemented by huge works of art by the likes of Alexander Calder. ⊠ *Western Ave. at Broad St., Belltown.*

(See also: Gas Works Park.)

BEST WALKING TRAILS

Green Lake. The almost-three-mile loop around the lake is a favorite spot for joggers, kids, and dog walkers alike. You can rent a paddleboat and explore the waters. ⊠ *E. Green Lake Dr. N and W. Green Lake Dr. N, Green Lake.*

Seward Park. Old-growth forest, views of the mountains and Lake Washington, and a very fun walking loop make this a beloved spot on the southwest side of Lake Washington. ⊠ *5902 Lake Washington Blvd.*

Warren G. Magnuson Park. Northeast of the University District, this large green space has great playgrounds, walkable trails, and one of the largest off-leash dog parks in the city (with a designated dog beach). ⊠ *Sand Point Way NE at 65th St., Sand Point.*

(See also: Discovery Park.)

BEST SOUND-SIDE PARKS

Lincoln Park. With old-growth forest and rocky beaches, as well as facilities like a pool and tennis courts, this is a West Seattle favorite. ⊠ *5551 SW Admiral Way, West Seattle.*

(See also: Alki Point, Discovery Park, Golden Gardens Park, Lincoln Park, and Myrtle Edwards Park.)

BEST PARKS ON THE EASTSIDE

Bellevue Botanical Gardens. Perennial borders, colorful rhododendron, rock gardens, and the lovely Lost Meadow Trail fill the 36 acres of this spot in Bellevue. ⊠ *510 Bellevue Way NE, Bellevue, Eastside.*

Marymoor Park. 640 acres of fun can be found at this huge Redmond green space, including a climbing rock, tennis courts, game fields, an off-leash dog area, and a path along the Sammamish River. ⊠ *6046 W. Lake Sammamish Pkwy. NE, Redmond, Eastside.*

Chapter 2

TRAVEL SMART

Updated by
Naomi Tomky

ỉỉ POPULATION:
733,919

💬 LANGUAGE:
English

$ CURRENCY:
U.S. Dollar

☎ AREA CODES:
206

⚠ EMERGENCIES:
911

🚗 DRIVING:
On the right

⚡ ELECTRICITY:
120–220 v/60 cycles;
plugs have two or three
rectangular prongs

🕐 TIME:
Three hours behind New
York

🌐 WEB RESOURCES:
www.visitseattle.com
www.thestranger.com

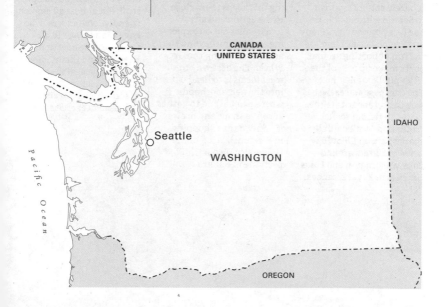

Know Before You Go

Take some trip-planning tips from locals to get prepared for your Seattle vacation. Wondering about the city's rainy reputation, which sights are free, and whether or not weed is legal? Answers to all that and more below.

IT ONLY RAINS MOST OF THE TIME

That might sound like a bad thing, but Seattle's bad rap is at odds with the city's rather pleasant year-round weather. Dry summers run from mid-June to mid-September, and while rain falls often in winter, it tends to be light, easily ignored, and at mild temperatures. The takeaway? Bring a raincoat, not an umbrella, to stay comfortable in Seattle.

BOATS ARE THE BEST

It barely counts as a visit to Seattle without at least one foray on the city's many waterways. Aside from the fun of floating around, boats make up part of the city's public transit mix. The cheapest and easiest way to hop aboard are the Water Taxis, but ferries, cruises, and sailboats all share space on Elliott Bay, while outfitters around Lake Washington and Lake Union rent kayaks, canoes, electric boats, and even boats with a hot tub built into them. Whatever the speed of the ship, the views from gliding along at water level offer a new angle to admire the region's drastic panoramas and natural wonders.

GET OUT OF (DOWN)TOWN

Seattle likes its neighborhoods, so most people don't go Downtown for much besides work or a special occasion. Visitors inclined to stay Downtown—thinking this keeps them close to the action and attractions—miss out on exploring everything beyond the area surrounding the Great Wheel. The best way to meet locals is to head out into the neighborhoods, where people tend to gather at coffee shops and breweries. Spend time shopping in Fremont, eating in the University District, and partying in Ballard.

REMEMBER: IT'S PIKE PLACE, NOT PIKE'S PLACE

Locals love the stunning market as much as the tourists, but they can spot an out-of-towner immediately when they hear people say "Pike's Place." To blend in, call it "Pike Place," or easier yet (and even more common), just "the Market." Equally importantly, avoid the summer afternoon crowds and instead join the folks who live here by grabbing breakfast and watching the vendors set up for the day.

MARIJUANA IS LEGAL, SO CHILL OUT

Sales of marijuana for recreational use are completely legal in Seattle (as long as you're 21 years or older), so pot shops pepper the town. Choosing the right spot for you to shop is like picking a liquor store: some higher-end stores carry nicer products, while divey ones sell the cheap stuff. But almost all employ friendly "budtenders" who have the answers to all your pressing questions. Keep in mind that it's not technically legal to smoke in any hotel rooms or public spaces, though, so visitors still need to exercise some caution.

IT'S COMMON TO KICK BACK AND BE CASUAL

Seattle's informality makes it almost impossible to feel out of place in a T-shirt and jeans. Grunge fizzled out in the '90s, but Seattleites really do wear a lot of flannel and fleece (basically the unofficial uniform of the Pacific Northwest), less for fashion than because the materials work perfectly for staying warm in the damp, cool weather. You rarely see anyone in formal attire, and only a few of the city's finest and most upscale restaurants encourage dressing up. Feel free to pack light by bringing only comfortable attire, or stop by REI in South Lake Union to buy something that blends in with the locals.

BRING ALONG BARKSLEY

Seattle's population includes more dogs than children, and businesses know that Fido wants to tag along, too. Hotels, bars, and even some restaurants make their dog-friendliness not just policy, but a point of pride. Even if you leave your own pup at home, expect to see a lot of them at Seattle's breweries, which almost all welcome furry friends. (If dogs aren't your thing, stick to brewpubs, which are less likely to have roaming Rovers.)

TRAFFIC IS TERRIBLE

Seattle's narrow geography, resistance to public transportation, and recent astronomic growth combine into a recipe for some horrific traffic. One small snafu can snarl roads for hours, anytime, so pack your patience and check in with the traffic cameras on ⊕ www.wsdot.com/traffic/seattle before hitting the road. Alternatively, stick to the parts of the city covered by light rail and look for the Rapid Ride buses (routes designated with a letter, rather than a number), as they run in their own lane during heavy traffic times.

THE BEST THINGS IN LIFE (AND SEATTLE) ARE FREE

Seattle's Space Needle gets the big press and the most attention from tourists, but the city hardly looks like herself from the top, since you can't see the needle itself. Take in another view by heading up to Kerry Park for the quintessential skyline scene without an entrance fee. In fact, many of Seattle's best activities cost nothing: dips in Lake Washington, visits to the Central Library, and walks in majestic Discovery Park. For folks on a strict budget, free museum days happen on the first Thursday of the month; the Center for Wooden Boats offers free sailing on Sundays; and the Pike Place Market never costs a dime (and you can probably even snag a few samples while you wander).

IT'S MORE SLEEPY THAN SLEEPLESS

For all the growth Seattle's had in recent years, it still keeps pretty sleepy hours: most restaurants close by 10 pm, and bars must completely shut down by 2 am. Only a few restaurants in the Chinatown–International District serve food past closing time and some scattered diners stay open around the clock. The flip side of this comes at 7 am, when the line already stretches to the door at local coffee shops.

DON'T MISS THE MOUNTAINS

In the Seattle area, you might hear the phrase "the mountain is out," which simply means that majestic Mt. Rainier showed up on the southern skyline. The bright and beautiful focal point makes a welcome distraction from the crowded freeway traffic, and seeing it makes most people smile. Find more stunning mountain views looking west from the city toward the Olympics, east toward the Cascades, or when Mt. Baker rises to the north.

Getting Here and Around

Hemmed in by mountains, hills, and multiple bodies of water, Seattle is anything but a linear, grid-lined city. Twisty, turny, and very long, the city can be baffling to navigate, especially if you delve into its residential neighborhoods—and you should. A good map or phone app can help you confidently explore, and you can use the transportation advice in this section to plan your wanderings around the city's sometimes confusing layout. One thing to keep in mind: Seattle's boomtown status shows in the construction sites that seem to dot every block, which can mean closed-off streets and extra traffic snarls. The Washington State Department of Transportation (WSDOT) features helpful real-time updates and camera footage of local traffic (⊕ www. wsdot.com/traffic).

 Air

Nonstop flying time from New York to Seattle is approximately five hours; flights from Chicago are about four hours; flights between Los Angeles and Seattle take 2½ hours; flights between London and Seattle are about 9½ hours; flights from Hong Kong are 13 hours.

Seattle is a hub for regional air service, as well as air service to Alaska, Hawaii, Canada, and Iceland. It's also a convenient North American gateway for flights to Australia, New Zealand, and the South Pacific. Nonstop flights between Seattle and Europe are available, though most transatlantic service involves a connection in Atlanta, Boston, Chicago, New York, or Washington, D.C. Several nonstop flights to Asia are offered.

AIRPORTS

A wide-ranging $650 million expansion plan for Sea-Tac airport has made some improvements but will not finish until 2024. In the meantime, travelers should leave plenty of time for long security lines and to reach faraway gates. Avoid the security line by reserving a time slot on the airport's website (⊕ www.portseattle.org/SEAspotsaver).

While the present Sea-Tac doesn't offer a particularly impressive array of shops and restaurants, there are enough sit-down cafés, fast-food joints, and quirky shops to keep you entertained between flights. Comfort-food lovers should proceed directly to Beecher's for their world-famous mac 'n' cheese, while Floret offers upscale vegan food. Sub Pop, the iconic Seattle music label that helped launch Nirvana, has a shop stocked with albums from bands on its roster. For longer layovers, stop into Butter London for a manicure or the Massage Bar for a quick, no-appointment-necessary back or foot massage. Charter flights and small carriers, such as Kenmore Air, that operate shuttle flights between the cities of the Pacific Northwest land at Boeing Field, which is between Sea-Tac and Seattle.

Paine Field, which until recently was mostly used by the nearby Boeing Company, reopened for commercial air service in 2019. With just three gates and nine destinations around the western United States, it's calm, clean, modern and a breeze to navigate. The only downside are the minimal amenities and almost nonexistent ground transportation.

FLIGHTS

American, Delta, Southwest, and United are among the many major domestic airlines that fly to Seattle from multiple locations. Alaska Airlines and its affiliate Horizon Air provide service from many states, including Alaska and Hawaii.

Frontier Airlines has direct flights from Denver to Seattle. JetBlue has nonstop service to Seattle from New York, Los Angeles, and Boston. Hawaiian Airlines flies daily from points in Hawaii. Air Canada flies between Seattle and Vancouver, Calgary, Toronto, and Montreal. Kenmore Air has scheduled and chartered floatplane flights from Seattle's Lake Union and Lake Washington to the San Juan Islands, Victoria, and the Gulf Islands of British Columbia.

Major global carriers such as Emirates, Cathay Pacific, and Air France, along with domestic and budget airlines serve 28 international destinations including Singapore, Dubai, and Paris.

Bicycling

Seattle's hills and its streets designed for cars seem inherently unfriendly for bikes, but recent expansions of separated bike lanes (like the one along 2nd Avenue through Downtown), bike paths, and the rise of electronic-assisted bikes make it much easier to get around by pedal power.

Bus

Greyhound Lines and Northwestern Trailways have regular service to points throughout the Pacific Northwest, the United States, and Canada from the regional Greyhound/Trailways bus terminal in SoDo, at 503 South Royal Brougham Way, making them convenient to all Downtown destinations. FlixBus, which serves Vancouver, Portland, Spokane, and points nearby and beyond, stops outside the International District light-rail station, at the University of Washington, and at Sea-Tac Airport. Quick Shuttle runs buses from Sea-Tac Airport and Downtown to Bellingham and Vancouver, BC. A public-private partnership on the Dungeness Line connects Downtown and Sea-Tac Airport to various parts of the Olympic Peninsula.

Car

Access to a car is helpful for exploring residential neighborhoods beyond their commercial centers and a necessity for trips to Mt. Rainier, the San Juan Islands, or pretty much any sight outside the Seattle limits without a group tour. Before you book a car for city-only driving, keep in mind that many high-end hotels offer complimentary town-car service around Downtown and the immediate areas, and that light rail, bus, and ferries keep it well connected to neighborhood hubs.

In the last seven years, Seattle's traffic improved from the fourth-worst in the country to barely in the top ten, thanks

Getting Here and Around

to improved public transit and a strong remote work culture. But that gives little relief when a single accident can snarl the city for the day. The worst tangles happen on the main highways (I-5 and I-90) and on the drawbridges across the Ship Canal that separates the north and south parts of the city (the Montlake, University, Fremont, and Ballard Bridges). Aurora Avenue/SR 99 gets very busy, especially where it crosses the Ship Canal. The section of Mercer Street between South Lake Union and I-5, improved as construction slowed and remote work kept Google, Amazon, and Facebook employees off the roads, but remains enough of bottleneck to keep the nickname "the Mercer Mess." Though you'll come across the occasional road-rager or oblivious driver who assumes driving an SUV makes one invincible, drivers in Seattle are generally courteous and safety-conscious. Be on the lookout for the city's many bicyclists and avoid blocking designated bike lanes, clearly marked throughout the city.

 Cruises

Seattle's expanding cruise industry now welcomes some of the world's largest ships to docks on Elliott Bay. The city's strategic location along the West Coast means that it's just a day's journey by water to Canada or California, and ships reach Alaska or Mexico in less than a week. In addition to the six major cruise lines that operate weekly service out of Seattle, local companies such as Argosy Cruises offer sailings around Elliott Bay, Lake Union, Lake Washington, or along a combination of waterways in smaller sightseeing boats.

Norwegian Cruise Line, Carnival Cruise Line, Celebrity Cruises, Holland America Line, Princess Cruises, and Royal

Caribbean all offer seven-day summer cruises from Seattle to Alaska. Some offer additional destinations, such as Princess's 16-day Hawaiian Island trip or Carnival's 17-day tri[p through the Panama Canal. Holland America Line, Princess Cruises, Celebrity Cruises, Carnival Cruise Line, Seabourn Cruise Line, and Royal Caribbean leave from the Smith Cove Cruise Terminal on Pier 91; Norwegian Cruise Line, Regent Seven Seas Cruises, Windstar Cruises, and Oceania Cruises depart from the Bell Street Pier Cruise Terminal at Pier 66. For a smaller, less traditional cruise experience, UnCruise leaves from Fisherman's Terminal for trips to Alaska and the San Juan Islands.

 Ferry

Washington State Ferries form a significant part of Seattle's transportation network and are the only way to reach points such as Vashon Island and the San Juans. Thousands of commuters hop a boat from Bainbridge Island, Bremerton, and other outer towns to their jobs in the city each day—which makes for a gorgeous and unusual commute. For visitors, ferries are one of the best ways to get a feel for the region and its ties to the sea. Plus, they're just plain fun and the Seattle routes give riders outstanding views of the skyline and the elusive Mt. Rainier.

Passenger-only King County Water Taxis depart from Seattle's Pier 50 weekdays during rush hours on runs to Vashon Island and West Seattle. In the summer, the West Seattle route sails throughout the day, seven days a week. The Vashon Water Taxi is $6.75 each way, and the West Seattle Water Taxi makes a quick journey from Pier 50 Seacrest Park in West Seattle for $5.75 each way. (Prices in cash; discounts for ORCA card users, seniors, and youth.) Several Metro bus routes stop at Pier 50—even if you've rented a car, it's a major hassle to park on the waterfront so busing is the way to go.

■TIP➔ Two free Metro shuttles take passengers directly from the West Seattle dock to the West Seattle Junction and Admiral neighborhoods.

For a great, inexpensive outing, hop on the water taxi to West Seattle, take the free shuttle, and spend the afternoon enjoying the great shopping and restaurants in West Seattle.

Clipper Navigation operates the passenger-only *Victoria Clipper* jet catamaran service between Seattle and Victoria year-round ($115–$204 round-trip). The company plans to restart its seasonal ferries between Seattle and the San Juan Islands, running May through October (prices to be announced, but previously starting at $100). Note that *Victoria Clipper* fares are less expensive on weekdays and if booked at least two days in advance, with another drop at seven days. Be sure to ask about any promotions or deals, and they also offer some great package deals online, which are, in general, your best bet for Clipper trips. Staying even one night in Victoria greatly reduces transportation rates.

The Washington State Ferry system, the largest ferry network in the country and the third largest in the world, serves the Puget Sound and San Juan Islands area (service to Sidney, BC, in Canada, is scheduled to return in 2023). Peak-season fares apply May 1 through September 30, but ferry schedules change quarterly, with the summer schedule running mid-June through mid-September. Ferries around Seattle get especially crowded during the city's weekday rush

hours and holiday events, while San Juan Islands ferries jam up on weekends, holidays, and throughout the summer. A tiered reservation system releases a portion of San Juan Island ferries at various increments leading up to travel dates. Check the Washington Department of Transportation's website (⊕ *www.wsdot. com/ferries*) as soon as you know your travel dates and prepare to book the minute they open to grab a coveted reservation. Without one, plan to be at the ferry, or have your car in line, at least 20 minutes before departure—but expect to wait several hours during heavily traveled times (on nice days, the ferry lines can take on something of a party feel, and impromptu, multicar Frisbee games are not unheard of). Walk-on and bike space is always available; if possible, leave your car behind.

You can pick up sailing schedules and tickets on board the ferries or at the terminals, and schedules are usually posted in local businesses around the docks. Note that schedules often differ from weekdays to weekends and holidays, and departure times may be altered due to ferry or dock maintenance, severe weather or tides, and high traffic volume. The Washington State Ferries website provides travel details, including weekly departure and arrival times, wait times, cancellations, and seasonal fare changes. To help guide your trip, regularly check it for service updates leading up to your trip, and keep an eye on the real-time ferry maps and the boarding status page, which gives live updates and views of the line.

Regular walk-on fares from Seattle are $9.25 to Bainbridge and Bremerton, and from Edmonds to Kingston; $6.10 from Fauntleroy in West Seattle, Point Defiance in Tacoma, or Southworth to Vashon Island; $5.65 from Mukilteo to Clinton,

Getting Here and Around

on Whidbey Island; $3.85 each way between Port Townsend and Coupeville; and $7.20 round-trip between Fauntleroy and Southworth. Round-trip rates from Anacortes to any point in the San Juan Islands run $14.85. If you'd rather head to Sidney, BC, from Anacortes when the service resumes in 2023, you need to make advanced reservations. Senior citizens (age 65 and over) and those with disabilities pay half fare; children 6-18 get a smaller discount, and those under age six ride free.

Peak-season vehicle fares (including one adult driver) are $20.90 from Seattle to Bainbridge and Bremerton, and from Edmonds to Kingston; $26.55 from Fauntleroy, Point Defiance, or South-worth to Vashon; $12.50 from Mukilteo to Clinton; and $16.20 from Fauntleroy to Southworth and Port Townsend to Coupeville. From Anacortes, peak-season vehicle and driver round-trip fares through the San Juans are $51.15 to Lopez Island, $61.25 to Orcas and Shaw Islands, and $72.65 to Friday Harbor. Shoulder-season rates are lower. The following routes accept reservations in advance (highly recommended) during summer and fall through the Save a Spot program (visit the ferries section of ⊕ *www.wsdot.wa.gov* for more information): Port Townsend/Coupeville, Anacortes/San Juans, and Anacortes/Sidney, British Columbia. For all fares, you can pay with cash, ORCA card, major credit cards, and debit cards with MasterCard or Visa logos.

⊕ Light Rail

The popular Central line runs from Angel Lake (just south of the airport) through Downtown, continues on to Capitol Hill and the University of Washington, then north to Northgate. By late 2024 or early 2025, that line is planned to expand north to Lynnwood and south to Federal Way, while a second line will run south from Lynnwood through Downtown, then turn east and stop in the Central District before crossing the lake to Mercer Island, Bellevue, and Microsoft's main campus in Redmond. More lines and stations are in the works, too, so eventually travelers should have a reliable rail route to get around instead of the hodgepodge of transit options currently offered. For now, definitely take advantage of the easy and inexpensive route from Sea-Tac Airport to Downtown, Capitol Hill, and the University District. Simply head to the Link light-rail station on the fourth floor of the airport parking garage and arrive in Downtown in 36 minutes for just $3 (youth fare is $1.50 and senior/disabled fare is $1). Trains depart every 6 or 15 minutes (depending on the time of day) and run from 5 am to 1 am Monday through Saturday and 6 am to midnight on Sunday.

⊕ Monorail

Built for the 1962 World's Fair, the country's first full-scale commercial monorail is a quick, convenient link for tourists, though it travels an extremely short route between Seattle Center and Downtown's Westlake Mall, located at 5th Avenue and Pine Street. Most travelers could walk the one-mile route without much of a struggle, but the Monorail is nostalgic, retro fun. Making the journey in just two minutes, the Monorail departs both points every 10 minutes. Hours vary by season, but in summer it runs Monday through Friday 7:30 am to 11 pm; Saturday and Sunday it runs 8:30 am to 11 pm; it's closed Thanksgiving and Christmas Day. The round-trip fare is $3.25; youth and senior citizens receive a discount and children age five and under ride free, and fares can be paid for with Orca Card or Transit Go Ticket app.

Streetcar

The city's cute-as-a-button Seattle Streetcars are a fun way to explore the Downtown core. The South Lake Union Streetcar (SLUS) links South Lake Union and Downtown, with seven stops along the 1½-mile line and connections to light rail and the Monorail. The 10-stop First Hill line connects Capitol Hill, First Hill, Yesler Terrace, Central Area, Chinatown–International District, and Pioneer Square. Streetcar frequencies vary; the South Lake Union line runs at 10-minute intervals from 7 am to 7 pm on weekdays, while the First Hill line runs every 15 minutes from 9 am to 4 pm. Both run more frequently during rush hour and less often in the late evening (the South Lake Union line stops service at 9 pm; First Hill runs until 10:30 pm). A single fare costs $2.25 (senior/disabled $1, youth $1.05, children under six are free). Tickets can be purchased from a ticket vending machine (coins and credit cards are accepted), on the Transit GO Ticket app, or deducted from an ORCA card. Streetcar-only unlimited day passes cost $4.50 ($2 senior/disabled, $3 youth).

Taxi

Seattle has a smaller taxi fleet than most major cities do, and it's not the most reliable. Taking a cab is not a major form of transportation in the city, and the city highly controls the number of taxis; accordingly, rates run high. Most people take cabs only to and from the airport and when they go out partying on weekends. You may be able to hail cabs on the street Downtown, but anywhere else, plan to call. Expect long waits on Friday and Saturday nights.

Metered taxis all run the same rate, $2.70 per mile, plus a $2.60 meter drop, and 50¢ per minute stuck in traffic. Unless you're going a very short distance, the average cost of a cab ride in the city is $10–$25 before tip. Taxis charge flat rates to and from the airport—how much varies by company, but usually starts around $45 to Downtown hotels. Conveniently, Seattle metered cabs almost always accept credit cards, and an automated system calls you on your cell phone to alert you when your cab arrives. Some of the taxi companies have apps, but none are very functional: it's still best to call, except at the airport, where taxis line up on the third floor of the parking garage.

Metered cabs are not the best way to visit the Eastside or any destination far outside the city—if you get stuck in traffic, you'll pay for it. Take the bus when possible, and ask your hotel for car-service quotes for short side trips outside city limits.

Many locals avoid cabs entirely and take advantage of app-based ride services like Uber or Lyft, both of which boast large fleets of drivers in Seattle. You'll need to download the apps in advance and

Getting Here and Around

register with a credit card; fares automatically deduct at the end of your ride. Before you book, check the current rates, which fluctuate with demand; during major events, even a short ride can cost a small fortune thanks to surge pricing.

🚈 Train

Amtrak runs daily service to Seattle from the Midwest, California, and Vancouver, BC. The *Empire Builder* takes a northern route from Chicago to Seattle, with a stop in St. Paul. The *Coast Starlight* begins in Southern California, makes stops throughout western Oregon and Washington, including Portland, and terminates its route in Seattle. The *Cascades* travels from Eugene, Oregon, up to Vancouver, BC, with several stops in between. If you want to spend a day or two in Portland, taking the train down instead of driving is a great way to do so. It's fast and comfortable, and the Amtrak station in Portland is centrally located. Sit on the left side of the train on the way down for stunning views of Mt. Rainier. All Amtrak trains to and from Seattle pull into King Street Station off South Jackson Street in the International District.

Trains to and from Seattle have regular and business-class compartments. Cars with private bedrooms are available for multiday trips (such as to Chicago), while business-class cars provide more legroom, quieter cars, and complimentary newspapers. Reservations are necessary (you can book up to 11 months in advance), and major credit cards are accepted.

Sounder Trains, run by Sound Transit, run between Seattle–Everett and Seattle–Lakewood and travel only during peak hours on weekdays. Trains leave Lakewood about every 20 minutes between 4:36 am and 6:46 am, with stops in Tacoma, Puyallup, Sumner, Auburn, Kent, and Tukwila, prior to Seattle. A shortened route from Tacoma runs a few more times in the morning and three times during evening rush hour. Southbound trains leave Seattle twice during early-morning rush hour and then regularly from 2:35 pm to 6:30 pm (some end at the Tacoma Dome). Sounder Trains from Everett offer two morning departure times at 6:15 and 7:15 am, stopping in Mukilteo and Edmonds, and two return trips from Seattle at 4:33 and 5:35 pm. (Note that there is daily Amtrak service from most of these cities, offering more departure times.)

Fares are based on distance traveled, starting at $3.25 and running up to $5.75 for the Seattle–Tacoma trip; youth, senior citizens, and the disabled receive a discounted fare, and kids under six ride free. Tickets can be purchased at machines inside the stations before you board, or you can use your ORCA card or the Transit GO Ticket app.

Essentials

Accommodations

Seattle's hotels run the gamut from high-end luxury high-rises to clever boutiques, and from historic properties to brand-new digs, but almost all of them are Downtown. Outside the city center and University District, the best options are the remaining bed-and-breakfasts scattered among the neighborhoods, though the few rooms there tend to go quickly.

For more information about lodging options and for prices, see hotel listings within each chapter.

Most hotels and other lodgings require your credit-card details before confirming your reservation. If you don't feel comfortable booking your hotel online, call the property to give them this information over the phone. However you book, get confirmation in writing and have a copy of it handy when you check in.

Be sure you understand the hotel's cancellation policy. Some places allow you to cancel without any kind of penalty—even if you prepaid to secure a discounted rate—if you cancel at least 24 hours in advance. Others require you to cancel a week in advance or penalize you the cost of one night. Small inns and B&Bs are most likely to require you to cancel far in advance. Most hotels allow children under a certain age to stay in their parents' room at no extra charge, but others charge for them as extra adults; find out the cutoff age for discounts.

■TIP➔ **Assume that hotels don't include breakfast in the cost of your room unless we specify that breakfast is included.**

Another option for visitors that continues to grow in popularity is Airbnb (⊕ *www.airbnb.com*). Using Airbnb's website or app, you can browse and book apartments and houses all over the city, from budget-friendly spare bedrooms to truly beautiful and spacious digs. Airbnb is a unique way to experience Seattle like a local and stay outside of commercial centers. Its vast offerings feature a broad range of amenities and prices. VRBO (Vacation Rental by Owner; ⊕ *www.vrbo.com*) offers a similar service.

Earthquakes

Seattle is earthquake country, and the impending "big one" could happen next week—or it could happen in 50 years. But far more likely, you might experience the regular gentle rustles. The last major earthquake in the area was in 2001 (magnitude 6.8) with only one related death (a heart attack). Following that, the city tore down the Alaskan Way Viaduct, a major earthquake hazard. The good news is that because it is earthquake country, most buildings are built to withstand a pretty severe shaking. If you experience an earthquake here, follow the locals, who train with earthquake protocols from a very young age: drop, cover, and hold on. Get as low as you can to the ground and try to stay under a table or at least between pieces of furniture. A major earthquake may bring aftershocks and tsunami warnings for the waterfront areas.

Essentials

Events

Visit Seattle keeps a full calendar of events at ⊕ *www.visitseattle.org/things-to-do/events*.

■TIP→ **Some area restaurants use alternative tipping models, including getting rid of it altogether in favor of slightly higher food prices. Menus and servers generally make a note of any untraditional policies.**

ⓢ Taxes

There is a 15.7% hotel tax in Seattle for hotels with more than 60 rooms, plus an additional $2 per room charge per night. In Bellevue the rate is 14.5%. Renting a car in Seattle will set you back 9.7% in tax, and there are additional taxes for renting cars at the airport.

The sales tax in Seattle is 10.25% and is applied to all purchases except groceries and prescription drugs.

ⓢ Tipping

Tips and service charges are usually not automatically added to a bill in the United States (except when your party is over six people). If service is satisfactory, customers generally give waitstaff, taxi drivers, barbers, hairdressers, and so forth, a tip of from 18% to 20% of the total bill. (Be aware that tipping waitstaff less than 20% is considered a sign that service was bad.) Bellhops, doormen, and porters at airports and railway stations are generally tipped $1 for each item of luggage. In Seattle, there is no recognized system for tipping concierges. A gratuity of $2–$5 is suggested if you have the concierge arrange for a service such as restaurant reservations, theater tickets, or car service, and $10–$20 if the service is more extensive or unusual, such as having a large bouquet of roses delivered on a Sunday.

Tours

Bike Tours

Seattle Bicycle Tours

BICYCLE TOURS | Explore the city by standard or electric bicycle, the latter of which makes even the local hills rideable for all levels. The Emerald City Tour covers 13 miles as it goes by the Olympic Sculpture Park, Ballard Locks, and Fremont, almost entirely on Seattle's car-free bike paths. Reservations are required and can be made online. ✉ *11 Vine St., Downtown* ☎ *206/697–9611* ⊕ *www.seattlebicycle-tours.com* From $65.

Boat Tours

Argosy Cruises

BOAT TOURS | Seattle's unique geography, with hills cascading down to the waterfront, means that some of the best views come from the water. Argosy's boats have indoor and outdoor spaces with seating and full-service bars. The one-hour harbor loop shows you the Downtown skyline and surrounding mountains, while a two-hour cruise goes through the Ballard Locks and passes by the Space Needle, Olympic Sculpture Park, and Gas Works Park. ✉ *1101 Alaskan Way, Pier 55, Suite 201, Downtown* ☎ *206/623–1445* ⊕ *www.argosycruises.com* From $35.

 Driving Tours

Show Me Seattle

DRIVING TOURS | Show Me Seattle offers a huge variety of tours; their basic orientation tour takes up to 14 people in vans on three-hour tours of the major sights. ✉ *8110 7th Ave. S, Seattle* ☎ *206/633–2489* ⊕ *showmeseattle.com* From $66.

Walking Tours

Beneath the Streets

WALKING TOURS | This guided tour of Seattle's underground and Pioneer Square above it takes an honest look at the city's history. Along with the daily one-hour tour, the company offers an adults-only tour on weekends, and a queer history tour every other Friday. ✉ *102 Cherry St., Pioneer Square* ☎ *206/624–1237* ⊕ *www.beneath-the-streets.com* From $27.

★ Chinatown Discovery Tours

WALKING TOURS | The Wing Luke Museum offers tours of the Chinatown–International District, some with food samples. Reserve ahead. ✉ *719 S. King Street, International District* ☎ *206/623–5124* ⊕ *www.wingluke.org* From $24.95 ⊗ *Closed Mon.–Tues.* ☞ *Food tours happen on Friday, and the theme changes quarterly. Most other tours outside the museum run on Saturday.*

Seattle Architecture Foundation

WALKING TOURS | These expert-led two-hour tours of Downtown cover specialized styles or neighborhoods, including art deco skyscrapers and hidden places; community tour options include Ballard's maritime history and the South Lake Union tech boom. Tours operate on Saturday year-round, and Thursday–Sunday in spring and summer. ✉ *1010 Western Ave., Downtown* ☎ *206/667–9184* ⊕ *seattlearchitecture.org/tours* From $20.

Seattle Free Walking Tours

WALKING TOURS | The two-hour Seattle 101 takes you through Downtown, the waterfront, and Pioneer Square; a shorter Pike Place Market tour includes samples. ✉ *Victor Steinbrueck Park, 2001 Western Ave, Seattle* ☎ *425/770–6928* ⊕ *www.seattlefreewalkingtours.org* Pay what you wish ☞ *Reservations required.*

Great Itineraries

Seattle in 5 Days

Though Seattle's not always the easiest city to navigate, it's small enough that you can see a great deal of it in a week. If you've only got a long weekend here, you can easily mix and match any of the days in this itinerary. Before you explore, you'll need three things: comfortable walking shoes, layered clothing, and a flexible mindset: it's easy and advisable to meander off track.

DAY 1: PIKE PLACE MARKET AND DOWNTOWN'S MAJOR SIGHTS

Spend the first day seeing some of the major sights around Downtown. Get up early and stroll to Pike Place Market. Grab a latte or have a hearty breakfast at a café, then spend the morning wandering through the fish, fruit, flower, and crafts stalls. When you've had your fill, head south to the Seattle Art Museum or take the steps down to the docks and visit the Seattle Aquarium. Alternatively, stroll to Belltown to take in the views at the Olympic Sculpture Park or getting a roving view of the landscape from atop the new Seattle Great Wheel. Stop for a simple lunch at Pasta Casalinga or Le Pichet. If you're not too tired, do some late-afternoon shopping at Nordstrom, Pacific Place Mall, Westlake Center, and the surrounding area. Eat dinner and get drinks in Downtown or in Belltown, where terrific restaurants give you a taste of that famous Pacific Northwest cuisine.

DAY 2: SEATTLE CENTER OR PIONEER SQUARE

Hop the two-minute monorail ride from Downtown's Westlake Center to the Seattle Center, then travel up the Space Needle for 360-degree city views. Take in one of Seattle Center's many ground-level attractions: the Pacific Science Center, the Children's Museum, the Chihuly Garden and Glass exhibit, or the Museum of Pop Culture (MoPOP). If you didn't visit it the day before, walk southwest down Broad Street to the Olympic Sculpture Park. From there, take a cab or bus to the Chinatown–International District. Visit the Uwajimaya Asian Market, stroll the streets, and have dinner in one of the neighborhood's many restaurants.

Option: If you don't want to start out with the Space Needle, skip Seattle Center and start your day in Pioneer Square. Tour a few galleries (most of which open late morning), peek into some shops, and then head to nearby International District for more exploring—don't miss the Wing Luke Museum of the Asian Pacific American Experience. If you still want to see the Space Needle, you can go after dinner; the observation deck stays open late in summer.

DAY 3: SIDE TRIPS FROM THE CITY

Now that you've seen some of the city, get out of town and get closer to nature. Hikers have almost too many options, but Mt. Rainier National Park never disappoints—though lines can get long to enter in the summer. Crystal Mountain, a popular ski resort (from Highway 410, turn left onto Crystal Mountain Boulevard just before the entrance to the national park), offers gondola rides to the summit, where you can take in unparalleled views of Mt. Rainier and the Cascade Range (to get back to the base, hop back on the gondola or hike down). Plan a whole day for a hiking excursion to this area. Closer and shorter hike options pepper I-90 from the suburbs to the other side of the

Cascades; Rattlesnake Ledge is a short, close hike (though sometimes this also means quite crowded). When you return to the city, tired and probably ravenous, grab a hearty, casual meal and check out some live music on Capitol Hill or the University District.

If you'd rather take to the water, get on a ferry and visit either Bainbridge or Vashon islands. Bainbridge is more developed, but the pretty island has large swaths of protected land with trails. At the Bloedel Reserve, trails pass through a bird refuge, forest, and themed gardens, including a Japanese garden and moss garden. The limit on the number of daily visitors keeps it serene (make reservations). Vashon is more agricultural and low-key. The most popular way to explore either island is by bicycle, though note that Bainbridge has some hills. Both islands have beach strolls, many shops, and good restaurants, so grab a bite before heading back into the city. Exploring the island takes less time than a hiking excursion, so you can probably see one or two sights Downtown before going to the dock. If you haven't made it to the Aquarium yet, its proximity to the ferry makes it a great option.

DAY 4: STEPPING OFF THE TOURIST TRAIL

Since you covered Downtown on days 1 and 2, today you can sleep in a bit and explore some of the different residential neighborhoods. Check out Capitol Hill for great shopping, strolling, café culture, and people-watching. Or head north of the Lake Washington Ship Canal to Fremont and Ballard. Wherever you end up, you can start your day by having a

leisurely breakfast or getting a coffee fix at an independent coffee shop. To stretch your legs, make the rounds at Volunteer Park in Capitol Hill or follow the Burke-Gilman Trail from Fremont Center to Gasworks Park. Both the Woodland Park Zoo (slightly north of Fremont) and the Hiram M. Chittenden Locks (also known as the Ballard Locks) are captivating. In Capitol Hill or in the northern neighborhoods, you'll have no problem rounding out the day by ducking into shops and grabbing a great meal. If you're looking for late-night entertainment, you'll find plenty of nightlife options in both areas, too.

DAY 5: LAST RAYS OF SUN AND LOOSE ENDS

Spend at least half of your last day in Seattle outdoors, exploring Discovery Park or renting kayaks in the University District, from Agua Verde Café and Paddle Club, for a trip around Portage Bay or into Lake Washington. Linger in your favorite neighborhood (you'll have one by now). Note that you can combine a park visit with kayaking if you head to the Washington Park Arboretum and Japanese Garden first. From there, it's a quick trip to the U-District.

Contacts

Air

AIRPORTS King County International Airport (Boeing Field). ☎ 206/296–7334 ✎ kciacustsvc@kingcounty.gov ⊕ www.kingcounty.gov/services/airport.aspx. **Paine Field.** ✉ 3300 100th Street SW, Everett ☎ 425/622–9040 ✎ info@propellerairports.com ⊕ www.flypainefield.com. **Seattle–Tacoma International Airport.** ✉ 17801 International Blvd., Seattle ☎ 206/787–5388, 800/544–1965 ⊕ www.portseattle.org/sea-tac.

AIRLINES Air Canada. ☎ 888/247–2262 ⊕ www.aircanada.com. **Alaska Airlines.** ☎ 800/252–7522 ⊕ www.alaskaair.com. **American Airlines.** ☎ 800/433–7300 ⊕ www.aa.com. **Delta Airlines.** ☎ 800/221–1212 for U.S. reservations, 800/241–4141 for international reservations ⊕ www.delta.com. **Frontier.** ☎ 602/333–5925 ⊕ www.flyfrontier.com. **Hawaiian Airlines.** ☎ 800/367–5320 ⊕ www.hawaiianairlines.com. **JetBlue.** ☎ 800/538–2583 ⊕ www.jetblue.com. **Kenmore Air.** ☎ 866/435–9524 ⊕ www.kenmoreair.com. **Southwest Airlines.** ☎ 800/435–9792 ⊕ www.southwest.com. **United Airlines.** ☎ 800/864–8331 ⊕ www.united.com.

Taxi

Green Cab. ☎ 206/575–4040 ⊕ greencab.me. **Orange Cab.** ☎ 206/522–8800 Seattle, 253/852-1607 South King County, 425/453–0919 Eastside ⊕ www.orangecab.net. **Yellow Cab.** ✉ Seattle ☎ 206/622–6500 for Seattle, 253/872-5600 for South King County, 425/455–4999 for Eastside ⊕ www.seattleyellowcab.com.

Train

Amtrak. ☎ 800/872–7245 ⊕ www.amtrak.com.

Bus

Metro Transit. ✉ Seattle ☎ 206/553–3000 for customer service, schedules, and information ⊕ metro.kingcounty.gov. **ORCA Card.** ☎ 888/988–6722 ⊕ www.myorca.com. **Shuttle Express.** ✉ Seattle ☎ 425/981–7000 ⊕ www.shuttleexpress.com. **Sound Transit.** ☎ 888/889–6368 ✎ main@soundtransit.org ⊕ www.soundtransit.org.

Ferry

Washington State Ferries. ☎ 206/464–6400, 888/808–7977 ⊕ www.wsdot.wa.gov/ferries. **King County Water Taxi.** ☎ 206/477–3979 ✎ watertaxi.info@kingcounty.gov ⊕ www.kingcounty.gov/depts/transportation/water-taxi.

♀ Visitor Information

Seattle Visitors Center. ✉ 701 Pike St., Suite 800, Downtown ☎ 206/461–1888 ⊕ www.visitseattle.org. **Washington State Parks.** ✉ 1111 Israel Rd. SW, Olympia ☎ 360/902–8844 for general information, 888/226–7688 for campsite reservations ⊕ www.parks.wa.gov. **Washington Tourism Alliance.** ☎ 800/544–1800 ⊕ www.experiencewa.com.

Chapter 3

DOWNTOWN
AND BELLTOWN

Updated by
AnnaMaria Stephens

● Sights	🍴 Restaurants	🛏 Hotels	🛍 Shopping	🍸 Nightlife
★★★★★	★★★★☆	★★★★★	★★★★★	★★★★☆

NEIGHBORHOOD SNAPSHOT

TOP REASONS TO GO

■ Find your perfect souvenir—along with yummy breakfast or lunch—at **Pike Place Market.**

■ Visit the **Seattle Art Museum**—consider doing it on a First Thursday or during a Remix event.

■ Hit the **shopping areas**: On Pike and Pine between 4th and 6th Avenues are favorite chains, department stores, and high-end labels. Belltown has boutiques, design stores, and a big branch of Patagonia. Western Avenue on the waterside of the market has upscale furniture stores that are fun to browse.

■ Take a stroll in the **Olympic Sculpture Park,** or, if you're traveling with kids, beeline for the **Seattle Aquarium** to watch sea otters frolic.

GETTING AROUND

Downtown and Belltown are easy to explore on foot, but if you head down to the waterfront, be prepared for some major hills on the way back up. Third Avenue is Seattle's bus transit corridor, and not very pedestrian-friendly; while it's fine for catching a bus, be aware the area also has problems with crime.

PLANNING YOUR TIME

All Downtown itineraries should include a stop at Pike Place Market, the Olympic Sculpture Park, and the Seattle Art Museum. If you have children, consider the aquarium, a ride on the Seattle Great Wheel, and the sights along the waterfront.

Try to arrive at Pike Place Market in the morning, before cruise ships have docked. The aquarium also gets crowded midday, but it's a happy chaos and preferable to negotiating the midday market crowds.

Even though the shops are concentrated in small areas, a comprehensive shopping tour will take all day—plan to hit Belltown when you get tired, as there are good cafés along 1st and 2nd Avenues.

VIEWFINDER

■ As you walk along Downtown's 1st Avenue, you'll notice view corridors and public stairways that connect to the waterfront tucked between some of the tall modern buildings. Right next to the posh Four Seasons Hotel (1st and Union Street) you'll find a small viewing deck that's a popular public spot for watching sunsets over Elliott Bay and the Seattle Great Wheel; the stairway leads down to Western Avenue and the waterfront. But the most pleasant public gathering spot and access point is actually a wide stairway park with multiple levels of café seating next to the Harbor Steps Apartments at 1st and University Avenue. It's a perfect place to rest and regroup while taking in lovely views and lots of great people-watching.

Except for the busy areas around the market and the piers, and the always-frenetic shopping district, a lot of Downtown can often seem deserted, especially at night. Still, while it may not be the soul of the city, it's definitely the heart, and there's plenty to do—nearly all of it easily reachable by foot.

There's the city's premier art museum, the eye-popping Rem Koolhaas–designed Central Library, lively Pike Place Market, and a major shopping corridor along 5th Avenue and down Pine Street. And, of course, there's the water: Elliott Bay beckons from every crested hill. Within the core of Downtown—which is bounded on the west by Elliott Bay and on the east by I–5, stretching from Virginia Street to Yesler Way—are several different experiences. The waterfront and much of 1st Avenue are lively and at times quite touristy, thanks to Pike Place Market, the Seattle Art Museum (SAM), and the piers, which have several kid-friendly sights as well as ferries to Bremerton and to Bainbridge Island. As you head east from Pike Place Market, you soon hit Downtown's shopping and entertainment district. The flagship Nordstrom department store is here, and the Westlake Center also offers some opportunities to part with your money. Heading south of Pike Street, the Central Business District holds mostly office and municipal buildings. There are a few sights scattered about, including the library, a handful of art galleries, and a sampling of higher-end shops. There are a few major cultural sights, too, including the Seattle Symphony's elegant concert venue, Benaroya Hall. North of Downtown, Belltown beckons with hip shops, bars, and restaurants, as well as the free waterfront Olympic Sculpture Museum, which has beach access and some of the best views in town.

Downtown

Sights

★ Pike Place Market
MARKET | **FAMILY** | One of the nation's largest and oldest public markets dates from 1907, when the city issued permits allowing farmers to sell produce from parked wagons. At one time the market was a madhouse of vendors hawking produce and haggling with customers over prices; now you might find fishmongers engaging in frenzied banter and hilarious antics, but chances are you won't get them to waver on prices. There are many restaurants, bakeries, coffee shops (including the flagship Starbucks, which usually has a long line), and lunch counters—go to Pike Place hungry and you won't be disappointed. The flower market is also a must-see—gigantic fresh arrangements can be found for around $12. It's well worth wading through dense crowds to

Sights ▼

1 Olympic
  Sculpture Park **A2**
2 Pike Place Market **E5**
3 Seattle Aquarium **E6**
4 Seattle Art Museum **F6**
5 Seattle Great Wheel **E7**
6 The Seattle
  Public Library **H6**
7 Steinbrueck
  Native Gallery **D4**
8 Suyama Peterson
  Deguchi **D3**
9 Traver Gallery **F6**

Restaurants ▼

1 Ben Paris **F5**
2 Charlotte Restaurant
  & Lounge **H7**
3 El Gaucho **D4**
4 Jerk Shack **C3**
5 Le Pichet **E5**
6 Lola **F3**
7 Matt's in the Market **E5**
8 Metropolitan Grill **G7**
9 The Pink Door **E5**
10 Place Pigalle **E6**
11 Serious Pie **E4**
12 Shiro's Sushi
   Restaurant **C3**
13 Six Seven **B4**
14 Sushi Kashiba **E5**
15 Tavolàta **C3**

Quick Bites ▼

1 Anchorhead Coffee **D5**
2 Cherry Street Coffee ... **G8**
3 Dahlia Bakery **E3**
4 Ellenos Real
  Greek Yogurt **E5**
5 Macrina Bakery **C3**
6 Mr. West Cafe Bar **G3**
7 Storyville Coffee **F5**

Hotels ▼

1 Ace Hotel **C3**
2 The Alexis Royal
  Sonesta Hotel **G7**
3 The Charter Hotel **F4**
4 The Edgewater **B4**
5 The Fairmont
  Olympic Hotel **H6**
6 Four Seasons Hotel
  Seattle **F6**
7 Grand Hyatt Seattle **H4**
8 Hilton Seattle **H5**
9 Hotel Ändra Seattle -
  MGallery **F3**
10 Hotel Max **G3**
11 Hotel Monaco **G6**
12 Hotel 1000 .... **G7**
13 Hotel Theodore **G4**
14 Hyatt at Olive 8 .... **G3**
15 Hyatt Regency **H3**
16 Inn at the Market **E5**
17 Kimpton Hotel Vintage . **H6**
18 Kimpton Palladian
   Hotel **E4**
19 Lotte Seattle **H7**
20 Mayflower Park Hotel ... **F4**
21 Motif Seattle **G5**
22 Palihotel **E5**
23 The Paramount Hotel ... **H3**
24 Renaissance Seattle
   Hotel **H6**
25 Seattle Marriott
   Waterfront **C5**
26 The State Hotel **F5**
27 Thompson Seattle **E4**
28 W Seattle **H6**
29 Warwick Seattle
   Hotel **E3**

3

Downtown and Belltown DOWNTOWN

enjoy the market's many corridors, where you'll find specialty-food items, quirky gift shops, tea, honey, jams, comic books, beads, eclectic crafts, and cookware.

In recent years, Pike Place Market debuted a significant expansion, fulfilling a decades-long vision for Seattle's Market Historic District. The market's newer digs feature artisanal-food purveyors, an on-site brewery, four public art installations, seasonal pop-up vendors, and a 30,000-square-foot open public space with a plaza and a viewing deck overlooking Elliott Bay and the Seattle waterfront. ■TIP➔ **The famous "flying fish" fishmonger is located at the main entrance on Pike Street. Just be patient and eventually someone will toss a big fish through the air. Nearby you'll also find Rachel the Piggy Bank, a life-size bronze pig that helps bring home the bacon for local social services; she's a favorite spot for Pike Place pics.** ✉ *Pike Pl. at Pike St., west of 1st Ave., Downtown* ☎ *206/682–7453* ⊕ *www. pikeplacemarket.org.*

★ **Seattle Aquarium**

AQUARIUM | FAMILY | Located right at the water's edge, the Seattle Aquarium is one of the nation's premier aquariums. Among its most engaging residents are the sea otters—kids, especially, seem able to spend hours watching the delightful antics of these creatures and their river cousins. In the Puget Sound Great Hall, "Window on Washington Waters," a slice of Neah Bay life is presented in a 20-foot-tall tank holding 120,000 gallons of water. The aquarium's darkened rooms and large, lighted tanks brilliantly display Pacific Northwest marine life, including clever octopuses and translucent jellyfish. The "Life on the Edge" tide pools re-create Washington's rocky coast and sandy beaches—kids can touch the starfish, sea urchins, and sponges. Huge glass windows provide underwater views of the harbor seal exhibit; go up top to watch them play in their pools. If you're visiting in fall or winter, dress

A Good Combo

If you plan to spend the morning exploring Pike Place Market or the Seattle Art Museum, but still have energy for a walk, head north into the Belltown neighborhood, grab lunch to go at Macrina Bakery, and stroll down to the Olympic Sculpture Park: views, works of art, and chairs aplenty await.

warmly—the Marine Mammal area is outside on the waterfront and catches all of those chilly Puget Sound breezes. The café serves Ivar's chowder and kid-friendly food like burgers and chicken fingers. ■TIP➔ **As of this writing, the aquarium is undergoing a major expansion. The new Ocean Pavilion will feature a massive 325,000-gallon tank with coral reefs, rays, sharks, and tropical fish.** ✉ *1483 Alaskan Way, Pier 59, Downtown* ☎ *206/386–4300* ⊕ *www.seattleaquarium.org* ⌨ *From $24.95–$34.95 (price varies by day; pre-buy online for best rate).*

★ **Seattle Art Museum**

ART MUSEUM | Sculptor Jonathan Borofsky's several-stories-high "Hammering Man" greets visitors to SAM, as locals call this pride of the city's art scene. SAM's permanent collection surveys American, Asian, Native American, African, Oceanic, and pre-Columbian art. Collections of African dance masks and Native American carvings are particularly strong. SAM's free floors have the best attractions for kids, including an installation of a massive tree-like sculpture hanging from the ceiling and the Chase Open Studio. If you're interested in checking a special exhibition, consider buying tickets in advance as they can sell out. ■TIP➔ **The listed admission price to see the museum's general collections and installations is suggested pricing, though the museum charges fixed pricing for tickets that include special exhibitions.** ✉ *1300*

The stunning Seattle Central Library

1st Ave., Downtown ☎ *206/654–3100* ⊕ *www.seattleartmuseum.org* ✉ *$32.99; free 1st Thurs. of month* ☾ *Closed Mon.–Tues.*

Seattle Great Wheel

AMUSEMENT RIDE | FAMILY | Want to hitch a ride to a soaring Seattle vantage point above the water? At the end of Pier 57, just steps from Pike Place Market and the Seattle Aquarium, the Seattle Great Wheel is a 175-foot (about 17 stories tall) Ferris wheel. As you round the top, enjoy views of the city skyline, Elliott Bay, the Olympic Mountains, and Mt. Rainier (on a clear day, of course). Rides are slow and smooth, lasting 15 to 20 minutes, with three revolutions total. Each climate-controlled gondola can hold six people (up to eight if some are children) and, generally speaking, parties will be able to sit together. The Seattle Great Wheel is also clad in more than 500,000 LED lights that put on an after-dark light show on summer weekends until 10 pm. Advance tickets are recommended— you'll still have to wait in line, but the line

is a lot shorter. ✉ *1301 Alaskan Way, Pier 56, Downtown* ☎ *206/623–8600* ⊕ *www. seattlegreatwheel.com* ✉ *$17.*

★ The Seattle Public Library

LIBRARY | The hub of Seattle's 26-branch library system is a stunning jewel of a building that stands out against the concrete jungle of Downtown. Designed by renowned Dutch architect Rem Koolhaas and Joshua Ramus, this 11-story structure houses more than one million books, a language center, terrific areas for kids and teens, hundreds of computers, an auditorium, a "mixing chamber" floor of information desks, and a café. The building's floor plan is anything but simple; stand outside the beveled glass-and-metal facade of the building and you can see the library's floors zigzagging upward. Tours are self-guided via a laminated sheet you can pick up at the information desk; there's also a number you can call on your cell phone for an audio tour. The reading room on the 10th floor has unbeatable views of the city and the water, and the building has Wi-Fi throughout (look for the network "spl-public"). Readings and free film screenings happen on a regular basis. ✉ *1000 4th Ave., Downtown* ☎ *206/386–4636* 🌐 *www.spl.org/locations/central-library.*

Traver Gallery
ART GALLERY | One block north of the Seattle Art Museum, Traver Gallery is like a little slice of SoHo in Seattle, with large picture windows and uneven wood floors. The focus is on contemporary studio glass, paintings, sculpture, and installation art from local and international artists. Pieces are exquisite—never whimsical or gaudy—and the staff is extremely courteous. After you're done tiptoeing around the gallery, head back downstairs and around the corner to Vetri (✉ *1404 1st Ave.*), which sells smaller-scale glass art and home objects from emerging artists at reasonable prices. ✉ *110 Union St., Suite 200, Downtown* ☎ *206/587–6501* 🌐 *www.travergallery.com* 🎫 *Free* 🕒 *Closed Sun.–Mon.*

🍴 Restaurants

After a day of exploring the museums, sights, and shops, what could be better than a perfect meal? Luckily, this area is filled with a wide range of eateries, from the offerings in and around Pike Place Market to happening spots inside boutique hotels.

Ben Paris
$$ | **AMERICAN** | Located in the hip State Hotel, Ben Paris has become a neighborhood favorite for elevated classic American fare—think shrimp cocktail, wedge salads, fried chicken, and crab Louie—dished up in a stylish space with graphic wallpaper and a bustling bar. Don't miss the outstanding grilled octopus or the creative cocktail list designed by Abigail Gullo, a star bartender from New Orleans (one drink is served in a darling copper bird mug). **Known for:** avocado or tuna confit toast for breakfast or lunch; craft cocktails with unique ingredients; inside one of Seattle's coolest hotels. [$] *Average main: $24* ✉ *The State Hotel, 130 Pike St., Downtown* ☎ *206/513–7303* 🌐 *www.benparis.com.*

Charlotte Restaurant & Lounge
$$$$ | **PACIFIC NORTHWEST** | The 16th-story, panoramic views of Downtown, Elliott Bay, and Smith Tower make Charlotte one of Seattle's newest special-occasion destinations. On the top floor of the luxury hotel Lotte (Charlotte is pronounced "Char-lot-tay"), the blonde-wood-heavy, mid-century-inspired dining room has a handful of spaced-out tables right by the floor-to-ceiling windows, making for a spectacular perch at sunset if you're lucky. **Known for:** excellent wine pairing options; exceptional service; epic views of Downtown Seattle and the bay. [$] *Average main: $150* ✉ *Lotte Hotel, 809 5th Ave., Downtown* ☎ *206/800–8117* 🌐 *www.charlotterestaurantseattle.com* 🕒 *No lunch. No dinner Sun.–Mon.*

Le Pichet
$$ | **FRENCH** | Slate tabletops, a tile floor, and a rolled-zinc bar will transport you out of Downtown Seattle and into the charming 6th arrondissement. The menu is quintessentially French: at lunch there are rustic pâtés and *jambon et fromage* (ham and cheese) sandwiches on crusty baguettes; dinner sees homemade sausages, daily fish specials, and steak tartare. **Known for:** authentic French food; roast chicken for two; bustling atmosphere. [$] *Average main: $22* ✉ *1933 1st Ave., Downtown* ☎ *206/256–1499* 🌐 *www.lepichetseattle.com.*

★ Matt's in the Market
$$$$ | **PACIFIC NORTHWEST** | One of the most beloved of Pike Place Market's restaurants, Matt's is all about intimate dining, fresh ingredients, and superb service. You can perch at the bar for pints and the signature deviled eggs or be seated at a table—complete with vases filled with flowers from the market—for a seasonal menu that synthesizes the

Matt's in the Market is a favorite eatery at Pike Place.

best picks from the restaurant's produce vendors and an excellent wine list. **Known for:** wonderful Market and water views; fresh catch of the day; late-night hours. $ *Average main: $42* ⊠ *94 Pike St., Downtown* ☎ *206/467–7909* ⊕ *www. mattsinthemarket.com* ⊘ *Closed Mon.*

Metropolitan Grill

$$$$ | **STEAKHOUSE** | This is a favorite lunch spot for the professional crowd but it's not for timid eaters: custom dry-aged mesquite-grilled steaks and chops— among the best in Seattle—are huge and come with a hearty side option. The Met's take on a steak house is either classic or a caricature, depending on how you take to the cigar-and-cognac vibe: servers wear tuxes and everything is clad in fine wood, brass, and velvet. **Known for:** splurge-worthy steaks; rich sides like lobster mac 'n' cheese; classic service. $ *Average main: $75* ⊠ *820 2nd Ave., Downtown* ☎ *206/624–3287* ⊕ *www. themetropolitangrill.com* ⊘ *No lunch weekends.*

The Pink Door

$$$ | **ITALIAN** | With its Post Alley entrance and meager signage, the Pink Door's speakeasy vibe draws Pike Place Market regulars almost as much as its savory, seasonal Italian food does. The food is good, and the pappardelle al ragù Bolognese and cioppino are reliably standout entrées, but people come here mostly for the atmosphere (which includes tasteful cabaret acts) and shaded outdoor deck with views of Elliott Bay. **Known for:** an entertaining atmosphere; classic Italian dishes; a large patio with an arbor, grapevines, and a view. $ *Average main: $28* ⊠ *1919 Post Alley, Downtown* ☎ *206/443–3241* ⊕ *www. thepinkdoor.net* ⊘ *No lunch Sun.*

Place Pigalle

$$$ | **MODERN AMERICAN** | Large windows look out on Elliott Bay in this cozy spot tucked behind a meat vendor in Pike Place Market's main arcade. In nice weather, open windows let in the fresh salt breeze. **Known for:** more Pacific Northwest than French; rich oyster stew;

local beer on tap. $ *Average main: $37* ✉ *81 Pike St., Downtown* ☎ *206/624–1756* 🌐 *www.placepigalle-seattle.com.*

★ Sushi Kashiba

$$$$ | SUSHI | After decades spent earning a reputation as one of Seattle's top sushi chefs, Shiro Kashiba opened his own spot in a location as notable as his skill with seafood deserves. Diners in the spare-but-elegant Pike Place Market space can opt for the *omakase* (chef's choice) selection of the best fish from around the world and just up the street, or order from the menu of Japanese classics and sashimi. **Known for:** local celebrity chef; memorable omakase; outstanding service. $ *Average main: $100* ✉ *86 Pine St., Suite 1, Downtown* ✥ *Inn at the Market* ☎ *206/441–8844* 🌐 *www.sushikashiba.com* ⏲ *No lunch.*

Coffee and Quick Bites

Anchorhead Coffee

$ | CAFÉ | Anchorhead is serious about coffee: everybody raves about their smooth roasts that need no doctoring, from pour-overs to perfectly pulled espresso. They also serve unique milk-substitute creations, like the popular creamy-green pistachio matcha and the Shy Bear Fog Latte (oolong, burnt honey, and oat milk) along with a menu of pastries and breakfast sandwiches. **Known for:** unique flavors; in the heart of Downtown; something for everyone. $ *Average main: $8* ✉ *2003 Western Ave., Ste 110A, Downtown* 🌐 *www.anchorheadcoffee.com.*

★ Ellenos Real Greek Yogurt

$ | GREEK | When people walk by the Pike Place Market booth, they might think they're passing a gelato stand from the artful display, but in fact Ellenos is serving up the best (and best-looking) yogurt in the city—and possibly the country. Thicker and smoother than most commercial Greek yogurts, the Australian-Greek family behind the brand uses local milk and a slow culturing process to create their nearly ice cream-like treat. **Known for:** Greek yogurt with a cult following; perfect on-the-go snack; fresh fruit toppings. $ *Average main: $6* ✉ *1500 Pike Pl., Downtown* ☎ *206/535–7562* 🌐 *www.ellenos.com.*

Mr. West Cafe Bar

$ | CAFÉ | Cozy leather bar seats surround the wide wood bar at the stylish, modern Mr. West Cafe Bar, where they've got you covered from morning pick-me-up to early-evening imbibing. The coffee menu offers the usuals, from drips and cortados to cappuccinos and lattes, as well as creative espresso-based options like coffee soda, coffee egg cream, and a cardamom tonic. **Known for:** tasty breakfast and lunch options; creative coffee and tea beverages; stylish digs. $ *Average main: $8* ✉ *720 Olive Way, Downtown* 🌐 *www.mrwestcafebar.com.*

Storyville Coffee

$ | CAFÉ | In addition to perfectly pulled espresso drinks, Storyville offers fresh pastries, light lunch items, and beer and wine in a welcoming space with ample comfy seating and Elliott Bay views. **Known for:** skilled baristas; house-made ingredients like chocolate syrup; cashew and other alt-milks. $ *Average main: $5* ✉ *94 Pike St. #34, Downtown* ☎ *206/780–5777* 🌐 *www.storyville.com.*

Hotels

Downtown has the greatest concentration of hotels, many of which are new or updated high-end high-rises, though there are also several boutique hotels and midrange properties in historic buildings. There aren't many budget properties in the area. All Downtown hotels are convenient (and within walking distance) to many major sights, including the Seattle Art Museum, Pike Place Market, and the Olympic Sculpture Park. Sights that aren't a short walk away are easily accessible via public transit, and there are plenty of buses, as well as the light

Staying with Kids

Children are welcome at most Seattle hotels; some even cater to your munchkins with kid-approved snacks and amenities. Most, but not all, hotels in Seattle allow children under a certain age to stay in their parents' room at no extra charge, so be sure to find out the cutoff age for children's discounts. Cribs are usually available upon request, and hotel staff can assist you in finding daycare. Always let hotel staff know you'll be traveling with children when you book your room so that they can be extra accommodating.

Some of the loveliest (and most expensive) hotels also cater to young ones:

The **Silver Cloud** hotels, especially the one on Lake Union, are all suitable for families. ✉ *South Lake Union.*

The **Fairmont Olympic Hotel** has a swimming pool and offers milk and cookies, kid-friendly movies (popcorn included!), and child-size bathrobes. ✉ *Downtown.*

Tweens and teens will love the virtual golf club and Xbox suites at **Hotel 1000**, while more Zen youngsters can luxuriate in child-size robes for the hotel's kid spa treatments. ✉ *Downtown.*

Both the **Pan Pacific Hotel Seattle** in South Lake Union and Downtown's **Four Seasons Hotel Seattle** have stuffed animals waiting on beds of small guests, while the Four Seasons also pampers kids with mini-robes, children's videos, and baby bath products. ✉ *South Lake Union and Downtown.*

rail and the Monorail in this part of town. Although the waterfront is an integral part of Downtown, there are surprisingly few hotels directly on the water. Many high-rises have water views, but make sure to specify that you want a room with a view. Hotel prices climb significantly during July and August, which are the two most reliably good weather months in Seattle.

★ The Alexis Royal Sonesta Hotel

$$$ | **HOTEL** | The stylish guestrooms received a recent top-to-bottom redo at the boutique Alexis Royal Sonesta, which occupies a pair of historic buildings (on the National Register of Historic Places, in fact) near the waterfront; the new design has a contemporary loft vibe, featuring handsome Northwest-inspired hues, textures, and furnishings that complement the hotel's high ceilings and walls of windows. **Pros:** a short walk to the waterfront; chic modern rooms that appeal to design lovers; suites aren't prohibitively expensive. **Cons:** small lobby; not entirely soundproofed against old building and city noise; some rooms can be a bit dark. [$] *Rooms from: $299* ✉ *1007 1st Ave., Downtown* ☎ *206/624–4844, 888/850–1155* 🌐 *www.alexishotel.com* 🛏 *88 rooms* 🍴 *No Meals.*

The Charter Hotel

$$$ | **HOTEL** | Part of the Hilton's upscale Curio Collection, the new Charter Hotel features chic, quiet rooms with floor-to-ceiling windows, marbled wallpaper, 50-inch TVs, and spacious bathrooms. **Pros:** quiet and immensely comfortable rooms; a treat for Hilton Honors loyalists; great location near Pike Place Market. **Cons:** not the best water views; the on-site restaurant is only so-so; showers only in some bathrooms. [$] *Rooms from: $289* ✉ *1610 2nd Ave., Downtown* ☎ *206/256–7500* 🛏 *229 rooms* 🍴 *No Meals.*

★ The Fairmont Olympic Hotel

$$$$ | **HOTEL** | **FAMILY** | The lobby and other social spaces (including the hotel's gorgeous The George restaurant) of this sophisticated 1920s icon have all been updated recently, melding the existing Old World glamour with modern luxury to stylishly complement contemporary guest rooms that feature mid-century-inspired furnishings and all-marble bathrooms with rain showers and designer toiletries. **Pros:** impeccable service; top-notch fitness center with an indoor pool; great on-site dining and amenities. **Cons:** not much in the way of views; valet parking is costly; some rooms on the small side. [$] *Rooms from: $399* ✉ *411 University St., Downtown* ☎ *206/621–1700, 888/363–5022* 🌐 *www.fairmont.com/seattle* 🛏 *450 rooms* 🍴 *No Meals.*

★ Four Seasons Hotel Seattle

$$$$ | **HOTEL** | **FAMILY** | Just south of Pike Place Market and steps from the Seattle Art Museum, this Downtown gem overlooking Elliott Bay is polished and elegant, with spacious light-filled guest rooms; after a recent renovation, the fresh new design features serene hues that nod to the hotel's surroundings, museum-quality art reproductions, and comfortable high-end modern furnishings. **Pros:** fantastic outdoor inifinity pool with views for miles; luxurious marble bathrooms with deep soaking tubs; lovely spa facility offering extensive treatments. **Cons:** Four Seasons regulars might not click with this modern take on the brand; street-side rooms not entirely soundproofed; some water-facing room views are partially obscured by industrial sites. [$] *Rooms from: $899* ✉ *99 Union St., Downtown* ☎ *206/749–7000, 800/332–3442* 🌐 *www.fourseasons.com/seattle* 🛏 *134 rooms* 🍴 *No Meals.*

Grand Hyatt Seattle

$$$ | **HOTEL** | Adjacent to the Washington State Convention Center, this view-centric hotel with spacious rooms appeals to business travelers, conventioneers, or brand loyalists who want a dependable Hyatt-level stay in a central Downtown location. **Pros:** city-and-water views from upper-floor rooms; large bathrooms with ample counter space; on-site brand-name restaurants. **Cons:** not a ton of personality; some traffic and construction noise; no lounge. [$] *Rooms from: $296* ✉ *721 Pine St., Downtown* ☎ *206/774–1234* 🌐 *www.grandseattle.hyatt.com* 🛏 *425 rooms* 🍴 *No Meals.*

Hilton Seattle

$$ | **HOTEL** | The Hilton Seattle is a popular site for meetings, conventions, and the summer cruise set, where the newly renovated rooms are tasteful but nondescript—you'll be paying for a brand name here, reliable though it may be. **Pros:** helpful staff; clean rooms, some with city views; comfortable beds. **Cons:** overpriced; small bathrooms; lacks personality. [$] *Rooms from: $247* ✉ *1301 6th Ave., Downtown* ☎ *206/624–0500, 800/426–0535* 🌐 *www.thehiltonseattle.com* 🛏 *240 rooms* 🍴 *No Meals.*

Hotel Max

$$ | **HOTEL** | Hip and art-forward, the Hotel Max (for "Maximalism") blends artsy decor with punchy minimalism for an

Dog-Friendly Seattle

Seattle ranks as one of the top dog cities in the country, with more canines living here than children. Pooches are pampered with 14 off-leash areas within city boundaries, including 9-acre Magnuson Park, which includes a stretch of beach on Lake Washington and a special area for small dogs. More than 70 hotels allow furry friends (for free or a fee), and some go out of their way to make pets feel as welcome as their human pals.

architect-office effect, and though most of the rooms are on the small side, they come with cushy trimmings. **Pros:** hip, youthful vibe; extra pet-friendly (it's OK to leave pets in the room unattended); 4-minute walk from Westlake Center transit hub. **Cons:** tiny rooms and even tinier elevator; traffic noise, thin walls, and late-night revelers; older and larger travelers may not be comfortable here. [$] *Rooms from: $250* ✉ *620 Stewart St., Downtown* ☎ *866/833–6299, 866/833–6299* 🌐 *www.hotelmaxseattle.com* 🛏 *163 rooms* 🍴 *No Meals.*

Hotel Monaco

$$$ | **HOTEL** | **FAMILY** | It only takes one glimpse of the global-modern lobby to know that this stylish boutique hotel in the heart of Downtown is a standout, and rooms carry on the eclectic feel, with a palette of soft reds and gunmetal grays, beds topped with Frette linens, floor-to-ceiling drapes in a Turkish motif, and floor lamps that recall telescopes. **Pros:** some rooms feature fabulous deep soaking tubs; welcoming public spaces; daily hosted wine reception with savory snacks. **Cons:** some street-facing rooms can be noisy; small gym; daily facilities fee. [$] *Rooms from: $286* ✉ *1101 4th Ave., Downtown* ☎ *206/621–1770, 800/715–6513* 🌐 *www.monaco-seattle.com* 🛏 *187 rooms* 🍴 *No Meals.*

Hotel 1000

$$$ | **HOTEL** | **FAMILY** | A short walk from Pioneer Square, the art museum, and the waterfront, Hotel 1000 features ultra-comfortable rooms with on-trend contemporary design elements and unexpected touches like large soaking tubs that fill from the ceiling. **Pros:** ideal location near Pike Place Market; golf simulator and lovely small spa; upper-floor rooms have great city and water views. **Cons:** bar attracts a lot of tourists; a handful of no-view rooms look out to a cement wall; not the most spacious for the price. [$] *Rooms from: $318* ✉ *1000 1st Ave., Downtown* ☎ *206/957–1000, 844/244–4973* 🌐 *www.hotel1000seattle.com* 🛏 *120 rooms* 🍴 *No Meals.*

Hotel Theodore

$$$ | **HOTEL** | The 90-year-old Roosevelt Hotel got a serious makeover before debuting as Hotel Theodore, a stylish boutique hotel with handsome industrial furnishings and artwork, soundproofed guest rooms. **Pros:** some rooms have Freeman Seattle raincoats available to borrow; right by freeway and great Downtown shopping; warm and welcoming lobby. **Cons:** standard rooms are small; though interior soundproofing is great, some street/construction noise gets through; lower-floor views can be drab. [$] *Rooms from: $288* ✉ *1531 7th Ave., Downtown* ☎ *206/621–1200* 🌐 *hoteltheodore.com* 🛏 *153 rooms* 🍴 *No Meals.*

★ **Hyatt at Olive 8**

$$$ | **HOTEL** | In a city known for environmental responsibility, being one of the greenest hotels in town is no small feat, and green is rarely this chic—rooms have floor-to-ceiling windows flooding the place with light along with enviro touches like dual-flush toilets, fresh-air vents, and low-flow showerheads. **Pros:** central location; serene indoor pool; one of Seattle's best day spas. **Cons:** standard rooms have showers only; hallway and traffic noise; translucent glass bathroom doors offer little privacy. [$] *Rooms from: $267* ✉ *1635 8th Ave., Downtown* ☎ *206/695–1234, 800/233 1234* 🌐 *www.olive8.hyatt.com* 🛏 *346 rooms* 🍴 *No Meals.*

Hyatt Regency

$$ | **HOTEL** | **FAMILY** | This newcomer to the Downtown hotel scene—right next door to the future Convention Center expansion—currently holds the title of the biggest hotel in the Pacific Northwest; the Hyatt's sophisticated 45-story tower practically feels like a small city, with multiple dining options, a large cutting-edge gym, and an especially swanky Regency Club. **Pros:** spacious rooms are brand-new, quiet, and very

Time to Relax

If serious pampering is your favorite part of traveling, you'll find world-class spa options at a few of Seattle's upscale hotels.

At the new Philippe Starck–designed Lotte Seattle, Le SPA de l'hôtel LOTTE feels like you've stepped into a cloud. Everything is white, ethereal, and soothing, including four spacious treatment rooms with impossibly comfortable massage tables. The spa offers a variety of treatments and includes use of the sauna and steam room.

The marble-clad spa at the Four Seasons books up well in advance for its outstanding signature massages and facials. Spa guests have access to the sauna and steam room (though the hotel's gorgeous infinity pool is reserved for Four Seasons guests).

At the eco-friendly Elaia Spa at Hyatt at Olive 8, organic treatments include seasonal offerings like an apple cider scrub as well as a CBD facial (with treatments over 60 minutes, guests have access to the relaxation room and saunas).

And finally, although it's on the petite side, the lovely Spa at Hotel 1000 offers luxurious expert treatments like massages and customized facials.

comfortable; expansive cityscape and water views; an outpost of Seattle steak house Daniel's Broiler. **Cons:** not as close to the waterfront action as many hotels; no single cozy lobby space for gathering; might feel a bit business-y for pleasure travelers. $ *Rooms from: $263* ⊠ *808 Howell St., Downtown* ☏ *206/973–1234* ⊕ *www.hyatt.com* ⇌ *1,260 rooms* ⦿ *No Meals.*

★ Inn at the Market

$$$$ | **HOTEL** | From its jaw-dropping bay views to the fabulous location just steps from Pike Place Market, this is a unique place you'll want to visit again and again; excellent service and dining options make it even more worth the splurge. **Pros:** outstanding views from most rooms; deals on rooms that don't have views, even in peak season; guests have access to the rooftop deck. **Cons:** not much indoor common space; some street and Market noise; not the easiest to get in and out by car. $ *Rooms from: $450* ⊠ *86 Pine St., Downtown* ☏ *206/443–3600, 800/446–4484* ⊕ *www. innatthemarket.com* ⇌ *70 rooms* ⦿ *No Meals.*

Kimpton Hotel Vintage

$$$ | **HOTEL** | Each of the serene, quiet rooms named after Washington wineries—some of which boast marvelous views of Seattle's iconic public library—feature a vineyard-inspired palette of burgundy, taupe, and green hues, with a focus on unique interior design and comfortable touches. **Pros:** truly pet-friendly (dogs get their own beds and bowls); daily hosted wine hour; on-site Tulio is a nice Italian restaurant. **Cons:** a short-but-steep uphill walk from Downtown could be tough on some travelers; lobby is attractive but small; bathrooms aren't particularly spacious. $ *Rooms from: $329* ⊠ *1100 5th Ave., Downtown* ☏ *206/624–8000, 800/853–3914* ⊕ *www. hotelvintage-seattle.com* ⇌ *125 rooms* ⦿ *No Meals.*

★ Lotte Seattle

$$$$ | **HOTEL** | Housed in a striking reflective tower that connects to a historic church (now an event space), Lotte Seattle (by the South Korean Lotte brand) debuted in 2020; Philippe Starck–designed, mid-century-inspired interiors feature sleek mirrored surfaces

(even in the bathroom), an eclectic mix of contemporary art, faux-bois motifs, and floor-to-ceiling windows, some with lovely views of Elliott Bay and Smith Tower. **Pros:** impeccable customer service; design aficionados will drool over the architecture and interiors; the soothing, ethereal spa is one of Seattle's best. **Cons:** a 15-minute walk to some attractions; valet parking costs $70; mirrored bathroom/shower rooms are love it or hate it. $\boxed{S}$ *Rooms from: $425 ⊠ 809 5th Ave., Downtown* ☎ *206/800–8110* ⊕ *www.lottehotelseattle.com* ⮑ *189 rooms* ⟊ *No Meals.*

★ Mayflower Park Hotel

$$$ | HOTEL | Comfortable, old-world charm comes with sturdy antiques, Asian accents, brass fixtures, and florals, and though the hotel's main draw is its central location, street noise isn't much of an issue thanks to the sturdy old construction of the historic 1927 building. **Pros:** close to light rail and Monorail; on-site Spanish restaurant Andaluca is well worth a visit; comfortable beds. **Cons:** some of the rooms are small; old-fashioned for some travelers; not all rooms have mini fridges. $\boxed{S}$ *Rooms from: $355 ⊠ 405 Olive Way, Downtown* ☎ *206/623–8700, 800/426–5100* ⊕ *www.mayflowerpark.com* ⮑ *189 rooms* ⟊ *No Meals.*

Motif Seattle

$$$ | HOTEL | With a colorful vibe and eye-catching design motifs throughout, this conveniently located urban property owned by Hyatt has a boutique feel despite its large size. **Pros:** in the heart of Downtown; water-and-mountain views in some upper-floor rooms; several cool communal spaces. **Cons:** rooms near terrace can be loud; small bathrooms; service can be slow and mediocre. $\boxed{S}$ *Rooms from: $325 ⊠ 1415 5th Ave., Downtown* ☎ *206/971–8015* ⮑ *329 rooms* ⟊ *No Meals.*

Palihotel

$$$ | HOTEL | A fabulous shade of dark green coats most of the interior walls and brick surfaces at this eclectic boutique hotel in a historic building (circa 1898) just a block up from Pike Place Market, and other vintage-modern design touches are equally memorable, like bold graphic tile in the bathrooms, chintz headboards and accent pillows, and Smeg tea kettles. **Pros:** fresh design perfectly suits the old architecture; good coffee shop and cocktail bar; cool, cozy lounge with a fireplace. **Cons:** no free coffee; some street noise; small bathrooms. $\boxed{S}$ *Rooms from: $300 ⊠ 107 Pine St., Downtown* ☎ *206/596–0600* ⊕ *www.palisociety.com* ⮑ *96 rooms* ⟊ *No Meals.*

★ The Paramount Hotel

$$ | HOTEL | Good value meets great location at this comfortable boutique hotel with friendly service and tasteful contemporary furnishings, including a decent-size desk for business travelers. **Pros:** close to the Convention Center; clean, quiet rooms; ice chests instead of machines mean less noise. **Cons:** not much in the way of amenities; tiny fitness center; small lobby. $\boxed{S}$ *Rooms from: $247 ⊠ 724 Pine St., Downtown* ☎ *206/292–9500* ⊕ *www.paramounthotelseattle.com* ⮑ *146 rooms* ⟊ *No Meals.*

Renaissance Seattle Hotel

$$$ | HOTEL | A bit of a walk uphill from Downtown, this high-rise has a calm feel to it, with contemporary decor, inviting common areas, and especially great views of Elliott Bay from rooms above the 20th floor. **Pros:** comfy beds; pool at the rooftop health club; good deals are often available online. **Cons:** freeway noise; some visitors won't enjoy the walk uphill; not much happening in the area at night. $\boxed{S}$ *Rooms from: $296 ⊠ 515 Madison St., Downtown* ☎ *206/583–0300, 800/546–9184* ⊕ *www.renaissanceseattle.com* ⮑ *553 rooms* ⟊ *No Meals.*

★ The State Hotel

$$ | **HOTEL** | From the huge exterior mural by artist Shepard Fairey to the gorgeous graphic wallpaper inspired by nearby Pike Place Market, every inch of this hip boutique hotel is eye candy, including stylish rooms with sleek, tiled rain showers, an eclectic and welcoming lobby, and vibrant Ben Paris bar and restaurant, where neighborhood locals are as likely to hang out as tourists. **Pros:** minimal but well-appointed guest rooms, some with nice water views; really friendly service; great lobby coffee. **Cons:** not the nicest corner at night; rooms on the small side; rooftop patio only has a few tables. $ *Rooms from: $221* ✉ *1501 2nd Ave., Downtown* ☎ *800/827–3900* ⊕ *www.statehotel.com* ⮑ *91 rooms* ⦿| *No Meals.*

★ Thompson Seattle

$$$ | **HOTEL** | Designed by local star architects Olson Kundig, the 12-story Thompson Seattle (a Hyatt hotel) makes an impression with a contemporary glass exterior and sophisticated guest rooms that feature floor-to-ceiling windows (some framing epic water views), hardwood floors, a crisp white-and-navy palette, and leather and smoked-glass accents. **Pros:** perfect for the style obsessed; very close to Pike Place Market; The Nest rooftop bar. **Cons:** blazing afternoon sun in some rooms; some small rooms; floor beneath rooftop bar can be noisy. $ *Rooms from: $318* ✉ *110 Stewart St., Downtown* ☎ *206/623–4600* ⊕ *www.thompsonhotels.com/hotels/thompson-seattle* ⮑ *158 rooms* ⦿| *No Meals.*

W Seattle

$$$ | **HOTEL** | With a club-like atmosphere that starts at the VIP-style lobby check-in, the W Seattle goes for a distinct "urban lodge" vibe, with guest rooms that feature a palette of Seattle-inspired grays and blues accented by bright pops of color, as well as headboards made from floor-to-ceiling backlit wood stacks and Northwest touches like plaid pillows and Pendleton-pattern wallpaper. **Pros:** lively late-night scene in lobby bar; comfortable beds; great city views. **Cons:** self-consciously trendy; a bit too youthful for some visitors; outrageous room service prices. $ *Rooms from: $284* ✉ *1112 4th Ave., Downtown* ☎ *206/264–6000, 877/946–8357* ⊕ *www.wseattle.com* ⮑ *433 rooms* ⦿| *No Meals.*

Nightlife

Downtown is a great place for anyone looking to dress up a bit and hit glam hotel bars, classy lounges, and wine bars where you don't have to be under the age of 30 to fit in. Downtown also has a smattering of pubs popular with the happy-hour crowd.

BARS

Alibi Room

DANCE CLUBS | Well-dressed locals head to this hard-to-find wood-paneled bar to sip double martinis while taking in peekaboo views of Elliott Bay or studying the scripts, handbills, and movie posters that line the walls. The lower level is more crowded and casual. Stop by for a drink or a meal (the pizza is great), and stay to listen and dance to live music. Happy hour—daily from 11:30 am to 6 pm—is quiet and a good respite from the Market. ✉ *85 Pike St., in Post Alley, at Pike Place Market, Downtown* ☎ *206/623–3180* ⊕ *www.seattlealibi.com.*

The Diller Room

COCKTAIL LOUNGES | Occupying the former lobby of the historic Diller Hotel, which was built in 1890, the Diller Room is a charming, worn-around-the-edges spot for cocktails in downtown, across the street from the Seattle Art Museum. Exposed brick, mismatched crystal chandeliers, a beat-up white tile floor, and a vintage neon Diller Hotel sign above the wood bar provide the atmosphere. The drink menu includes cocktails and a section devoted to tallboys. Happy hour runs 2–7 pm every day, and the food menu offers various sliders, pizzas, and bar snacks. ⊠ *1224 1st Ave., Downtown* ☎ *206/467–4042* ⊕ *www.dillerroom.com.*

Fog Room

BARS | Perched on the 16th floor of The Charter Hotel, Fog Room is the latest arrival to Seattle's small rooftop bar scene and it's a classy modern one, from the decor to the cocktails. A chic indoor lounge with expansive windows opens to an outdoor terrace with seating and a fire pit; the city and water views aren't the best of the bunch, but you don't need to reserve outdoor seating. ⊠ *The Charter Hotel, 1610 2nd Ave., Downtown* ☎ *206/256–7525* ⊕ *www.fogroomseattle. com.*

The Nest at Thompson Seattle

COCKTAIL LOUNGES | Yes, the Nest has carefully crafted cocktails and tasty snacks, but the real draw is the breathtaking, unobstructed view of Elliot Bay. On a clear evening, the outdoor deck, with ample seating and fireplaces, is the perfect spot to gaze across Puget Sound at the Olympic Mountains. This place gets busy, though, so reservations—available for parties of four to 20 guests—are a good idea. ⊠ *110 Stewart St., Downtown* ☎ *206/623–4600* ⊕ *www.thompsonhotels.com.*

Oliver's

COCKTAIL LOUNGES | The most important question here: shaken or stirred? This sophisticated bar in the Mayflower Park Hotel is famous for its martinis. Wing chairs, low tables, and lots of natural light make it easy to relax after a hectic day. The likes of Frank Sinatra or Billie Holiday may be playing in the background; expect an unfussy crowd of regulars and hotel guests. ⊠ *405 Olive Way, Downtown* ☎ *206/623–8700* ⊕ *oliverstwistseattle. com.*

Phởcific Standard Time

COCKTAIL LOUNGES | The owners call it a "Viet tree house" and the speakeasy-style cocktail bar certainly nailed

its hideaway vibe. Look for Phở Bắc (the fourth location for the popular Seattle restaurant opened in 2022) and a sandwich sign pointing you to "PST," then head upstairs. Inventive cocktails at the cozy, plant-filled bar feature Vietnamese ingredients and flavors, like an egg coffee or a pickled leek martini, as well nibbles such as crab dip and a phở cup of noodles. ⊠ *1923 7th Ave., Downtown* ⚓ *Enter through Phở Bắc, go up the stairs* ⊕ *instagram.com/pst.seattle* ⊗ *Closed Sun.–Tues.*

Purple Café and Wine Bar

WINE BARS | Wine lovers come for the massive selection—the menu boasts 90 wines by the glass and some 600 bottles—but this place deserves props for its design, too. Despite the cavernous quality of the space and floor-to-ceiling windows, all eyes are immediately drawn to the 20-foot tower ringed by a spiral staircase that showcases thousands of bottles. Full lunch and dinner menus feature American and Pacific Northwest fare—the lobster mac 'n' cheese is especially tasty—and servers know their ideal pairings. ⊠ *1225 4th Ave., Downtown* ☎ *206/829–2280* ⊕ *www.thepurplecafe. com.*

★ Zig Zag Café

BARS | A mixed crowd of mostly locals hunts out this unique spot at Pike Place Market's Street Hill Climb (walk past the Gum Wall to find a nearly hidden stairwell leading down to the piers). In addition to pouring a perfect martini, Zig Zag features a revolving cast of memorable cocktails and a Mediterranean-inspired food menu with plenty of tasty bites. A small patio is the place to be on a summery happy-hour evening. Zig Zag is friendly—retro without being obnoxiously ironic—and very Seattle, with the occasional live music show to boot. ⊠ *1501 Western Ave., Downtown* ☎ *206/625–1146* ⊕ *zigzagseattle.com.*

BREW PUBS
Old Stove Brewing Co.
BREWPUBS | FAMILY | Part of Pike Place Market's recent expansion, Old Stove Brewing—which is brewed on-site—might be the kid-friendliest taproom in town. Choose from 24 drafts at the award-winning brewery and restaurant; try to nab a seat on the patio or by the window (especially at sunset) so you can watch ferries glide across the Puget Sound from the 80-foot west-facing window that frames Elliott Bay and the mountains. ⊠ *Pike Place Market, 1901 Western Ave., Downtown* ☎ *206/602–6120* ⊕ *www.oldstove.com.*

The Pike Brewing Company
BREWPUBS | True to its location, you might find more tourists than locals at the Pike Brewing Company, though it is popular with the Downtown after-work crowd. The cavernous bar and restaurant, operated by the brewers of the Pike Place Pale Ale, also houses the Seattle Microbrewery Museum and an excellent shop with home-brewing supplies. Pints of beer are cold and satisfying—the pale ale and the Kilt Lifter Scottish ale have been local favorites for decades. ⊠ *1415 1st Ave., Downtown* ☎ *206/622–6044* ⊕ *www.pikebrewing.com.*

COMEDY CLUBS
Unexpected Productions Improv
COMEDY CLUBS | Unexpected Productions Improv, adjacent to Pike Place Market, hosts tons of different improv events; shows may have holiday or seasonal themes or be done in the style of a certain TV or film genre like sci-fi or noir. On Friday and Saturday at 10:30, the troupe presents the long-running "TheatreSports" show, in which the skits are based entirely on audience suggestions. ⊠ *Market Theater, 1428 Post Alley, Downtown* ☎ *206/587–2414* ⊕ *www.unexpectedproductions.org.*

LIVE MUSIC
Dimitriou's Jazz Alley
LIVE MUSIC | Seattleites dress up to see nationally known jazz artists at Dimitriou's. The cabaret-style theater, where intimate tables for two surround the stage, runs shows nightly. Those with reservations for cocktails or dinner, served during the first set, receive priority seating. ⊠ *2033 6th Ave., Downtown* ☎ *206/441–9729* ⊕ *www.jazzalley.com.*

Owl N' Thistle Irish Pub
LIVE MUSIC | This affable pub near Pike Place Market presents acoustic folk music on a small stage in a cavernous room. It's often loaded with regulars, who appreciate the well-drawn pints of Guinness, the talent, and the Tuesday-night jazz jam. ⊠ *808 Post Ave., Downtown* ☎ *206/621–7777* ⊕ *www.owlnthistle.com.*

Showbox
LIVE MUSIC | Just across from Pike Place Market, this venue—which is more than 80 years old—is a great spot to see some pretty big-name acts. The room's small enough that you don't feel like you're miles away from the performers, and the terraced bar areas flanking the main floor provide some relief if you don't want to join the crush in front of the stage. ⊠ *1426 1st Ave., Downtown* ☎ *888/929–7849* ⊕ *www.showboxpresents.com.*

The Triple Door
LIVE MUSIC | Come here for live world music and jazz. The seating is half-moon booths giving it a cabaret lounge feel. They also host a bawdy burlesque show during the holidays. ⊠ *216 Union St., Downtown* ☎ *206/838–4333* ⊕ *www.thetripledoor.net.*

🔴 Performing Arts

The tech boom created an enthusiastic and philanthropic audience for Seattle's arts community, which continues to grow. The gorgeous Benaroya Hall is a national benchmark for acoustic design.

Musical Seattle

Seattle buzzes with musical energy—and has for years. The symphony gave its first performance in 1903. The Cornish College of the Arts, which has an extensive music program, was founded in 1914. As early as 1918, a vibrant jazz scene was developing in the Central District.

Clubs clustered around Jackson Street and 12th Avenue attracted big names like Jelly Roll Morton, Duke Ellington, and Charlie Parker. Quincy Jones and Ray Charles both started their careers at the tail end of the city's jazz era—Jones was a Seattle native and Charles moved here at age 17. The jazz scene peaked in the early '50s, though it received a fleeting boost again in the late '80s and early '90s after guitarist Bill Frisell and keyboardist-composer Wayne Horvitz moved here from New York.

The '60s and '70s brought soul, garage rock, and punk to the city. The Wailers were an influential group with a national hit "Tall Cool One." Legendary rock band Heart was gigging around Seattle in the mid-'70s. Jimi Hendrix grew up in Seattle and attended Garfield High School, which today produces one of the nation's top high-school jazz ensembles. Although Hendrix wouldn't become famous until he left his hometown, Seattle still holds this rock icon dear.

In 1988, rapper Sir Mix-a-Lot released *Swass*, with its memorable hit "Baby Got Back." In the '90s, Seattle's hip-hop scene belonged to the b-boys, with the Oldominion Crew and the Massive Monkees being the major players.

Seattle's best-known contribution—grunge—started in the late 1980s. By 1992, with local bands Nirvana, Pearl Jam, and Soundgarden gracing the album collection of nearly every rock fan in the nation, *Rolling Stone* dubbed Seattle "the new Liverpool." Belltown was one of Nirvana's favorite early places to perform (the club The Crocodile is still kicking) and hang out. By the mid-'90s, Seattleites were starting to move away from the movement that put the city on the map; Kurt Cobain's suicide in 1994 felt to many like the last nail in the coffin of the grunge scene. However, Sub Pop Records, the major independent label that was instrumental in the grunge scene, continues to flourish. KEXP, the local nonprofit radio station, is an integral part of the music scene in Seattle, hosting concerts at its home at Seattle Center, and organizing and promoting music events throughout the city.

FILM
Big Picture
FILM | Enjoy the same first-run films that are playing down the street at the multiplex—minus the crowds, screaming kids, and sensory overload—at Big Picture. This small, elegant theater has a full bar (you can order refills during the screening), and it's 21 and older only. ⊠ *2505 1st Ave., Belltown* ☎ *206/256–0572* ⊕ *www.thebigpicture.net.*

ARTS CENTERS
Benaroya Hall
CONCERTS | The acoustics are good from every one of the main hall's 2,500 seats—great news if you want to check out the Seattle Symphony, which is based here, or any of a number of world-class speakers, musicians, and other performers who appear here throughout the year. The four-story lobby has a curved glass facade that makes intermissions

The Grammy-nominated Seattle Symphony performs in Benaroya Hall.

almost as impressive as performances. ✉ *200 University St., Seattle* ☎ *206/215–4800* ⊕ *www.seattlesymphony.org/benaroya.*

CLASSICAL MUSIC
★ Seattle Symphony
MUSIC | The symphony performs from September through June in the stunning Benaroya Hall. The group has been nominated for numerous Grammy Awards and is well regarded nationally and internationally. ✉ *Benaroya Hall, 200 University St., Downtown* ☎ *206/215–4747* ⊕ *www.seattlesymphony.org.*

THEATER
A Contemporary Theatre (ACT)
THEATER | Dedicated to launching exciting works by emerging dramatists, ACT has four staging areas, including a theater-in-the-round and an intimate downstairs space for small shows. The season runs from April to November. ✉ *700 Union St., Downtown* ☎ *206/292–7676* ⊕ *www.acttheatre.org.*

The 5th Avenue Theatre
THEATER | Even if you don't plan on seeing anything here, this Asian fantasia is worth a peek—it's one of the most beautiful venues in the world. The 5th Avenue Theatre opened in 1926 as a silent-movie house and vaudeville stage, complete with a giant pipe organ and ushers who dressed as cowboys and pirates. Today it has its own theater company, which stages lavish productions October through May. At other times it hosts concerts, lectures, and films. ✉ *1308 5th Ave., Downtown* ☎ *206/625–1900* ⊕ *www.5thavenue.org.*

👜 Shopping

Much of the Downtown core is given over to chains like North Face and Anthropologie, but you'll find Nordstrom's lovely flagship store here as well as a packed Nordstrom Rack and Westlake Center. An outdoor urban atmosphere of street musicians and the bustle of industry make for an enjoyable, walkable retail experience. Independent gems are scattered throughout, particularly in and around Pike Place Market and along Western Avenue—although for a greater concentration of indie stores, head to Capitol Hill, Belltown, or the northern neighborhoods. Downtown is a great area for wandering, browsing, and people-watching along the way, but we've listed the shops that are worth a special visit.

■ TIP→ Find the best shopping on 4th, 5th, and 6th Avenues between Pine and Spring Streets, and 1st Avenue between Virginia and Madison Streets.

ANTIQUES AND COLLECTIBLES
Seattle Antiques Market
ANTIQUES & COLLECTIBLES | For antiques lovers, this market should not be missed. A funky warehouse offering everything from modern furniture to gemstones and bicycles, there is an unmistakable charm that keeps Seattleites coming back. Parking is tricky, so if you are already shopping in Pike Place Market, we recommend soaking up the fresh salty breeze and walking to this hidden gem. ⊠ 1400 Alaskan Way, Downtown 🕾 206/623–6115 ⊕ www.seattleantiques-market.com.

APPAREL
Alhambra
WOMEN'S CLOTHING | Sophisticated yet casual, this pricey boutique delivers quality, European-style looks for women of all ages. Pop into the Moorish-inspired shop for a party dress, elegant jewelry, or separates, and be sure to check out the house line, designed by the owners. ⊠ 101 Pine St., Downtown 🕾 206/621–9571 ⊕ www.alhambrastyle.com.

Marios
MIXED CLOTHING | Known for fabulous service and designer labels, this high-end boutique treats every client like a superstar. Men shop the ground floor for Armani, Etro, and Zegna; women ascend the ornate staircase for Prada, Emilio

Pucci, and Lanvin. A freestanding Hugo Boss boutique sells the sharpest tuxedos in town. ⊠ 1513 6th Ave., Downtown 🕾 206/223–1461 ⊕ www.marios.com.

Pirkko
WOMEN'S CLOTHING | A petite, colorful boutique by Pike Place Market, Pirkko carries a selection of high-quality Finnish and Scandinavian clothing and accessories, including famously bold pieces by Marimekko. ⊠ 1407 1st Ave., Downtown 🕾 206/223–1112.

BOOKS
Metsker Maps of Seattle
BOOKS | Whether you're searching for a laminated pocket map of Seattle or a world map made up of music notes, stop here for a massive selection of books, globes, charts, atlases, antique reproduction maps, and local satellite images. Don't let the store's location in the middle of Pike Place Market fool you: this is a Seattle institution, not a tourist trap. ⊠ 1511 1st Ave., Downtown 🕾 206/623–8747 ⊕ www.metskers.com.

DEPARTMENT STORES
★ Nordstrom
DEPARTMENT STORE | Seattle's own retail giant sells quality clothing, accessories, cosmetics, jewelry, and lots of shoes—in keeping with its roots in footwear—including many hard-to-find sizes. Peruse the various floors for anything from trendy jeans to lingerie to goods for the home. A sky bridge on the store's fourth floor will take you to Pacific Place Shopping Center. Deservedly renowned for its impeccable customer service, the busy Downtown flagship has a concierge desk and valet parking. **■ TIP→ The Nordstrom Rack store at 1st Avenue and Spring Street, close to Pike Place Market, has great deals on marked-down items.** ⊠ 500 Pine St., Downtown 🕾 206/628–2111 ⊕ shop.nordstrom.com.

Continued on page 80

PIKE PLACE MARKET
Nine Acres of History & Quirky Charm

With more than a century of history tucked into every corner and plenty of local personality, the Market is one spot you can't miss. Office workers hustle past cruise-ship crowds to take a seat at lunch counters that serve anything from pizza to piroshkies to German sausage. Local chefs plan the evening's menu over stacks of fresh, colorful produce. At night, couples stroll in to canoodle by candlelight in tucked-away bars and restaurants. Sure, some residents may bemoan the hordes of visitors, and many Seattleites spend their dollars at a growing number of neighborhood farmers' markets. But the Market is still one of Seattle's best-loved attractions.

The Pike Place Market dates from 1907. In response to anger over rising food prices, the city issued permits for farmers to sell produce from wagons parked at Pike Place. The impromptu public market grew steadily, and in 1921 Frank Goodwin, a hotel owner who had been quietly buying up real estate around Pike Place for a decade, proposed to build a permanent space.

More than 250 businesses, including 70 eateries. Breathtaking views of Elliott Bay. A pedestrian-friendly central shopping arcade that buzzes to life each day beginning at 6:30 AM. Strumming street musicians. Cobblestones, flying fish, and the very first Starbucks. Pike Place Market —the oldest continuously operated public market in the United States and a beloved Seattle icon—covers all the bases.

The Market's vitality ebbed after World War II, with the exodus to the suburbs and the rise of large supermarkets. Both it and the surrounding neighborhoods began to deteriorate. But a group of dedicated residents, led by the late architect Victor Steinbrueck, rallied and voted the Market a Historical Asset in the early 1970s. Years of subsequent restoration turned the Market into what you see today.

Pike Place Market is many buildings built around a central arcade (which is distinguished by its huge red neon sign). Shops and restaurants fill buildings on Pike Place and Western Avenue. In the main arcade, dozens of booths sell fresh produce, cheese, spices, coffee, crafts, and seafood—which can be packed in dry ice for flights home. Farmers sell high-quality produce that helps to set Seattle's rigorous dining standards. The shopkeepers who rent store spaces sell art, curios, clothing, beads, and more. Most shops cater to tourists, but there are gems to be found.

EXPLORING THE MARKET

TOP EATS

❶ THE PINK DOOR. This adored (and adorable) Italian eatery is tucked into Post Alley. Whimsical decor, very good Italian food (such as the scrumptious *linguine alla vongole*), and weekend cabaret and burlesque make this gem a must-visit.

❷ LE PANIER. It's a self-proclaimed "Very French Bakery" and another Seattle favorite. The pastries are the main draw, but sandwiches on fresh baguettes and stuffed croissants offer more substantial snacks.

❸ PIROSHKY PIROSHKY. Authentic piroshky come in both standard varieties (beef and cheese) and Seattle-influenced ones (smoked salmon with cream cheese). There are plenty of sweet piroshky, too, if you need a sugar fix.

❹ CAMPAGNE. This French favorite and its charming attached café have you covered, whether you want a quick Croque Madame for lunch, a leisurely and delicious weekend brunch, or a white-tablecloth dinner.

❺ BEECHER'S. Artisanal cheeses—and mac-n-cheese to go—make this a spot Seattleites will brave the crowds for.

❻ THREE GIRLS BAKERY. This tiny bakery turns out piles of pastries and sandwiches on their fresh-baked bread (the baked salmon is a favorite).

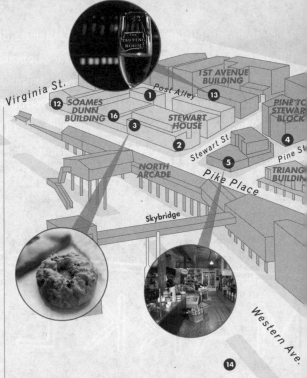

❼ MATT'S IN THE MARKET. Matt's is the best restaurant in the Market, and one of the best in the city. Lunch is casual (try the catfish po'boy), and dinner is elegant, with fresh fish and local produce showcased on the small menu. Reservations are essential.

❽ DAILY DOZEN DONUTS. Mini-donuts are made fresh before your eyes and are a great snack to pick up before you venture into the labyrinth.

❾ MARKET GRILL. This no-frills counter serves up the market's best fish sandwiches and a great clam chowder.

❿ CHUKAR CHERRIES. Look for handmade confections featuring—but not restricted to—local cherries dipped in all sorts of sweet, rich coatings.

TOP SHOPS

⓫ MARKET SPICE TEA. For a tin of the Market's signature tea, Market Spice Blend, which is infused with cinnamon and clove oils, seek out Market Spice shop on the south side of the main arcade.

⓬ PIKE & WESTERN WINE SHOP. The Tasting Room in Post Alley may be a lovely place to sample Washington wines, but Pike and Western is the place where serious oenophiles flock.

⓭ THE TASTING ROOM. With one of the top wine selections in town, the Tasting Room offers Washington wines for the casual collector and the experienced connois-

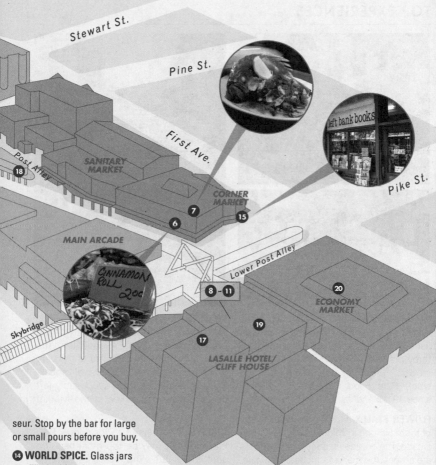

seur. Stop by the bar for large or small pours before you buy.

14 WORLD SPICE. Glass jars are filled with spices and teas from around the world here: Buy by the ounce or grab a pre-packaged gift set as a souvenir.

15 LEFT BANK BOOKS. A collective in operation since 1973, this tiny bookshop specializes in political and history titles and alternative literature.

16 THE ORIGINAL STAR-BUCKS. At 1912 Pike Place, you'll find the tiny store that opened in 1971 and started an

empire. The shop is definitely more quaint and old-timey than its sleek younger siblings, and it features the original, uncensored (read: bare-breasted) version of the mermaid logo.

17 RACHEL'S GINGER BEER. The flagship store for Seattle's wildly popular ginger beer serves up delicious variations on its homemade brew, including boozy cocktails.

18 PAPPARDELLE'S PASTA. There's no type of pasta you could dream up that isn't already in a bin at Pappardelle's.

19 DELAURENTI'S. This amazing Italian grocery has everything from fancy olive oil to digestifs and wine to meats and fine cheeses.

TOP EXPERIENCES

Pike Place Flowers

Pike Place Fish Co.

Market buskers

FISHMONGERS. There are four spots to visit if you want to see some serious fish: Pike Place Fish Co. (where the fish-throwers are—look for the awestruck crowds); City Fish (the place for fresh crab); Pure Food Fish Market (selling since 1911); and Jack's Fish Spot.

FLOWER STALLS. Flower growers, many of them Hmong immigrants, dot the main arcade. The gorgeous, seasonal bouquets are among the market's biggest draws.

PILES OF PRODUCE. The bounty of the agricultural valleys just outside Seattle is endless. In summer, seek out sweet peaches and Rainier cherries. In fall, look for cider made from Yakima Valley apples. There are dozens of produce vendors, but Sosio's and Manzo Brothers have been around the longest.

BUSKERS. The market has more than 240 street entertainers in any given year; the parade of Pacific Northwest hippie quirkitude is entertainment in itself.

POST ALLEY. There are some great finds in the alley that runs the length of the Market, paralleling First Avenue, from the highbrow (The Tasting Room) to the very lowbrow (the Gum Wall, a wall speckled with discarded gum supposedly left by people waiting in line at the Market Theater).

GHOSTS. If you listen to local lore, Pike Place Market may be the most haunted spot in Seattle. The epicenter seems to be 1921 First Avenue, where Butterworths & Sons Undertakers handled most of Seattle's dead in the early 1900s. You might see visitors sliding flowers into the building's old mail slot.

***SLEEPLESS IN SEATTLE* STOP.** Though it's been more than a decade since Rob Reiner and Tom Hanks discussed dating mores at the bar of The Athenian Inn, tourists still snap pictures of the corner they occupied. Look for the bright red plaque declaring: *TOM HANKS SAT HERE.*

A DAY AT THE MARKET

6:30 AM: Delivery vans and trucks start to fill the narrow streets surrounding Pike Place Market. Vendors with permanent stalls arrive to stack produce, arrange flowers, and shovel ice into bins for displaying salmon, crab, octopus, and other delicacies.

7:30 AM: Breakfast is served! ■TIP→ **For freshly made pastries head to Three Girls and Le Panier.**

9 AM: Craftspeople vying for day stalls sign in and are assigned spots based on seniority.

10 AM: Craftspeople set up Down Under —the levels below the main arcade— as the main arcade officially opens. The Heritage Center on Western Avenue opens. ■TIP→ **See available market tours at ⊕ *pikeplacemarket.org/tours-market*.**

11 AM: The Market madness begins. In summer, midday crowds make it nearly impossible to walk through the street-level arcades. ■TIP→ **Head Down Under where things are often a bit quieter.**

12 PM–2 PM: Lunch counters at places like the Athenian Inn and the Market Grill fill up.

Pike Place Market

5 PM: Down Under shops close and the cobblestones are hosed down. (The Market closes at 6 pm Mon.–Sat. and 5 pm on Sun.)

7 PM–2 AM: Patrons fill the tables at the Alibi Room, Zig Zag Café, the Pink Door, Matt's at the Market, and Maximilien's.

RACHEL THE PIG

Rachel, the 550-pound bronze pig that greets marketgoers at the main entrance on Pike and 1st Avenue, is a popular photo stop. But she's also a giant piggy bank that contributes up to $9,000 per year to the Market Foundation. Rachel was sculpted by Georgia Gerber, of Whidbey Island, and was named for the 750-pound pig that won the 1985 Island County Fair.

PARKING

There are numerous garages in the area, including one affiliated with the market itself (the Public Market Parking Garage at 1531 Western Avenue), at which you can get validated parking from many merchants; some restaurants offer free parking at this garage after 5 pm. You'll also find several pay lots farther south on Western Avenue and north on 1st Avenue Street parking is next to impossible to find midday. From Downtown hotels, the Market is easy to reach on foot or on city buses in the "Ride Free Zone."

GIFTS AND HOME DECOR

Sur La Table

HOUSEWARES | Need a brass-plated medieval French duck press? You've come to the right place. Culinary artists and foodies have flocked to this popular Pike Place Market destination since 1972. The chain's flagship shop is packed to the rafters with thousands of kitchen items, including an exclusive line of copper cookware, endless shelves of baking equipment, tabletop accessories, cookbooks, and a formidable display of knives. ✉ *84 Pine St., Downtown* ☎ *206/448–2244* ⊕ *www.surlatable.com.*

Watson Kennedy Fine Living

HOUSEWARES | This small store in the courtyard of the Inn at the Market is worth a visit just for how heavenly it smells. With a lovely line of artisanal jewelry, luxurious bath products, and enticing—and often aromatic—gifts, it makes for a relaxing stop in the Pike Place tour. A standout favorite is Seattle-based fragrance brand Antica Farmacista—you'll want every scent of their luxury reed diffusers. Watson Kennedy's sister store is located on 1st Avenue and Spring Street (✉ *Watson Kennedy Fine Home, 1022 1st Ave.*) and includes vintage furniture, tableware, gourmet foods, and its own line of beeswax candles. ✉ *86 Pine St., Downtown* ☎ *206/443–6281* ⊕ *www. watsonkennedy.com.*

JEWELRY

Turgeon Raine Jewelers

JEWELRY & WATCHES | Offering an art-forward take on gems and jewelry in a spacious contemporary gallery, Turgeon Raine employs only staff with a design background—you can work with them to create a one-of-a-kind piece, or pick from house-made items on display. It's also Washington's exclusive representative for Patek Philippe watches. ✉ *1407 5th Ave., Downtown* ☎ *206/447–9488* ⊕ *www. turgeonraine.com.*

SHOES

A Mano

SHOES | The store's name means "by hand," and that ethos of handmade, high-quality craftsmanship seems soaked into the very (exposed brick) walls of this charming shop. A small selection of shoes from all over the world, along with some jewelry and handbags from local designers can be found here—all of it lovingly selected and much of it unique. ✉ *1115 1st Ave., Downtown* ☎ *206/292–1767* ⊕ *www.shopamano.com.*

John Fluevog Shoes

SHOES | You'll find the store's own brand of fun and funky boots, chunky leather shoes, and urbanized wooden sandals here in men's and women's styles. ✉ *205 Pine St., Downtown* ☎ *206/441–1065* ⊕ *www.fluevog.com.*

WINE AND SPECIALTY FOODS

★ DeLaurenti Specialty Food and Wine

WINE/SPIRITS | Attention foodies: clear out your hotel minibars and make room for delectable treats from DeLaurenti (open until 5 pm daily). And, if you're planning any picnics, swing by here first. Imported meats and cheeses crowd the deli cases, and packaged delicacies pack the aisles. Stock up on hard-to-find items like truffle-infused olive oil or excellent Italian vintages from the wine shop upstairs. ✉ *Pike Place Market, 1435 1st Ave., Downtown* ☎ *206/622–0141* ⊕ *www. delaurenti.com.*

★ Fran's Chocolates

CHOCOLATE | This Seattle institution (helmed by Fran Bigelow) has been making quality chocolates for decades. Its world-famous salted caramels are transcendent—a much-noted favorite of the Obama family—as are delectable truffles, which are spiked with oolong tea, single-malt whiskey, or raspberry, among other flavors. This shop is housed in the elegant Four Seasons on 1st Avenue. ✉ *1325 1st Ave., Downtown* ☎ *206/682–0168* ⊕ *www.franschocolates.com.*

Pike and Western Wine Shop

WINE/SPIRITS | These folks have spent more than four decades carving out a reputation as one of the best wine markets in the city. With more than 1,000 wines personally selected from the Pacific Northwest and around the world, this shop offers expert advice from friendly salespeople. ✉ *1934 Pike Pl., Downtown* ☎ *206/441–1307* ⊕ *www.pikeandwestern.com* ⊘ *Closed Sun.*

Sotto Voce Inc

OTHER SPECIALTY STORE | This Italian-inspired local company has taken savory infusions to the next level with its assortment of "made from scratch" oils and vinegars. Each bottle is produced by hand, from flavoring to filling and labeling. Tastings are encouraged at the Pike Place Market storefront. The red-chili-and-horseradish-infused olive oil and the lemon-, tarragon-, and dill-infused balsamic vinegar are perfect Pacific Northwest mementos you can enjoy in your own home for many meals to come. ✉ *1532 Pike Pl., Downtown* ☎ *206/624–9998* ⊕ *www.sottovoce.com.*

The Tasting Room

WINE/SPIRITS | When you're ready for a break from sightseeing, make a detour into this relaxing tasting room and wine store in the northern end of Post Alley. Several Washington State boutique wineries are represented; most of the bottles are handcrafted and/or reserve vintages. Taste the offerings, then buy a bottle or two—you can sit and enjoy your pick in the wine bar without paying for corkage. ✉ *1924 Post Alley, Downtown* ☎ *206/770–9463* ⊕ *www.winesofwashington.com.*

World Spice Merchants

FOOD | Many of the city's best chefs get their herbs, spices, and salts at this aromatic shop under Pike Place Market. Many teas are also available. ✉ *1509 Western Ave., Downtown* ☎ *206/682–7274* ⊕ *www.worldspice.com.*

Belltown

Belltown is Downtown's younger sibling, just north of Virginia Street (up to Denny Way) and stretching from Elliott Bay to 6th Avenue. Not so long ago, Belltown was home to some of the most unwanted real estate in the city. Today, Belltown is increasingly hip, with luxury condos, trendy restaurants, swanky bars, and a number of boutiques. (Most of the action happens between 1st and 4th Avenues and between Bell and Virginia Streets.) You can still find plenty of evidence of its edgy past—including a gallery exhibiting urban street art, a punk-rock vinyl shop, and a major indie rock music venue that was a cornerstone of the grunge scene—but today Belltown is almost unrecognizable to long-term residents. Except for the stunning Olympic Sculpture Park—which, especially on a gorgeous day, is not to be missed—the area doesn't have much in terms of traditional sights, but it's an interesting extension of Downtown. Though the number of homeless people in the neighborhood can be off-putting, Belltown is generally safe during the day and is very pleasant to explore.

◉ Sights

Belltown doesn't have much in the way of sights other than the magnificent Olympic Sculpture Park, which is truly a waterfront show-stopper. On the way, be sure to pop into Steinbrueck Gallery, which features artwork from indigenous Northwest Coast artists.

★ Olympic Sculpture Park

PUBLIC ART | An outdoor branch of the Seattle Art Museum is a favorite destination for picnics, strolls, and quiet contemplation. Nestled at the edge of Belltown with views of Elliott Bay, the gently sloping green space features native plants and walking paths that wind past larger-than-life public artwork. On

A steel sculpture by Richard Serra at the Olympic Sculpture Park

sunny days, the park frames an astounding panorama of the Olympic Mountains, but even the grayest afternoon casts a favorable light on the site's sculptures. The grounds are home to works by such artists as Richard Serra, Louise Bourgeois, and Alexander Calder, whose bright-red steel *Eagle* sculpture is a local favorite (and a nod to the bald eagles that sometimes soar above). *Echo*, a 46-foot-tall elongated girl's face by Spanish artist Jaume Plensa, is a beautiful and bold presence on the waterfront. The park's PACCAR Pavilion has a gift shop, café, and information about the artworks. ✉ *2901 Western Ave., between Broad and Bay Sts., Belltown* ☎ *206/654–3100* ⊕ *www.seattleartmuseum.org* ✉ *Free.*

Steinbrueck Native Gallery

ART MUSEUM | Prints, masks, drums, sculptures, baskets, and jewelry by local Native artists fill the space of this elegant Belltown gallery near Pike Place Market. Alaskan and Arctic art is also on display, including beautiful sculptural pieces carved from ivory, wood, and soapstone. ✉ *2030 Western Ave., Belltown* ☎ *206/441–3821* ⊕ *www.steinbruecknativegallery.com* ✉ *Free.*

Suyama Peterson Deguchi

ART GALLERY | The brainchild of art advocate and noted local architect George Suyama, this nonprofit gallery located within the architecture firm of Suyama Peterson Deguchi exhibits large-scale, site-specific contemporary installations three times a year. Unlike many of Seattle's galleries, this is not a commercial venue—its programming is made possible through grants and donations—which is just another reason to stroll through the lofty space. When you visit, ring the bell at 2324 2nd Avenue for entry. ✉ *2324 2nd Ave., Belltown* ☎ *206/256–0809* ⊕ *www.suyamaspace.org* ✉ *Free* ⊗ *Closed Sat.-Sun.*

🍴 Restaurants

Belltown is home to several restaurants from Seattle restaurateur Tom Douglas, including some of the eateries recommended below. Since Douglas put down roots here, Belltown has continued to expand, with hip new places to eat and drink continually cropping up alongside new luxury condos.

El Gaucho

$$$$ | STEAKHOUSE | Waistcoated waitstaff coolly navigate the packed floor of this retro steak house serving satisfying fare in a swanky, expansive room. King crab legs, crispy seared chicken, and cool tableside Caesar salads (possibly the city's best) all tantalize, but the eatery is best known for perfectly cooked steaks—and the virtuoso presentation seems to make everything taste better. **Known for:** luscious steaks; tableside Caesar salad; live piano. [$] *Average main: $75* ✉ *2200 Western Ave Ste. 101, Belltown* ☎ *206/728–1337* 🌐 *www.elgaucho.com* 🕓 *No lunch.*

Jerk Shack

$$ | CARIBBEAN | Stepping inside feels like a temporary island getaway, from the cheery yellow walls and rum barrels repurposed as palm planters to the complex aromas wafting through the air. The Caribbean food here is the real deal—Seattle-born chef Trey Lamont has Jamaican roots—with a menu featuring signature jerk-spice-dredged meats and seafood as well Cuban sandwiches, black beans, collard greens, tropical fruit salads, and fried plantains. **Known for:** big flavors and even bigger portions; sun-dappled fenced-in patio; island-style cocktails. [$] *Average main: $20* ✉ *2510 1st Ave., Belltown* ☎ *206/441–7817* 🌐 *www.jerkshackseattle.com.*

Tom's Corner 🍴

Restaurateur Tom Douglas is a household name for foodies in Seattle. Over the last three decades, he's opened 13 full-service restaurants and a convivial cooking school, Hot Stove Society, that's tucked inside the Hotel Ändra (visit for a list of upcoming classes). The James Beard Outstanding Restaurateur also launched Rub With Love, a spice blend line carried at stores all over the city. At the corner of 4th Avenue and Virginia Street, you'll find Hot Stove Society and Lola, his ever-popular Mediterranean-inspired eatery, as well as Serious Pie and Dahlia Bakery across the street.

Lola

$$$ | MEDITERRANEAN | Tom Douglas dishes out his signature Northwest style, spiked with Greek and Mediterranean touches—another huge success for the local celebrity chef. Try a spice-rubbed lamb chop or the eggplant shakshuka, which elevates the humble eggplant to new heights. **Known for:** Greek flavors; popular brunch; made-to-order pillowy square doughnuts. [$] *Average main: $24* ✉ *Hotel Ändra, 2000 4th Ave., Belltown* ☎ *206/441–1430* 🌐 *www.lolaseattle.com* 🕓 *Closed Mon.-Tues.*

Serious Pie

$$ | PIZZA | Serious artisanal pizzas are worth the wait here—and there will be a wait at this tiny Belltown restaurant. Famed local restaurateur Tom Douglas delivers chewy, buttery crusts anchored by such toppings as fresh arugula, guanciale (cured pork jowl), and a soft egg; or Meyer lemon, chili, and buffalo mozzarella. **Known for:** fun atmosphere; egg-topped pizza; local wine and beer selections. $ *Average main: $22* ✉ *2001 4th Ave., Belltown* ☎ *206/838–7388* ⊕ *www.tomdouglas.com.*

★ Shiro's Sushi Restaurant
$$$ | JAPANESE | Founder Shiro Kashiba is no longer here (he's now at Downtown's Sushi Kashiba), but this sushi spot is still the best in Belltown, with simple decor, ultra-fresh fish, and an omakase service that's a bit more affordable than at other spots. **Known for:** chef's choice omakase; affordable sushi; simple ambience. $ *Average main: $30* ✉ *2401 2nd Ave., Belltown* ☎ *206/443–9844* ⊕ *www. shiros.com* ☉ *No lunch.*

Six Seven
$$$$ | SEAFOOD | Like the Edgewater Hotel that houses it, Six Seven would be noteworthy for its views of Elliott Bay and the Puget Sound alone, especially if you opt to dine at the café tables lining the deck at sunset. Regionally sourced seafood such as planked salmon, miso-glazed black cod, and a flavorful bouillabaisse take top billing on the menu, which also features dishes like lamb ragout pasta and Roquefort-crusted filet mignon alongside an award-winning wine list. **Known for:** budget-friendly brunch; classic shareable sides; nice alternative to touristy waterfront seafood restaurants. $ *Average main: $60* ✉ *Edgewater Hotel, 2411 Alaskan Way, Pier 67, Downtown* ☎ *206/728–7000* ⊕ *www.edgewaterhotel.com.*

Tavolàta
$$ | ITALIAN | This Belltown favorite is helmed by superstar-chef Ethan Stowell (also of How to Cook a Wolf and Staple & Fancy), who is known for his way with fresh pasta. Serving up Italian goodness by the plateful in an industrial-chic bi-level space, Tavolàta is a decidedly lively, loud, and delicious night out on the town. **Known for:** community-style dining; housemade pasta; elegant cocktails. $ *Average main: $28* ✉ *2323 2nd Ave., Belltown* ☎ *206/838–8008* ⊕ *www. tavolata.com.*

☕ Coffee and Quick Bites

Cherry Street Coffee
$ | CAFÉ | With a handful of locations throughout Seattle, this local roaster gets coffee just right: smooth, bold, and full of flavor. Breakfast items at the laid-back café include same-day-fresh Seattle Bagels with schmear and bagel (or pita) egg sandwiches, while the lunch menu features gyro and falafel sandwiches as well as a signature Persian rice bowl with house-made yogurt, pickled vegetables, and a choice of beef or eggplant. **Known for:** friendly service; bagels and Middle Eastern fare; reliably good coffee. $ *Average main: $10* ✉ *2719 1st Ave., Belltown* ⊕ *www.cherryst.com.*

Dahlia Bakery
$ | BAKERY | Attached to Serious Pie, this fragrant bakery will make you reconsider cookies as a valid breakfast choice. The coffee, fresh pastries, and breakfast sandwiches here are delicious, but Dahlia is particularly famous for its peanut butter sandwich cookies. **Known for:** convenient lunch options; coconut cream pie; peanut butter sandwich cookies. $ *Average main: $12* ✉ *2001 4th Ave., Belltown* ⊕ *www.dahliabakery.com.*

Macrina Bakery
$ | BAKERY | One of Seattle's favorite bakeries is also popular for breakfast and brunch and an excellent place to take a delicious break on your way to or from the Olympic Sculpture Park. With its perfectly executed breads and pastries— from Nutella brioche and ginger cookies to almond croissants and dark chocolate, sugar-dusted brownies—it's become a true Belltown institution. **Known for:** breakfast and lunch options; baguettes; pastries. $ *Average main: $7* ✉ *2408 1st Ave., Belltown* ☎ *206/448–4032* ⊕ *www. macrinabakery.com* ☉ *No dinner.*

Hotels

Belltown, slightly north and within walking distance of Downtown, has some of the city's trendiest hotels. It's a great place to stay if you plan to hit the bars and clubs in the neighborhood. Belltown hotels are convenient (and within walking distance) to many major sights—including the Seattle Art Museum, Pike Place Market, and the Olympic Sculpture Park.

★ Ace Hotel

$$ | HOTEL | The Ace is a dream come true for anyone who appreciates unique minimalist decor, with touches like army-surplus blankets, industrial metal sinks, and street art breaking up any notion of austerity; the cheapest rooms share bathrooms, which have enormous showers. **Pros:** ultratrendy but affordable; good place to meet other travelers; free Wi-Fi. **Cons:** half the rooms have shared bathrooms; not for people who want pampering; lots of stairs to get to lobby. $ *Rooms from: $229* ✉ *2423 1st Ave., Belltown* ☎ *206/448–4721* ⊕ *www.ace-hotel.com* ⤳ *28 rooms* ⊚ *No Meals.*

The Edgewater

$$$$ | HOTEL | Literally perched over Elliott Bay, the rustic-chic Edgewater has spectacular west-facing views of ferries and sailboats, seals and seabirds, and the distant Olympic Mountains, so don't even think of booking a city-view room. **Pros:** one of Seattle's most unique properties; stunning public lobby lounge; complimentary bikes. **Cons:** a long walk from some attractions; expensive and rooms without views might not be worth it; thin walls and some noise from the busy waterfront. $ *Rooms from: $399* ✉ *Pier 67, 2411 Alaskan Way, Belltown* ☎ *206/728–7000, 800/624–0670* ⊕ *www.edgewaterhotel.com* ⤳ *213 rooms* ⊚ *No Meals.*

★ Hotel Ändra Seattle – MGallery

$$$$ | HOTEL | Scandinavian modern design lovers will swoon over Hotel Ändra, from the striking double-height lobby lounge that still feels cozy thanks to plush seating and a large fireplace, to the freshly renovated rooms, which feature stylish furnishings in an on-trend palette of grays, ochres, and pinks. **Pros:** unique boutique hotel style and luxurious touches; Tom Douglas restaurant Lola on ground level; in a walkable area and close to attractions. **Cons:** some street noise late at night; old building with slow elevators; bathrooms on the small side. $ *Rooms from: $464* ✉ *2000 4th Ave., Belltown* ☎ *206/448–8600, 877/448–8600* ⊕ *www.hotelandra.com* ⤳ *115 rooms* ⊚ *No Meals.*

Kimpton Palladian Hotel

$$ | HOTEL | At this hip Kimpton hotel in a 1910 Belltown landmark, the unpretentious vibe is masculine-chic, from the tufted-leather front desk to the Napoleonic-style pop-art portraits of local icons like Jimi Hendrix, Bill Gates, and Frasier Crane that hang in the lobby and appear again as pillows in the guest rooms. **Pros:** tons of bold style; a short walk from Pike Place Market; Shaker + Spear restaurant serves fab seafood. **Cons:** rooms are on the small side; awkward bathroom layout; street noise. $ *Rooms from: $210* ✉ *2000 2nd Ave., Belltown* ☎ *206/448–1111* ⊕ *www.palladianhotel.com* ⤳ *97 rooms* ⊚ *No Meals.*

Seattle Marriott Waterfront

$$$ | HOTEL | With views of Elliott Bay from most rooms (half have small Juliet balconies), proximity to the cruise terminals, comfy beds, and a great location near the tourist spots and the financial district, this property is a hot spot for groups and cruise travelers. **Pros:** relaxing lobby invites lounging; elevator takes you directly to Pike Place Market; outdoor pool. **Cons:** train noise; expensive restaurant and bar; uphill walk to most sights. $ *Rooms from: $349* ✉ *2100 Alaskan Way, (between Piers 62/63 and Pier 66), Belltown* ☎ *206/443–5000, 800/455–8254* ⊕ *www.marriott.com/seawf* ⤳ *358 rooms* ⊚ *No Meals.*

Warwick Seattle Hotel

$$$ | HOTEL | Space Needle views, vintage charm, and family-friendly service abound at this renovated classic hotel in Belltown, which features contemporary guest rooms with soundproofed sliders and patios and Italian marble-clad bathrooms. **Pros:** great walkable location; Juliet balconies in most rooms; heated indoor pool and whirlpool. **Cons:** slow Wi-Fi; small fitness room; expensive valet parking. $ *Rooms from: $271* ⊠ *401 Lenora St., Belltown* ☎ *206/443–4300, 206/443–4300* ⊕ *www.warwickwa.com* ⇨ *230 rooms* ⫯⊙⫯ *No Meals.*

▼ Nightlife

Belltown can be an absolute madhouse on weekends. That said, there are some lovely spaces, a few of which stay relatively low-key even during the Saturday-night crush, as well as some quirky old neighborhood dives left over from Belltown's former life. Belltown can get gritty late at night around the Pike–Pine Corridor, so stick to busy, well-lit areas.

BARS AND LOUNGES

Bathtub Gin & Co.

BARS | The speakeasy trend has produced some lovely, intimate bars, including this one, which is reached via a wooden door in an alley next to the Humphrey Apartments (it's actually in the basement of the building). The tiny, shabby-chic bar is a laid-back spot to settle into a couch for a few drinks. Note that despite being a pain in the neck to find, the bar still attracts the hard-partying Belltown crowd on weekends, so go midweek for maximum serenity. ⊠ *2205 2nd Ave., Belltown* ☎ *206/728–6069* ⊕ *bathtubgin-seattle.com.*

Black Bottle

PUBS | This sleek and sexy gastro-tavern makes the northern reaches of Belltown look good. The interior is simple but stylish, with black chairs and tables and shiny wood floors. It gets crowded on nights and weekends with a laid-back but often dressed-up clientele. A small selection of beers on tap and a solid wine list (with Washington, Oregon, California, and beyond well represented) will help you wash down the sustainably sourced and creatively presented snacks and shareable dishes, including house-smoked wild boar ribs, pork belly with kimchi, and oysters on the half shell. Vegan and nut-, dairy-, and gluten-free options are plentiful. ⊠ *2600 1st Ave., Belltown* ☎ *206/441–1500* ⊕ *www.black-bottleseattle.com.*

List

PUBS | A Belltown favorite for great happy-hour deals, this hip, dimly lit space has a come-hither glow thanks to red and white backlighting. An all-day happy hour on Sunday and Monday (or Tuesday to Saturday from 4–6:30 pm and 9–11) means you get half off the yummy food menu (local clams, Angus beef burgers, bacon-wrapped prawns, spicy calamari), plus $22 bottles of wine. ⊠ *2226 1st Ave., Belltown* ☎ *206/441–1000* ⊕ *www.listbelltown.com.*

The Rendezvous

GATHERING PLACES | Since it opened in 1926 as an elite screening room for film stars and moguls, Rendezvous has done time as both a porn theater and a dive bar. Today it's settled down as a multipurpose hub with a small theater, a basement bar, a lounge, and a classic dining room. While maintaining the building's 1920s charm, it's been spruced up just enough to suit the new wave of wealthy locals without alienating everyone else. The Jewelbox Theater (live music, comedy, film, burlesque shows) sets it apart from the neighborhood's string of cookie-cutter trendy spots. ⊠ *2322 2nd Ave., Belltown* ☎ *206/441–5823* ⊕ *www.therendezvous.rocks.*

Rob Roy

COCKTAIL LOUNGES | With its deep selection of dark liquor, low-light ambience, and black leather walls, Rob Roy is a serious-but-inviting cocktail bar. Their original concoctions change four to five times a year, and include drinks like a Saffron Sandalwood Sour. They also feature nonalcoholic cocktails for teetotalers and designated drivers. Goldfish crackers, beef jerky, and chicken meatballs are among the options on the limited food menu, which is half-off during a daily 4–6 pm happy hour that also features drink specials. ⊠ *2332 2nd Ave., Belltown* ☎ *206/956–8423* ⊕ *www.robroyseattle. com.*

Shorty's

BARS | It may be one of the diviest bars in Belltown, but Shorty's is a bright spot in a neighborhood where most bars serve $15 cocktails (and the bathrooms happen to be spotless). Along with a come-as-you-are atmosphere, the grown-up arcade features pinball machines and video games, cheap beer and gourmet hot dogs, and lots of no-frills fun. ⊠ *2316 2nd Ave., Belltown* ☎ *206/441–5449* ⊕ *www. shortydog.com.*

Umi Sake House

BARS | Choose from a wide selection of sake and sake-based cocktails in a space designed to look like someone shoehorned a real *izakaya* (a sake house that also serves substantial snacks) into a Belltown building—there's even an enclosed patio and a tatami room that can be reserved for larger parties. The sushi is good, and there's a very long happy hour offered at one of the bar areas. Umi is less of a meat market than some Belltown spots—unless you're here late on a Friday or Saturday night. ⊠ *2230 1st Ave., Belltown* ☎ *206/374–8717* ⊕ *www.umisakehouse.com.*

The Whisky Bar

BARS | One of Belltown's reigning dive bars, this aptly named spot has a jaw-dropping selection of whisky, bourbon, and rye. They also have 24 beers on tap, mostly from West Coast brewers, and a bottle list with beers from around

the world. The food menu includes comfort food such as wings, giant pretzels, and burgers. Daily happy hour runs from 3:30 to 5:30 pm. ⊠ *2122 2nd Ave., Belltown* ☎ *206/443–4490* ⊕ *www. thewhiskybar.com.*

MUSIC VENUES
★ The Crocodile

LIVE MUSIC | The heart and soul of Seattle's music scene since 1991 has hosted the likes of the Beastie Boys, Pearl Jam, and Mudhoney, along with countless other bands. There's a reason *Rolling Stone* once called The Crocodile one of the best small clubs in America. Even now, in new, much larger digs (the main room has a 750-person capacity) not far from the original, The Croc retains its old-school Seattle vibe. ⊠ *2505 1st Ave., Belltown* ☎ *206/441–7416* ⊕ *www. thecrocodile.com.*

🛍 Shopping

Stroll along 1st Avenue to find an eclectic mix of high-end clothing boutiques, custom tailoring shops, artsy gift stores, and gritty standouts. A few local, independent designers are represented here, although the clothing tends to be more upmarket than the crafty, DIY goods offered in Capitol Hill or Ballard.

■ **TIP→** Find the best shopping along 1st Avenue between Cedar and Virginia Streets.

BOOKS
★ Peter Miller Architectural & Design Books and Supplies

BOOKS | Aesthetes and architects haunt this shop, which is stocked with all things design. Rare, international architecture, art, and design books (including titles for children) mingle with high-end products from Alessi and Iittala; sleek notebooks, bags, portfolios, and drawing tools round out the collection. This is a great shop for quirky, unforgettable gifts, like a pentagram typography calendar, an Arne Jacobsen wall clock, or an

3

Downtown and Belltown **BELLTOWN**

aerodynamic umbrella. ⊠ *304 Alaskan Way South, Post Alley, Belltown ⊹ Entrance off alley* ☎ *206/441–4114* ⊕ *www. petermiller.com* ⊗ *Closed Sun.*

CLOTHING
Kuhlman

MIXED CLOTHING | This tiny store tucked inside the Ace Hotel has a careful selection of urban street wear that includes hard-to-find designers like Nudie Jeans Co., Barbour, and Fred Perry—it's sophisticated while still maintaining an edge. Kuhlman is best known for creating custom clothing, often from superb European and Japanese fabrics. ⊠ *2419 1st Ave., Belltown* ☎ *206/441–1999* ⊕ *www. kuhlmanseattle.com.*

Patagonia

MIXED CLOTHING | If the person next to you on the bus isn't wearing North Face, they're probably clad in Patagonia. This popular and durable brand excels at functional outdoor wear—made with earth-friendly materials such as hemp and organic cotton—as well as technical clothing hip enough for mountaineers or urban hikers. The line of whimsically patterned fleece wear for children is particularly cute. ⊠ *2100 1st Ave., Belltown* ☎ *206/622–9700* ⊕ *www.patagonia.com.*

Sassafras

WOMEN'S CLOTHING | Find locally made fashions from eight in-house designers and some 60 local designers in this charming Belltown storefront, including a popular obi wrap dress that seems to flatter everybody and stylish jewelry and accessories. ⊠ *2307 1st Ave., Belltown* ☎ *206/420–7057* ⊕ *www.sassafras-seattle.com* ⊗ *Closed Sun.-Tues.*

MUSIC
Singles Going Steady

MUSIC | If punk rock is more to you than anarchy symbols sewn on Target sweatshirts, then stop here. Punk and its myriad subgenres on CD and vinyl are specialties, though they also stock rockabilly, indie rock, and hip-hop. It's a nice foil to the city's indie-rock-dominated record shops, and a good reminder that Belltown is still more eclectic than its rising rents may indicate. ⊠ *2219 2nd Ave., Belltown* ☎ *206/441–7396* ⊗ *Closed Sun.-Mon.*

Activities

SPAS
Spa Noir

SPAS | If you're not into the new-age earthy vibe found in so many day spas, head to Spa Noir, a hip Belltown spot done up in black, red, and gold. The spa specializes in facials, manicures, pedicures, and other beauty treatments, but it also offers a small menu of reasonably priced massage treatments. ⊠ *2120 2nd Ave., Belltown* ☎ *206/448–7600* ⊕ *www. spanoir.net.*

Chapter 4

SOUTH LAKE UNION AND QUEEN ANNE

Updated by
Naomi Tomky

⊙ **Sights**
★★★★☆

🍴 **Restaurants**
★★★★☆

🛏 **Hotels**
★★★☆☆

🛍 **Shopping**
★★☆☆☆

🍸 **Nightlife**
★☆☆☆☆

NEIGHBORHOOD SNAPSHOT

TOP REASONS TO GO

■ Visit (or gaze up at) the **Space Needle** and rock out at **MoPOP**; leave a couple of hours to visit **Chihuly Garden and Glass**, the **Children's Museum**, or the nearby **Bill & Melinda Gates Visitor Center**.

■ **Kerry Park** has outstanding views of the skyline and Elliott Bay. It's an all-time favorite spot for snapshots and public displays of affection.

■ Seattle Center houses the opera, ballet, and the headquarters of **SIFF Cinema**. Don't miss **On the Boards**, a small but important performing-arts space.

■ **Climate Pledge Arena** hosts concerts by international headliners and the home games of two Seattle pro sports teams: the WNBA's Storm (basketball) and the NHL's Kraken (hockey).

■ Rent a small boat at the **Center for Wooden Boats** to tour Lake Union, and go back in time with a visit to the **Museum of History and Industry**.

GETTING HERE AND AROUND

The monorail runs from Westlake Center (5th Avenue and Pine Street) for easy access from Downtown. It runs from 7:30 am (8:30 am weekends) to 11 pm (extended for events at Climate Pledge Arena), with departures every 10 minutes. Traffic and parking around the Center can be nightmarish during special events, so walk or take public transportation if you can. Walking to Seattle Center from the Olympic Sculpture Park is a half-mile stroll northeast on Broad Street.

From Downtown, multiple bus lines run up 3rd and 1st Avenues to Seattle Center. Buses also climb Queen Anne Avenue, making the commercial districts easy to reach from Downtown or Seattle Center; the rest of that neighborhood requires a car.

From Downtown, South Lake Union is served by the Seattle Streetcar. The #8 bus connects South Lake Union to Seattle Center and Lower Queen Anne.

FUN FACT

■ In the 1990s, Seattle voters rejected the idea of turning the then largely industrial area south of Lake Union into a Central Park-style greenspace. The property ownership reverted to the person who donated the money for its purchase, Microsoft co-founder Paul Allen. His company developed the area, which struggled until Amazon announced it would become their headquarters in 2007.

PLANNING YOUR TIME

■ Depending on your endurance, you can combine a visit to the Space Needle with one museum visit before exhaustion sets in. Schedule more time for the Pacific Science Center and MoPOP than other sights—the former includes a laser show and the latter has a lot of interactive exhibits. The Space Needle is open late in summer.

South Lake Union

South Lake Union, on the east side of Seattle Center, is a destination in itself. Though it's still in transition (construction is underway in many areas), Amazon's headquarters and major tech company offices draw more amenities, such as boutiques and upscale restaurants, and hotels with great views. The biggest attractions are Lake Union itself, the Museum of History and Industry, and the incredible REI megastore.

Sights

Amazon Spheres

GARDEN | Three giant glass spheres filled with indoor gardens anchor the Amazon campus in South Lake Union. Living walls, 40,000 plants, and a café are part of the lounge space at Amazon's headquarters. The public must admire from afar most of the time; however, on the first and third Saturday of each month, the spheres open to the public by reservation only. Book online up to 15 days ahead of your visit, and make sure to bring government ID (for all adults in the party) and no large bags. ✉ *2111 7th Ave., South Lake Union* 🌐 *www.seattlespheres.com.*

Lake Union Park

CITY PARK | This 12-acre green space along Lake Union's southern shore includes a model boat pond, a boardwalk, a beach where you can launch small craft like kayaks and rowboats to paddle past the houseboats, a spray area for little kids, plus the Museum of History & Industry and the Center for Wooden Boats. Several historic ships sit in the dock, and cruise options also depart from the park. A 45-minute narrated Ice Cream Cruise on the Seattle mini ferry is a family favorite on Sundays year-round (on the hour from 11 to 5; $15), with additional Saturday sailings in summer. ✉ *860 Terry Ave. N, South Lake Union* ☎ *206/684–4075* 🌐 *www.atlakeunionpark.org.*

Museum of History & Industry

HISTORY MUSEUM | **FAMILY** | Located in the Lake Union Park's converted Naval Reserve Building, the 20,000-square-foot MOHAI offers visitors an in-depth slice of regional history with a permanent collection featuring more than 100,000 objects ranging from vintage souvenirs to everyday household items. Permanent exhibitions include the Center for Innovation, which showcases Seattle's role as a place where invention and entrepreneurship flourish; the exhibit is supported by a $10 million gift from Jeff Bezos, founder of Amazon (which has its corporate headquarters a few blocks away). Special temporary exhibitions examine everything from chocolate to stories of Jewish merchants in Washington State. ✉ *860 Terry Ave. N, at Lake Union Park, South Lake Union* ☎ *206/324–1126* 🌐 *www.mohai.org* 🎟 *$22, free first Thurs. of month.*

Restaurants

Bar Harbor

$$$ | **MODERN AMERICAN** | Straddling an indoor space and outdoor patio of the large 400 Fairview building, this lobster specialist channels a Maine shoreline shack into an urban west coast landscape. Seafood is the star here, particularly in the lobster roll, but also in other sandwiches, a range of salads, and the clam dip. **Known for:** frozen drinks in summer; big outdoor patio; many styles of lobster roll. [$] *Average main: $28* ✉ *400 Fairview Ave. N, Suite 105, South Lake Union* ☎ *206/922–3288* 🌐 *www.barharborbar.com* 🕒 *Closed Sun.–Mon.*

Tanoor

$$$ | **MIDDLE EASTERN** | This elegant Lebanese restaurant serves an enormous menu of Halal cuisine, including flavorful mezze, all-day breakfasts, and plenty of meat on a stick. For more casual meals, they have a few Middle Eastern street foods and sandwiches. **Known for:** huge selection of Lebanese food; spacious dining room;

The giant glass spheres at the Amazon campus are open to the public by reservation.

fresh-baked pita. $ Average main: $26 ⊠ 803 Dexter Ave. N, South Lake Union ☎ 206/457–5272 ⊕ www.tanoor.com.

Teinei

$$ | **JAPANESE** | A narrow gem tucked into the office building landscape of South Lake Union, this spot opened by the former chef of the local Japanese consulate specializes in ramen, but executes a huge variety of Japanese specialties. The izakaya food works well for a small snack with a drink, while heartier dishes make a great dinner. **Known for:** fun menu; good cocktail snacks; delicate ramen broths. $ Average main: $20 ⊠ 1256 Republican St., South Lake Union ☎ 206/420–4500 ⊕ www.teinei-seattle.com.

★ White Swan Public House

$$ | **SEAFOOD** | Weaving local seafood into gastropub-style favorites, this waterfront restaurant makes food as good as the view, which stretches up to the Space Needle to the west and over to Lake Union to the north. Seafood chowder, both on its own and over fries as "Poutine o' the Sea," Dungeness Crab Louie

salad, and amazing oysters show off the kitchen's skill with the local treasures. **Known for:** inventive seafood dishes; seafood happy hour; jaw-dropping views. $ Average main: $20 ⊠ 1001 Fairview Ave. N, South Lake Union ☎ 206/588–2680 ⊕ www.whiteswanpublichouse. com ☉ No lunch weekdays.

☕ Coffee and Quick Bites

Espresso Vivace

$ | **CAFÉ** | A large outpost of the famed Capitol Hill roaster, the Vivace coffee shrine in South Lake Union is right across from the REI megastore. Grab a seat, order an expertly prepared espresso beverage, and munch on a small variety of snacks—this is a perfect stop after an exhausting jaunt through REI. **Known for:** great latte art; café Nico; precisely pulled espresso. $ Average main: $4 ⊠ 227 Yale Ave. N, South Lake Union ☎ 206/388–5164 ⊕ www.espressovivace.com.

Great State Burger

$ | BURGER | This update to the classic American burger shop manages to be both an ode to the Northwest and an example of how fast food can be done right. Organic, grass-fed beef is broken down and ground in-house, organic milkshakes are made from local ice cream, and the crinkle-cut fries feel like a nostalgic nod to childhood. **Known for:** organic burgers; cheerful decor; local ingredients. $ *Average main: $8* ⊠ *2014 7th Ave., South Lake Union* ⊕ *www. greatstateburger.com.*

 # Hotels

Seemingly everlasting construction projects have finally begun to yield an influx of new hotels. Though they lean corporate, the area makes a good base for exploring the city and the views are generally excellent.

Astra Hotel Seattle

$$ | HOTEL | Taking cues from the tech industry, this hotel aims to be "innovation-inspired." The crisp, attractive rooms include upscale touches like Jonathan Adler toiletries, colorful ombre blinds, and wallpaper meant to look like a birds-eye view of the Space Needle. **Pros:** great views from upper floors; good fitness amenities; attractive lobby with good coffee shop. **Cons:** impersonal feel; small rooms; uninspired lobby. $ *Rooms from: $241* ⊠ *300 Terry Ave. N, South Lake Union* ☎ *206/693–6000* ⊕ *www. astrahotelseattle.com* 🛏 *265 rooms* ⊚ *No Meals.*

citizenM

$$ | HOTEL | The first location of this Dutch hotel to land on the West Coast wears its design-forward mindset on the facade, adorned with a mural by local Native American artist Jeffrey Veregge. **Pros:** friendly communal spaces; clean and modern; fun, arty design. **Cons:** bare-bones amenities in rooms; small rooms; guests complain of hard beds. $ *Rooms from: $187* ⊠ *201 Westlake Ave. N, South Lake Union* ⊕ *www.citizenm.com* 🛏 *264 rooms* ⊚ *No Meals.*

Level Seattle

$$$ | HOTEL | Though Level is geared toward longer stays—with a full kitchen, washer, and dryer in each room—it offers nightly stays too and all guests share access to the excellent facilities with the property's residents. **Pros:** full kitchens; spare, modern design; incredible fitness amenities. **Cons:** amenity and parking fees add up; staff struggle to keep up with size; street noise on lower levels. $ *Rooms from: $305* ⊠ *110 Boren Ave. N, South Lake Union* ☎ *206/455–9077* ⊕ *www.stayinglevel.com/destinations/ seattle* 🛏 *299 rooms* ⊚ *No Meals.*

Pan Pacific Hotel

$$$ | HOTEL | In the very heart of South Lake Union, this hotel is conveniently located for tourist attractions and dining, as well as for business. **Pros:** central location; soaking tubs; free shuttle. **Cons:** lacks local character; needs updating; guests report understaffing. $ *Rooms from: $331* ⊠ *2125 Terry Ave., South Lake Union* ⊹ *Above Whole Foods* ☎ *206/264–8111* ⊕ *www.panpacificseat- tle.com* 🛏 *153 rooms* ⊚ *No Meals.*

ⓨ Nightlife

A mix of a few clubs left from the area's previous life as a no-man's land between Downtown and Capitol Hill have long anchored evenings in the neighborhood, but snazzy new cocktail bars have begun to fill in the gaps.

BARS AND LOUNGES

Deep Dive

COCKTAIL LOUNGES | Renowned local chef Renee Erickson opened an enchanting nautical-themed speakeasy inside the Amazon spheres. The immersive decor adds to the swanky feel. Aside from the luxurious setting, guests are drawn by the fancy and creative cocktails using ingredients such as fig-infused

South Lake Union and Queen Anne

Lake Union

KEY
- **1** Sights
- **1** Restaurants
- **1** Quick Bites
- **1** Hotels

QUEEN ANNE

SEATTLE CENTER

SOUTH LAKE UNION

DOWNTOWN

1/4 mi

1/4 km

Sights ▼

1 Amazon Spheres **D5**
2 Bill & Melinda Gates Foundation Discovery Center **C4**
3 Chihuly Garden and Glass **B4**
4 Climate Pledge Arena.. **B4**
5 Discovery Park........... **C1**
6 Kerry Park **A3**
7 Lake Union Park **D3**
8 Museum of History & Industry **D3**
9 Museum of Pop Culture (MoPop).................. **C4**
10 Pacific Science Center **B4**
11 Seattle Children's Museum **B4**
12 Space Needle........... **B4**

Restaurants ▼

1 Bar Harbor.............. **D4**
2 Canlis Restaurant........ **C1**
3 Eden Hill **B1**
4 How To Cook A Wolf.... **B1**
5 Paju..................... **B4**
6 Tanoor.................. **C3**
7 Taylor Shellfish Oyster Bar **B4**
8 Teinei..................... **E4**
9 wa'z **C5**
10 White Swan Public House **D3**

Quick Bites ▼

1 Dick's Drive-In........... **B4**
2 Espresso Vivace **E4**
3 Great State Burger **D5**
4 Queen Cà Phê........... **B1**
5 Seattle Center Armory **B4**

Hotels ▼

1 Astra Hotel Seattle **D4**
2 citizenM.................. **D4**
3 Level Seattle **D5**
4 MarQueen Hotel........ **B3**
5 The Maxwell Hotel **B3**
6 Pan Pacific Hotel **D5**

grappa. The short but sexy food menu includes a high-end version of the cream cheese-garnished Seattle dog and a caviar service. ⊠ *620 Lenora St., South Lake Union* ⊕ *Under the small, barely marked single door on the Lenora side of the spheres.* ☎ *206/900–9390* ⊕ *www. deepdiveseattle.com.*

Mbar

BARS | One of Seattle's few rooftop bars, the colorful, partially covered patio overlooks the entire South Lake Union neighborhood. Guests gaze at the Space Needle as they sip glasses of Prosecco or look out at the lake over pink-hued cocktails while swinging in the hanging chairs. In winter, the 14th-floor spot stays open with blankets and the fire pits roaring as guests dig into the Middle Eastern–influenced small plates. ⊠ *400 Fairview Ave. N, 14th Floor, South Lake Union* ⊕ *Hop on the designated elevator in the lobby, which will whisk you straight up to the bar.* ☎ *206/457–8287* ⊕ *nadima-ma.com/mbar.*

DANCE CLUBS

Kremwerk + Timbre Room Complex

DANCE CLUBS | This queer-centric nightclub that combines modern fixtures and an industrial space is known for electronic music and theatrical performances that draw fun crowds. Tickets to shows by local and out-of-town DJs, musicians, and multidisciplinary artists are often available in advance. Upstairs, the Timbre Room hosts smaller, more intimate shows, and a third space, Cherry, has more electronic music as well as drag shows. ⊠ *1809 Minor Ave., #10, South Lake Union* ☎ *206/682–2935* ⊕ *www.kremwerk.com* ⊗ *Closed Tues.*

Lo-Fi Performance Gallery

DANCE CLUBS | The two rooms of Lo-Fi host small shows by up-and-coming local hip-hop groups, national DJs, and anything else that benefits from a crowd of committed fans. A regular venue for the Emerald City Soul Club, a fun monthly dance party of classic funk and soul, and a

Chief Seattle

At the southeast side of Seattle Center (on the corner of 5th Avenue and Denny Way) stands a statue of Chief Seattle (originally Si'ahl), of the Duwamish tribe. The chief was among the first Native Americans to have contact with the white explorers of the region. His fellow tribesmen considered him to be a great leader and peacemaker. The sculpture was created by local artist James Wehn in 1912 and dedicated by the chief's great-great-granddaughter, Myrtle Loughery.

variety of music acts and DJ nights, Lo-Fi Performance Gallery is a laid-back space that's a stark contrast to velvet-rope clubs. Its divey, warehouse-chic feel makes it a favorite among Seattleites. ⊠ *429 Eastlake Ave., South Lake Union* ☎ *206/254–2824* ⊕ *www.thelofi.net.*

🛍 Shopping

While there are a few perfunctory shops that fill in the main drag along Westlake, the biggest shopping destination is the flagship store of Seattle's giant outfitter, REI, and the smaller outdoors stores nearby that hope to ride its coattails.

★ REI

SPORTING GOODS | The enormous flagship for Recreational Equipment, Inc. (REI) has an incredible selection of outdoor gear—polar-fleece jackets, wool socks, down vests, hiking boots, rain gear, and much more—as well as its own 65-foot climbing wall. The staff is extremely knowledgeable, and there always seems to be enough help on hand, even when the store is busy. You can test things out on the mountain-bike test trail or in the simulated rain booth. REI also rents gear such as tents, sleeping bags, skis, snow-shoes, and backpacks. Bonus: they offer an hour of free parking. ⊠ *222 Yale Ave. N, South Lake Union* ☎ *206/223–1944* ⊕ *www.rei.com.*

Activities

While the land side of the lake is dominated with office buildings and condos, the lakefront is a bit of outdoor paradise.

★ The Center for Wooden Boats

BOATING | FAMILY | Located on the southern shore of Lake Union, Seattle's free maritime heritage museum is a bustling community hub. Thousands of Seattleites rent kayaks, canoes, rowboats, and small wooden sailboats here every year; the center also offers workshops, demonstrations, and classes. Rentals for nonmembers start at $25 per hour, and sailboats require a prescheduled sailing checkout test. They also offer free one-hour rowboat rentals by reservation. ⊠ *1010 Valley St., South Lake Union* ☎ *206/382–2628* ⊕ *www.cwb.org* ☉ *Closed Mon.–Tues. and from mid-Dec. to early Jan.*

★ Hot Tub Boats

BOATING | Yes, it's real, and yes, it's as cool as it sounds. Grab up to five friends and spend an afternoon or evening motoring (somewhat slowly) around Lake Union from the comfort of your own private hot tub. You can bring your own picnic on board and connect the stereo to your phone to play tunes throughout the journey. The custom-made wooden boats can be rented for $400 for two hours. ⊠ *2520 Westlake Ave. N, South Lake Union* ☎ *206/771–9883* ⊕ *www. hottubboats.com.*

Northwest Outdoor Center

BOATING | This center on Lake Union's west side rents one- or two-person kayaks (it also has a few triples) by the hour or day, including equipment and wetsuits (much needed outside of summer). The hourly rate is $23 for a single and $30 for a double (pro-rated after the first hour). For the more vertically inclined, the center also rents stand-up paddleboards

for $23 an hour. NWOC also runs classes, sunset tours near Golden Gardens Park, and full moon moonlight paddles. Reservations recommended in summer. ⊠ *2100 Westlake Ave. N, Suite 1, South Lake Union* ☎ *206/281–9694* ⊕ *www. nwoc.com.*

Queen Anne

Just west of Seattle Center, the neighborhood of Queen Anne stretches all the way up formidable Queen Anne Hill to the ship canal on the other side. The neighborhood is split into Upper and Lower Queen Anne, the latter now officially called Uptown. The two are quite different: Uptown is a mixed-income neighborhood with an interesting mix of restaurants and bars. Past Aloha Street, the neighborhood starts to look more upscale, with the snazzy Galer Street commercial strip and the urban village along Queen Anne Avenue at the top of the hill. Queen Anne doesn't have many sights, but the residential streets west of Queen Anne Avenue in Upper Queen Anne are fun to stroll, and sunny days offer gorgeous views. This ribbon of residential turf extends to the Magnolia neighborhood. There's only one sight to see in off-the-beaten-path Magnolia, but it's a terrific one: Discovery Park.

At the bottom of the hill, Uptown abuts Seattle Center, home to Seattle's version of the Eiffel Tower—the Space Needle—and is anchored by Frank Gehry's wild MoPOP building, the acclaimed Pacific Science Center, and the dazzling Chihuly Garden and Glass. This area is a key destination for the museums or to catch a show at one of the many performing arts venues.

Seattle Center's 74-acre complex was built for the 1962 World's Fair. A rolling green campus with multiple venues is organized around the massive International Fountain. Among the arts groups based here are the Seattle Repertory Theatre, Intiman Theatre, the Seattle Opera, and the Pacific Northwest Ballet. It's also the site of three of summer's largest festivals—Northwest Folklife Festival, Bite of Seattle, and Bumbershoot. Climate Pledge Arena hosts pro sports and major music acts, and the Pacific Science Center, Seattle Children's Museum, and nearby Bill & Melinda Gates Visitor Center offer engaging activities for visitors of all ages.

Sights

Bill & Melinda Gates Foundation Discovery Center

VISITOR CENTER | FAMILY | The Bill & Melinda Gates Foundation has some lofty goals, and across the street from Seattle Center you can witness their plans in action. Exhibits are thought-provoking and interactive, inviting you to offer up your own solutions to complex global problems like poverty and climate change. Fight disease, design a media campaign, and take part in a featured project to make a difference during your visit. ⊠ 440 5th Ave. N, South Lake Union ☎ 206/709–3100 ⊕ www.discovergates. com ⊗ Closed Sun.–Wed. ♿ Reservations recommended via website.

Chihuly Garden and Glass

ART GALLERY | Just steps from the base of the Space Needle, fans of Dale Chihuly's glass works will be delighted to trace the artist's early influences—neon art, Native American Northwest Coast trade baskets, and Pendleton blankets, to name a few—to the vibrant chandelier towers and architectural glass installations he is most known for today. There are eight galleries total, plus a 40-foot-tall "Glasshouse," and an outdoor garden that serves as a backdrop for colorful installations that integrate with a dynamic Northwest landscape, including native plants and a 500-year-old western cedar that washed up on the shores of Neah Bay. Chihuly, who was born and raised

in Tacoma, was actively involved in the design of the exhibition. So many of his personal touches are part of the exhibition space, you can almost feel his presence in every room (look for the guy with the unruly hair and the black eye patch). Chihuly is kid-friendly for all but the littlest ones. ■ TIP→ If you're also planning to visit the Space Needle, the combination ticket can save you some money. ⊠ 305 Harrison St., under Space Needle, South Lake Union ☎ 206/753–4940 ⊕ www. chihulygardenandglass.com ⊠ $32.

Climate Pledge Arena

SPORTS VENUE | Formerly KeyArena, this zero-carbon, renewable-energy powered arena hosts basketball (Seattle Storm) and hockey (Seattle Kraken) matches, as well as major concerts and other performances. ⊠ 334 1st Ave. N, Queen Anne ⊕ climatepledgearena.com.

★ Discovery Park

CITY PARK | FAMILY | You won't find more spectacular views of Puget Sound, the Cascades, and the Olympics. Located on Magnolia Bluff, northwest of Downtown, Seattle's largest park covers 534 acres and has an amazing variety of terrain: shaded, secluded forest trails lead to meadows, saltwater beaches, sand dunes, a lighthouse, and two miles of protected beaches. The North Beach Trail, which takes you along the shore to the lighthouse, is a must-see. Head to the South Bluff Trail to get a view of Mt. Rainier. The park has several entrances if you want to stop at the visitor center to pick up a trail map before exploring, use the main entrance at Government Way. The North Parking Lot is much closer to the North Beach Trail and to Ballard and Fremont, if you're coming from that direction. First-come, first-served beach parking passes for the disabled, elderly, and families with small children are available at the Learning Center. Note that the park is easily reached from Ballard and Fremont. It's easier to combine a park day with an exploration of those

The view from Kerry Park

neighborhoods than with a busy Downtown itinerary. ✉ *3801 W. Government Way, Magnolia* ✛ *From Downtown, take Elliot Ave. W (which turns into 15th Ave. W), and get off at Emerson St. exit and turn left onto W Emerson. Make a right onto Gilman Ave. W (which eventually becomes W Government Way). As you enter park, road becomes Washington Ave.; turn left on Utah Ave.* ☎ *206/386–4236* ⊕ *www.seattle.gov/parks/find/parks/discovery-park.*

★ **Kerry Park**

VIEWPOINT | While in Seattle, if the mood strikes you to "pop the question" (any question will do, really), you'll find the answer at Kerry Park. Famous for engagements, sweeping views of the city skyline and, on clear days, Mt. Rainier, camera buffs and romantic types can't help but linger at this 1¼-acre sliver of a city park, which is a short but steep walk up from the shops and restaurants of Lower Queen Anne. The sculpture *Changing Form* by Doris Chase was added in 1971. There's a terrific little park and

play area for kiddos at Bayview-Kinnear Park, just below the viewpoint of Kerry Park. ✉ *211 W. Highland Dr., Queen Anne* ☎ *206/684–4075* ⊕ *www.seattle.gov/parks/find/parks/kerry-park.*

Museum of Pop Culture (MoPOP)

OTHER MUSEUM | FAMILY | What started as the Experience Music Project first expanded to include science fiction and fantasy, then took on all of pop culture. The 140,000-square-foot complex is a controversial architectural statement; architect Frank Gehry drew inspiration from electric guitars to achieve the building's curvy metallic design. It's a fitting backdrop for rock memorabilia from the likes of Bob Dylan and the grunge-scene heavies.

The 35-foot tower of guitars (and other instruments) traces the instrument's history in America and includes 20 guitars from music legends. A permanent exhibit provides a primer on the evolution of Seattle's music scene. *Nirvana: Taking Punk to the Masses* features rare and unseen artifacts and photography from the band, their crews, and families.

The interactive space has 12 ministudio rooms where you can jam with friends on real or MIDI-compatible instruments. You can also channel your inner rock star in front of a virtual audience in the *On Stage* exhibit, complete with smoke, hot lights, and screaming fans.

In the Science Fiction and Fantasy Hall of Fame and related exhibits, you'll find iconic artifacts from sci-fi literature, film, television, and art, including an Imperial Dalek from *Doctor Who,* the command chair from the classic television series *Star Trek,* and Neo's coat from *The Matrix Reloaded.* ⊠ *325 5th Ave. N, between Broad and Thomas Sts., Lower Queen Anne* ☎ *206/770–2700* ⊕ *www.mopop. org* ✉ *MoPop uses dynamic pricing, so tickets are cheaper when purchased ahead and during less busy times. Expect to pay about $30.*

★ **Pacific Science Center**
SCIENCE MUSEUM | FAMILY | If you have kids, this nonprofit science center in the heart of Seattle is a must-visit; it's home to more than 200 indoor and outdoor hands-on exhibits, two IMAX theaters, a Laser Dome, a butterfly house, and a state-of-the-art planetarium. The dinosaur exhibit—complete with moving robotic reproductions—is a favorite, and tots can experiment with water at the ever-popular stream table. Follow the journey of a drop of water through an interactive outdoor maze, then warm up in the Tropical Butterfly House, the 80°F home to colorful butterflies from South and Central America, Africa, and Asia. Look for the giant white arches near the Space Needle and make a day of the surrounding sights. ■TIP➔ **Pacific Science Center offers a number of lectures, forums, and "Science Cafes" for adults, plus a variety of educational programs for kids, including camp-ins, monthly parents' night outs, workshops, and more. See website for schedule information.** ⊠ *200 2nd Ave. N, Queen Anne* ☎ *206/443–2001* ⊕ *www. pacificsciencecenter.org* ✉ *$27.95,*

discounts for advance purchase, IMAX shows extra ☉ *Closed Mon.–Tues.*

Seattle Children's Museum
CHILDREN'S MUSEUM | FAMILY | If you're traveling with kids, you already know that a good children's museum is like gold at the end of a rainbow. This colorful, spacious museum, located on the lower level of The Armory in the heart of Seattle Center, provides hours of exploration and fun. The 2022 renovation added more Northwest touches to the exhibits, including Tribal Tales puppet play area and local artist murals There's a small play area called Orca Cove for toddlers and plenty of crafts to keep everyone engaged. ⊠ *305 Harrison St., Central District* ☎ *206/441–1768* ⊕ *www.seattle-childrensmuseum.org* ✉ *$12* ☉ *Closed Mon.–Tues.*

Space Needle
NOTABLE BUILDING | FAMILY | Seattle's most iconic building is as quirky as ever, and a 2018 remodel restored and improved it. The distinctive, towering, 605-foot-high structure is visible throughout much of Seattle—but the view from the inside is also great. A less-than-one-minute ride up to the observation deck yields 360-degree vistas of Downtown Seattle, the Olympic Mountains, Elliott Bay, Queen Anne Hill, Lake Union, and the Cascade Range through floor-to-ceiling windows, the open-air observation area, and the rotating glass floor. Built for the 1962 World's Fair, the Needle has an app to guide you around and interactive experiences to leave your own mark. Schedule your visit for a day with a sunny forecast if you're lucky enough to have one. If you can't decide whether you want the daytime or nighttime view, buy the day/night pass that allows you to visit twice in one day. Also look for package deals with Chihuly Garden and Glass. ⊠ *400 Broad St., Lower Queen Anne* ☎ *206/905–2100* ⊕ *www.spaceneedle.com* ✉ *From $35.*

Did You Know?

You can snap photos of the Space Needle framed by Chihuly sculptures from the Glasshouse, a 40-foot-tall conservatory, at the Chihuly Garden and Glass.

🍴 Restaurants

Canlis Restaurant

$$$$ | **AMERICAN** | Canlis has been setting the standard for opulent dining in Seattle since the 1950s, and the food, wine, practically clairvoyant service, and views overlooking Lake Union are still remarkable. Executive chef Aisha Ibrahim draws on local flavors and her own experience at Asia's top restaurants to flavor the finest meat and freshest produce. **Known for:** stunning views; impeccable service; unbeatable entrées. $ *Average main: $165 ✉ 2576 Aurora Ave. N, Queen Anne ☎ 206/283–3313 ⊕ www.canlis.com ⊙ Closed Sun.–Mon. No lunch 🍸 Jacket required.*

Eden Hill

$$$ | **MODERN AMERICAN** | This tiny, 24-seat restaurant quietly turns out exciting and innovative food in the form of visually stunning small plates. Tables are seated beside wide windows overlooking the serene side of Queen Anne. **Known for:** signature dessert "lick the bowl" made with foie gras; grand tasting menu requires reservations; daily changing menus. $ *Average main: $25 ✉ 2209 Queen Anne Ave. N, Queen Anne ☎ 206/708–6836 ⊕ www.edenhillrestaurant.com ⊙ No lunch.*

How to Cook a Wolf

$$$ | **ITALIAN** | This sleek eatery features fresh, artisanal ingredients. Starters run the gamut from cured-meat platters to roasted almonds, pork terrine, chicken-liver mousse, and arugula salad, while tasty mains focus on simple handmade pastas, like orecchiette with sausage, garlic, and ricotta. **Known for:** seasonal ingredients; small plates; fresh pasta. $ *Average main: $30 ✉ 2208 Queen Anne Ave. N, Queen Anne ☎ 206/838–8090 ⊕ www.ethanstowellrestaurants.com ⊙ No lunch.*

Paju

$$ | **KOREAN** | This small restaurant brings together the flavors and techniques of Korean cuisine and cutting-edge global style to create a unique, innovative combination. The concise menu features intriguing combinations such as pistachio cream and lettuce, along with new spins on comforting classics, like the beloved house fried rice with squid ink. **Known for:** beautiful presentation; pairs well with beer; progressive Korean cuisine. $ *Average main: $23 ✉ 11 Mercer St., Queen Anne ☎ 206/829–8215 ⊕ www.pajurestaurant.com ⊙ Closed Mon. No lunch weekdays.*

★ Taylor Shellfish Oyster Bar

$$ | **PACIFIC NORTHWEST** | When the family behind a fifth-generation shellfish farm decides to open a restaurant devoted to their signature products, the result is a temple to those oysters, mussels, and clams. Cool colors, a metal bar, and big windows give the urban restaurant a distinctly beachy feel, which seems appropriate for digging into dozens of the region's acclaimed bivalves. **Known for:** the Salish sampler—a giant tray of chilled seafood; tide-to-table seafood; soul-warming chowder. $ *Average main: $20 ✉ 124 Republican St., Queen Anne ☎ 206/501–4442 ⊕ www.taylorshellfish-farms.com/location/queen-anne ⊙ No lunch weekdays.*

★ wa'z

$$$$ | **JAPANESE** | Art meets seasonal ingredients in the traditional multi-course *kaiseki* meal, and here, it also intersects with the bounty of the Pacific Northwest. Eight courses of local seafood, premium meat, and foraged treasures show off the chef's mastery of various techniques. **Known for:** fresh seafood; kaiseki-style meal; luxury ingredients. $ *Average main: $150 ✉ 411 Cedar St., South Lake Union ☎ 206/441–7119 ⊕ www.wazseattle.com ⊙ Closed Sun.–Mon. No lunch.*

Coffee and Quick Bites

Dick's Drive-In

$ | **BURGER** | You won't find a quicker or more affordable snack than a few burgers and a milkshake at this Seattle classic. The only location of the local chain (dating back to 1954) that offers indoor dining, its bargain-basement prices and late-night hours make it an enduring favorite. **Known for:** fair pay for employees; Seattle institution; beloved burgers (even if they're not the best in town). [$] *Average main: $3* ✉ *500 Queen Anne Ave. N, Lower Queen Anne* ☎ *206/285–5155* 🌐 *www.ddir.com.*

Queen Cà Phê

$ | **VIETNAMESE** | Quick and sleek, this bubble tea and banh mi shop makes it easy to pop in for a customized beverage or flavorful sandwich. The screen menu shows the extensive tea and coffee options, including pink salt cheese crema. **Known for:** strong coffee; quick service; customizable bubble tea. [$] *Average main: $12* ✉ *2231 Queen Anne Ave. N, Queen Anne* ☎ *206/457–8998* 🌐 *www.queencaphe.com* 🕓 *Closed Mon.*

Seattle Center Armory

$ | **AMERICAN** | A complete remodel changed the Seattle Center food court from an only-if-you're-desperate stop into a quick-bite destination. Several local restaurant groups have erected walk-up windows or shops here, from skillet burgers to Seattle fudge. **Known for:** beautiful space; quick service; variety. [$] *Average main: $10* ✉ *305 Harrison St., Queen Anne* ☎ *206/684–7200* 🌐 *www.seattlecenter.com.*

Hotels

Queen Anne is a mostly residential neighborhood spread out over a large hill just to the north of Belltown and close to Seattle Center. Upper Queen Anne is posh, quiet, and scenic. Lower Queen Anne, where all the lodging options lie, is very walkable to Belltown, Downtown, and Seattle Center—but it's considerably less elegant than the top of the hill.

MarQueen Hotel

$$ | **HOTEL** | Fans of historic boutique hotels will love this reasonably priced 1918 brick property at the foot of Queen Anne Hill. **Pros:** in-room kitchens and living room areas; free Wi-Fi; central locations. **Cons:** street-side rooms can be loud; housekeeping not always consistent; no elevator. [$] *Rooms from: $221* ✉ *600 Queen Anne Ave. N, Queen Anne* ☎ *206/282–7407* 🌐 *www.marqueen.com* 🛏 *58 rooms* 🍴 *No Meals.*

The Maxwell Hotel

$$ | **HOTEL** | Colorful and funky rooms, with argyle-print chairs and outlines of chandeliers painted on the walls, are *the* choice for visitors frequenting the Seattle Center for opera or the ballet. **Pros:** free parking and shuttle; complimentary bikes; some rooms have great views of the Space Needle. **Cons:** hotel is on a busy street; pool and gym are tiny; guests complain of low water pressure. [$] *Rooms from: $235* ✉ *300 Roy St., Queen Anne* ☎ *206/286–0629, 866/866–7977* 🌐 *www.themaxwellhotel.com* 🛏 *139 rooms* 🍴 *No Meals.*

Start your Seattle aquatic adventures at the Center for Wooden Boats.

Nightlife

Queen Anne is a diffuse and mostly residential neighborhood, so while there are a few bars scattered around the formidable hill, most are on the lower reaches, near Seattle Center and Key Arena.

BARS AND LOUNGES

Bar Miriam

BARS | On the quiet side of the hill, this cute European-style café-bar feels like it's been around forever despite opening in 2022. The craft cocktails feel like classics but include a number of creative originals, and the menu offers plenty of low- and no-alcohol options. The terrific food menu reads like a high-end restaurant menu, but the upscale, gastropub-style snacks come out bistro casual. ✉ *307 W. McGraw St., Lower Queen Anne* ☎ *206/708–1213* ⊕ *www.barmiriam.com.*

Queen Anne Beer Hall

BEER GARDENS | In a city known for icing out strangers, this classic European beer hall tries to get them to cozy back up with its communal tables, frosty mugs of beer from 30 taps, and a menu of hearty drinking foods, like pretzels, poutine, and burgers. Everybody's invited to the party here, including kids up until 10 pm. ✉ *203 W. Thomas St., Lower Queen Anne* ☎ *206/420–4326* ⊕ *www.queenannebeerhall.com.*

The Sitting Room

COCKTAIL LOUNGES | With its European-café vibe and excellent mixed drinks, the Sitting Room lures residents of both the lower and upper parts of Queen Anne. It's quite an accomplishment to get those two very different demographics to agree on anything, but this sweet, relaxed little spot has done it with its eclectic furniture, zinc bar, sexy lighting, and friendly staff. ✉ *108 W. Roy St., Queen Anne*

☎ *206/285–2830* ⊕ *www.the-sitting-room.com* ⊘ *Closed Sun.–Mon.*

Targy's Tavern

BARS | Iconic and historic, Targy's Tavern hangs onto one of the last vestiges of true dive bar in central Seattle in a 1902 building originally designed as trolley worker housing. The U-shaped bar has been serving up strong drinks, cold pints, and pulltabs, with just a smattering of surliness, since 1937. Though it gets packed on weekends with a newer crowd, the real fun comes on slower nights when the regulars and bartenders get to chit-chatting. ⊠ *600 W. Crockett St., Queen Anne* ☎ *206/352–8882* ⊕ *www.thestedmangroup.com/targystavern.*

 Performing Arts

ARTS CENTERS

Marion Oliver McCaw Hall

ARTS CENTERS | The home of the Seattle Opera and the Pacific Northwest Ballet is an opulent, glass-enclosed structure reflecting the skies and the Space Needle nearby. The facility houses two auditoriums and a four-story main lobby area where several artworks are on display. Look for Sarah Sze's *An Equal and Opposite Reaction*, an enormous sculpture of found objects, hanging over the stairs at the north end of the Kreielsheimer Promenade. ⊠ *321 Mercer St., Lower Queen Anne* ☎ *206/684–7200* ⊕ *www.mccawhall.com.*

Seattle Center

ARTS CENTERS | Several of the Seattle Center's halls are used for theater, opera, dance, music, and performance art. Public radio station KEXP frequently hosts concerts in their home on the Seattle Center campus, and the center is also the site of many of Seattle's major cultural festivals. ⊠ *305 Harrison St., Queen Anne* ☎ *206/684–7200* ⊕ *www.seattlecenter.org.*

THEATER

Cornish Playhouse at Seattle Center

THEATER | This performance and education venue run by the Cornish College of the Arts hosts public music and theater programs, produced by students and professionals, throughout the year in a 432-seat auditorium on the Seattle Center Campus. ⊠ *Seattle Center, 201 Mercer St., Queen Anne* ☎ *206/726–5176* ⊕ *www.cornish.edu/facilities/cornish-playhouse.*

Seattle Children's Theatre

THEATER | **FAMILY** | Top-notch productions of new works join adaptations from classic children's literature here. After the show, actors come out to answer questions and explain how the tricks are done. ⊠ *201 Thomas St., Lower Queen Anne* ☎ *206/441–3322* ⊕ *www.sct.org* 🖃 *From $15.*

Seattle Repertory Theater

THEATER | During its season (September through June), the Seattle Repertory Theater brings new and classic plays to life. Adoring fans flock to new takes on choice classics as well as works fresh from the New York stage, but the overall mission is to produce shows that reflect the experiences and perspectives of people in the region. You can preorder your drinks from the lobby bar to enjoy during intermission. ⊠ *155 Mercer St., Lower Queen Anne* ☎ *206/443–2222* ⊕ *www.seattlerep.org.*

SIFF Cinema Uptown

FILM | Festival films, independent releases, and arthouse flicks pepper the schedule of this cinema run as a year-round extension of the Seattle International Film Festival. The three screens vary between new releases and themed selections, the concession stand serves beer and alcohol, and the old-school marquee adds charm to the neighborhood. ⊠ *511 Queen Anne Ave. N, Queen Anne* ⊕ *www.siff.info/uptown.*

DANCE
On the Boards

MODERN DANCE | Since 1978, On the Boards has been presenting contemporary dance performances, as well as theater, music, and multimedia events. The main subscription series runs from September through May, but events are scheduled year-round. ⊠ *100 W. Roy St., Lower Queen Anne* ☎ *206/217–9886* ⊕ *www.ontheboards.org.*

Pacific Northwest Ballet

BALLET | The lineup of Seattle's resident ballet company and school includes works from celebrated contemporary choreographers as well as a mix of classic and international productions (think *Swan Lake* and *Carmina Burana*). Fans of *The Nutcracker* can rest assured that the timeless production is still part of the company's repertoire. Its season runs from September through June. ⊠ *Mc-Caw Hall at Seattle Center, 301 Mercer St., Lower Queen Anne* ☎ *206/441–2424* ⊕ *www.pnb.org.*

OPERA
Seattle Opera

OPERA | Housed in the beautiful Marion Oliver McCaw Hall, the opera stages productions from August through May. National and international stars make their way to the stage as part of the wide-ranging schedule of classic and new operas, drawn from around the world. Additional educational and community events aim to bring diverse crowds out to enjoy the genre. ⊠ *McCaw Hall at Seattle Center, 321 Mercer St., Lower Queen Anne* ☎ *206/389–7676* ⊕ *www.seattleopera.org.*

🛍 Shopping

There are actually two shopping areas in this hillside neighborhood—the more urban-feeling Lower Queen Anne, near the Seattle Center campus, and the more neighborhood-feeling Upper Queen Anne, along Queen Anne Avenue North at the top of the hill. The cluster of businesses at the top of the hill includes a bookshop, gift stores, clothing boutiques, and a heralded wine shop.

■ **TIP→ Find the best shopping along Queen Anne Avenue North between West Galer and McGraw Streets.**

McCarthy & Schiering Wine Merchants

WINE/SPIRITS | One of the oldest wine shops in the city is attitude-free and offers an amazing selection of wines from around the world. Check out the selection of local wines to experience the true flavor of the Northwest. Free tastings are held on Saturday. ⊠ *2401B Queen Anne Ave. N, Queen Anne* ☎ *206/282–8500* ⊕ *www.mccarthyand-schiering.com* ⊗ *Closed Sun.–Mon.*

Queen Anne Dispatch

SOUVENIRS | In the tradition of the general store, this shipping spot also operates a sweet boutique with fashionable women's clothes, jewelry, and gifts. Come here for locally made goods, shirts emblazoned with the neighborhood name, and a unique souvenir (and ship it home, if you need). ⊠ *2212 Queen Anne Ave. N, Queen Anne* ☎ *206/286–1025* ⊕ *www.queenannedispatch.com* ⊗ *Closed Sun.*

SpaceBase Gift Shop

SOUVENIRS | The SpaceBase Gift Shop has the city's ultimate icon, the Space Needle, rendered in endless ways. Among the officially licensed goods are bags of Space Needle Noodles, towering wooden pepper grinders, and artsy black T-shirts. ⊠ *400 Broad St., Queen Anne* ☎ *206/905–2100* ⊕ *www.spaceneedle. com.*

Chapter 5

PIONEER SQUARE

Updated by
AnnaMaria Stephens

👁 **Sights**
★★★☆☆

🍴 **Restaurants**
★★☆☆☆

🛏 **Hotels**
★☆☆☆☆

🛍 **Shopping**
★★★☆☆

🍸 **Nightlife**
★★☆☆☆

NEIGHBORHOOD SNAPSHOT

TOP REASONS TO GO

■ Leave the Space Needle to the masses and check out the observation deck and speakeasy-style bar at 38-story **Smith Tower**.

■ Gallery hop on First Thursday Art Walks—perhaps the best time to see Pioneer Square, when animated crowds walk from gallery to gallery. It claims to be the oldest art walk in the country, with around 35 participating spaces including Greg Kucera and the Tashiro-Kaplan Building. Architecture lover? Check out the exterior of the temporarily closed Arctic Club Hotel Seattle, which features famous terra-cotta walruses on the facade.

■ Soak up some weird and wonderful historic Seattle tidbits on the zany **Bill Speidel's Underground Tour**.

■ Catch your reflection in the hood of an antique fire truck at **Last Resort Fire Department Museum**.

■ Cheer for one of the home teams at **Lumen Field** or **T-Mobile Park**.

GETTING HERE AND AROUND

Pioneer Square is directly south of Downtown, which means you can easily walk here. However, the stretch between the two neighborhoods is not the most scenic trip, so you can also hop on a bus heading south on 1st Avenue.

Pioneer Square is pretty small; you'll easily be able to walk to all the galleries. If you've driven in from a more distant neighborhood, most of the pay parking lots and garages are on South Jackson Street.

Most people combine Pioneer Square with a trip to the Chinatown–International District, which together would make for a full day of sightseeing. Pioneer Square is also the closest neighborhood to Lumen Field and T-Mobile Park, so it also makes sense to end a touring day here before heading to a game.

PAUSE HERE

■ In the heart of Pioneer Square, the tree-lined Occidental Square is home to the Occidental Square Pavilion, which includes a stylish modern kiosk that's open to visitors year-round. You can pick up a booklet that outlines walking tours around the historic buildings of Pioneer Square or take a break from the elements under the large, timber-and-glass pavilion. You'll also find colorful cafe tables and ping-pong tables, as well as shops, a cafe, and a wine shop.

TOURS

■ Sports fans can get their major-league fix with behind-the-scenes tours at both Lumen Field (Seattle Seahawks and the Seattle Sounders) and T-Mobile Park (Seattle Mariners). The Underground Tour shows you the remnants of passageways and buildings buried when the city regraded the streets in the 1880s. The tour is fun and full of Seattle-history tidbits, though younger kids might be bored as there's not much to see.

The Pioneer Square district, directly south of Downtown, is Seattle's oldest neighborhood. It attracts visitors for elegantly renovated (or in some cases replica) turn-of-the-20th-century redbrick buildings and art galleries. It's the center of Seattle's arts scene, and the galleries in this small neighborhood make up the majority of its sights.

Today's Yesler Way was the original "Skid Road," where, in the 1880s, timber was sent to the sawmill on a skid of small logs laid crossways and greased so that the cut trees would slide down to the mill. The area later grew into Seattle's first center of commerce. Many of the buildings you see today are replicas of the wood-frame structures destroyed by fire in 1889.

The role Pioneer Square plays in the city today is harder to define. Despite the concentration of galleries, the neighborhood is no longer a center for artists per se, as rents have risen considerably; only established gallery owners can rent loft-like spaces in heavily trafficked areas.

By day, you'll see a mix of Downtown workers and tourists strolling the area. The neighborhood also has one of the highest concentrations of homeless people in Seattle, and though they don't typically aggressively panhandle, they do tend to congregate at public parks. Pioneer Square has a well-known nightlife scene, but these days it's much-derided, thanks to the meat-market vibe of many of the clubs. If you want classier venues,

head north up 1st Avenue to Belltown or to select spots on Capitol Hill.

When Seattleites speak of Pioneer Square, they usually speak of the love they have for certain neighborhood spots—Zeitgeist coffeehouse, a beloved art gallery, a friend's vintage loft apartment—not the love they have for the neighborhood as a whole. Pioneer Square is always worth a visit, but reactions vary. Anyone seriously interested in doing the gallery circuit will be impressed, and foodies will find a few buzzworthy options. Smith Tower, once the tallest building on the West Coast, beckons with an observation deck and a bar on the 35th floor. That said, those looking for a vibrant, picture-perfect historic district will be underwhelmed.

Pioneer Square is a gateway of sorts to the stadium district, which segues into SoDo (South of Downtown). First comes Lumen Field, where the Seahawks and the Sounders play. Directly south of that is T-Mobile Park, where the Mariners play. There's not much to see in this industrial area, but if you're a sports fan you can easily make a run from Pioneer Square to one of the stadiums' pro shops.

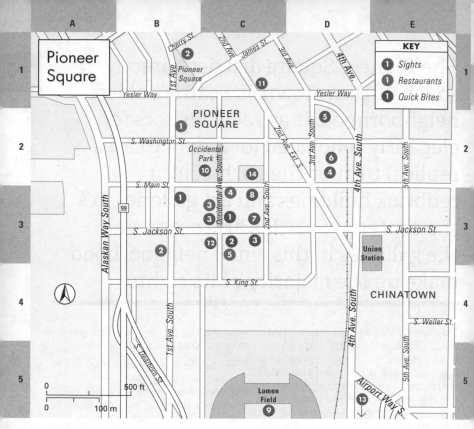

Pioneer Square

KEY
- ① Sights
- ① Restaurants
- ① Quick Bites

The popular Foster/White Gallery has 7,000 square feet of exhibition space.

Sights

AXIS Pioneer Square

ART GALLERY | Soaring 18-foot ceilings, classic brick arches, and antique wood floors make a dramatic backdrop for monthly rotating exhibits with a contemporary bent. Part of a multitasking, 6,000-square-foot studio space, the gallery features a roster of local, national, and international artists and photographers. AXIS hosts new shows with entertainment during First Thursday Art Walk. ⊠ *308 1st Ave. S, Pioneer Square* ☎ *206/681–9316* ⊕ *www.axispioneer-square.com* ✉ *Free* ⊘ *Closed Sat.*

Bill Speidel's Underground Tour

HISTORIC SIGHT | Present-day Pioneer Square is actually one story higher than it used to be. After the Great Seattle Fire of 1889, Seattle's planners regraded the neighborhood's streets, which had been built on filled-in tide lands and regularly flooded. The result? There is now an intricate and expansive array of subterranean passageways and basements beneath Pioneer Square, and Bill Speidel's Underground Tour is the only way to explore them. Speidel was an irreverent historian, PR man, and former *Seattle Times* reporter who took it upon himself to preserve historic Seattle, and this 75-minute tour is packed with his sardonic wit and playful humor. It's very informative, too—if you're interested in the general history of the city or salty anecdotes about Seattle's early denizens, you'll appreciate it that much more. Younger kids will almost certainly be bored, as there's not much to see at the specific sites, which are more used as launching points for the stories (some of the tour is above ground, as well). Comfortable shoes, a love for quirky historical yarns, and an appreciation of bad puns are musts. Several tours are offered daily, and schedules change month to month: call or visit the website for a full list of tour times. ⊠ *608 1st Ave., Pioneer Square* ☎ *206/682–4646* ⊕ *www.undergroundtour.com* ✉ *$22.*

Davidson Galleries

ART GALLERY | Davidson has several different departments in one building: the Contemporary Print & Drawing Center, which holds the portfolios of 50 print artists; the Antique Print Department; and the Painting and Sculpture Department. Though the Antique Print Department is more of a specialized interest, the contemporary print exhibits are always interesting and worth a look. ⊠ *313 Occidental Ave. S, Pioneer Square* ☎ *206/624–7684 contemporary prints, 206/624–6700 antique prints, 206/624–7684 painting and sculpture* ⊕ *www.davidsongalleries. com* 🖃 *Free* ⊗ *Closed Sun.–Mon.*

Foster/White Gallery

ART GALLERY | One of the Seattle art scene's heaviest hitters has digs as impressive as the works it shows: a century-old building with high ceilings and 7,000 square feet of exhibition space. Works by internationally acclaimed Northwest masters Kenneth Callahan, Mark Tobey, Alden Mason, and George Tsutakawa are on permanent display. ⊠ *220 3rd Ave. S, Pioneer Square* ☎ *206/622–2833* ⊕ *www.fosterwhite. com* 🖃 *Free* ⊗ *Closed Sun.–Mon.*

Gallery 110

ART GALLERY | Gallery 110 works with a collective of 30 contemporary artists (primarily Northwest-based) showing pieces in its small space that are energetic, challenging, and fresh. On-site exhibitions change monthly, and once a year the gallery hosts a juried exhibition. ⊠ *110 3rd Ave. S, Pioneer Square* ☎ *206/624–9336* ⊕ *www.gallery110.com* 🖃 *Free* ⊗ *Closed Sun.–Wed.*

★ Greg Kucera Gallery

ART GALLERY | One of the most important destinations on the First Thursday gallery walk, this gorgeous space is a top venue for national and regional artists. Be sure to check out the outdoor sculpture deck on the second level. If you have time for only one gallery visit, this is the place to go. You'll see big names that

Gallery Walks

It's fun to simply walk around Pioneer Square and pop into galleries. South Jackson Street to Yesler between Western and 4th Avenue South is a good area. The first Thursday of every month, galleries stay open late for First Thursday Art Walk, a neighborhood highlight.

you might recognize—along with newer artists—and the thematic group shows are always thoughtful and well presented. ⊠ *212 3rd Ave. S, Pioneer Square* ☎ *206/624–0770* ⊕ *www.gregkucera. com* 🖃 *Free* ⊗ *Closed Sun.–Mon.*

Klondike Gold Rush National Historical Park

HISTORY MUSEUM | A tiny yet delightful free museum illustrating Seattle's role in the 1897–98 Gold Rush in the Klondike region, this gem is located inside a historic redbrick building with wooden floors and soaring ceilings. Walls are lined with photos of gold miners, explorers, and the hopeful families who followed them. Some of the national historical park's more interactive components (ranger talks, gold-panning demonstrations) are still on hold indefinitely. ⊠ *319 2nd Ave. S, Pioneer Square* ☎ *206/220–4240* ⊕ *nps.gov/klse/index.htm* 🖃 *Free.*

Last Resort Fire Department Museum

OTHER MUSEUM | If you're in Pioneer Square on a Thursday between 11 am and 3 pm, this museum occupying the bottom floor of the Seattle Fire Department's headquarters includes eight historic rigs from Seattle dating from the 19th and early 20th centuries, as well as artifacts (vintage helmets and uniforms, hose nozzles, and other equipment) and photos, logs, and newspaper clippings recording historic fires. ⊠ *301 2nd Ave. S, Pioneer Square* ☎ *206/783–4474* ⊕ *www.lastresortfd.org* 🖃 *Free* ⊗ *Closed Fri.–Weds.*

The Seattle Seahawks play at the state-of-the-art Lumen Field.

Lumen Field

SPORTS VENUE | Located directly south of Pioneer Square, Lumen Field hosts two professional teams, the Seattle Seahawks (football) and the Seattle Sounders FC (soccer). The open-air stadium has 67,000 seats; sightlines are excellent thanks to a cantilevered design and the close placement of lower sections. Tours start at the pro shop (be sure to arrive at least 30 minutes prior to purchase tickets) and last an hour and a half. You'll get a personal look at behind-the-scenes areas as well as the famous 12th Man Flag Pole, and have a chance to sink your feet into the same playing surface as your favorite Seahawks and Sounders stars. ⊠ *800 Occidental Ave. S, SoDo* ☎ *206/381–7582* ⊕ *www.centurylinkfield. com* ✉ *$18.*

Occidental Park

PLAZA/SQUARE | This shady, picturesque cobblestone park is the geographical heart of the historic neighborhood—on first Thursdays it's home to a variety of local artisans setting up makeshift booths. Grab a sandwich or pastry at the London Plane and people watch from one of the colorful cafe tables dotting the tree-lined square. Note that this square is a spot where homeless people congregate; you're likely to encounter more than a few oddballs. The square is best avoided at night. ⊠ *Occidental Ave. S and S. Main St., Pioneer Square.*

Smith Tower

NOTABLE BUILDING | When this iconic landmark opened in 1914, it was the tallest office building outside New York City and the fourth-tallest building in the world. (It remained the tallest building west of the Mississippi for nearly 50 years.) The Smith Tower Observatory on the 35th floor is an open-air wraparound deck providing panoramic views of the surrounding historic neighborhood, ball fields, the city skyline, and the mountains on clear days. It's also a superb spot to take in a sunset. The top floor includes the speakeasy-themed Observatory Bar, which features striking original architectural details and a cocktail and nibbles menu that pays homage

Seattle's Pro Sports

Seattle Seahawks

When Seahawks mania hits Seattle, it's off the charts. Or rather on them—seismologists at the University of Washington have registered actual earthquakes caused by the cheering, clapping, and foot-stomping of the crowd at big games. The team, which joined the National Football League in 1976, hit peak popularity when it won the Super Bowl in 2014, with household-name players like Marshawn "Beast Mode" Lynch (cause of the first "Beast Quake") and Russell Wilson on the roster (neither are with the team anymore). Tickets to games at Pioneer Square's Lumen Field cost a fortune, to the chagrin of many locals: they technically start at $59 but you're more likely to pay around $500.

Seattle Mariners

Another longtime Seattle fixture, the Mariners joined Major League Baseball in 1977. And although the team has never made it to the World Series (the only active MLB team with that distinction), it's been home to several famous players, including Ken Griffey Jr., Alex Rodriguez, and Ichiro Suzuki. Despite their lack of big wins, the Mariners maintain a fiercely loyal fanbase and T-Mobile Park makes a fine place to enjoy a warm summer day (the ballpark food options are terrific). Mariners tickets aren't as hard to come by as football or hockey; with dynamic pricing, they start at $13 but average around $51.

Seattle Kraken

The latest addition to Seattle's pro sports scene is the Seattle Kraken, who made their hotly anticipated National Hockey League debut season in 2021-22. Playing at the sustainable Climate Pledge Arena, the team—named for the mythical Scandinavian sea beast—is still hitting its stride, with a lackluster record of 16-22-3 its first year. Tickets are among the highest priced in the league, though, starting at around $80 but more frequently falling in the $200 to $300 range.

Seattle Sounders

In Seattle, soccer gives football a run for its money. Locals are loudly supportive of their home team, the Seattle Sounders FC, who play at Lumen Field. The soccer club won Major League Soccer Cup titles in 2016 and 2019. On the current roster, standouts include Justin Morris, who grew up locally on Mercer Island. Tickets start at around $17 and average $64.

OL Reign

Seattle's women's soccer team, OL Reign, is among the eight founding members of the Women's National Soccer League. The team, which plays at Lumen Field, includes star forward Megan Rapinoe, who won gold with the U.S. team at the 2012 Summer Olympics and bronze at the 2020 Olympics. Tickets average $31.

Seattle Storm

Seattle long-timers still lament the loss of the Seattle SuperSonics to Oklahoma in 2008, but basketball fans can get their fix with the women's team, Seattle Storm, who play at Climate Pledge Arena. The Storm's star player, Sue Bird, retired in 2022 but was considered to be one of the greatest players in the league's history. Tickets average $42.

to the Prohibition era. Smith Tower's ground-floor retail shop packed with locally made goods is also worth a visit. ■ **TIP→ Can't make it to Pioneer Square? Check out Downtown's Sky View Observatory & Bar at the Columbia Center. What the sleek skyscraper lacks in vintage architectural charm, it more than makes up for with epic views.** ✉ *506 2nd Ave. S, Pioneer Square* ☎ *206/622–4004* 🌐 *www.smithtower.com* 🎟 *$19* 🕓 *Closed Mon.-Tues.*

Stonington Gallery
ART GALLERY | You'll see plenty of cheesy tribal art knockoffs in tourist-trap shops, but this elegant gallery will give you a real look at the best contemporary work of Northwest Coast and Alaska tribal members (and artists from these regions working in the Native style). Three floors exhibit wood carvings, paintings, sculpture, and mixed-media pieces from the likes of Robert Davidson, Joe David, Preston Singeltary, Susan Point, and Rick Barto. ✉ *119 S Jackson St., Pioneer Square* ☎ *206/405–4040* 🌐 *www.stoningtongallery.com* 🎟 *Free* 🕓 *Closed Sun.-Mon.*

T-Mobile Park
SPORTS VENUE | This 47,000-seat, open-air baseball stadium with a state-of-the-art retractable roof is the home of the Seattle Mariners. If you want to see the stadium in all its glory, take the one-hour tour, which brings you onto the field, into the dugouts, back to the press and locker rooms, and up to the posh box seats. Tours depart from the Team Store on 1st Avenue, and you purchase your tickets there, too (at least 15 minutes prior to the scheduled tour). ✉ *1250 1st Ave. S, SoDo* ☎ *866/800–1275* 🌐 *www.mlb.com/mariners/ballpark/tours* 🎟 *$15.*

Waterfall Garden
GARDEN | A tranquil spot to take a break, this small garden with a few cafe tables surrounds a 22-foot artificial waterfall that cascades over large granite stones. ✉ *219 2nd Ave. South, Pioneer Square* ☎ *206/624–6096.*

🍴 Restaurants

Damn the Weather
$$ | **AMERICAN** | In addition to its navy-blue exterior and cheeky name, this small, upscale gastropub is known for simple craft cocktails made by devoted mixologists and a small but spot-on menu of comfort foods. The bar offers several snacks (olives, nuts, fries) and small plates ideal for sharing as well as heartier options including a shrimp po'boy and classic burger with fries at lunch. **Known for:** chicken fat fries; booze expertise; cool historic building. [$] *Average main: $22* ✉ *116 1st Ave. S, Pioneer Square* ☎ *206/946–1283* 🌐 *www.damntheweather.com.*

Il Terrazzo Carmine
$$$ | **ITALIAN** | Tuscan and southern Italian cooking blend to create soul-satisfying dishes such as veal *osso buco*, homemade ravioli, linguine *alle vongole* (with clams), and eggplant Parmesan. Ceiling-to-floor draperies lend the dining room understated dignity, and intoxicating aromas waft from the kitchen to the restaurant's small outdoor patio that sits beneath a canopy of lights. **Known for:** veal osso buco; elegant space; classic Italian fare. [$] *Average main: $35* ✉ *411 1st Ave. S, Pioneer Square* ☎ *206/467–7797* 🌐 *www.ilterrazzocarmine.com* 🕓 *Closed Sun., no lunch Sat.*

Locus Wines
$ | **WINE BAR** | Already a familiar name in the Seattle wine scene, Locus Wines recently debuted a bright, modern tasting room that showcases food-and-wine pairings. The small menu features flights served with a small bite that perfectly complements each pour—like a caramelized onion and lamb pastry square matched with the signature Locus Red—although Locus also offers wine by the glass and a few light snacks, including a kale salad and pillowy meatballs, as well as a brunch on weekends. **Known for:** Rhône-style wines; food-focused flights;

DID YOU KNOW?

Grapevines must be stressed to give their best; their fruit becomes the most complex when grown in well-drained soils with little water. Many parts of Washington, on either side of the mountains, meet these basic requirements.

friendly, knowledgeable service. $ *Average main: $16* ✉ *307 Occidental Ave. S, Pioneer Square* ☎ *206/682–1760* ⊕ *www. locuswines.com.*

The London Plane
$ | BAKERY | In an airy building right on the corner of Occidental Square, The London Plane is a gorgeous multipurpose space that also includes a small artisanal shop, florist, and bakery. The daytime menu (until 3 pm) features mostly vegetarian light bites, many with Mediterranean-inspired flavors, from classic pastries and quiches to grain-enriched salads and seared albacore. **Known for:** fresh coffee and pastries; focus on fresh vegetables; a lovely space to explore. $ *Average main: $12* ✉ *300 Occidental Ave. S, Pioneer Square* ☎ *206/624–1374* ⊕ *www. thelondonplaneseattle.com* ☾ *No dinner.*

★ Taylor Shellfish Oyster Bar
$$ | PACIFIC NORTHWEST | Oysters don't get any fresher than this: Taylor, a fifth-generation, family-owned company, opened its own restaurant in order to serve their products in the manner most·befitting such pristine shellfish. The simple preparations—raw, cooked, and chilled—are all designed to best show off the seafood with light broths and sauces and a few accoutrements. **Known for:** popular with locals; expert shucking; unlikely pre-stadium tailgating stop. $ *Average main: $17* ✉ *410 Occidental Ave., Pioneer Square* ☎ *206/501–4060* ⊕ *www.taylorshellfishfarms.com.*

☕ Coffee and Quick Bites

Caffè Umbria
$ | CAFÉ | Enjoy traditional Italian-style espresso, pastries, and paninis at this full-service wholesale roaster and flagship retail location for the local brand. Set in a historic brick building with indoor and sidewalk seating, the café also serves Italian beer and wine. **Known for:** expertly pulled espresso; gelato (because it's always time for gelato); good

people-watching. $ *Average main: $5* ✉ *320 Occidental Ave. S, Pioneer Square* ☎ *206/624-5847* ⊕ *www.caffeumbria. com.*

★ Salumi Deli
$ | ITALIAN | The lines are long for hearty, unforgettable sandwiches filled with superior house-cured meats and more at this shop, originally founded by famed New York chef Mario Batali's father Armandino. The oxtail sandwich special is unbeatable, but if it's unavailable or sold out (as specials often are by the lunchtime peak) order a salami, bresaola, porchetta, meatball, sausage, or lamb prosciutto sandwich with onions, peppers, cheese, and olive oil. **Known for:** cured meats; oxtail sandwich; famous chef. $ *Average main: $10* ✉ *404 Occidental Ave. S, Pioneer Square* ☎ *206/621–8772* ⊕ *www.salumicuredmeats.com* ☾ *Closed Sun.-Mon.*

Zeitgeist Coffee
$ | CAFÉ | A colorful local favorite among coffee shops: even Seattleites who don't haunt Pioneer Square will happily hunt for parking to spend a few hours here. In one of Pioneer Square's great brick buildings, with high ceilings and a few artfully exposed ducts and pipes, Zeitgeist has a simple, classy look that's the perfect backdrop for the frequent art shows held in this space. **Known for:** strong coffee; great place to work; eye-catching art. $ *Average main: $7* ✉ *171 S. Jackson St., Pioneer Square* ☎ *206/583–0497* ⊕ *www. zeitgeistcoffee.com.*

Nightlife

Pioneer Square is changing. The area is still home to dance clubs that attract a young crowd, many of whom come in from the suburbs. But with new offices opening, and new bars, restaurants, and coffee shops catering to after-work and sports crowds, Pioneer Square is a place worth visiting. As always, First Thursdays attracts a more varied crowd participating in the art walk. Galleries provide another focal point, and an additional reason to spend the evening here.

Despite the development, transients and drug use remain a part of the Pioneer Square scene, and it can feel unsafe at times. On weekends, disturbances from the hard-partying crowd make this a less-attractive neighborhood for some.

BARS AND LOUNGES
Collins Pub

BARS | The best beer bar in Pioneer Square features 22 rotating taps of Northwest (including Boundary Bay, Chuckanut, and Anacortes) and California beers and a long list of bottles from the region. Its upscale pub menu features local and seasonal ingredients. ✉ *526 2nd Ave., Pioneer Square* ☎ *206/623–1016* ⊕ *www. collinspubseattle.com.*

Flatstick Pub

PUBS | The original idea was a clever one for a perennially drizzly city: indoor mini golf for grownups and a great local draft beer list. Flatstick Pub's fun-focused concept was such a hole-in-one that it's since expanded to six locations total around the region, including this underground Pioneer Square spot. Set in an industrial-cool space with brick walls, exposed ducts, and colorful artwork, Flatstick features a mini golf course that spells out "Seattle" and a 12-foot tall Space Needle that lights up if you sink it on your first try. You can also try your hand at Stick Putt (think skee-ball meets putting) and Duffleboard, a Flatstick-invented tabletop golf game.

The quirky murals at all Flatstick locations were painted by local artist Ryan Henry Ward. If you spend any time driving around Seattle, you're sure to see his art and prominent simple signature on a building or wall; he's the city's most prolific muralist, with works sometimes featuring Pacific Northwest subjects,

including Sasquatch. Not everyone appreciates his widespread whimsy, but nobody can deny his art is a memorable part of the cityscape. ✉ *240 2nd Ave. S, Pioneer Square* ☎ *206/682–0608* ⊕ *www. flatstickpub.com.*

Good Bar

BARS | This bright, high-ceilinged space in a historic building in Pioneer Square still features the safe doors of the former Japanese Commercial Bank that once occupied the building. Post-work crowds and pre-game sports fans mix at the U-shape marble bar and a few small tables during a daily 4–7 pm happy hour. There's a rotating list of classic cocktails, newly developed libations featuring house-made infusions, and a beer and wine list. Small plates like pork terrine, wings, and sardines come out of an open kitchen. ✉ *240 2nd Ave. S, Pioneer Square* ☎ *206/624–2337* ⊕ *www.good-barseattle.com.*

DANCE CLUBS
Trinity

DANCE CLUBS | This multilevel, multiroom club plays hip-hop, reggae, disco, and Top 40. It gets packed on weekends—arrive early to avoid lines or to snag a table for some late-night snacks. This is the most appealing and interesting of the Pioneer Square megaclubs—in terms of decor, anyway. ✉ *107 Occidental Ave. S, Pioneer Square* ☎ *206/697–7702* ⊕ *www. trinitynightclub.com.*

⬤ Shopping

Gritty, eccentric, artsy, and fabulous, Pioneer Square is an eclectic blend of what makes Seattle, Seattle. Although this neighborhood has more than a few tourist traps hiding in its attractive brick buildings, it also has some wonderful shops with unique wares that range from antiques to heritage clothing. As Pioneer Square has been redeveloped over the

Continued on page 126

SEATTLE'S SIPPING CULTURE
ARTISAN COFFEES, CRAFT MICROBREWS, AND BOUTIQUE WINES

by Carissa Bluestone

Seattle's beverage obsession only begins with coffee. Whether you're into hoppy microbrews, premium wines, or expertly crafted cappuccinos, prepare to devote much of your visit to sipping the best Seattle and Washington State have to offer.

Seattle may forever be known as the birthplace of Starbucks, but nowadays foodies are just as likely to talk about Washington state's wine industry as the city's coffeehouses. Not to pronounce coffee dead, however. After a few years of inertia, the coffee scene is growing again with more independent roasters and shops than ever.

In fact, in the past few years the city's seen a profusion of potables: New microbreweries and wineries are opening, and hip new bars, taprooms, and tasting rooms are thriving more than ever. Like its sister city, Portland, Seattle is a hotspot for entrepreneurial spirit—it's this energy, mixed with a passion for local and organic ingredients, that has raised the bar on everything artisan.

COFFEE

Although Seattle owes much of its coffee legacy to Starbucks, the city's independent coffee shops rule the roast here. Their ardent commitment to creating premium artisanal blends from small batches of beans is what truly defines the scene. The moment you take your first sip of an expertly executed cappuccino at a coffeehouse such as **Caffé Vita** or **Espresso Vivace** you realize that the drink is never an afterthought here. Perfectly roasted beans ground to specification and pulled into espresso shots using dual-boiler machines and velvety steamed milk are de rigueur. In most restaurants, your coffee is likely to be a personal French press filled with a brew roasted just a few blocks away.

LATTE ART

Latte art is a given in Seattle. Designs vary by barista, but the most common flourish is the rosetta, which resembles a delicate fern. Here's how it's done:

1. THE BASE. A latte consists of a shot (or two) of espresso and hot, frothy milk.

2. THE POUR. First the shot is poured. The milk pitcher gets a few gentle swirls and taps (to burst the largest bubbles), then the milk is poured at a steady pace into the center of the tilted cup.

3. THE SHAKE. When the cup's about three-quarters full, the milk is streamed with tiny side-to-side strokes up and down the cup's center line. The "leaves" will start to fan out.

4. THE TOP. When the cup's almost full, the milk is drawn towards the bottom. With the last stroke the "stem" is drawn through the center of the leaves.

The "rosetta," a common latte design.

BEST COFFEEHOUSES

Many Seattle roasters obtain their beans through Direct Trade, sourcing directly from growers rather than brokers. They travel across the globe to meet with farmers, often paying them well above Fair Trade prices to ensure the highest-quality beans. Local roasters are also intensely community-minded: Caffé Vita, for example, recently partnered with the much-loved local chocolate factory Theo to produce sublime espresso-flavored chocolate bars.

CAFFÉ VITA. Though now a mini-chain (with locations in Fremont, Queen Anne, Pioneer Square, and Seward Park), Vita's roasting operations (and heart and soul) are in Capitol Hill. ✉ *1005 E. Pike St., Capitol Hill* ☎ *206/709–4440* ⊕ *www.caffevita.com*

ESPRESSO VIVACE. A top roaster, Vivace has two tidy coffee shops (the other's by REI in South Lake Union), and a sidewalk espresso stand at Broadway and Harrison. ✉ *532 Broadway Ave E, Capitol Hill* ☎ *206/860–2722* ⊕ *www.espresso-vivace.com*

FREMONT COFFEE COMPANY. Known for its awesome wraparound porch and exceptional brews, this friendly shop is the city's latest small-batch roaster. ✉ *459 N. 36th St., Fremont* ☎ *206/632–3633* ⊕ *www.fremontcoffee.net*

HERKIMER. This cheerful small-batch roaster is a northern neighborhoods favorite. ✉ *7320 Greenwood Ave. N, Phinney Ridge* ☎ *206/784–0202* ⊕ *www.herkimercoffee.com*

VICTROLA COFFEE. The original branch on 15th Avenue is a favorite standby, but the newer branch at 310 E. Pike St. in the Pike-Pine Corridor has a great view of the roasting room from its cafe tables. ✉ *411 15th Ave. E, Capitol Hill* ☎ *206/462–6259* ⊕ *www.victrolacoffee.com*.

Victrola Coffee

BEER

Craft brews have fewer ingredients than you might think.

Next time you drink a beer, thank the state of Washington. More than 70% of the nation's hops is grown in the Yakima Valley, and Washington is the fourth-largest producer of malting barley. The state's 80-plus breweries combine top-notch ingredients with crystal-clear snowpack waters to make high-quality craft beers. Seattle has at least a dozen breweries within its city limits, plus many fine gastropubs with standout locals on tap.

GREAT BREWERIES

ELLIOTT BAY BREWING. A dozen of Elliott Bay's beers are certified organic. The pub is a neighborhood favorite for its good, locally sourced food. ☒ *4720 California Ave NW, West Seattle* ☎ *206/932–8695* ⊕ *www.elliottbaybrewing.com*

PIKE PUB. The most touristy of the local breweries, Pike Pub also has a small microbrewery museum. The pale ale and the Kilt Lifter Scottish ale have been local favorites for two decades. There's a full pub menu. ☒ *1415 1st*

Ave, Downtown ☎ *206/622–6044* ⊕ *www.pikebrewing.com*

ELYSIAN BREWING COMPANY. Known for its Immortal IPA and good seasonal brews and pub grub, Elysian has branches in Capitol Hill and across from Lumen Field. ☒ *1221 E. Pike St., Capitol Hill* ☎ *206/860–1920* ⊕ *www.elysian-brewing.com*

Elysian Brewing Company

Elliot Bay Brewing

FREMONT BREWING. This brewery makes small-batch pale ales using organic hops. The Urban Beer Garden is open daily 11–9. ⊠ *1050 N 34th St, Seattle* ☎ *206/420-2407* ⊕ *www.fremontbrewing.com*

GEORGETOWN BREWING CO. This brewery offers a very small list, including Manny's Pale Ale and a special namesake porter for neighborhood bar the Nine Pound Hammer. Visit the store to pick up souvenirs or a growler of beer. ⊠ *5200 Denver Ave. S., Georgetown* ☎ *206/766–8055* ⊕ *www.georgetownbeer.com*

REUBEN'S BREWS. One of the pioneers of the current generation of Ballard breweries, Reuben's Brews specializes in IPAs like the World Beer Cup Gold Medal–winning Hazelicious IPA. ⊠ *5010 14th Ave NW, Ballard* ⊕ *www.reubensbrews.com.*

REDHOOK. This brewery specializes in amber ales—their ESB is an award-winner. The Redhook Brewlab in the Pike Motorworks building is open daily. It's open Wednesday–Thursday 5-10, Friday–Saturday 5–11, and Sunday 3–9. ⊠ *714 E Pike St.* ☎ *206/823-3026* ⊕ *www.redhook.com.*

TWO BEERS BREWING CO. A small list of ales and IPAs, and interesting seasonal experiments—such as a summer ale with coriander and sweet orange peel. Tasting room open Monday–Thursday 12–9, Friday–Saturday 12–10, and Sunday 12–8. ⊠ *4700 Ohio Ave. S., SoDo* ☎ *206/762-0490* ⊕ *www.twobeersbrewery.com*

BEER FESTIVALS

Washington Brewers Festival (⊕ washingtonbeer.com; June/Father's Day weekend).

Fremont Oktoberfest (⊕ www.fremontoktoberfest.com; September).

Washington Cask Beer Festival (⊕ www.washingtonbrewersguild.org, end of March).

Pike Pub

Fremont Oktoberfest

WASHINGTON STATE WINE REGIONS

Second only to California in U.S. wine production, Washington has more than 500 wineries and 11 official American Viticultural Areas. The state is increasingly becoming known for its fine cabernet sauvignons after decades-strong on its crisp chardonnays and complex merlots. Here's a sampling of some of the state's best grape varieties.

Orchards and vineyard near Wishram, WA

WHITE WINES

CHARDONNAY. The French grape widely planted in eastern Washington, where the wines range from light to big and complex.

GEWÜRTZTRA-MINER. A German-Alsatian grape in the Columbia Gorge and the Yakima Valley that produces a spicy, aromatic wine.

RIESLING. A German grape that makes a delicate, floral wine.

Chateau Ste. Michelle

SAUVIGNON BLANC. Herbal, dry wine from this Bordeaux grape, fermented in oak, is sold as fumé blanc.

VIOGNIER. A Rhône Valley grape that in eastern Washington makes fragrant wine with a good acid content.

WINERY SAMPLING

Amavi Cellars
(🌐 www.amavicellars.com)

Chateau Ste. Michelle
(🌐 www.ste-michelle.com)

Columbia Crest
(🌐 www.columbiacrest.com)

Cote Bonneville
(🌐 www.cotebonneville.com)

DeLille (🌐 www.delillecellars.com)

Gramercy Cellars
(🌐 www.gramercycellars.com)

L'Ecole no. 41 (🌐 www.lecole.com)

Long Shadows
(🌐 www.longshadows.com)

Mark Ryan
(🌐 www.markryanwinery.com)

Maryhill (🌐 www.maryhillwinery.com)

àMaurice (🌐 www.amaurice.com)

RED WINES

CABERNET FRANC. A Bordeaux grape that produces well-balanced wine in the Walla Walla and Yakima Valleys and Columbia Gorge.

CABERNET SAUVIGNON. The famed Bordeaux grape grows well in the Columbia Valley and makes deeply tannic wines in Walla Walla and Yakima.

MERLOT. A black grape yielding a softer, more supple wine than cabernet sauvignon, merlot has recently experienced a boom, espe-

Columbia Crest

cially in the Walla Walla Valley.

SYRAH. A Rhône grape that produces complex, big-bodied wines; increasingly planted in the Yakima and Walla Walla Valleys.

ZINFANDEL. A hot-climate grape that in the Yakima Valley and the Columbia Gorge makes big, powerful wines.

BEST TASTING ROOMS AND WINE BARS

Almost every wine list in Seattle includes at least some regional choices, even when the cuisine has origins far from the Pacific Northwest.

POCO WINE ROOM. Feels like both a date spot and a friendly neighborhood hangout. Reasonably priced Pacific Northwest wines are the focus. ✉ 1408 E. Pine St., Capitol Hill ☎ 206/322–9463 🌐 www.pocowineroom.com

PORTALIS. A cozy wine bar and well-stocked shop, Portalis has happy hours, prix-fixe dinners, and regular thematic tastings. ✉ 5205 Ballard Ave NW, Ballard 🌐 www.portaliswines.com

CHEZ PHINNEY WINE BAR. This charming neighborhood wine bar focuses on smaller Pacific Northwest wineries. ✉ 7400 Greenwood Ave N, Phinney Ridge ☎ 206/656-7400 🌐 chezphinney.com

PURPLE CAFE AND WINE BAR. Rumor has it that the imposing tower at this lofty wine bar contains more than 5,000 bottles. It should be no surprise, then, that this sprawling downtown spot has one of the largest local wine selections in the city, with more than 50 choices from Washington state alone and hundreds from around the globe. Try the wines on their own or with snacks like Gorgonzola-stuffed dates, beef tartare, or meat and cheese plates. ✉ 1225 4th Ave., Downtown ☎ 206/829-2280 🌐 www.purple-cafe.com

THE TASTING ROOM. Wine shop and tasting bar with hard-to-find boutique Washington wines. ✉ 1924 Post Alley, Downtown 🌐 www.tastingroomseattle.com

Cabernet Sauvignon, Chateau Ste. Michelle

recent years, many of the area's longtime antique and furniture shops have shuttered, but you'll still find old classics like the flagship Filson store.

■ TIP→ **Find the best shopping on 1st Avenue South between Yesler Way and South Jackson Street, and Occidental Avenue South between South Main and Jackson Streets.**

Agate Designs

SOUVENIRS | Amateur geologists, curious kids, and anyone fascinated by fossils and gems should make a trip to this store that's almost like a museum (but a lot more fun). Between the 500-million-year-old fossils and the 250-pound amethyst geodes, there's no shortage of eye-popping items on display. ⊠ *120 1st Ave. S, Pioneer Square* ☎ *206/621–3063* ⊕ *www.agatedesigns.com.*

Arundel Books

BOOKS | Since 1984, this bastion of bibliophilia has offered new, used, and collectible titles to discerning shoppers. Its shelves are especially strong in art, photography, and graphic design. This eclectic assortment will satisfy both the avid reader and discriminating collector. ⊠ *212 1st Ave. S, Pioneer Square* ☎ *206/624–4442* ⊕ *www.arundelbookstores.com.*

Filson

SPORTING GOODS | Seattle's 6,000-square-foot flagship Filson store is a shrine to meticulously well-made outdoor wear for men and women. The hunting-lodge decor of the space, paired with interesting memorabilia and pricey, made-on-site clothing, makes the drive south of Pioneer Square worth it (we recommend catching a cab, not hoofing it). The attention to detail paid to the plaid vests, oil-treated rain slickers, and fishing outfits borders on the fetishistic. ⊠ *1741 1st Ave. S, Pioneer Square* ☎ *206/622–3147* ⊕ *www.filson.com.*

Glass House Studio

GLASSWARE | Seattle's oldest glassblowing studio and gallery lets you watch fearless artisans at work in the "hot shop." Some of the best glass artists in the country work out of this shop, and many of their impressive studio pieces are for sale, along with around 40 other Northwest artists represented by the shop. ⊠ *311 Occidental Ave. S, Pioneer Square* ☎ *206/682–9939* ⊕ *www.glasshouse-studio.com.*

Magic Mouse Toys

TOYS | FAMILY | Since 1977, this two-story, 7,000-square-foot shop in the heart of Pioneer Square has been supplying families with games, toys, puzzles, tricks, candy, and figurines. They claim a professional child runs this friendly store—and it shows. ⊠ *603 1st Ave., Pioneer Square* ☎ *206/682–8097* ⊕ *www.magicmousetoys.com.*

Saké Nomi

WINE/SPIRITS | Whether you're a novice or expert, you'll appreciate the authentic offerings here. The shop and tasting bar is open from 2–8 pm, Tuesday through Saturday. Don't be shy—have a seat, try a few of the rotating samples, and ask a lot of questions. Sake can be served up in a variety of temperatures and styles. ⊠ *106 Cherry St., Pioneer Square* ☎ *206/682–1117* ⊕ *www.sakenomi.us.*

Velouria

WOMEN'S CLOTHING | The ultimate antidote to mass-produced, unimaginative women's clothes can be found in this exquisitely feminine shop where independent West Coast designers rule. Much on offer is one of a kind: handmade, '70s-inspired jumpsuits; romantic, demure eyelet dresses; and clever screen-printed tees. Superb bags, delicate jewelry, and fun cards and gifts are also on display. It's worth a look just to check out all the wearable art. ⊠ *145 S. King St., Pioneer Square* ☎ *206/788–0330* ⊕ *shopvelouria.com* ⊙ *Closed Sun.–Mon.*

Chapter 6

THE CHINATOWN–
INTERNATIONAL
DISTRICT

Updated by
Naomi Tomky

👁 **Sights**
★★☆☆☆

🍴 **Restaurants**
★★★★☆

🛏 **Hotels**
★☆☆☆☆

🛍 **Shopping**
★★★☆☆

🍸 **Nightlife**
★☆☆☆☆

NEIGHBORHOOD SNAPSHOT

TOP REASONS TO GO

■ Browse for unique gifts, souvenirs, and trinkets at **Uwajimaya** and **Kobo at Higo**. Uwajimaya offers an amazing array of foods from around East and South-east Asia, along with deep home and beauty sections. Kobo, a gallery for local artists, sells cool clothes, unique gifts, and classy mementos.

■ Get a history lesson with your tea at the **Panama Hotel**. Although not one of our top choices for lodging, this hotel is a must-see for its lovely ground-floor teahouse and window into the lives of Japanese Americans forced into internment camps during World War II.

■ Tour the neighborhood with docents from the **Wing Luke Museum of the Asian Pacific American Experience**. The museum casts a no-nonsense eye on the story of Asian and Pacific Islander communities, and themed guided tours point out the living history in the neighborhood.

■ Sample something from a wide variety of East and Southeast Asian cuisines.

GETTING AROUND

The International District is southeast of Pioneer Square, and the neighborhoods are often combined in one visit—you may find yourself wandering into the I.D. anyway, along South Jackson Street, which is the main thoroughfare connecting the two.

From the center of Downtown, walking to the I.D. takes about 20 minutes. However, it's not a scenic route, so unless you need the leg stretch, take the light rail, which whisks you straight there.

FUN FACTS

■ Plenty of famous faces spent time in the I.D.'s beloved restaurants:

■ Former Japanese prime minister Takeo Miki worked as a dishwasher at Maneki while he went to school at the University of Washington.

■ The Bruce Lee booth in the back of Tai Tung gives customers a chance to sit in the same spot as the martial arts star once did, at his favorite restaurant.

■ Fans of author Jamie Ford's *Hotel on the Corner of Bitter and Sweet* will recognize the Panama Hotel from the book.

PLANNING YOUR TIME

■ The International District is a very popular lunchtime spot with Downtown office workers and a popular dinner spot with many Seattleites. You should definitely make a meal here part of your visit. You'll need at least an hour at the Wing Luke Museum, longer if you plan to do one of the tours. A stop at Uwajimaya is essential. Don't plan on spending a full day here—a morning or an afternoon will suffice.

Bright welcome banners, 12-foot fiberglass dragons clinging to lampposts, and a traditional Chinese gate confirm you're in the Chinatown–International District. It's synonymous with delectable dining—it has many Chinese restaurants (this is the neighborhood for barbecued duck and dumplings), including regional specialists, along with eateries whose cuisines reflect its Pan-Asian spirit: Vietnamese, Japanese, Filipino, and Korean.

With the endlessly fun Uwajimaya shopping center, the gorgeous and informative Wing Luke Museum, several walking tours, and some terrific shopping, it also keeps you well entertained between bites.

The neighborhood used to be called Chinatown; it began as a haven for Chinese workers who came to the United States to work on the transcontinental railroad. It was later a hub for Seattle's growing Japanese population, and now features a lot of Vietnamese influence, both in the center of the I.D. and in "Little Saigon," on the eastern edge of the neighborhood. A complicated compromise that nobody really loved resulted in its official name being "The Chinatown–International District," though most people these days just call it the I.D.

The neighborhood weathered anti-Chinese riots and the forced eviction of Chinese residents during the 1880s, and

the internment of Japanese-Americans during World War II, but it has become increasingly less vital to its communities. Many of the people who actually live in the neighborhood are older—newer generations of immigrants start their lives and raise their children in the northern and southern suburbs. (Though everyone still makes the I.D. an obligatory snack stop before heading home after a night out in Seattle).

The I.D. stretches from 4th Avenue to 14th Avenue and between Yesler Way and South Dearborn Street. The main business anchor is the Uwajimaya Asian Market, and there are other small businesses scattered among the restaurants, including herbalists, acupuncturists, antiques shops, and private clubs. The area is more diffuse than similar communities in cities like San Francisco and New York. You won't find the densely packed streets chockablock with tiny storefronts and markets that spill out onto

The Seattle Pinball Museum has at least 50 games from all different eras.

the sidewalk—scenes that have become synonymous with the word "Chinatown."

As the I.D. increasingly becomes a destination for disparate communities, the neighborhood has worked to foster a more lively community feel. The 2021 remodel of Hing Hay Park added a central seating area, while annual parades and regular night markets have given it new life.

Sights

Kobe Terrace Park

CITY PARK | Follow pathways adorned by Mt. Fuji trees at this lovely hillside pocket park. The trees and a 200-year-old stone lantern were donated by Seattle's sister city of Kobe, Japan. Despite being so close to I-5, the terrace is a peaceful place to stroll and enjoy views of the city, the water, and, if you're lucky, Mt. Rainier; a few benches line the gravel paths. The herb gardens you see are part of the Danny Woo Community Gardens, tended to by neighborhood residents. Across

the street from the park is the historic Panama Hotel, featured in the novel *Hotel on the Corner of Bitter and Sweet* by Jamie Ford. Artifacts from the days of Japanese internment are on display, including a window on the floor showing a basement storage space containing a time capsule of unclaimed belongings. ✉ *Main St. between 6th Ave. S and 7th Ave. S, International District* ☎ *206/684–4075* 🔁 *Free.*

Seattle Pinball Museum

OTHER MUSEUM | FAMILY | More arcade than museum, this space puts a collector's life's work in play: more than 50 pinball games line up on the two floors, all included in the price of admission. The games rotate out frequently, and the collection includes machines as old as 1934 right up to recent releases. Entrance includes unlimited games, so take a break to chat with the staff, who can point out interesting features like the cigarette holders on the older machines. ⚠ **Children under 7 not permitted to play.** ✉ *508 Maynard Ave. S, International*

District ☎ 206/623–0759 ⊕ www.seat-tlepinballmuseum.com ☎ $20 ⊗ Closed Tues.–Wed.

★ Uwajimaya

STORE/MALL | FAMILY | This huge, fascinating Japanese supermarket is a feast for the senses, and a 2020 remodel makes it easier to navigate the colorful mounds of fresh produce and aisles of delicious packaged goods, with unique sweets and savory treats from countries throughout East and Southeast Asia. A busy food court serves sushi, Japanese bento-box meals, Chinese stir-fry combos, Vietnamese spring rolls, and an assortment of teas and tapioca drinks. You'll also find authentic housewares, cosmetics, toys, and more. There's also a fantastic branch of the famous Kinokuniya bookstore chain. The large parking lot is free for one hour with a minimum $10 purchase or two hours with a minimum $20 purchase—don't forget to have your ticket validated by the cashiers. ☒ 600 5th Ave. S, International District ☎ 206/624–6248 ⊕ www.uwajimaya.com.

★ Wing Luke Museum of the Asian Pacific American Experience

HISTORY MUSEUM | FAMILY | One of the only museums in the United States devoted to the Asian Pacific American experience provides a sophisticated and often somber look at how immigrants and their descendants have transformed (and been transformed by) American culture. The evolution of the museum has been driven by community participation—the museum's library has an oral history lab, and many of the rotating exhibits are focused on stories from longtime residents. Museum admission includes a guided tour through the East Kong Yick building, where scores of immigrant workers from China, Japan, and the Philippines first found refuge in Seattle (check the schedule, as this is the only way to see this section). The museum also offers weekly guided food tours of the neighborhood along rotating themes.

A Good Combo

For a great day of walking and exploring, start your day with breakfast at Pike Place Market, then bus, cab, or stroll down 1st Avenue to Pioneer Square (you'll pass SAM along the way). After visiting some art galleries—which generally open between 10:30 and noon—and stopping at any of the neighborhood's coffee shops (such as Zeitgeist or Grand Central Bakery), walk southeast to the International District for some retail therapy at Uwajimaya and a visit to the Wing Luke Museum. Then cab it back to your hotel.

☒ 719 S. King St., International District ☎ 206/623–5124 ⊕ www.wingluke.org ☎ $17 ⊗ Closed Mon. and Tues.

🍴 Restaurants

Famed for its many varieties of restaurants—from dim sum palaces to hole-in-the-wall noodle shops—the International District is a cultural and culinary destination. Along Main Street, the restaurants hold the history of Nihonmachi, or Japantown—sometimes literally, in the case of the Panama Hotel. Moving east along Jackson, the old Chinatown fades into what's now called Little Saigon, and the signs for Chinese barbecue become ones for banh mi. Around the neighborhood, the latest trendy food imports pop up, sporting spiffy signs for the hottest boba teas or coolest shave ice desserts.

Dough Zone Dumpling House

$ | CHINESE | What started as a small dumpling restaurant has grown into a juggernaut local chain, with this location as its flagship. Crowds pack in for juicy pork dumplings, crisp-bottomed q-bao, and artfully arranged noodles and vegetables.

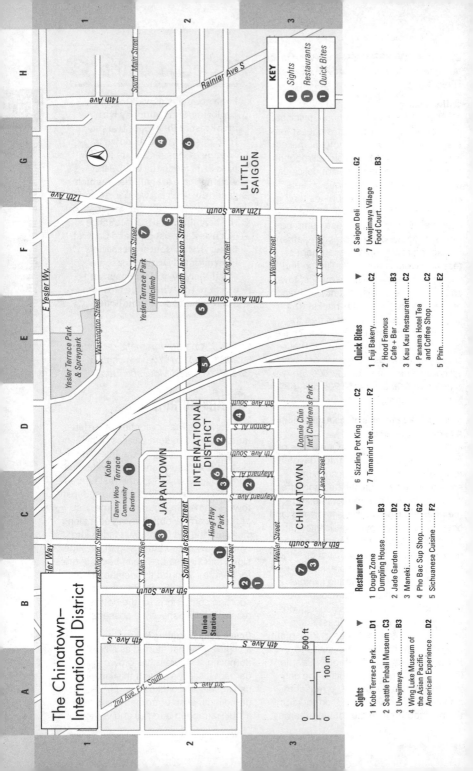

The Chinatown–International District

KEY

- ● Sights
- ● Restaurants
- ● Quick Bites

LITTLE SAIGON

Yesler Terrace Park & Spraypark

Yesler Terrace Park Hillclimb

Kobe Terrace

Danny Woo Community Garden

JAPANTOWN

Hing Hay Park

INTERNATIONAL DISTRICT

CHINATOWN

Donnie Chin Int'l Children's Park

Union Station

Streets: E Yesler Wy, E Yesler Way, S Washington Street, S Main Street, South Main Street, South Jackson Street, S Jackson Street, South Jackson Street, S King Street, S Weller Street, S Lane Street, Rainier Ave S, 14th Ave, 12th Ave, 12th Ave South, 10th Ave South, 8th Ave South, 7th Ave South, Maynard Ave S, Canton Al S, Maynard Al S, 6th Ave South, 5th Ave South, 4th Ave S, 4th Ave. S, 3rd Ave. S, 2nd Ave Ext South

0 — 500 ft
0 — 100 m

Sights ▶

1 Kobe Terrace Park......**D1**
2 Seattle Pinball Museum . **C3**
3 Uwajimaya.................**B3**
4 Wing Luke Museum of the Asian Pacific American Experience....**D2**

Restaurants ▶

1 Dough Zone Dumpling House.........**B3**
2 Jade Garden...............**D2**
3 Maneki.....................**C2**
4 Pho Bac Sup Shop.......**G2**
5 Sichuanese Cuisine.......**F2**
6 Sizzling Pot King..........**C2**
7 Tamarind Tree.............**F2**

Quick Bites ▶

1 Fuji Bakery.................**C2**
2 Hood Famous Cafe + Bar.............**B3**
3 Kau Kau Restaurant......**C2**
4 Panama Hotel Tea and Coffee Shop.......**C2**
5 Phin........................**E2**
6 Saigon Deli................**G2**
7 Uwajimaya Village Food Court............**B3**

Known for: juicy pork dumplings; traditional flavors; friendly and efficient service. $ *Average main: $12* ✉ *504 5th Ave. S, Suite 109, International District* ☎ *206/285–9999* ⊕ *www.doughzone-dumplinghouse.com.*

Jade Garden

$ | **CHINESE** | This is a longtime favorite for dim sum enthusiasts, who also come for fluffy barbecue pork buns, walnut shrimp, chive dumplings, congee, and sticky rice. The waits are long and the atmosphere is lacking, but when you're craving dim sum, this is the place to go. **Known for:** extensive dim sum; dumplings; barbecue pork buns. $ *Average main: $13* ✉ *424 7th Ave. S, at King St., International District* ☎ *206/622–8181.*

Maneki

$$ | **JAPANESE** | The oldest Japanese restaurant in Seattle, Maneki is no longer a hidden gem catering to in-the-know locals and chefs, but that doesn't mean the food is any less impressive. Though the James Beard American Classic winner serves good sushi, it's better known for home-style Japanese dishes, which can be ordered as small plates and accompanied with sake. **Known for:** "Mom," the most wonderful elderly bartender; giant pieces of nigiri sushi; tatami rooms great for mini-parties. $ *Average main: $20* ✉ *304 6th Ave. S, International District* ☎ *206/622–2631, 503/662-2814* ⊕ *www.manekiseattle.com* ⊗ *Closed Mon. No lunch.*

★ Phở Bắc Sup Shop

$ | **VIETNAMESE** | Phở Bắc first brought its eponymous noodle soup to Seattle in the early 1980s; now, the children of the original owners proffer an equally pioneering Vietnamese restaurant. The recipes and flavors hew tightly to tradition, but the space and style come wholly from a young, modern perspective. **Known for:** excellent pho; fun versions of Vietnamese classics; absurdly big beef ribs. $ *Average main: $14* ✉ *1240 S. Jackson St., International District* ☎ *206/568-0882* ⊕ *www.thephobac.com.*

Sichuanese Cuisine

$ | **CHINESE** | For budget-friendly and oh-so-good Sichuan cooking, head to this simple spot in the Asian Plaza strip mall east of I–5. The atmosphere is ordinary, but the service is friendly and the food here is as traditional as it gets. **Known for:** house-made noodles; spicy Sichuanese ravioli; ma po tofu. $ *Average main: $15* ✉ *1048 S. Jackson St., International District* ☎ *206/399–8242* ⊕ *www.sichuan-cuisine.com.*

Sizzling Pot King

$$ | **HUNAN** | The attentive service at this quiet spot makes the enormous menu of searingly spicy and mostly traditional Hunan dishes easy to navigate. Customize your own sizzling dry pot with a choice of meat, flavoring, and vegetables, or stick to the menu of standards from the renowned cuisine of Hunan. **Known for:** huge menu with plenty of variety; dry pot; spicy traditional Hunan dishes. $ *Average main: $23* ✉ *660 S. King St., International District* ☎ *206/624-0314* ⊕ *www.spkorder.com* ⊗ *Closed Weds.*

Tamarind Tree

$$ | **VIETNAMESE** | Wildly popular with savvy diners from across the city, this Vietnamese haunt *really* doesn't look like much from the outside—and the entrance is through a cramped parking lot (which it shares with Sichuanese Cuisine restaurant)—but once you're inside, the elegantly simple space is extremely welcoming. Try the spring rolls, which are stuffed with fresh herbs, fried tofu, peanuts, coconut, jicama, and carrots; authentic *bánh xèo* (a crispy, stuffed rice pancake); spicy pho; the signature "seven courses of beef"; and, to finish, grilled banana cake with warm coconut milk. **Known for:** great service; delicious cocktails; authentic Vietnamese dishes. $ *Average main: $18* ✉ *1036 S. Jackson St., International District* ☎ *206/860–1404* ⊕ *www.tamarindtreerestaurant.com.*

☕ Coffee and Quick Bites

Fuji Bakery

$ | **BAKERY** | For a nice pastry or quick lunch, pop by this street corner window for passionfruit malasadas or a chicken *katsu sando*. A Japanese artisan bakery at its core, Fuji happily (and expertly) dabbles across cultures and styles, making everything from twice-baked almond croissants to bacon-and-cheese breads, plus stunning desserts such as filled cream puffs, fruit tarts, and soufflé cheesecakes. **Known for:** huge variety; fluffy baked goods; Japanese-style sandwiches. $ *Average main: $6* ⊠ *526 S. King St., #2834, International District* ☎ *206/623-4050* ⊕ *www.fujibakeryinc. com.*

★ Hood Famous Cafe + Bar

$ | **FILIPINO** | Starting out small and growing on word of mouth, Chera Amlag's bakery and bar sprouted from the desserts she made for her husband's Filipino pop-up dinners. A 2022 expansion grew this elegant I.D. space where she serves her dazzling purple ube cheesecake, alongside cafe foods with Filipino touches, like hot dog *ensaymadas* and *pan de sal* sandwiches. **Known for:** bright purple cheesecake; Filipino flavors; Asian coffee. $ *Average main: $8* ⊠ *504 5th Ave. S, Suite 107A, International District* ☎ *206/485–7049* ⊕ *www.hoodfamous bakeshop.com* ⊗ *Closed Mon. and Tues.*

Kau Kau Restaurant

$ | **CHINESE** | This simple spot serves the best Chinese barbecue in the I.D. Large cuts of meat hang in the window, enticing customers to try the famous BBQ pork. **Known for:** roasting dozens of ducks a day; fast service; crispy pork. $ *Average main: $15* ⊠ *656 S. King St., International District* ☎ *206/682–4006* ⊕ *www. kaukaubbq.com* ⊟ *No credit cards.*

Panama Hotel Tea and Coffee Shop

$ | **ASIAN** | This serene teahouse on the ground floor of the historic Panama Hotel has tons of personality and a subtle Asian flair that reflects its former life as a Japanese bathhouse. The space is lovely, with exposed-brick walls, shiny hardwood floors, and black-and-white photos of old Seattle (many of them relating to the history of the city's Japanese immigrants). **Known for:** glimpse into history; calm ambience; wide variety of tea. $ *Average main: $3* ⊠ *607 S. Main St., International District* ☎ *206/515–4000* ⊕ *www.pan amahotelseattle.com.*

Phin

$ | **VIETNAMESE** | Part café and part love letter to Vietnamese coffee tradition, all the drinks here are brewed on the small metal filter from which the coffee shop takes its name. The commitment to quality shows in the house-made condensed milks (dairy or oat) used for the *cà phê sữa*—classic Vietnamese coffee—and various related drinks. **Known for:** beautiful plant-filled space; house-made dairy and non-dairy products; crisp waffles. $ *Average main: $5* ⊠ *913 S. Jackson St., Suite D, International District* ⊕ *www. phinseattle.com* ⊗ *Closed Tues.*

Saigon Deli

$ | **VIETNAMESE** | Every Seattleite knows their favorite banh mi shop, and this quick, convenient spot is often a winner; try the "three kinds of ham" sandwich here to see if you agree. Tables brim with colorful Vietnamese sweets and grab-and-go meals. **Known for:** big flavors; easy on the budget; fast meals. $ *Average main: $10* ⊠ *1237 S. Jackson St., International District* ☎ *206/322–3700* ⊟ *No credit cards* ⊗ *Closed Wed.*

Uwajimaya Village Food Court

$ | **ASIAN** | Uwajimaya has a lively food court offering a quick tour of Asian cuisines at lunch-counter prices. The

Kobe Terrace Park's Mt. Fuji trees and centuries-old stone lantern were gifts from Seattle's sister city of Kobe, Japan.

deli offers sushi, teriyaki, and barbecued duck; fresh spring rolls served with hot chili sauce at Saigon Streets; plus tacos and a poke counter. **Known for:** great dessert options; food from around the world; prepared lunch at reasonable prices. $ *Average main: $9* ✉ *600 5th Ave. S, International District* ☎ *206/624–6248* ⊕ *www.uwajimaya.com.*

Shopping

Seattle's primarily Asian neighborhood offers plenty of ways to bring the experience home with you. Sample tea at Seattle Best Tea, leaf through books at Kinokuniya, check out Asian antiques, and stop for dim sum along the way. Megamarket Uwajimaya is the major shopping attraction of the International District, but the rest of the neighborhood is packed with shops worth visiting, too. Wander the neighborhood for bubble tea

(milky tea with tapioca pearls), Chinese pastries, jade and gold jewelry, Asian produce, and Eastern herbs and tinctures. Little souvenir shops sell plants, Japanese kites, Vietnamese bowls, Chinese slippers, Korean art, and tea or dish sets. The best shopping is from South Jackson Street to South Lane Street, between 5th and 8th Avenues South.

Kinokuniya Book Stores of America

BOOKS | Japanophiles, get thee to this Tokyo-based chain for a huge collection of books, magazines, office supplies, collectibles, clothes, and gifts. Their manga selection is particularly impressive—nearly every title you could want is represented, and they'll happily order anything you don't find in the store. ✉ *525 S. Weller St., International District* ⊕ *Enter through Uwajimaya's Weller St. entrance* ☎ *206/587–2477* ⊕ *usa.kinokuniya.com.*

★ Kobo at Higo

SOUVENIRS | Housed in what used to be a 75-year-old five-and-dime store, this distinctive gallery has fine ceramics, textiles, and exquisite crafts by Japanese and Northwest artists; you can also see artifacts from the old store, a part of the original Nihonmachi (Japantown). Items range from something as simple as incense from Kyoto to an enormous painted antique chest. Clothes, books, and gift options abound, all with ties to Japan or the local Japanese community. ⊠ *604 S. Jackson St., International District* ☎ *206/381–3000* ⊕ *www.koboseattle.com* ⊗ *Closed Sun.–Tues.*

★ Sairen

MIXED CLOTHING | Locally designed dresses, hand-made ceramics featuring East Asian ingredients, and cute children's toys from Hawaii somehow all make sense in this small boutique. The owners, both named Kaitlin and from Hawaii, curate an amazing selection of clothes, crafts, jewelry, and home goods, mostly produced in Seattle or by Asian American makers. Their eye for everything classy and cute, from boba tea-shaped cat toys to elegant Czech glass earrings makes shopping fun, and they stock European raincoats and cozy hoodies for men and women if you forgot to bring the right outfit for the weather. ⊠ *600 S. Jackson St., International District* ☎ *206/588-6144* ⊕ *www.shopsairen.com* ⊗ *Closed Mon.-Tues.*

Seattle Best Tea

OTHER FOOD & DRINK | If you haven't been introduced to the wonders of Asian tea, you need to make a trip here, where the experience is as enriching as the tea itself. Helpful staff will walk you through the selection of oolong, pouchong, jasmine, and green teas. All the teas are available to try, and you can pick up a cute teapot while you're at it. They also offer bubble tea and ice cream (in tea flavors, of course). ⊠ *506 S. King St., International District* ☎ *206/749–9855* ⊕ *www.seattlebesttea.com.*

Chapter 7

FIRST HILL AND THE CENTRAL DISTRICT

Updated by
AnnaMaria Stephens

👁 Sights	🍴 Restaurants	🛏 Hotels	🛍 Shopping	🍸 Nightlife
★★☆☆☆	★★☆☆☆	★☆☆☆☆	★☆☆☆☆	★☆☆☆☆

NEIGHBORHOOD SNAPSHOT

TOP REASONS TO GO

■ Spend a quiet, art-filled afternoon at the free **Frye Art Museum**, the only real attraction in First Hill and one of Seattle's best museums. The Frye mixes representational art with rotating exhibits of folk and pop art, so there's something for everyone.

■ Settle into an overstuffed chair for a drink at the Hotel Sorrento's delightfully fussy **Fireside Room**. This is an especially pleasant stop on a chilly, rainy day—a few leather easy chairs are parked in front of a crackling fireplace.

■ Redefine dinner theater at **Central Cinema**. This off-the-beaten-path movie house serves beer, wine, burgers, pizzas, and salads. Screenings are a mix of classics (e.g. *The Shining, Animal House*) and small independent films.

GETTING AROUND

Because the sights are so spread out here, having a car is essential. This is especially true if you want to tool around the Central District to see the landmark buildings and houses, or if you want to visit the Northwest African American Museum, which is far south of everything else, in the Rainier Valley area. If you're busing to the Northwest African American Museum from Downtown, take Bus 7 to Rainier Avenue South and South State Street. From Capitol Hill take Bus 48 from 23rd Avenue and East Madison Street to 23rd Avenue and South Massachusetts Street, which is right in front of the museum. If you're visiting the Frye and the Sorrento Hotel, you can walk from either Downtown or Capitol Hill. By bus, take the 3 from Downtown to James Street and 8th Avenue or hop on the First Hill Streetcar (which runs between Pioneer Square and Capitol Hill); the closest stop for the museum is at Broadway and Marion.

PAUSE HERE

■ Seattle's reputation as a highly literary city is bolstered by its beautiful libraries, including the Douglass-Truth branch in the Central District. Take a break from the elements after you've admired the architecture, a stylish mashup of the original 1914 brick-and-terra-cotta facade and a modern expansion. Inside, you'll find grand reading rooms, gleaming oak bookcases, free Wi-Fi, and a large collection of African American literature. Like many old buildings in the C.D., the library reflects the ever-changing nature of the neighborhood and its rich cultural history.

PLANNING YOUR TIME

■ Both of these neighborhoods are best as detours from other itineraries. First Hill is adjacent to Downtown, and the Central District is close to the International District. The Northwest African American Museum requires at least an hour. A visit to the small but captivating Frye Art Museum could take anywhere from one to three hours.

The little-visited neighborhoods of First Hill and the Central District are important pieces of the city's fabric. First Hill is an eastern extension of Downtown, and one tree-lined street has the truly spectacular Frye Art Museum. The mostly residential Central District is the historic hub of Seattle's local community, though the neighborhood is rapidly gentrifying.

First Hill

First Hill earned its unimaginative moniker because it's the first big hill that you encounter while heading east from Downtown toward Lake Washington. Starting in the early 1890s, many of Seattle's wealthiest residents built homes atop the steep hill, which was close to Downtown but still offered some distance from the busy urban core. Today the neighborhood is a mix of stately old mansions, dense high-rises, and modern hospitals (which explains the nickname "Pill Hill"). There isn't much for tourists to see in First Hill with a couple of notable exceptions: the Frye Art Museum and Hotel Sorrento, which features lovely Italianate architecture and a fabulous outdoor patio with black-and-white-striped umbrellas.

Sights

Frye Art Museum
ART MUSEUM | In addition to its beloved permanent collection—predominately 19th- and 20th-century pastoral paintings—the Frye hosts eclectic and often avant-garde exhibits, putting this elegant museum on par with the Henry in the University District. No matter what's going on in the stark, brightly lighted back galleries, it always seems to blend well with the permanent collection, which is rotated regularly. Thanks to the legacy of Charles and Emma Frye, the museum is always free, including parking. ⊠ *704 Terry Ave., First Hill* ☎ *206/622–9250* ⊕ *www.fryemuseum. org* 🎟 *Free* ⊘ *Closed Mon.-Tues.*

Town Hall
PERFORMANCE VENUE | First Hill's recently renovated Town Hall cultural center hosts scores of events in its spacious yet intimate Great Hall, chief among them talks and panel discussions with leading politicians, authors, scientists, and academics. ⊠ *1119 8th Ave., Downtown*

The Frye Art Museum has permanent and rotating collections and is always free to visit.

☎ *206/652–4255* 🌐 *www.townhallseattle.org.*

Coffee and Quick Bites

Most of the restaurants in First Hill cater to the neighborhood's working crowd, so you'll find plenty of budget-friendly places to grab a coffee or quick bite if you're visiting the museum or staying at Hotel Sorrento. For more dining options, head north to Capitol Hill, a seven-minute drive or 20-minute bus or streetcar ride.

George's Sausage and Delicatessen
$ | **SANDWICHES** | For nearly 40 years, George's has sold delicious deli sandwiches in a small market filled with Polish and Eastern European groceries. **Known for:** pierogi plate; Eastern European deli; housemade sausages. [$] *Average main: $8* ✉ *907 Madison St., First Hill* ☎ *206/622–1491* 🕐 *Closed Sun. No dinner.*

Italian Family Pizza
$ | **PIZZA** | New Yorkers say this family-owned place comes close to the pizza they know and love, with thin crusts and just the right proportions of red sauce and cheese. **Known for:** real-deal NYC-style pizza; homemade lasagna and meatballs; huge family-size pies. [$] *Average main: $16* ✉ *1028 Madison St., First Hill* ☎ *206/538–0040* 🌐 *italianfamilypizza.juisyfood.com.*

Sugar Bakery & Cafe
$ | **BAKERY** | An early-morning crowd lines up here for flaky pastries, bagels, coffee, and sweet treats; the freshly made soups and sandwiches are also tasty. **Known for:** gluten-free-friendly; nondairy choices; cookies and cakes. [$] *Average main: $7* ✉ *1014 Madison St., First Hill* ☎ *206/749–4105* 🌐 *www.sugarbakerycafe.com.*

Hotels

★ Hotel Sorrento

$$$$ | **HOTEL** | Built in 1906, the historic and serene Hotel Sorrento hits the perfect note between traditional and modern, with lovely Italianate architecture, carved wood moldings, white marble bathrooms, antique furnishings in sumptuous fabrics, and chic original contemporary artwork in the common spaces. **Pros:** the elegant wood-paneled Fireside Room is perfect for cocktail hour; courteous guest service; comfortable beds. **Cons:** not central; rooms are a bit small (though corner suites are commodious); ho-hum views. [$] *Rooms from: $424* ✉ *900 Madison St., First Hill* ☎ *206/622–6400, 800/426–1265* 🌐 *www.hotelsorrento.com* 🔑 *76 rooms* 🍴 *No Meals.*

Central District

The predominantly residential Central District, or the "C.D.," lies south of Capitol Hill and northeast of the International District. Its boundaries are roughly 12th Avenue on the west, Martin Luther King Jr. Boulevard on the east, East Madison to the north, and South Jackson Street to the south. As Seattle continues to develop at a rapid pace and the transit options connecting the city expand, the C.D. faces a transitional period. Community groups are working hard to ensure that the "revitalization" of the area doesn't come at the expense of stripping the city's oldest residential neighborhood of its history or breaking up and pricing out the community that's hung in there during years of economic blight. It has a few monuments honoring the city's Black community, as well as some notable restaurants and landmarks that provide an interesting survey of architectural trends throughout the decades.

■ TIP→ Several pop-culture icons hail from the C.D., including Jimi Hendrix, Quincy Jones, Bruce Lee, and Sir Mix-a-Lot.

Sights

Crespinel Martin Luther King Jr. Mural

PUBLIC ART | Heading west on Cherry Street in the Central District, you'll see a 17-foot-tall mural of Dr. Martin Luther King Jr. on the side of Fat's Chicken & Waffles restaurant. Pacific Northwest artist James Crespinel painted the mural on the eastern face of the building in 1995 and touched up his faded work two decades later while the community gathered to watch. ✉ *Corner of Martin Luther King Jr. Way and Cherry St., Central District.*

Douglass-Truth Neighborhood Library

LIBRARY | A city landmark that offers a little something for history buffs, architecture fans, and public-art lovers alike, this 1914 library was the first to be funded entirely by the city. After a lauded remodel and expansion a decade ago that followed strict historic preservation guidelines, Douglass-Truth remains a cherished community gathering spot. It also houses one of the largest collections of African American literature and history on the West Coast. Local artists Marita Dingus and Vivian Linder created sculptures and three-dimensional relief panels for the branch, which can be seen in the spacious corridor connecting the two buildings. Paintings of former slaves and abolitionists Frederick Douglass and Sojourner Truth by artist Eddie Ray Walker are also on display. Don't miss the recently restored Soul Pole, a totem pole depicting African American history, located outside on the grassy area on the corner of 23rd Avenue and East Yesler Way. ✉ *2300 E. Yesler Way, Central District* ☎ *206/684–4704* 🌐 *www.spl.org/locations/douglass-truth-branch.*

First African Methodist Episcopal Church

CHURCH | Founded in 1886, the state's oldest African American church and the community's nexus has operated out of this historic building since 1912. FAME's gospel choirs are among the city's best, and discussions with intellectuals,

First Hill, Central District, and South Seattle

Sights ▼

1 Crespinel Martin Luther King Jr. Mural.................. **I3**
2 Douglass-Truth Neighborhood Library............. **H5**
3 First African Methodist Episcopal Church................... **E1**
4 Frye Art Museum **C4**
5 Jimi Hendrix Park................. **H9**
6 Kubota Garden..................... **G9**
7 Mount Zion Baptist Church....... **G1**
8 Northwest African American Museum **H9**
9 Seward Park **G9**
10 Town Hall **B3**

Restaurants ▼

1 Cafe Selam **I3**
2 COMMUNION Restaurant & Bar.................. **H2**
3 Ezell's Famous Chicken **H4**
4 Fat's Chicken & Waffles **I3**
5 Jackson's Catfish Corner **H6**
6 Reckless Noodle House **H6**

Quick Bites ▼

1 Broadcast Coffee.................. **G5**
2 George's Sausage and Delicatessen **C3**
3 Italian Family Pizza **C3**
4 Katy's Corner Café................. **G2**
5 Raised Doughnuts and Cakes.... **H2**
6 Sugar Bakery & Cafe............... **C3**

Hotels ▼

1 Hotel Sorrento **C3**

authors, artists, and the community are regularly scheduled. ✉ *1522 14th Ave., Central District* ☎ *206/324–3664* ⊕ *www.fameseattle.org.*

Jimi Hendrix Park

CITY PARK | Adjacent to the Northwest African American Museum, Jimi Hendrix Park pays homage to one of the Central District's most famous sons. The 2½-acre park features walking paths, landscaping, interpretive signs about Hendrix's legacy, and a colorful 100-foot-long outdoor public art piece called the Shadow Wave Wall. The sculpture, which consists of undulating sections of gray and purple metal with cut-out designs, has a huge mural of the musical icon engraved at the center. ■ TIP→ **A short walk from the park, the under-construction Judkins Park Station also features two large-scale public artworks of a teen Jimi Hendrix. The light rail station, the only Seattle stop on the new East Link light rail line that will connect Seattle to Bellevue and Redmond, is slated to open in winter 2024.** ✉ *2400 S. Massachusetts St., Central District* ☎ *206/684-4075* ⊕ *www.seattle.gov/parks/find/parks/jimi-hendrix-park.*

Mount Zion Baptist Church

CHURCH | Gospel-music fans are drawn to the home of the state's largest Black congregation. The church's first gatherings began in 1889; back then its prayer meetings were held in homes and in a store. The church, which was recently designated an official Seattle landmark, was incorporated in 1903, and after a number of moves, settled in its current simple but sturdy brick building. Eighteen stained-glass windows, each with an original design that honors a key Black figure, glow within the sanctuary. Beneath the bell tower, James Washington's sculpture *The Oracle of Truth,* a gray boulder carved with the image of a lamb, is dedicated to children struggling to find truth. ✉ *1634 19th Ave., Central District* ☎ *206/322–6500* ⊕ *www.mountzion.net.*

Jazzy School

Garfield High School (✉ *400 23rd Avenue*) is one of the Central District's historic landmarks. Alumni include Quincy Jones and Jimi Hendrix; today the school enjoys national attention for its jazz program. The 30-piece ensemble often performs at local festivals, including Earshot Jazz Festival in October and Folk Life in May. ⊕ *www.garfieldjazz.org.*

Northwest African American Museum

HISTORY MUSEUM | Focusing on the history of African Americans in the Northwest, this museum housed in an old school building tells stories through a diverse collection of well-curated and insightful photos, artifacts, and compelling narratives. Past exhibits have included *Xenobia Bailey: The Aesthetics of Funk*, and *The Test: The Tuskegee Project*, focusing on the first African American aviation units in the U.S. military to serve in combat. One gallery is dedicated to the work of local artists. NAAM also hosts film screenings, talks, and other community events. ✉ *2300 S. Massachusetts St., Central District* ☎ *206/518–6000* ⊕ *www.naamnw.org* ✉ *$7* ⊙ *Closed Mon.–Tues.*

🍴 Restaurants

The C.D. isn't a culinary destination per se, largely because it's spread out and residential, but it does have a big star on the map: COMMUNION, a "Seattle soul" restaurant that has landed on local and international best-of lists since it opened (make your reservations now). Also noteworthy are the authentic Ethiopian restaurants (there are several on East Cherry Street), fast-casual soul food spots, and new small eateries cropping up as the neighborhood grows.

Cafe Selam

$$ | ETHIOPIAN | Don't let the modest digs dissuade you: the Ethiopian cuisine here is delicious. Open all day, Cafe Selam serves specialties like beef or lamb *tibs* (cubed meat sautéed with onions and spices) and *ketfo* (steak tartare), but is particularly known for its *ful*, a spicy breakfast dish of lightly pureed fava beans topped with eggs, onions, peppers, and feta cheese, served with two fluffy French loaves. **Known for:** butter-brushed injera bread; spicy ful with eggs; a tangy and complex berbere sauce. Ⓢ *Average main: $20* ✉ *2715 E. Cherry St, Central District* ☎ *206/328–0404* ⊕ *www.cafeselam.com.*

★ COMMUNION Restaurant & Bar

$$ | SOUTHERN | An instant Central District classic upon opening in late 2020, this acclaimed Black-owned restaurant dishes up "Seattle soul" in a vibrant setting. Think exquisitely prepared soul food that pays homage to family traditions—fried chicken, mac 'n' cheese, greens, and cornbread—alongside creative fare honoring Seattle's multicultural intersections, like the Fried Catfish Po'mi, a mashup of po'boy and bánh mi sandwiches. **Known for:** Pacific Northwest-inflected soul food; craft cocktails; international accolades. Ⓢ *Average main: $22* ✉ *2350 E. Union St., Seattle* ☎ *206/391-8140* ⊕ *www.communionseattle.com* ⊙ *Closed Mon.-Tues.*

Ezell's Famous Chicken

$ | AMERICAN | Though slammed at lunch time thanks to the high school across the street, this fast-food restaurant (the original location of a popular local chain) serves up some of the best fried chicken in Seattle—Oprah once had the founders fly to Chicago to make it for her birthday. Both original and spicy flavors are terrific, but be warned that the spicy is exactly that. **Known for:** fluffy rolls; perfectly crispy fried chicken; classic sides like coleslaw. Ⓢ *Average main: $10* ✉ *501 23rd Ave., Central District* ☎ *206/324–4141* ⊕ *www.ezellschicken.com.*

Fat's Chicken & Waffles

$ | SOUTHERN | Offering a taste of New Orleans in the Central District, Fat's Chicken & Waffles serves authentic Southern cuisine in a hip spot filled with furniture and murals made by local artists. Helmed by a chef with deep Louisiana roots, Fat's serves shrimp and grits, fried okra, red beans and rice, and other soul food classics in addition to the namesake chicken and waffles. **Known for:** New Orleans–style fare; trendy space; filling comfort food. Ⓢ *Average main: $16* ✉ *2726 Cherry St., Central District* ⊕ *www.fatschickenandwaffles. com* ⊙ *Closed Mon.*

Jackson's Catfish Corner

$$ | SOUTHERN | Not surprisingly, catfish dominates the menu at Jackson's, a neighborhood fast-casual fixture that recently reopened in a new spot. Run by the grandson of the restaurant's founders, Jackson's carries on the legacy of deep-fried catfish (as well as snapper and prawns), hush puppies, and other soul-food staples that have made it a local favorite for decades. **Known for:** friendly service; a crisp fish fry; longtime neighborhood fixture. Ⓢ *Average main: $20* ✉ *2218 S. Jackson St., Central District* ☎ *206/420-3911* ⊕ *www.jacksonscatfish-corner.com* ⊙ *Closed Mon.*

Reckless Noodle House

$$ | VIETNAMESE | Traveling around Vietnam together led two friends to open Reckless, which taps Vietnamese and other Asian flavors for its inventive street food–style noodle and rice bowls, salads, and crispy rolls. The craft cocktail list is just as creative as the culinary offerings at this cozy spot with dark walls, rustic wood booths, and eclectic artwork. **Known for:** sustainable ingredients; hip ambience; authentic pan-Asian flavors. Ⓢ *Average main: $18* ✉ *2519 S. Jackson St., Central District* ☎ *206/329–5499* ⊕ *www.reck-lessnoodles.com.*

☕ Coffee and Quick Bites

Broadcast Coffee

$ | CAFÉ | A popular neighborhood coffee-house, Broadcast roasts its own ethically sourced coffee; many locals pick up bags of coffee beans here (purchase includes a free cup of drip coffee). Choose from well-made standard espresso drinks or more creative options like the Disco Pony (espresso with Perrier, half 'n' half, and a lemon twist over ice) as well as seasonal offerings. **Known for:** stylish space with A/C and decent amount of stay-awhile seating; delicious coffee drinks; fresh pastries. $ *Average main: $7* ⊠ *1918 E. Yesler Way, Central District* ☎ *206/322–0807* ⊕ *www.broadcastcoffee.com.*

Katy's Corner Café

$ | SANDWICHES | This tiny, unpretentious neighborhood espresso bar has a classic coffeehouse vibe, with red walls, eclectic local art, a comfy worn sofa, and a few small tables. You'll find standard coffee drinks here along with homemade pastries, quiches, and sandwiches. **Known for:** dog-friendly (look for the jar of cookies); very good customer service; no-frills caffeine fix. $ *Average main: $6* ⊠ *2000 E. Union St., Central District* ☎ *206/329–0121.*

Raised Doughnuts and Cakes

$ | BAKERY | You can order ahead online so you won't experience the heartbreak of an empty bakery case—doughnuts go fast here. Tucked into the ground floor of one of the Central District's newest multi-use developments, Raised Doughnuts and Cakes turns out simple but perfectly airy classics like a basic glazed, maple and chocolate bars, and creative monthly specials with seasonal flavors and a mochi-flour gluten-free option. **Known for:** airy doughnuts; gluten-free options; creative seasonal flavors. $ *Average main: $3* ⊠ *2301 E. Union St., Suite L, Central District* ☎ *206/420-4077* ⊕ *www.raiseddoughnuts.com.*

🎭 Performing Arts

Central Cinema

FILM | Forget about 40-ounce Cokes and popcorn with neon-yellow butter—Central Cinema makes movie night a more elegant experience. The first few rows of this charming, friendly, little theater consist of diner-style booths; place your order for pizzas, salads, and snacks (including popcorn with inventive toppings like curry or brewer's yeast), and servers will deliver your food unobtrusively during the first few minutes of the movie. Wash it down with a normal-size soda, a cup of coffee, or better yet a cocktail or a glass of wine or beer. The theater shows a great mix of favorites and local indie and experimental films. ⊠ *1411 21st Ave., Central District* ☎ *206/328–3230* ⊕ *www.central-cinema.com.*

Langston Hughes Performing Arts Institute

ARTS CENTERS | A community hub that celebrated its 50th anniversary in 2022, the Central District's Langston Hughes Performing Arts Institute (LHPAI) offers a gathering place for Seattle's Black community—even as it's become more dispersed—through a variety of programming like classes, film screenings, readings, and theater. Housed in an elegant historic domed building, LHPAI also hosts the annual Seattle Black Film Festival in the spring. ⊠ *104 17th Ave. S, Central District* ☎ *206/323-7067* ⊕ *www.langstonseattle.org.*

South Seattle

Visitors looking for some outdoor time a short drive from the Central District should visit two parks in the southern portion of the city—Seward Park and Kubota Garden.

Did You Know?

At Seward Park you'll find trails through old-growth forest, mountain views, eagles' nests, an art studio, and a small swimming beach.

Sights

Kubota Garden

GARDEN | About 20 minutes south of the International District by car, sit 20 serene acres of streams, waterfalls, ponds, and rock outcroppings created by Fujitaro Kubota, a 1907 emigrant from Japan. (Other examples of his work show up in the gardens on the Seattle University campus, and the Japanese Garden at the Bloedel Reserve on Bainbridge Island.) The designated historical landmark of the city of Seattle is free to visitors, and tours are self-guided, though you can go on a docent-led tour on the fourth Saturday of every month, April through October, at 10 am (reservations required). ⊠ *9817 55th Ave. S, Mt. Baker* ✛ *From I–5, take Exit 158 and turn left toward Martin Luther King Jr. Way; continue up hill on Ryan Way. Turn left on 51st Ave. S, then right on Renton Ave. S, and right on 55th Ave. S to parking lot.* ☎ *206/684–4584* ⊕ *www.kubotagarden.org* ⊡ *Free.*

Seward Park

CITY PARK | Seward Park, about 15 minutes from the C.D., is a relatively undiscovered gem on the shores of Lake Washington. The 300-acre park includes trails through old-growth forest, mountain views, eagles' nests, a 2½-mile biking and walking path, a native plant garden, art studio, and a small swimming beach. For an informative self-guided tour of the park, available as a printable PDF, visit ⊕ *www.seattleolmsted.org/self-guided-tours.* ■ **TIP→ Turn your park visit into a bike tour on select summer weekends for Bicycle Weekends, when Lake Washington Boulevard (south of Mount Baker Beach to the entrance of Seward Park) is closed to motorized traffic from Friday evening to Monday morning. Check** ⊕ **www.parkways.seattle.gov.** ⊠ *5895 Lake Washington Blvd. S, Columbia City–Seward Park, Mt. Baker* ⊕ *www.sewardpark.org, www.seattle.gov/parks/bicyclesunday.*

Activities

Jefferson Park

GOLF | This golf complex has views of the city skyline and Mt. Rainier. The par-27, nine-hole course has a lighted driving range with heated stalls that's open from dusk until midnight. And the 18-hole, par-69 main course is one of the city's best. Greens fees start around $35 but are dynamic based on demand, so you could get a great deal on an off-time or weekday option. ⊠ *4101 Beacon Ave. S, Beacon Hill* ☎ *206/762–4513* ⊕ *www.seattlegolf.com.*

Chapter 8

CAPITOL HILL AND MADISON PARK

8

Updated by
Naomi Tomky

 Sights
★★★☆☆

 Restaurants
★★★★★

 Hotels
★★★☆☆

 Shopping
★★★★☆

 Nightlife
★★★★★

NEIGHBORHOOD SNAPSHOT

TOP REASONS TO GO

■ Browse the stacks at **Elliott Bay Book Company**, Seattle's biggest independent bookstore. Then find a sunny reading spot in **Cal Anderson Park**, a block away.

■ After you've stocked up on books, visit the surrounding shops, ice-cream shops, coffeehouses, and restaurants that make the **Pike–Pine Corridor** so hip and happening.

■ Browse the art collection at the **Seattle Asian Art Museum**, then relax in the surrounding **Volunteer Park**.

■ Rock out at **Neumos**, to anything from indie music to national touring acts.

■ Sample fantastic restaurants and coffeehouses, including **Altura**, **Taku**, and **Cascina Spinasse** for food; and **Vivace** or Analog Coffee for caffeine.

■ See the season's colors at nearby **Washington Park Arboretum**.

GETTING HERE AND AROUND

You can walk from Downtown, taking Pine or Pike Street across I–5 to Melrose Avenue, but keep in mind that touring the neighborhood itself will require a lot of walking, and it's uphill from Downtown.

Light rail runs from Westlake Center to Capitol Hill before continuing north to the University District and beyond. The First Hill Streetcar connects the International District, and First Hill to Capitol Hill. Buses 10, 11, 43, and 49 all pick up on Pike Street Downtown and head to various parts of Capitol Hill. This is the easiest crosstown route to Capitol Hill's Pike–Pine Corridor. The 10 and the 49 continue up toward Volunteer Park. The 8 connects Seattle Center to Capitol Hill via Denny Way. The 11 will get you to Madison Park and the Washington Park Arboretum, which is technically several neighborhoods out of Capitol Hill (most people usually drive or bike there).

Street parking here is difficult. Keep an eye out for pay lots, which are numerous.

VIEWFINDER

■ The view from the Volunteer Park Water Tower is one of the best in town, but if you lack the time, mobility, or motivation to climb more than 100 stairs, head across 15th Avenue East at the north end of the park to the Louisa Boren Lookout. The tree-framed view east over Lake Washington and toward the Bellevue skyline comes with plenty of benches for resting while you admire it, and accessible parking nearby.

PLANNING YOUR TIME

■ Spend the morning at the Seattle Asian Art Museum or at Washington Park Arboretum, or visit in the afternoon, then stay for dinner and barhopping.

The Hill has two faces: on one side, it's young and edgy, full of artists, musicians, and students. Tattoo parlors and coffeehouses abound, as well as thumping music venues and bars. On the other side, it's elegant and upscale, with tree-lined streets, 19th-century mansions, and John Charles Olmsted's Volunteer Park and the Seattle Asian Art Museum.

Converted warehouses, modern high-rises, colorfully painted two-story homes, and brick mansions all occupy the same neighborhood. There are parks aplenty and cute, quirky shops to browse, including one of the best bookstores in the city.

The Pike–Pine Corridor (Pike and Pine Streets running from Melrose Avenue to 15th Avenue) is the heart of the Hill. Pine Street is a slightly more pleasant walk, but Pike Street has more stores—and unless you're here in the evening (when the area's restaurants come to life), the stores and coffee shops will be the main draw. The architecture along both streets is a mix of older buildings with small storefronts, a few taller buildings that have lofts and office spaces, and garages and warehouses (some converted, some not). Pine skirts Cal Anderson Park—a small, pleasant park with an unusual conic fountain and reflecting pool—a lovely place to take a break after walking and shopping. Depending on weather, the park can be either very quiet or filled with all kinds of activities from softball games to impromptu concerts.

The Hill's other main drag is Broadway, a north-south avenue that crosses both Pike and Pine. Seattle's youth culture, old money, gay scene, and everything in between all converge on its lively stretch between East Denny Way and East Roy Street. Although it's got a few spots of note (Nathan Lockwood's ode to Northwestern ingredients, Altura, for one), it's still mostly a cluttered stretch of cheap restaurants, even cheaper clothing stores, and a few bars. Many people still find the area compelling for its people-watching. If you really want to see Seattle in all its quirky glory, head to Dick's Drive-In around midnight on a weekend.

The neighborhood's reputation as one of the city's hippest and most vibrant brought Seattle's beloved Elliott Bay Book Company up the hill from its original Pioneer Square location, and it's now within walking distance of several great pizzerias, ice-cream shops, and coffeehouses.

Climb the spiral staircase to the top of the Volunteer Park water tower for views of the city.

Capitol Hill

 Sights

AMcE Creative Arts

ART GALLERY | Nestled into a residential neighborhood, this spacious fine art gallery features both big national names with ambitious works in the main gallery and smaller local artists in its "Niche Market" space. The gallery focuses on contemporary art, with an eye to inclusivity and diversity. The exhibits tend to lean toward works with big, bold uses of color, such as by Gegam Kacherian, Johanna Goodman, and Chris Natrop. ✉ 612 19th Ave. E, Capitol Hill ☎ 206/518–1046 ⊕ www.amcecreativearts.com ⊘ Closed Mon.-Tues. Wed. by appt. only.

Lake View Cemetery

CEMETERY | One of the area's most beautiful cemeteries, dating back to 1872, looks east toward Lake Washington from its elevated hillside directly north of Volunteer Park. Several of Seattle's founding families are interred here (names you will likely recognize from street names and public places); the graves of Bruce Lee and his son Brandon are also among the most-visited sites. ✉ 1554 15th Ave. E, Capitol Hill ☎ 206/322–1582 ⊕ www. lakeviewcemeteryassociation.com.

Vermillion Gallery and Bar

ART GALLERY | While Vermillion is a fine bar, it is a very good art gallery, and excels most at the way it combines the two into a space that celebrates art, often with a glass of wine in hand. Vermillion takes the spirit of art openings—the way they combine an evening out with the appreciation of beautiful works—and presents it as a nightly event. Visual art exhibits take up the front room, while the back and bar area often host live music or performance art. ✉ 1508 11th Ave., Capitol Hill ☎ 206/709-9797 ⊕ www.vermillionseattle.com ⊘ Closed Sun.–Tues.

Lakeside Beaches Nearby

Madison Park. In the late 19th century, Madison Park was the most popular beach in the city, with a promenade, floating bandstands, gambling halls, and ship piers. Now it's a lakefront park with sloping lawns, a swimming area, playgrounds, and tennis courts. The whole area is usually bustling with activity—there are a number of upscale coffee shops, restaurants, and boutiques nearby. As the closest beach to densely populated Capitol Hill, it serves a wide audience. The beach has picnic tables, restrooms, and showers, and lifeguards on duty in summer, and a children's playground across the street. From Downtown, go east on Madison Street; it'll take you straight down to the lake. ⊠ *Madison St. and 43rd Ave., Madison Park.*

Madrona Park. Several beach parks and green spaces front the lake along Lake Washington Boulevard; Madrona Park is one of the largest. Lifeguards are on duty in the summer, and young swimmers have their own roped-in area, while teens and adults can swim out to a floating raft with a diving board. The trail along the shore is a great jogging spot. Grassy areas encourage picnicking; there are grills, picnic tables, phones, restrooms, and showers. From Downtown, go east on Yesler Way about two miles to 32nd Avenue. Turn left onto Lake Dell Avenue and then right; go to Lake Washington Boulevard and take a left. ⊠ *853 Lake Washington Blvd., Madrona.*

Volunteer Park and the Seattle Asian Art Museum

ART MUSEUM | Nestled among the grand homes of North Capitol Hill sits this 45-acre grassy expanse that's perfect for picnicking, sunbathing (or stomping in rain puddles), and strolling. You can tell this is one of the city's older parks by the size of the trees and the rhododendrons, many of which were planted more than a hundred years ago. The Olmsted Brothers, the premier landscape architects of the day, helped with the final design in 1904; the park has changed surprisingly little since then. In the center of the park is the Seattle Asian Art Museum (SAAM), housed in a 1933 art moderne–style edifice. It fits surprisingly well with the stark plaza stretching from the front door to the edge of a bluff, and with the lush plants of Volunteer Park. The museum's collections include thousands of paintings, sculptures, pottery, and textiles from China, Japan, India, Korea, and several Southeast Asian countries.

The Victorian-style Volunteer Park Conservatory greenhouse, across from the museum, has a magnificent collection of tropical pants. The five houses include the Bromeliad House, the Palm House, the Fern House, the Seasonal Display House, and the Cactus House.

A focal point of the park, at the western edge of the hill in front of the Asian Art Museum, is Isamu Noguchi's sculpture, *Black Sun,* a natural frame from which to view the Space Needle, the Puget Sound, and the Olympic Mountains. ⊠ *Park entrance, 1400 E. Prospect St., Capitol Hill* ☎ *206/654–3210 museum, 206/684–4743 conservatory* ⊕ *www.seattle.gov/parks/find/parks/volunteer-park* ☒ *Conservatory from $4; museum $5, free the last Friday of each month.* ☺ *Conservatory closed Mon., museum closed Mon.-Thurs.*

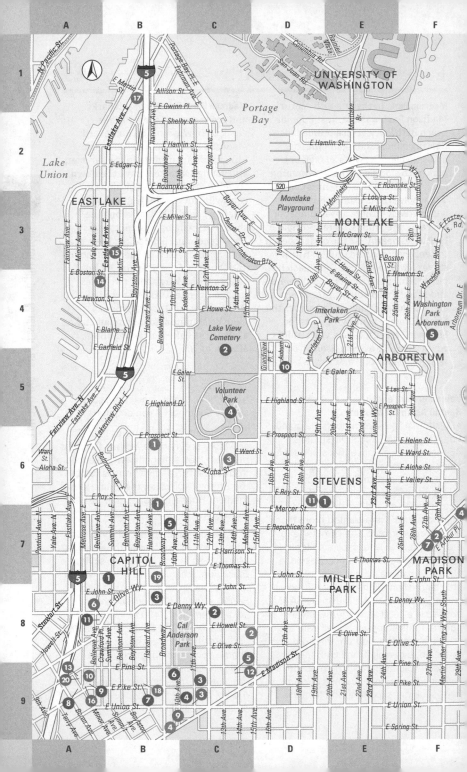

Capitol Hill and Madison Park

Union Bay

520

Evergreen Pt. Floating Bridge

Broadmoor Golf Course

Broadmoor Dr. E

E. Blenheim Dr. E

Parkside Dr. E

Shenandoah Dr. E

Lexington Wy. E

E. Saint Andrews Way

E. Morley Wy.

38th Ave. E
39th Ave. E
40th Ave. E
41st Ave. E
42nd Ave. E
43rd Ave. E
McGilvra Blvd.

E Lynn St.
E Newton St. E
E Blaine St
E Garfield St.
E Highland Dr.
E Prospect St.
E Lee St.

MADISON PARK

37th Ave. E

WASHINGTON PARK

McGilvra Blvd. E

31st Ave. E
32nd Ave. E
33rd Ave. E

E Valley St.
E Mercer St.
Lake Washington Blvd. E
E Republican St.
E Harrison St.
E John St.
E Denny Wy.
E Howell St.

Lake Washington

39th Ave. E
Dorffel Dr. E
Lake Washington Blvd.

MADRONA

31st Ave.
32nd Ave.
33rd Ave.
34th Ave.
35th Ave.
36th Ave.
38th Ave.

Madrona Dr.

0 ____ 1/4 mi
0 ____ 1/4 km

8

8

Capitol Hill and Madison Park CAPITOL HILL

KEY

1 *Sights*
1 *Restaurants*
1 *Quick Bites*
1 *Hotels*

★ Washington Park Arboretum

GARDEN | **FAMILY** | This 230-acre arboretum may be the most beautiful of Seattle's green space. On calm weekdays, the place feels really secluded. The seasons are always on full display: in warm winters, flowering cherries and plums bloom in its protected valleys as early as late February, while the flowering shrubs in Rhododendron Glen and Azalea Way bloom March through June. In autumn, trees and shrubs glow in hues of crimson, pumpkin, and lemon; in winter, plantings chosen specially for their stark and colorful branches dominate the landscape. A 1¼-mile trail that connects to an existing path to create a 2½-mile accessible loop, giving all guests access to areas that were previously hard to reach.

March through November, visit the peaceful Japanese Garden, a compressed world of mountains, forests, rivers, lakes, and tablelands. The pond, lined with blooming water irises in spring, has turtles and brightly colored koi. An authentic Japanese tea house reserved for tea ceremonies is open to the public on Saturdays and some additional days (check 🌐 *www.seattlejapanesegarden.org* for details). Visitors who would like to enjoy a bowl of tea and sweets can purchase a $10 "Chado" tea ticket at the Garden ticket booth.

The Graham Visitors Center at the park's north end has descriptions of the arboretum's flora and fauna (which include 130 endangered plants), as well as brochures, a garden gift shop, and walking-tour maps. Free tours are offered on the first Thursday of each month at 11:30 am. There is a pleasant playground at the ball fields on the south end of the park. ✉ *2300 Arboretum Dr. E, Capitol Hill* ☎ *206/543–8800 arboretum, 206/684–4725 Japanese garden* 🌐 *botanicgardens.uw.edu/washington-park-arboretum* 🎟 *Japanese garden from $8* 🕒 *Visitor center closed Mon.–Tues.; Japanese Garden closed Mon. and Dec.-Feb.*

🍴 Restaurants

Capitol Hill has become Seattle's major culinary destination. The greatest concentration of restaurants is around the Pike–Pine Corridor—Pike and Pine Streets from Melrose Avenue to 15th Avenue. All-day cafés like Oddfellows are all the rage, as are smaller, posh new American and Italian-inspired eateries like Lark, Altura, and Cascina Spinasse. On the west edge of the hill, smaller shops like Dino's Tomato Pie and Yalla have created a more casual restaurant corridor.

★ Altura

$$$$ | **ITALIAN** | A hand-carved cedar angel statue watches over diners at this lively spot, where chef-owner Nathan Lockwood lends a Northwest focus to seasonal Italian cuisine. The set tasting menu weaves rare, intriguing, and fascinating local and global ingredients into classic Italian techniques. **Known for:** great wine list; tasting menu; interesting ingredients. [$] *Average main: $175* ✉ *617 Broadway E, Capitol Hill* ☎ *206/402–6749* 🌐 *www.alturarestaurant.com* 🕒 *Closed Sun.–Mon. No lunch.*

★ Boat Bar

$$$ | **SEAFOOD** | Renee Erickson made her name serving Seattle's seafood, and takes a new spin on the same at this cool, marble-topped ode to Parisian fish and shellfish bistros. The menu offers seafood both raw and cooked, as well as meaty continental classics like steak tartare and a burger (and steaks borrowed from Bateau next door). **Known for:** fresh oysters; great drink options; delightful interior. [$] *Average main: $25* ✉ *1060 E. Union St., Capitol Hill* ☎ *206/900-8808* 🌐 *www.boatbarseattle.com* 🕒 *Closed Tues.–Wed. No lunch.*

Cascina Spinasse

$$$$ | **ITALIAN** | With cream-colored lace curtains and Italian soul, Spinasse brings the cuisine of Piedmont to Seattle. Chef Stuart Lane makes pasta fresh daily with fillings such as short rib ragu, eggplant, and anchovies, or simply dressed in butter and sage. **Known for:** classic Italian cuisine; handmade pasta; plentiful amaro. [$] *Average main: $45* ✉ *1531 14th Ave., Capitol Hill* ☎ *206/251-7673* 🌐 *www.spinasse.com* 🕒 *No lunch.*

★ Dino's Tomato Pie

$ | **PIZZA** | Long hailed as the creator of Seattle's best pizza at his first shop, Delancey, Brandon Pettit perhaps even improves on his previous recipe as he re-creates the neighborhood joints of his New Jersey childhood. The thick, crisp corners of the square Sicilian pies caramelize in the hot oven into what is practically pizza candy, while lovers of traditional round pizza will enjoy the char on the classics. **Known for:** square pizza; creative cocktails; adults only. [$] *Average main: $6* ✉ *1524 E. Olive Way, Capitol Hill* 🌐 *www.dinostomatopie.com* 🕒 *Closed Mon.–Tues. No lunch.*

Lark

$$$$ | **AMERICAN** | The Central Agency Building, a converted 1917 warehouse, is the setting for mouthwateringly delicious set menus with seasonally inspired main dishes. The expert servers can help you choose from an impressive wine list, and will happily help you decide two or three options for each course. **Known for:** welcoming space and service; set menu; local ingredients. [$] *Average main: $120* ✉ *952 E. Seneca St., Capitol Hill* ☎ *206/323-5275* 🌐 *www.larkseattle.com* 🕒 *Closed Sun.–Mon. No lunch* ☞ *Strongly recommend no children under 8.*

Mamnoon

$$$ | **MIDDLE EASTERN** | The sophistication, elegance, and excitement of Mamnoon are rare in Seattle's excessively casual restaurant culture. Try inventive Middle Eastern foods like pumpkin dumplings, chicory salad with sour mint dressing, and labneh cheesecake, in a transportive environment that matches the enchanting menu. **Known for:** fluffy housemade bread; stunning interior; superior drinks. [$] *Average main: $30* ✉ *1508 Melrose Ave., Capitol Hill* ☎ *206/906-9606* 🌐 *www.nadimama.com/mamnoon* 🕒 *Closed Sun.–Mon.*

Monsoon

$$$ | **VIETNAMESE** | With an elegant bar and laid-back roof deck, this serene Vietnamese restaurant on a tree-lined residential stretch of Capitol Hill is a better bet than ever. Upscale fare blends Vietnamese and Pacific Northwest elements, including wild prawns with lemongrass, catfish clay pot with fresh coconut juice and green onion, and lamb with fermented soybeans and sweet onions. **Known for:** crab dishes; excellent wine list; weekend brunch. [$] *Average main: $29* ✉ *615 19th Ave. E, Capitol Hill* ☎ *206/325-2111* 🌐 *www.monsoonrestaurants.com.*

Omega Ouzeri

$$$ | **GREEK** | Open the door into Greece and be welcomed by the white-washed walls, blond-wood tables, bold-blue chairs, and most importantly, the open kitchen full of grilling and olive oil. Greek classics dominate here, with lots of seafood. **Known for:** fresh seafood; Mediterranean ambience; Greek spirits. [$] *Average main: $27* ✉ *1529 14th Ave., Capitol Hill* ☎ *206/257-4515* 🌐 *www.omegaouzeri.com* 💳 *No credit cards* 🕒 *Closed Sun.–Mon.*

Qin Xi'an Noodles

$ | **CHINESE** | Silky, chewy noodles, named biang biang for the noise made when they're slapped on a counter as they're stretched by hand, are the specialty at this tiny spot—and you can watch them being prepared while you eat. Aside from the signature hot oil–seared noodles, the shop serves Xi'an delicacies such as stewed pork sandwiches and cold spicy appetizers. **Known for:** hot oil–seared biang biang noodles; quick service; Xi'an delicacies. [$] *Average main: $11* ✉ *1203 Pine St., Capitol Hill* ☎ *206/332-0220* 🌐 *www.qinxiannoodleswa.com* 🕒 *Closed Tues.*

Serafina

$$$ | ITALIAN | To many loyal patrons, Serafina is the perfect neighborhood restaurant: burnt-sienna walls topped by a dark ceiling convey the feeling of a lush garden villa, a sense heightened by the small sheltered courtyard out back. Menu highlights include grilled eggplant rolled with ricotta and basil; asparagus with an egg and truffle oil; and gnudi with rotating ingredients such as mushrooms, nettle, or beef cheeks. **Known for:** live music on some nights; eggplant rolls; handmade gnudi. $ *Average main: $29* ✉ *2043 Eastlake Ave. E, Capitol Hill* ☎ *206/323–0807* ⊕ *www.serafinaseattle. com* ☾ *No lunch.*

Son of a Butcher

$$$ | KOREAN BARBECUE | Forget smoke and mirrors, this Korean barbecue spot fills up every night with smoke and meat-eaters. While most of the city's Korean food scene sits in the suburbs, this quality-focused restaurant presents trays of impeccable sliced beef, pork, and chicken. **Known for:** assortment of sauces; Korean drinking snacks; high-quality meats. $ *Average main: $26* ✉ *2236 Eastlake Ave. E, Eastlake* ☎ *206/946-6574* ⊕ *www.sobseattle.com* ☾ *Closed Sun.– Mon. No lunch.*

Stateside

$$$ | VIETNAMESE | Low lights, ceiling fans, and palm-patterned wallpaper combine with weathered gold fixtures to evoke a sense of Vietnam with nearly the same precision as the chef's rendition of *bun cha* Hanoi. The setting transports, while the food impresses: great Vietnamese food isn't hard to find around town, but chef Eric Johnson brings an outsider's playfulness—as well as a pedigree at Michelin-starred restaurants—to the cuisine. **Known for:** great ambience; inventive takes on Vietnamese cuisine; bun cha Hanoi. $ *Average main: $30* ✉ *300 E. Pike St., Suite 1200, Capitol Hill* ☎ *206/557-7273* ⊕ *www.statesideseattle. com* ☾ *Closed Sun.-Tues. No lunch.*

Sushi Kappo Tamura

$$$$ | SEAFOOD | The seafood is as blindingly fresh as one would hope for at a Seattle sushi bar, but chef Taichi Kitamura ups the ante by adding seasonal, sustainable, and Northwest touches such as pork loin from sustainable Skagit River Ranch with organic watercress. Order a series of small plates at the blond-wood tables, like oysters from nearby Totten Inlet in ponzu sauce, or impeccable spot prawns in soy-butter sauce—or put yourself in Kitamura's more-than-capable hands for omakase at the 13-seat bar. **Known for:** Pacific Northwest touches; high-quality fish; creative sushi. $ *Average main: $39* ✉ *2968 Eastlake Ave. E, Capitol Hill* ☎ *206/547-0937* ⊕ *www. sushikappotamura.com* ☾ *Closed Sun.– Mon. No lunch.*

Taku

$ | JAPANESE FUSION | After closing two fine-dining restaurants and landing as runner up on Bravo's *Top Chef*, Shota Nakajima decided to use his talents to create this laid-back, super casual, fun-focused Japanese-style fried chicken shop. Though technically a bar (sorry, kiddos, this one is 21+), most people don't come for the kegged cocktails, sake, or Jell-O shots. **Known for:** late-night eats; crispy Japanese fried chicken; celebrity chef Shota Nakajima. $ *Average main: $18* ✉ *706 E. Pike St., Capitol Hill* ☎ *206/829-9418* ⊕ *www.takuseattle.com* ☾ *Closed Mon.–Tues. No lunch.*

Taneda Sushi in Kaiseki

$$$$ | JAPANESE | This tiny space hidden inside an aging mall is modern and lovely and the food is transportive. Reserve far in advance for one of the few coveted spots at Hideki Taneda's counter where each diner receives a progression of dishes, built from seasonal ingredients transformed into elaborate flavors and stunning presentations. **Known for:** Kaiseki service; see the food as it's prepared; coveted reservations. $ *Average main: $215* ✉ *219 E. Broadway, Suite 14,*

Capitol Hill ✥ *Enter through the center of the building, between American and Hana, and it will be on your left on the first floor.* 🌐 *www.tanedaseattle.com* 🕒 *Closed Mon.–Tues. No lunch.*

★ Taylor Shellfish Oyster Bar

$$ | **SEAFOOD** | The first oyster bar from a fifth-generation family-owned aquaculture farm, it's designed to give the diner the ultimate experience of eating a raw oyster. The elegant but casual wood bar and subway-tiled walls frame big tubs of bubbling water keeping the shellfish alive. **Known for:** live shellfish; family-owned business; oyster-focused dining. [$] *Average main: $20* ✉ *1521 Melrose Ave., Capitol Hill* ☎ *206/501-4321* 🌐 *www.taylorshellfishfarms.com.*

☕ Coffee and Quick Bites

Analog Coffee

$ | **CAFÉ** | The hipster and third-wave coffee dreams combine at this picture-perfect café on the Capitol Hill's west slope. Bright, light, and with big windows onto a quiet street, it invites coffee drinkers in to sit for a spell. **Known for:** quality coffee; cold brew on tap; attractive decor. [$] *Average main: $7* ✉ *235 Summit Ave. E, Capitol Hill* 🌐 *www.analogcoffee.com.*

Blotto

$$ | **PIZZA** | When a pizza obsessive decided to turn his pop-up into a proper restaurant, he recruited an accomplished chef to help him out, and the result is this delightful and precise mini-market, pie counter, and wine shop. Parmesan-sprinkled crusts decorate each of the pizzas, and while the selection is small, chef touches like confit cherry tomatoes keep the toppings interesting. **Known for:** pizza counter seating; natural wine bottles; chef touches on pizza. [$] *Average main: $23* ✉ *1830 12th Ave., Capitol Hill* ☎ *206/403–1809* 🌐 *www.blottoseattle.com* 🕒 *Closed Mon.–Tues.*

Dick's Drive-In

$ | **BURGER** | This local chain of hamburger drive-ins with iconic orange signage has changed little since the 1950s. The fries are hand-cut, the shakes are hand-dipped (made with hard ice cream), and the burgers hit the spot. **Known for:** fun scene; classic burgers; iconic local staple. [$] *Average main: $3* ✉ *115 Broadway E, Capitol Hill* ☎ *206/323–1300* 🌐 *www.ddir.com.*

Drip Tea

$ | **CAFÉ** | This hypebeast destination calls itself a concept store and sells sneakers and streetwear, but the lines stretching out the door are for its popular bubble tea and soft-serve stand. Eye-catching three-color beverages, bear-shaped takeout bottles, and "designer blend" smoothies show off creative combinations of fruit, boba, syrup, and ice cream. **Known for:** colorful drinks and ice cream; over-the-top bubble tea; bear-shaped bottles. [$] *Average main: $6* ✉ *416 10th Ave., Capitol Hill* ☎ *206/457–4374* 🌐 *www.thedriptea.com.*

Espresso Vivace at Brix

$ | **CAFÉ** | Vivace is widely considered to be the home of Seattle's finest espresso. The long, curving bar and a colorful mural add some character to a space in the upscale Brix condo complex. **Known for:** lively space; excellent espresso; classic coffeeshop feel. [$] *Average main: $4* ✉ *532 Broadway Ave. E, Capitol Hill* ☎ *206/860–2722* 🌐 *www.espressovivace.com.*

Oddfellows Cafe + Bar

$$ | **AMERICAN** | Right in the center of the Pike–Pine universe, this huge, ultrahip space anchoring the Oddfellows Building, across from Cal Anderson Park, serves inspired American food from morning coffee to evening drinks. The day might start with breakfast biscuits and thick brioche French toast; later on you can order the "Oddball" sandwich of meatballs in marinara sauce with provolone and Parmesan and roasted free-range

chicken. **Known for:** baked goods; trendy space; dependable cuisine. $ *Average main: $20* ✉ *1525 10th Ave., Capitol Hill* ⊕ *www.oddfellowscafe.com.*

Salt and Straw

$ | ICE CREAM | FAMILY | Though the Portland-based ice-cream chain has since opened stores up and down the West Coast, it found a welcoming home on Capitol Hill, where its "farm-to-cone" style of ice cream is respected, and the creative, sometimes a little out-there monthly specials don't scare anyone. **Known for:** creative flavors; generous sampling; long lines in summer. $ *Average main: $7* ✉ *7414 Pike St., Suite A, Capitol Hill* ☎ *206/258–4574* ⊕ *www. saltandstraw.com.*

Starbucks Reserve Roastery & Tasting Room

$ | CAFÉ | You could call it a coffee amusement park for its many ways to keep audiences entertained, but the sprawling combination café and showroom is deadly serious about its beans. Fans of the chain, and the coffee curious, will find lots to taste and explore here in 15,000 square feet of coffee culture. **Known for:** educational signage; variety of drinks; brewing and roasting methods on display. $ *Average main: $8* ✉ *1124 Pike St., Capitol Hill* ☎ *206/624–0173* ⊕ *www. starbucksreserve.com.*

Victrola Coffee Roasters

$ | CAFÉ | Victrola is one of the most loved of Capitol Hill's many coffeehouses, and it's easy to see why: the sizable space is pleasant and the walls are hung with artwork by local painters and photographers. The coffee is fantastic, the baristas are skillful, and everyone, from soccer moms to indie rockers, is made to feel like this neighborhood spot exists just for them. **Known for:** art-decked walls; laid-back feel; fresh-roasted beans. $ *Average main: $4* ✉ *411 15th Ave. E, Capitol Hill* ☎ *206/325-6520* ⊕ *www. victrolacoffee.com.*

Volunteer Park Café

$ | BAKERY | Cute as a button, and beloved by the locals who flock here, VPC gives off a general store/farmhouse feeling. Wholesome, decadent pastries, cookies, and breads are piled high at the counter, and the breakfast sandwiches are legendary. **Known for:** light lunches; great breakfast sandwiches; sweet space. $ *Average main: $10* ✉ *1501 17th Ave. E, Capitol Hill* ☎ *206/822–6566* ⊕ *www. volunteerpark.cafe* ⊗ *Closed Mon.–Tues.*

Yalla

$ | MIDDLE EASTERN | Conveniently located in the heart of the Olive Way bar scene, this walk-up window caters to the drinking crowd with its late-night hours but serves its Middle Eastern sandwiches all day. The menu centers on *saj*, a thin bread that wraps around eggplant, meat, cheese, or falafel like a burrito, or comes with dips like muhummara, baba ghanouj, or hummus. **Known for:** saj sandwiches; late night eats; take-out only. $ *Average main: $12* ✉ *1510 E. Olive Way, Capitol Hill* ⊕ *www.yallaseattle.com.*

Hotels

To experience a true Seattle neighborhood, stay in Capitol Hill. Close to Downtown but with its own distinct scene, "the Hill" offers character-rich bed-and-breakfasts in old mansions and oversized Craftsmans run by thoughtful proprietors. Airbnb also has a wealth of offerings in this hip neighborhood. Seattle's historically LGBTQ+ neighborhood is chock-full of live-music venues, true foodie establishments, and little retail gems. While the Pike–Pine Corridor and much of Broadway are alive until the wee hours, most of the neighborhood's lodging spots are set in quiet, tree-lined side streets off the main drags. Most B&Bs require multinight stays.

The Cecil Bacon Manor

$$ | **B&B/INN** | Serene and traditional, this 1909 Tudor home is surrounded by opulent gardens and is near both Volunteer Park and Broadway—and it also has some rooms and suites that welcome children or pets. **Pros:** friendly service; lovely patio and porch; quiet, relaxing retreat. **Cons:** no a/c; some rooms need updating; small showers in some rooms. [$] *Rooms from: $239* ✉ *959 Broadway E, at E. Prospect St., Capitol Hill* ☎ *206/717–5959* 🌐 *www.baconmanor.com* 🛏 *11 rooms* 🍴 *Free Breakfast.*

Gaslight Inn

$$ | **B&B/INN** | The architecture in this historic landmark building, from the fireplaces to the stained-glass windows, makes for a stunning place to stay. **Pros:** recent refresh to many parts; in-ground heated pool; free Wi-Fi. **Cons:** breakfast is unimpressive; street parking not always easy to find; some shared bathrooms. [$] *Rooms from: $218* ✉ *1727 15th Ave., Capitol Hill* ☎ *206/627–0531* 🌐 *www.seattlegaslightinn.com* 🛏 *7 rooms* 🍴 *Free Breakfast.*

Shafer Baillie Mansion Bed & Breakfast

$ | **B&B/INN** | The opulent guest rooms and suites on the second floor are large, with private baths, antique furnishings, Oriental rugs, huge windows, and lush details like ornate four-poster beds; third-floor rooms, while lovely, have a more contemporary country feel, but still have private baths and large windows. **Pros:** wonderful staff; great interior and exterior common spaces; free Wi-Fi. **Cons:** no elevator and the walk to the third floor might be hard for some guests; while children are allowed, some guests say the mansion isn't kid-friendly; three-night minimum stay during summer weekends. [$] *Rooms from: $179* ✉ *907 14th Ave. E, Capitol Hill* ☎ *206/322–4654* 🌐 *www.sbmansion.com* 🛏 *8 rooms* 🍴 *Free Breakfast.*

Silver Cloud Hotel Broadway

$ | **HOTEL** | **FAMILY** | If you want to stay on Capitol Hill and don't like B&Bs, this is your only option—and it does the job. **Pros:** better than expected from mid-range chain; central location; only non-B&B lodging on the Hill. **Cons:** immediate location is uninspiring; some rooms are a bit dark; not a great value when high season prices spike. [$] *Rooms from: $189* ✉ *1100 Broadway, Capitol Hill* ☎ *206/325–1400, 800/590–1801* 🌐 *www.silvercloud.com* 🛏 *179 rooms* 🍴 *No Meals.*

Nightlife

Capitol Hill has a lot of music venues and interesting watering holes—it's one of the city's best areas for nightlife. The Pike–Pine Corridor was always base camp for hipsters drinking Pabst out of the can, but the changing face of the neighborhood has brought some edgy, upscale gastropubs and appearance-conscious lounges. The Hill is also the center of the city's LGBTQ+ community, with the majority of gay bars and dance clubs along Pike, Pine, and Broadway. A short stretch of East Olive Way from Denny to Melrose is another mini–nightlife district, which is a bit more subdued.

As with Downtown, most of the neighborhood's restaurants double as nightspots. Quinn's (on Pike Street) and Smith (on 15th Avenue), for example, both get kudos for tasty food but are also notable as drinking spots (in Quinn's case for its excellent beer list).

BARS AND LOUNGES

Artusi

COCKTAIL LOUNGES | Sit at the white tile bar—or on the patio on a sunny day—of this Italian cocktail bar and order delicious antipasti and desserts to go with expertly prepared drinks. Beer selection is limited, but Artusi has great wine options. Make it to the 5–7 pm happy hour. ✉ *1535 14th Ave., Capitol Hill* ☎ *206/251–7673* 🌐 *www.artusibar.com.*

The Pine Box beer hall is housed in a former funeral home.

★ La Dive

BARS | In an area full of bars with themes, styles, and hooks, La Dive stand outs as simply an excellent and fun bar for absorbing the neighborhood vibes. A long, L-shaped bar opens the room for conversation, while the booths allow for small gatherings. The sidewalk tables in front are prime people-watching spots and give the feel of a popular Parisian bistro. The drinks menu focuses on natural wine, with a few classic cocktails, plus their signature alcoholic slushies. As the evening goes on, more customers turn to the Cham-bong to slurp their sparkling wine. Thankfully, a strong food menu, with late-night options, keeps things from getting too wild. Look for upscale bar snacks with a slight Eastern European tinge, as in the dumplings section. ✉ *721 E. Pike St., Capitol Hill* ⊕ *www. ladiveseattle.com.*

Life on Mars

BARS | Calm, classic, and inviting, this bar is like if one of the city's top radio personalities invited you into his living room to browse his record collection. Opened by KEXP *Morning Show* host John Richards, the bar sits in a room with walls covered in shelves of vinyl. The bar has cushy blue seats, while the rest of the room opens to big soft booths and a couch-seating area. The drinks include both alcoholic and non, each labeled with the ABV, and all of the food (typical bar apps, burgers, and sandwiches) is vegan. They serve brunch on weekends, and late-night tacos on Fridays and Saturdays. ✉ *722 E. Pike St., Capitol Hill* ☎ *206/323–9166* ⊕ *www.lifeonmarsseattle.com.*

Linda's Tavern

BARS | Welcome to one of the Hill's iconic dives—and not just because it was allegedly the last place Kurt Cobain was seen alive. The interior has a vaguely Western theme, but the patrons are pure Capitol Hill indie-rockers and hipsters. The bartenders are friendly, the burgers are good (brunch is even better), and the always-packed patio is one of the liveliest places to grab a happy-hour drink. ⊠ *707 E. Pine St., Capitol Hill* ☎ *206/325–1220* ⊕ *www.lindastavern.com.*

Montana

BARS | Lived-in booths and a welcoming atmosphere keep this place packed with everyone from couples on a first date to groups of old friends. As an anchor to the East Olive bar strip, it makes for excellent people-watching, either from the inside looking out or from the co-opted piece of sidewalk called a "parklet" that serves as the patio. The specialty is the cocktails on tap, particularly the Moscow Mule, owing in part to co-owner Rachel Marshall's other businesses, a ginger beer company. ⊠ *1506 E. Olive Way, Capitol Hill* ⊕ *www. instagram.com/montanainseattle.*

The Pine Box

BARS | The clever name is just one reason to visit this beer hall housed in a former funeral home. The churchlike interior is stately, with soaring ceilings, dark woodwork, and custom furniture made from huge Douglas fir timbers found in the basement—they were supposedly used to shelve coffins many years ago. The place is rumored to be haunted, but that doesn't stop a trendy crowd from congregating to sample from 30-plus taps of craft beer and a menu of wood-fired pizza (morgue-rita, anyone?), pickles ("embalmed veggies"), and plenty more. ⊠ *1600 Melrose Ave., Capitol Hill* ☎ *206/588–0375* ⊕ *www.pineboxbar.com.*

Revolver

BARS | Revolver stands out from a row of bars on this crowded block of Capitol Hill with a vinyl-only music policy, classic cocktails, draft beer, and boozy snow cones. Laid-back and welcoming, this is as close to a neighborhood classic as a place with the occasional (analog) DJ on a bustling bar street can get (that's a

good thing). ⊠ *1514 E. Olive Way, Capitol Hill* ☎ *206/860–7000.*

★ Rumba

COCKTAIL LOUNGES | A spot of Caribbean sunshine in the Northwest, Rumba stocks hundreds of rums which they offer in a half-dozen styles of daiquiri, various punches, and other assorted cocktails. Staffed by many of the best bartenders in town, this is a place for serious spirit aficionados to dig deep, but even rum rookies will feel welcome in the bright, friendly space with its turquoise bar stools and banquettes.

Cocktail nerds should reserve ahead for the immersive bar-within-a-bar, Inside Passage, where Kiki, a tentacled sea monster, greets them for drinks served in unique vessels, including a camera lens and a rice cooker. ⊠ *1112 Pike St., Capitol Hill* ☎ *206/583–7177* ⊕ *www.rumbaonpike.com.*

Smith

BARS | Great for people-watching and very Capitol Hill, Smith is a large, dark space with portraits of ex-presidents and taxidermied birds all over the walls, plus a mixture of booth seating and large communal tables. A bit outside the Pike–Pine heart, and filled to brimming with tattooed hipsters on weekends, this is a super-friendly and inviting space with a solid food menu (including a top-notch burger and sweet-potato fries) and a full bar. Beer selection is small but good, and the cocktail list is decent. ⊠ *332 15th Ave. E, Capitol Hill* ☎ *206/709–1099* ⊕ *www.smithseattle.com.*

Tavern Law

COCKTAIL LOUNGES | Take a trip back in time to the golden age of cocktails before Prohibition and the speakeasies that followed it. Tavern Law is dark and tucked away, and houses a "secret" upstairs area (accessed by picking up the phone next to the old bank-vault door). The drinks are impeccably made, often with surprising ingredients. ⊠ *1406 12th Ave.,*

Capitol Hill ☎ *206/322–9734* ⊕ *www.tavernlaw.com* ⊙ *Closed Mon.*

The Tin Table

COCKTAIL LOUNGES | Upstairs from Oddfellows and across from Cal Anderson Park, The Tin Table is part of the Century Ballroom, a welcoming little lounge with lots of exposed brick and a long, glossy bar. Its three-course, $45 menu is very popular and so is the Chimay that's on tap. It's also beloved for its good à la carte food, like dynamite steak frites. Try the "floozy burger" (with caramelized onion, bacon, cheese, and shoestring fries) and a creative cocktail. ⊠ *915 E. Pine St., Capitol Hill* ☎ *206/320–8458* ⊕ *www.thetintable.com* ⊙ *Closed Sun.–Wed.*

Unicorn

THEMED ENTERTAINMENT | Welcome to the carnival... or at least the carnival-themed bar. Walking in feels like ducking into a flamboyant, chaotic big top: striped blue walls, an elaborate bar with plenty of flashing lights, arrows overhead, and an assortment of taxidermied animal heads. The drinks stay on theme, with plenty of colors and names like "Unicorn Jizz," "Capri Sun," and "The Cereal Killer," while the food goes all-in on childhood nostalgia. Corn dogs, chicken nuggets, and meatballs masquerading as "Unicorn Balls," hold down the savory side, while desserts include funnel cake and fruity fried ice cream. Narwhal, a sibling bar in the same location, holds events throughout the week, including karaoke on Monday and drag queen bingo on Tuesday. ⊠ *1118 E. Pike St., Capitol Hill* ☎ *206/325–6492* ⊕ *www.unicornseattle.com.*

BREWPUBS

Optimism Brewing Company

BEER GARDENS | Optimism, like so many of the city's breweries, acts as a multifunctional third place for locals. What sets it apart is how deftly it serves as beer-nerd haven, gathering space for parties and events, bar, and even indoor playspace for kids and dogs. There are 16 beers on tap in a variety of styles (plus sparkling water) to keep drinkers happy, while food trucks keep them fed. ⚠ **Optimism is a cash-free establishment.** ⊠ *1158 Broadway, Capitol Hill* ⊕ *www.optimismbrewing.com.*

Quinn's

BARS | Capitol Hill's original gastropub has friendly bartenders, a large selection of beers on tap (with the West Coast and Belgium heavily represented), an extensive whiskey list, and a menu of rib-sticking food, which you can enjoy at the long bar or at a table on either of the two floors of the industrial-chic space. A pretzel and some French fries are good ways to start—then you can choose from beef tartare with pumpernickel crisps and perfect marrow bones with baguette and onion jam. Heartier mains, like the signature wild boar sloppy Joe, are available at dinnertime. A pared-down pub menu is also available from 4 pm to midnight or later. The folks here take their libations seriously, so chat up the bartenders about their favorites. ⊠ *1001 E. Pike St., Capitol Hill* ☎ *206/325–7711* ⊕ *www.quinnspubseattle.com* ⊙ *Closed Mon.–Tues.*

DANCE CLUBS

Century Ballroom

DANCE CLUBS | This is an elegant place for dinner and dancing, with a polished, 2,000-square-foot dance floor. Salsa and swing events often include lessons in the cover charge. There's swing dancing on Tuesday and Wednesday, a bachata social on Thursday, and salsa on Monday and Saturday. ⊠ *915 E. Pine St., 2nd fl., Capitol Hill* ☎ *206/324–7263* ⊕ *www.centuryballroom.com.*

LGBTQ+ SPOTS

Cuff Complex

DANCE CLUBS | The Cuff Complex is one of the city's oldest LGTBQ+ bars and also one of the broadest, with four bars, billiards, darts, and all sorts of events.

It strives to be a manly leather bar but attracts all shapes, sizes, and styles. The loud, crowded dance floor is tucked away downstairs; the main-floor bar, with its patio, is the place to be on warm nights. ✉ *1533 13th Ave., Capitol Hill* ☎ *206/323–1525* ⊕ *www.cuffcomplex.com.*

Madison Pub

PUBS | Regulars shoot pool, hang out with groups of friends, and chat up the friendly bartenders at this laid-back, anti-scenester joint. In an area where gay bar often becomes synonymous with dance club, this sports bar and pub offers an inclusive, relaxed hang-out spot. ✉ *1315 E. Madison St., Capitol Hill* ☎ *206/325–6537* ⊕ *www.madisonpub.com.*

Neighbours

DANCE CLUBS | Neighbours is an institution thanks in part to its drag shows, theme DJ nights, and relaxed atmosphere (everyone, including the straightest of the straights, can feel welcome here). It's no longer the center of the gay and lesbian scene, but the dance floor and the rest of this large club is still usually packed all weekend. After-hours parties open the dance floor to ages 18 and up. ✉ *1509 Broadway, Capitol Hill* ☎ *206/420–2958* ⊕ *www.neighboursnightclub.com* ☾ *Closed Mon.-Thurs.*

Pony

DANCE CLUBS | The original and short-lived Pony, which got bulldozed along with the rest of the 500 block of Pine Street, was notorious for wild fun. The current incarnation, just a bit more polished and with an amazing patio, retains some of the former space's decorating touches (including vintage nude photos). There's a small dance floor and a mix of gays, lesbians, and their friends, and the patio is open year-round, thanks to a retractable roof and gas firepit. ✉ *1221 E. Madison St., Capitol Hill* ⊕ *www.ponyseattle.com.*

Queer/Bar

CABARET | Drag fans, assemble: for a very queer, very good time, head to this inclusive performance space and bar. Live drag shows feature local talent and nationally known queens up to five days a week, and other nights, the calendar fills with viewing parties for *RuPaul's Drag Race*, queer burlesque shows, and "queeraoke." Big name events can get crowded, so reservations are recommended for large groups, and smaller ones should plan on lines. ✉ *1518 11th Ave., Capitol Hill* ⊕ *www.thequeerbar.com* ☾ *Closed Mon.*

Union Bar

DANCE CLUBS | Big, young, fun, and modern, it can sometimes feel like you need to be beautiful to get in here, just based on the crowds packing the indoor bar, dance floor, and outdoor patio. From the service to the security, everything here is super friendly and professional, leaving the crowd to relax and keep the party going, which it does almost every hour that this spot is open. Great DJs fill the dance floors, and partiers can take breaks at the firepits in front. ✉ *1009 E. Union St., Capitol Hill* ☎ *206/328-1318* ⊕ *www.unionseattle.com.*

Wildrose

BARS | One of the last dedicated lesbian bars in the entire country, Wildrose draws a mob nearly every night. The crowd at weeknight karaoke is fun and good-natured, cheering for pretty much anyone. Weekends are raucous, so grab a window table early and settle in for perpetual ladies' night. ✉ *1021 E. Pike St., Capitol Hill* ☎ *206/324–9210* ⊕ *www.thewildrosebar.com* ☾ *Closed Mon., Wed.*

MUSIC CLUBS
Chop Suey

LIVE MUSIC | One of the city's defining music venues of the early 21st century continues to put on terrific shows, book acts that will make headlines in the future, and support local artists. The eclectic mix of performers defies categorization, and nights without shows offer dance parties and DJs. The venue underwent a much-needed remodel in 2015 that improved the space and removed some of the questionable "Asian" decor, though the name, to the chagrin of many, remains. ⊠ *1325 E. Madison St., Capitol Hill* ⊕ *www.chopsuey.com.*

Neumos

LIVE MUSIC | One of the grunge era's iconic clubs (then named Moe's) has managed to reclaim its status as a staple of the Seattle rock scene. And it is a great rock venue: acoustics are excellent, and the roster of cutting-edge indie rock bands is one of the best in the city. Their intimate downstairs venue, Barboza, often brings in great lesser-known acts. ⊠ *925 E. Pike St., Capitol Hill* ⊕ *www. neumos.com.*

🎭 Performing Arts

Capitol Hill is a rabbit warren of small theaters and arts organizations, many of which make for a nice night out. The best way to navigate them is to check event listings in *The Stranger* (⊕ *www.thestranger.com*) or on the local blog Capitol Hill Seattle (⊕ *www.capitolhillseattle. com*). If you're in town on the second Thursday of a month, the Capitol Hill Art Walk (5–8 pm) features all types of art and performances (⊕ *www.capitolhillartwalk.com*).

ARTS CENTERS

12th Avenue Arts

THEATER | Developed by Community Roots Housing, 12th Avenue Arts is designed to keep the arts in the neighborhood. It plays host to two theaters with rotating shows from various local troupes, including the excellent Strawberry Theatre Workshop and Washington Ensemble Theatre. The building itself also provides low-cost housing, office space

for nonprofits, and holds a few restaurants. ⊠ *1620 12th Ave., Capitol Hill* ⊕ *12avearts.org.*

FILM

Northwest Film Forum

FILM | A cornerstone of the city's independent film scene, the two screening rooms here show classic repertory, cult hits, experimental films, and documentaries. Workshops, curated film series, and festivals fill the schedule. ⊠ *1515 12th Ave., Capitol Hill* ☎ *206/329–2629* ⊕ *www.nwfilmforum.org* ✉ *From $7.*

READINGS AND LECTURES

Hugo House

READINGS/LECTURES | This writers' haven has classes and readings by Northwest luminaries and authors on their way up. From Q&A sessions with local novelists to lectures by Pulitzer Prize winners, community writing sessions to guided memoir classes, this organization uses its building to encourage and enable everyone's literary side. ⊠ *1634 11th Ave., Capitol Hill* ☎ *206/322–7030* ⊕ *www.hugohouse.org.*

🛍 Shopping

If you always make sure that your clothes are on trend, embody the DIY ethos, or just like to people-watch, head to Capitol Hill for some of the best shopping in town. Broadway is popular among college students because of its cheap clothing stores. The Pike–Pine Corridor holds the majority of the neighborhood's most interesting shops.

■TIP➔ **Find the best shopping on East Pike and East Pine Streets between Bellevue Avenue and Madison Avenue, East Olive Way between Bellevue Avenue and Broadway, and Broadway between East Denny Way and East Roy Street.**

CLOTHING

Indian Summer

SECOND-HAND | Nominally a vintage clothing store with a focus on inclusive styles and sizes, Indian Summer is a fashion community destination for anyone who has ever struggled to fit into traditional clothes or trends. The unique vintage clothes curated by owner Adria Garcia show off impeccable taste that caters to nobody's beauty ideals, filling the shelves with the kinds of dresses, pants, hats, and more that so many people always dreamt of but never thought they could wear. ✉ *543 Summit Ave. E, Capitol Hill* ⊕ *www.instagram.com/indiansummervintage* ☉ *Closed Mon.–Thurs.*

LIKELIHOOD

SHOES | With designers ranging from Mihara Yasuhiro to Nike, this sneaker store has an extensive brand selection that's perfect for the eclectic Capitol Hill neighborhood. With its emphasis on "less is more," the clean white space creates the illusion of art gallery rather than shoe retailer. They also have a wide variety of apparel and bags. ✉ *1101 E. Union St., Capitol Hill* ☎ *206/257–0577* ⊕ *www.likelihood.us* ☉ *Closed Wed.*

Revival Shop

JEWELRY & WATCHES | Vintage shopping meets modern style in this consignment shop. Mixing used women's clothing with a collection of jewelry and art from local designers and other miscellaneous items, the store winds up with just the kind of eclectic collection that feels curated enough not to be slogging through junk, but haphazard enough to feel like your next treasure could be right in front of you. ✉ *233 Broadway E, Seattle* ☎ *206/395–6414* ⊕ *www.revivalshopseattle.com* ☉ *Closed Mon.*

★ Standard Goods

MIXED CLOTHING | If you want to get a true sense of Pacific Northwest style, this men's and women's clothing shop embodies it all, from casual plaid button-down shirts to wood-framed sunglasses. Carrying local brands like Filson, Shwood, and Capitol Hill Candles, this trendy local shop sources only quality goods. ✉ *501 E. Pike St., Capitol Hill* ⊕ *www.thestandardgoods.com.*

BOOKS

Big Little News

NEWSSTAND | Browse through low-budget zines and carefully crafted journals to explore your niche interests or discover new ones: not only is print not dead, it's thriving at this tiny but huge-hearted new-era newsstand. Opened in 2021, it inhabits an old elevator shaft remodeled to hold more than 200 different magazines and publications. Carrying everything from super-high-end imported fashion journals to the latest tabloid, Big Little News refuses to stick to either half of their moniker. ✉ *1102 E. Pike St., Capitol Hill* ⊕ *www.biglittlenews.com.*

★ Elliott Bay Book Company

BOOKS | A major reason to visit this landmark bookstore—formerly a longtime haunt in Pioneer Square—is the great selection of Pacific Northwest history books and fiction titles by local authors, complete with handwritten recommendation cards from the knowledgeable staff. A big selection of bargain books, lovely skylights, and an appealing café all sweeten the deal—and the hundreds of author events held every year mean that nearly every day is exciting. ✉ *1521 10th Ave., Capitol Hill* ☎ *206/624–6600* ⊕ *www.elliottbaybook.com.*

Madison Park is a quaint residential neighborhood.

Twice Sold Tales

BOOKS | It's hard to miss this excellent used-book store: simply look for the six-foot neon cat waving his Cheshire tail. Inside, you'll find plenty more kitties winding their way through the maze of stacks. The specialties here are rare books and out-of-print treasures, but they've got a smattering of everything and the employees (feline and human) care deeply about finding you the right books. ⊠ *1833 Harvard Ave., at Denny, Capitol Hill* ☎ *206/324–2421* ⊕ *www. twicesoldtales.com.*

HOME AND GIFTS
Kobo

SOUVENIRS | This lovely store sells artisan crafts from studios in Japan and the Northwest. As at the International District branch, you'll find tasteful home wares, cute but functional gifts, and quirky pieces of furniture. After a long day of looking at retro and ironic items, this place will cleanse your palate. ⊠ *814 E. Roy St., Capitol Hill* ⊕ *www.koboseattle.com* ⊗ *Closed Sun.*

MARKETS
★ Capitol Hill Farmers Market

MARKET | One of the city's liveliest and most interesting farmers' markets fills a plaza and spills onto a side street. There's fresh produce galore, prepared foods including Ethiopian cuisine and ice pops, plus music, samples, and plenty of cut flowers. The market is open Sunday from 11 am to 3 pm. ⊠ *E. Denny Way between Broadway & 10th Ave E (aka E. Barbara Bailey Way), Capitol Hill* ⊕ *www.seattlefarmersmarkets.org.*

Melrose Market

FOOD | Seattle is famously foodie-friendly, and this historic building packs several of the city's best culinary shops under one roof. Browse and sample artisanal meats, cheeses, shellfish, and liquor, all with locavore leanings. Unlike Pike Place, the pint-size Melrose is more a hipster haunt than a tourist trap: Anthony Bourdain and the Seattle *Top Chef* contestants used to be spotted here. ⊠ *1501–1535 Melrose Ave., Capitol Hill* ⊕ *www.melrosemarket-seattle.com.*

MUSIC

Wall of Sound

MUSIC | If you're on the hunt for Japanese avant-rock on LP, antiwar spoken word, spiritual reggae with Afro-jazz undertones, or old screen-printed show posters, you've found the place. They carry new and used CDs and LPs of all sorts, specializing in the kinds of things you probably won't find anywhere else. ✉ *1205 E. Pike St., #1C, Capitol Hill* ☎ *206/441–9880* 🌐 *www.wosound.com.*

Madison Park

🍴 Restaurants

★ Azuki

$$ | **JAPANESE** | Enormous bowls filled with light, complex broths and the star of the show—handmade udon noodles—grace the tables at this tiny Madison Valley shop. Along with the various noodle dishes, the surprisingly large menu includes Japanese specialties including sushi, salads, tofu, and rice bowls. **Known for:** good combo meal options; traditional Japanese dishes; handmade udon noodles. [$] *Average main: $23* ✉ *2711 E. Madison St., Madison Park* ☎ *206/328-4910* 🌐 *www.azukimadison.com.*

Café Flora

$$ | **VEGETARIAN** | **FAMILY** | The vegetarian and vegan menu changes frequently at Café Flora, but the chefs tend to keep things simple, with dishes like black-bean burgers topped with spicy aioli, polenta with leeks and spinach, and the popular tacos dorados (corn tortillas filled with potatoes and four types of cheese). You can eat in the Atrium, which has a stone fountain, skylight, and garden-style café tables and chairs. **Known for:** delightful outdoor patio; vegan fare; crowd-pleasing brunch. [$] *Average main: $22* ✉ *2901 E. Madison St., Madison Park* ☎ *206/325–9100* 🌐 *www.cafeflora.com.*

The Harvest Vine

$$$ | **SPANISH** | Arrive early for a perch at the upstairs kitchen-side bar of this tiny tapas-and-wine bar, because the downstairs room isn't nearly as atmospheric (though you can get a reservation there). Though no longer the citywide destination it was in its heyday, it remains a sweet spot and cheerful place to enjoy often-delicious Basque tapas, including chorizo with grilled bread, pan-seared tuna belly with vanilla bean-infused oil, grilled sardines, or duck confit. **Known for:** small, flavorful bites; friendly, welcoming vibes; true tapas bar style. [$] *Average main: $25* ✉ *2701 E. Madison St., Capitol Hill* ☎ *206/320–9771* 🌐 *www.harvest-vine.com.*

★ The Independent Pizzeria

$$ | **PIZZA** | Across the street from the popular Madison Park Beach, this worker-owned shop quietly and consistently turns out some of the city's best pies. Chewy, thin, crispy, and full of flavor, the crusts defy a specific style, beyond "a New Yorker would approve." Toppings include classics as well as creative combinations like the No Brainer, with morel mushrooms and house-made cultured cream. **Known for:** blistered-crust pizzas; worker owned; beachfront location. [$] *Average main: $16* ✉ *4235 E. Madison St., Madison Park* ☎ *206/860-6110* 🌐 *www.theindiepizzeria.com* ⏲ *Closed Mon.–Wed.* ☞ *Currently takeout only.*

FREMONT, PHINNEY RIDGE, AND GREENWOOD

Updated by
AnnaMaria Stephens

👁 **Sights**
★★☆☆☆

🍴 **Restaurants**
★★★★☆

🛏 **Hotels**
★☆☆☆☆

🛍 **Shopping**
★★★★★

🍸 **Nightlife**
★★★☆☆

NEIGHBORHOOD SNAPSHOT

TOP REASONS TO GO

■ Follow the **Burke-Gilman Trail** along the Fremont section of the Lake Washington Ship Canal.

■ Indulge in retail therapy at the area's **boutiques.** Mandatory stops on the shopping tour include Les Amis and Burnt Sugar.

■ Sip some brews at a **neighborhood tap house.**

■ Take a spin on a historic wooden carousel, then hang out with snow leopards at **Woodland Park Zoo.**

■ Tour an artisanal-chocolate factory: **Theo Chocolate**'s confections are best sampled after seeing chocolate makers at work.

GETTING HERE AND AROUND

From Downtown, buses 28 and 5 will drop you in Fremont center. Driving, take either Aurora Avenue North (Route 99) and exit right after you cross the bridge, or take Westlake Avenue North and cross the Fremont Bridge into the neighborhood's core. Phinney is at the top of a big hill. If you want to walk it, the best strategy is to thread your way up through the charming residential streets. If not, take Bus 5 bus up Fremont Avenue.

FREMONT SOLSTICE PARADE

If you want to know where all of Fremont's legendary weirdness has retreated, look no further than the Fremont Arts Council's warehouse on Fremont Avenue North. For months leading up to the Fremont Solstice Parade (held on the summer solstice weekend in June), half-finished parade floats spill out of the workshop. The parade is Seattle's most notorious summer event—some of the floats and costumes are political and/or wacky, and the "highlight" is a stream of naked bicyclists, only some of whom don elaborate body paint. And the professionally built floats and puppets are truly spectacular: past participants have included giant robots and a papier-mâché Flying Spaghetti Monster.

VIEWFINDER

■ Phinney Ridge sits atop a high ridge that runs north-south. If you stroll north from the zoo to the heart of the neighborhood, you'll get a sampling of the views that have made Phinney one of Seattle's most coveted places to live. To the west, behold the Olympic Mountains, which on clear days make a spectacular backdrop for sunsets. To the east, catch views of Green Lake, a glacial lake created 50,000 years ago, and the snow-capped Cascade Mountains in the distance. When you reach the Phinney Neighborhood Center at 67th Street, there's a pocket park with benches and a unique piece of history: a Cold War-era air raid tower topped with the most powerful siren in existence when it was erected (it no longer works, but once blasted out test warnings weekly).

The charming neighborhoods of Fremont and Phinney Ridge are great side trips when you've done your major Seattle sightseeing and are in the mood for shopping, strolling along the canal, or sampling artisanal goodies.

Fremont

 Sights

For many years, Fremont enjoyed its reputation as Seattle's weirdest neighborhood, home to hippies, artists, bikers, and rat-race dropouts. But Fremont has lost most of its artist cachet as the stores along its main strip turned more upscale, luxury condos and townhouses appeared above the neighborhood's warren of small houses, and rising rents sent many longtime residents reluctantly packing. Today it's denser than ever, with large new developments going up on the edges of Fremont to accommodate Seattle's unstoppable growth. On weekend nights, Fremont's main strip sometimes looks like one big party, as a bunch of bars draw in a young crowd from Downtown, the University District, and the suburbs.

The mixed bag of "quintessential sights" in this neighborhood reflects the intersection of past and present. Most of them, like Seattle's favorite photo stop—the Fremont Troll—are works of public art created in the 1980s and '90s. Others, like Theo Chocolate and Fremont Brewing, celebrate the independent spirit of the neighborhood but suggest a much different lifestyle than the founders of the "republic of Fremont" espoused. Still others are neutral and timeless, like a particularly lovely section of the Burke Gilman Trail along the Lake Washington Ship Canal.

Theo Chocolate Factory Experience
STORE/MALL | FAMILY | If it weren't for a small sign on the sidewalk and the faint whiff of cocoa in the air, you'd never know that Fremont has its own artisanal chocolate factory with daily tours. Since it opened in 2005, Theo has become one of the Northwest's most familiar chocolate brands, sold in shops across the city. Theo uses only organic, fair-trade cocoa beans, usually in high percentages—yielding darker, less sweet, and more complex flavors than some of their competitors. Stop by the factory to buy exquisite "confection" truffles—made daily in small batches—with unusual flavors like basil-ganache, lemon, fig-fennel, and burnt sugar. The friendly staff is generous with samples. You can go behind the scenes as well, with informative, hour-long tours, reservations are highly recommended, especially on weekends and during peak tourist season. ⊠ *3400 Phinney Ave. N, Fremont* ☎ *206/632–5100* ⊕ *www.theo-chocolate.com* ▣ *Tour $14.*

🍴 Restaurants

Friendly neighborhood joints, Thai restaurants, good pubs, and a few swankier eateries worth making the trek to the northern part of the city round out the options in these quirky adjacent neighborhoods.

Tour the Theo Chocolate factory and sample Seattle's signature artisanal treat.

Joule

$$$ | **KOREAN** | Married chef-owners Rachel Yang and Seif Chirchi have wowed Seattle diners with their French-fusion spins on Asian cuisine. Joule's nouvelle take on a Korean steak house serves meat options like Wagyu bavette steak with truffled pine nuts and short rib with Kalbi and grilled kimchi. Nonmeat menu items include Chinese broccoli with walnut pesto and mackerel with green curry cilantro crust and black currant. **Known for:** classic brunch buffet; Korean-inflected flavors; lively vibe. $ *Average main: $30 ⊠ 3506 Stone Way N, Fremont ☎ 206/632–1913 ⊕ www.joulerestaurant. com ⊗ No lunch.*

Kamonegi

$$ | **JAPANESE** | Specializing in soba noodles, this tiny spot feels like it was dropped stateside from Japan, but the menu also embraces local ingredients and creative riffs on classics. Seasonal starters might include zucchini coins dusted with Japanese "happy powder"—the sweet and salty flavoring from rice crackers—and

small plates like duck meatballs and tempura. **Known for:** a mix of traditional and fusion dishes; packed dining room; a happy place for authentic noodle aficionados. $ *Average main: $22 ⊠ 1054 N 39th St, Fremont ☎ 206/632–0185 ⊕ www. kamonegiseattle.com ⊗ Closed Sun.– Mon. No lunch.*

★ Manolin

$$$ | **SEAFOOD** | Walking into the light-filled dining room of Manolin, with its horseshoe-shape bar framing the open kitchen, transports you straight to the sea. Blue tiles, the wood-fired oven in the center, the cool marble bar, and the seafood-laden menu all bring diners to an ambiguous maritime destination where ceviches are inspired by coastal Mexico, plantain chips come from the Caribbean, smoked salmon has vaguely Scandinavian flavors, and the squid with black rice and ginger is as if from Asia, all mingling on one menu. **Known for:** a celebration of ceviche; creative cocktails; global flavors. $ *Average main: $34 ⊠ 3621 Stone Way N, Fremont ☎ 206/294–3331 ⊕ www.*

Fremont Like a Local

Wacky Public Art

Kick-start your tour under the north end of the Aurora Bridge at North 36th Street, where you'll find the **Fremont Troll**, a 2-ton, 18-foot-tall concrete troll clutching a real Volkswagen Beetle in his massive hand. The troll appeared in 1991, commissioned by the Fremont Arts Council. Pose for a shot atop his head or pretending to pull his beard.

Next head west down the hill to the statue of **Lenin** (North 36th Street at Fremont Place and Evanston Avenue N). Constructed by Bulgarian sculptor Emil Venkov for the Soviets in 1988, the 16-foot, 7-ton statue was removed shortly after the Velvet Revolution and eventually made its way to Seattle. Visitors here during Gay Pride Week might catch a glimpse of him in drag. The annual Lenin lighting, part of the Fremont Festivus in early December, is also a popular tradition.

A few blocks away you'll find the **Fremont Rocket** (⊕ *North 35th Street and Evanston Avenue N*), a 53-foot Cold War–era rocket nonchalantly strapped to the side of a retail store—which just may mark the official "center of the universe." This Seattle landmark was rescued from a surplus store in 1991 and successfully erected on its current locale in '94, when neon lights were added, along with the crest "De Libertas Quirkas," meaning "Freedom to Be Peculiar."

Walk along the water toward the Fremont Bridge, past the offices of Adobe, Getty Images, and Google (among others) to visit the cast-aluminum sculpture *Waiting for the Interurban* (⊕ *North 34th Street and Fremont Avenue N*). Artist Richard Beyer created this depiction of six people and a dog waiting for a trolley in 1979. Observe that the dog's face is actually that of a man—story goes this is the face of recycling pioneer (and onetime honorary mayor of Fremont) Armen Stepanian, who made disparaging remarks about the statue. It's been a long local tradition to "vandalize" the sculpture with anything from brightly colored umbrellas to signs congratulating newlyweds.

Also nearby: A much more recent statue of J. P. Patches, a television clown who delighted the Pacific Northwest for decades, with his sidekick Gertrude. It's called *Late for the Interurban*, a wink to its public art predecessor.

Lunch, Shopping, Beer? Yes, Please!

Once you've finished your circuit of Fremont's famous photo ops, take a load off with a bite to eat. **Manolin** is a destination-worthy option for lunch; just make sure you have reservations. Or grab a to-go meal at **Paseo** and bring it with you to **Fremont Brewing's Urban Beer Garden** (bring-your-own food is encouraged!)—the Caribbean sandwiches pair nicely with a pint, and you're on vacation!

Next up: Browsing Fremont's quirky boutiques. There are hipper shopping options in Capitol Hill and more luxury goods Downtown, but in Fremont you'll find an approachable mix of cool boutiques and offbeat offerings.

Check out the neighborhood's website (⊕ *www.fremontuniverse.com*) for more information.

manolinseattle.com ▭ *No credit cards* ⏲ *Closed Sun.-Tues. No lunch.*

Paseo

$ | CUBAN | The centerpiece of this Cuban-influenced menu is the mouthwatering Famous Caribbean Roast sandwich: marinated pork topped with sautéed onions and served on a chewy baguette. It's doused with an amazing top-secret sauce that keeps folks coming back for more. **Known for:** baguette sandwiches; Cuban-style entrées; takeout if you can't score a table. [$] *Average main: $13* ✉ *4225 Fremont Ave. N, Fremont* ☎ *206/545–7440* 🌐 *www.paseoseattle.com.*

★ Revel

$$ | ASIAN | Adventurous enough for the most committed gourmands but accessible enough to be a neighborhood favorite, Revel starts with Korean street food and shakes it up with a variety of influences, from French to Americana. Noodle dishes at this sleek industrial-chic spot with ample outdoor seating might feature smoked tea noodles with roast duck or seaweed noodles with Dungeness crab, while irresistibly spicy dumplings might be stuffed with bites of short ribs, shallots, and scallions, or perhaps chickpeas, roasted cauliflower, and mustard yogurt. **Known for:** playful desserts; fusion flavors that work; creative rice bowls. [$] *Average main: $22* ✉ *401 N. 36th St., Fremont* ☎ *206/547–2040 Reservations* 🌐 *www.revelseattle.com* ⏲ *No lunch.*

RockCreek

$$$ | SEAFOOD | A temple to uniquely prepared seafood, this is the restaurant that locals want to bring visitors to: an example of the casual way seafood weaves into all sorts of dishes when you live so close to such bounty. The mix of appetizers, oyster shooters, small plates, and full entrées makes the long menu an epic adventure filled with fresh local, domestic, and global fish—from local oysters to Hawaiian tuna, and back to black cod from Washington's own Neah Bay. **Known for:** unexpected but spot-on flavors; fun atmosphere; craft cocktails. [$] *Average main: $32* ✉ *4300 Fremont Ave. N, Fremont* ☎ *206/557–7732* 🌐 *www.rockcreekseattle.com* ⏲ *No lunch weekdays.*

Uneeda Burger

$ | BURGER | FAMILY | A casual burger shack from a fine-dining chef means flavor and execution that are always on point. The controlled chaos of this family-friendly joint can make it hard to get an outdoor table on sunny days, but the lines and wait are worth it for the perfectly cooked burgers that range from a classic beef patty to a house-made vegetarian option. **Known for:** perfect for hungry kids; fine-dining quality burgers; a place to sit outside. [$] *Average main: $11* ✉ *4302 Fremont Ave. N, Fremont* ☎ *206/547–2600* 🌐 *www.uneedaburger.com.*

The Whale Wins

$$$ | AMERICAN | James Beard Award–winning chef and restaurateur Renee Erickson focuses on the Pacific Northwest's bounty of farm-fresh produce, seafood, and local meats (she raises beef on her own Whidbey Island farm), aided here by the hard-working wood-fired oven at the front of the bright, whimsical space. The vegetable plates are unfailingly excellent, but everything that comes out of the kitchen seems blessed, whether it's a juicy roast chicken with capers and preserved lemons, a roasted whole trout, or a delicious slab of rabbit terrine. **Known for:** gourmet local and imported goods (including wine) for sale; cozy, convivial atmosphere; very good wine selection. [$] *Average main: $25* ✉ *3506 Stone Way N, Fremont* ☎ *206/632–9425* 🌐 *www.thewhalewins.com* ⏲ *No lunch.*

Coffee and Quick Bites

Lighthouse Roasters

$ | **CAFÉ** | Just stepping in to this cozy corner coffeehouse awakens the senses. Lighthouse Roasters roasts its beans on-site in a vintage cast-iron roaster, filling the space with a heady aroma. **Known for:** freshly roasted coffee; beloved neighborhood spot; plenty of seating. [$] *Average main: $5* ✉ *400 N. 43rd St., Fremont* ☎ *206/633–4775* 🌐 *www.lighthouseroasters.com.*

Milstead & Co.

$ | **CAFÉ** | Seattle's premier multiroaster café would be a parody of coffee culture if it weren't so good at what it does: curate a lineup of the country's best coffees and pour them expertly in a variety of methods. Baristas here coach customers through the process of picking a bean (origin, type, and roast) and method, so this is not the place to come for a quick caffeine hit. **Known for:** "snobby" in the best way; helpful and knowledgeable baristas; lots of choices. [$] *Average main: $6* ✉ *754 N. 34th St., Fremont* ☎ *206/659–4814* 🌐 *www.milsteadandco.com.*

PCC Community Markets

$ | **AMERICAN** | PCC Community Markets, an upscale food co-op, has all the fixings you need for a picnic along the canal, including sandwiches and salads. You can also order fresh coffee from the deli. **Known for:** focus on natural and organic items; large selection of to-go foods; terrific deli with seasonal items and pizza. [$] *Average main: $9* ✉ *600 N. 34th St., Fremont* ☎ *206/632–6811* 🌐 *www.pccmarkets.com.*

Royal Grinders

$ | **SANDWICHES** | Just steps from Fremont's Stalin statue, Royal Grinders serves hearty hot subs on pillowy rolls. We're talking classic combos of meat, cheese, and veggies piled high and baked in the oven. **Known for:** right in the heart of Fremont; old-school subs; unfussy fare. [$] *Average main: $8* ✉ *3526 Fremont Pl. N, behind Lenin statue, Fremont* ☎ *206/545–7560* 🌐 *www.royalgrinders.com* 💳 *No credit cards* 🕘 *Closed Mon.-Tues.*

Nightlife

Fremont has quite a few bars lining its main commercial drag of North 36th Street, including a few spots for live music. Unfortunately, Fremont suffers from Dr. Jekyll and Mr. Hyde syndrome. During the week, almost any of its simple bars is a fine place to grab a quiet drink with a friend. Come Friday night, however, the neighborhood can transform into an extended frat party—so consider yourself warned.

BARS AND LOUNGES

Brouwer's

BREWPUBS | It may look like a trendy Gothic castle, but in fact this is heaven for Belgian-beer lovers. Set in a former warehouse with two floors and lots of seating (as well as an outdoor patio), Brouwer's has 64 drafts in total—though not all dedicated to Belgium's legendary suds. Also on tap: German and American/Northwest beers, as well as English, Czech, and Polish selections. Brouwer's serves food too, with several Belgian dishes among the options. ✉ *400 N. 35th St., Fremont* ☎ *206/267–2437* 🌐 *www.brouwerscafe.com.*

The George & Dragon Pub

PUBS | Beloved by locals, this divey English pub attracts grizzled old Brits watching soccer, hipsters looking for cheap beer and whiskey, a frat crowd that clogs up the front patio area on weekends, and know-it-alls hoping to crush the competition at the popular Thursday trivia night. Major soccer events like the World Cup bring in huge crowds. ⊠ *206 N. 36th St., Fremont* ☎ *206/545–6864* ⊕ *www.theegeorge.com.*

Stampede Cocktail Club

COCKTAIL LOUNGES | Talk about a perfect fit for Fremont. A funky modern saloon with a Western vibe that doesn't take itself too seriously, Stampede delights the eyes with a gold-plated ceiling, antique lamps, and cowboy decor in the main bar and a more whimsical Jungle Room bedecked in tropical wallpaper and a wall-mounted head. Locals come here for the vibe and the killer cocktails. Choose from a changing menu of creative signature drinks or the legacy menu of past favorites; you can also order dumplings. ⊠ *119 N. 36th St., Fremont* ☎ *206/420–2792* ⊕ *www.stampedecocktailclub.com.*

BREWPUBS

Fremont Brewing

BREWPUBS | Fremont Brewing makes small-batch pale ales using organic hops. Locals (including their kids and dogs) crowd into the communal tables at the Urban Beer Garden, which includes both indoor and outdoor space, and a fireplace. Lines for beer move quickly, and visitors are encouraged to order or bring in outside food, though the brewery provides free pretzels and apples to snack on. ⊠ *1050 N. 34th St., Fremont* ☎ *206/420–2407* ⊕ *www.fremontbrewing.com.*

MUSIC CLUBS

Nectar Lounge

LIVE MUSIC | Reggae fans—and, really, any music fans—should pay attention to the event calendar at Nectar Lounge. The club regularly hosts big-name stars of the genre, while also mixing in hip-hop, pop, rock, bluegrass, world music, and other forms. The narrow floor can be tough to navigate on crowded evenings, but the outdoor patio with views of the stage provides some relief for patrons who want to relax while they enjoy the show. ⊠ *412 N. 36th St., Fremont* ☎ *206/632–2020* ⊕ *www.nectarlounge.com.*

🛍 Shopping

Fremont is full of the sort of stores perfectly suited to browsing and window-shopping—lots of pretty, pricey nonessentials and fun junk shops, in a cute and quirky north-end neighborhood. The weekly summer Sunday market along the waterfront (with free parking nearby) is hit or miss, but worth a look if you're in the area.

■ TIP→ **Find the best shopping on the blocks bound by Fremont Place North and Evanston Avenue North to North 34th Street and Aurora Avenue North.**

CLOTHING

Blue Owl Workshop

MEN'S CLOTHING | A short stroll from the big tech companies based along the canal, Blue Owl encourages male shoppers to go beyond the ubiquitous khakis and polos of the tech world with high-end denim, leather goods, and other clothing and accessories from Japan, Canada, Europe, and the USA. The Pacific Northwest-friendly flannel shirts may cost a small fortune but they're the softest you've ever felt. Blue Owl also has a reputation for carrying Seattle's best selection of raw denim—once broken in, the highly coveted small-batch jeans supposedly provide an unsurpassed look and fit. ⊠ *124 N.W. Canal St., Fremont* ☎ *206/849–6500* ⊕ *www.blueowl.com.*

Essenza

SOUVENIRS | A gurgling stone fountain stands in the center of this light-filled boutique, where airy displays showcase delicately scented European bath products by Santa Maria Novella, Tocca, and Cote Bastide. You'll find the complete line of Fresh cosmetics, handmade bed linens, women's loungewear and lingerie, delicate jewelry, and exquisitely detailed children's clothing. ⊠ *615 N. 35th St., Fremont* ☎ *206/547–4895* ⊕ *www.essenza-inc.com* ⊗ *Closed Sun.-Tues.*

evo Seattle

SPORTING GOODS | For outdoor gear with an edgy vibe, locals head to evo, which specializes in snow-sports and also carries a solid selection of seasonal street clothes for men and women. You'll find everything you need to shred Washington's big mountains in style, from fat powder skis and snowboards with wild graphics to flashy ski jackets and thick woolen beanies. (Since opening in 2011, evo has gone binational with 11 locations in the USA and Canada.) ∎TIP→ **evo shares its industrial-modern "campus" with the restaurants Joule and The Whale Wins. Seattle's only indoor skatepark, All Together Skatepark, is also right next door.** ⊠ *3500 Stone Way N, Fremont* ☎ *206/973–4470* ⊕ *www.evo.com.*

Les Amis

WOMEN'S CLOTHING | Women whose sartorial leanings go beyond basic will adore the sophisticated dresses, gorgeous handknits, and the makings of great work outfits here, much of it from Europe and Japan. Younger fashionistas come here, too, for unique summer skirts and ultrasoft T-shirts. Everyone seems to love the whimsical lingerie collection. Les Amis carries some top designers, such as Dosa, Isabel Marant, and Nanette Lepore. ⊠ *3420 Evanston Ave. N, Fremont* ☎ *206/632–2877* ⊕ *www.lesamis-inc.com* ⊗ *Closed Mon.-Tue.*

Pipe and Row

WOMEN'S CLOTHING | Modern, minimalist clothing feels effortlessly stylish when it's good quality like the looks you'll find at this chic boutique, a surprisingly friendly place to browse. Think basic tees, on-trend denim, simple jewelry, and pieces with edgier details that are still highly wearable. Brands include Richer Poorer, AGOLDE, Ganni, and Mandinga, a Uruguayan line known for signature bold prints. ⊠ *611 N. 35th St., Fremont* ☎ *206/632–0720* ⊕ *www.pipeandrow.com.*

Show Pony

WOMEN'S CLOTHING | With a mix of new, used, and locally designed clothing, Show Pony is a great spot to grab reasonably priced girly frocks and fabulous accessories. Especially good is the used/vintage section upstairs, which mostly stocks designer labels. Jewelry, perfume, gifts, and home-decorating items round out the collection. ⊠ *702 N. 35th St., Fremont* ☎ *206/706–4188* ⊕ *www.showponyseattle.com.*

BOOKS

Ophelia's Books

BOOKS | With a tiny spiral staircase leading to the basement, and resident cats wandering through the tightly packed aisles, Ophelia's offers a classic used-bookstore experience in an age when so many are disappearing. The owner is known for her excellent taste, and it shows—you'll find major titles from notable authors as well as obscure works and poetry books. Be sure to ask for recommendations—she'll be happy to help. ⊠ *3504 Fremont Ave. N, Fremont* ☎ *206/632–3759* ⊕ *www.opheliasbooks.com.*

Outsider Comics and Geek Boutique
BOOKS | Comics and geek culture may be more popular than ever but many fans still feel underserved by the shops catering to the traditional audience. Enter Outsider Comics and Geek Boutique, a small, welcoming space that showcases comics and more created by and for women, minorities, and the LGBTQ+ community. The unique selection might even make a new comics appreciator out of you. ⊠ *223 N. 36th St., Fremont* ☎ *206/535–8886* ⊕ *www.outsidercomics. com* ⊗ *Closed Mon.*

MUSIC
Dusty Strings
MUSIC | A Seattle institution since 1979, Dusty Strings has long been delighting folk and roots music lovers with beautifully crafted hammered dulcimers, harps, guitars of all stripes, banjos, ukuleles, and mandolins. The relaxed shop invites hands-on browsing, and the lilting strains of traditional melodies often fill the space. ⊠ *3406 Fremont Ave. N, Fremont* ☎ *206/634–1662* ⊕ *www.dustystrings. com* ⊗ *Closed Sun.–Mon.*

Daybreak Records
MUSIC | Few things have made a bigger comeback in recent years than vinyl records. Daybreak Records, a small, stylishly outfitted shop with a roll-up door for warm days, stocks a great, varied selection of mint used vinyl, including deep-catalog albums, plus a lot of 45s. Local audiophiles adore this place. ⊠ *4323 Fremont Ave. N, Fremont* ☎ *206/268–0702* ⊕ *www.daybreakrecordstore.com.*

MISCELLANEOUS
Burnt Sugar
SOUVENIRS | If there's a rocket on the roof, then you've found Burnt Sugar—or you've gone too far and are in Cape Canaveral. This hip and funky shop focuses on cool shoes but also offers a mélange of handbags, greeting cards, soaps, candles, jewelry, toys, children's gifts, makeup, and other eclectic baubles you never knew you needed. ⊠ *601 N. 35th St., Fremont* ☎ *888/545–0699* ⊕ *www. burntsugarfrankie.com.*

Fremont Vintage Mall
ANTIQUES & COLLECTIBLES | Goods from about 25 vendors are crammed into every conceivable corner of this bi-level space, so you'll likely score at least something to take home (or giggle at in nostalgia). Clothing, furniture, and collectible art are among the finds, and the mall's eye-catching assortment of kitschy retro stuff is fun to look through whether you're a serious collector or just an innocent bystander. The Jive Time Records Annex is also a tenant. It's easy to walk right past this place—look carefully for the door and then proceed down the flight of stairs. ⊠ *3419 Fremont Pl. N, Fremont* ☎ *206/548–9140* ⊕ *www. fremontvintagemall.com.*

The Uncommon Cottage
OTHER SPECIALTY STORE | Painted classic gothic purple on the outside, this charming cottage shop is stuffed with the "weird and whimsical." From candles with cheeky, not-safe-for-work names to locally made jewelry and funny socks, you'll find loads of quirky gift items here, especially for the goths in your life—the Furrybones figurines with skeletal smiles are darkly adorable. ⊠ *465 N. 36th St., A, Fremont* ☎ *206/483–7949* ⊕ *www. theuncommoncottage.com.*

Phinney Ridge and Greenwood

Sights

Mostly residential Phinney Ridge and its nearby sister neighborhood of Greenwood are just north of Fremont and east of Ballard. Though most visitors come to Phinney for the Woodland Park Zoo, located on the main street of Phinney Avenue North (which turns into Greenwood Avenue North), the area around the zoo is worth exploring if you have time. Phinney Ridge, with its handsome original Craftsman homes and towering mature trees, is the quieter of the two neighborhoods with a few coffee shops, eateries, and boutiques; on a clear day, you'll glimpse gorgeous views of the Cascade Mountains to the east and the Olympics to the west as you walk along Phinney Avenue. Farther north on Greenwood Avenue, the denser Greenwood, one of Seattle's more affordable neighborhoods, boasts a bustling commercial district with a range of dining options and a few interesting shops. It's easy to get from downtown Seattle to the Phinney/Greenwood neighborhoods; the No. 5 bus travels all along Phinney Avenue and Greenwood Avenue, with stops at the zoo and beyond.

Woodland Park Zoo

ZOO | FAMILY | Ninety-two acres are divided into bioclimatic zones, allowing many animals to roam freely in habitat areas. A jaguar exhibit is the center of the Tropical Rain Forest area, where rare cats, frogs, and birds evoke South American jungles. The Humboldt penguin exhibit is environmentally sound—it uses geothermal heating and cooling to mimic the climes of the penguins' native home, the coastal areas of Peru. With authentic thatch-roof buildings, the African Village has a replica schoolroom overlooking animals roaming the savanna; the Trail of Vines takes you through tropical Asia; and the Northern Trail winds past rocky habitats where wolves, mountain goats, a grizzly bear, and otters scramble and play. The Zoomazium is a nature-themed indoor play space for toddlers and kids under eight, and the Woodland Park Rose Garden is also worth a stroll. ■**TIP**→ **Check out Woodland Park's ZooTunes lineup of summertime outdoor concerts at** ⊕ *www.zoo.org/zootunes* **(tickets sell out in advance, so plan ahead).** ✉ *5500 Phinney Ave. N, Phinney Ridge* ☎ *206/548–2000* ⊕ *www.zoo.org* ✉ *Oct.–Apr. $18.25, May–Sept. $26.25* ⚠ *Advance ticket purchase recommended during peak season.*

🍴 Restaurants

★ FlintCreek Cattle Co.

$$$ | STEAKHOUSE | Ethically sourced meats, from steak cuts to gamier dishes such as bison, wild boar, and duck, headline the menu at FlintCreek, where floor-to-ceiling windows overlook a busy corner of Greenwood. A small-plates section features a cumin-dusted lamb tartare as well as mussels bathed in charred jalapeño-lime butter, while main-dish standouts include a brined pork chop on grits and a hanger steak topped with onion marmalade. **Known for:** sustainable ingredients; fancy chops and à la carte sides; hip vibe. Ⓢ *Average main: $34* ✉ *8421 Greenwood Ave. N, Greenwood* ☎ *206/457–5656* ⊕ *www.flintcreekseattle.com* ⊗ *No lunch.*

Valhalla Sandwiches

$ | SANDWICHES | If you visit Valhalla for lunch, be sure to bring a Viking-size appetite. The sandwiches are enormous, like the piled-high house BBQ pork with chipotle sauce, or El Duderino, which features chicken topped with chorizo, avocado, and jack cheese. **Known for:** hearty sandwiches; fast and filling lunch spot; lots of covered outdoor seating. $ *Average main: $13* ✉ *8202 Greenwood Ave. N, Greenwood* ☎ *206/257–0658* ⊕ *www.valhallasandwiches.com* ⊘ *Closed Sun. No dinner.*

⚫ Coffee and Quick Bites

★ Coyle's Bakeshop

$ | **BAKERY** | One of the city's neighborhood charmers, this beloved bakery churns out the best of French, British, and American pastry traditions, as well as their own unique treats. Mornings mean the espresso bar is busy and the croissants are flying off the shelves, while midday offers light salads, quiches, and their savory signature, the cretzel—a buttery, crisp, pretzel-knotted treat. **Known for:** cretzels; full tea service; cake. $ *Average main: $5* ✉ *8300 Greenwood Ave. N, Greenwood* ☎ *206/257–4736* ⊕ *www.coylesbakeshop.com* ⊘ *Closed Mon.–Tues.*

Herkimer Coffee

$ | **CAFÉ** | Herkimer Coffee's Greenwood outpost is a favorite of coffee connoisseurs, with baristas who know their stuff but won't give you side-eye for dumping sweetener in their creations. The coffee shop has some seating, but it's also a great spot to grab a cup to go. **Known for:** perfectly pulled espresso; knowledgeable baristas; locally roasted beans. $ *Average main: $5* ✉ *7320 Greenwood Ave. N, Phinney Ridge* ☎ *206/784–0202* ⊕ *www.herkimercoffee.com.*

Nutty Squirrel Gelato

$ | **ICE CREAM** | A neighborhood favorite that now has two additional locations, this artisan shop isn't quite a trip to Italy but the gelato is the real deal, including stracciatella, pistachio, and other classic flavors, all with high-quality ingredients. The namesake-for-a-reason Nutty Squirrel swirls salty peanut butter with dulce de leche caramel and chocolate chips. **Known for:** house-made Italian gelato and sorbetto; a summertime neighborhood favorite; outdoor café tables perfect for people-watching. $ *Average main: $5* ✉ *7212 Greenwood Ave. N, Phinney Ridge* ⊕ *www.nuttysquirrel.com.*

Red Mill

$ | **BURGER** | People line up out the door for juicy burgers and milkshakes in yummy flavors like mandarin-chocolate and butterscotch. Order ahead if you want to avoid a long wait during the busy lunch and dinner rushes. **Known for:** family-friendly atmosphere; affordable prices; classic burgers and fries. $ *Average main: $10* ✉ *312 N. 67th St., Greenwood* ☎ *206/783–6362* ⊕ *www.redmillburgers. com* ▭ *No credit cards* ⊘ *Closed Mon.*

Nightlife

Phinney Ridge is a residential neighborhood with a few laidback nightlife options.

BARS AND LOUNGES

Chuck's Hop Shop

BARS | Were it not for the awning, picnic tables, and rotating food trucks routinely parked outside, this place might look like just another corner convenience store—which it used to be before owner Chuck transformed it into one of North Seattle's favorite spots for sampling craft beer. With 50 taps, Chuck's features an especially good selection of IPAs and ciders on draft, many of local origin. Families love this extremely kid-friendly spot— there's an ice-cream counter, ample seating inside and out, and stacks of board games. Chuck's also offers a huge selection of bottled beers from all over the world, including gluten- and alcohol-free options. ⊠ *656 N.W. 85th St., Greenwood* ☎ *206/297–6212* ⊕ *www. chuckshopshop.com.*

Oliver's Twist

BARS | Down the street from the Woodland Park Zoo, Oliver's Twist is a welcoming spot with cozy leather booths and tons of local art on the walls. Drinks are expertly poured with house-made shrubs and syrups, and the tapas menu includes tasty snacks (garlic truffle popcorn, grilled cheese and tomato soup). It makes for a fun evening slightly off the beaten path. ⊠ *6822 Greenwood Ave. N, Phinney Ridge* ☎ *206/706–6673* ⊕ *www.oliverstwistseattle.com* ☻ *Closed Sun.-Mon.*

Prost!

PUBS | German beer fans will raise a stein to this popular neighborhood bar that features 10 imported German drafts in a variety of styles, including pilsner, weissbier, dunkel, and more. They also offer cocktails and wine as well as a menu of tasty German fare, from pretzels to locally made brats. Dark and cozy, Prost! is a laid-back spot most weeknights but gets packed on weekends and around Oktoberfest. ⊠ *7311 Greenwood Ave. N, Phinney Ridge* ☎ *206/706–5430* ⊕ *www. prosttavern.net.*

⚭ Shopping

None of the shops in this area are particularly destination-worthy, but there are a handful of places to browse if you're out strolling. Stick to Phinney Avenue and Greenwood Avenue North for the best offerings.

Greenwood Pencil Box

STATIONERY | Greenwood Pencil Box— which is fairly new but truly feels like old-school Seattle—carries a range of fun writing-related items like T-shirts, notebooks, creative prompts, books, games, and other novelties. And of course, pencils: the shop is an authorized dealer of "feathery smooth" Blackwing Pencils. The seemingly anachronistic Pencil Box benefits two local nonprofit organizations that foster learning and creativity in youth and young adults. ⊠ *8414 Greenwood Ave. N, Greenwood* ⊕ *www.greenwoodpencilbox.com* ☻ *Closed Sun.-Mon.*

Phinney Books

BOOKS | A gem of an independent bookstore, Phinney Books is owned by local eight-time *Jeopardy!* champ and reading enthusiast Tom Nissley, who's stocked his charming shop with an expertly curated selection of books, including many titles by local authors and a whimsical section for kids. ⊠ *7405 Greenwood Ave. N, Seattle* ☎ *206/297–2665* ⊕ *www. phinneybooks.com.*

Chapter 10

BALLARD

Updated by
Naomi Tomky

👁 **Sights**	🍴 **Restaurants**	🛏 **Hotels**	💼 **Shopping**	🍸 **Nightlife**
★★☆☆☆	★★★★★	★★☆☆☆	★★★★★	★★★★☆

NEIGHBORHOOD SNAPSHOT

TOP REASONS TO GO

■ The **Ballard Farmers' Market**, on Ballard Avenue every Sunday from 9 to 2 (rain or shine, year-round), is one of the city's finest farmers' markets.

■ See a show at the **Sunset Tavern**. Ballard has its own music scene, with several small clubs on Ballard Avenue; the Tractor Tavern is a small venue with a big reputation.

■ Explore Ballard's **booming beer scene** at one or a few of the kid- and dog-friendly breweries in the area. Among the best: Reuben's, Stoup, and the Bale Breaker and Yonder Cider Taproom.

■ Get some **retail therapy**, Ballard-style: the area's artsy galleries, many boutiques, and shoe and clothing stores offer tempting reasons to drop some dough.

■ Dip your toes in the water at **Golden Gardens Park**.

GETTING HERE AND AROUND

Ballard's main drags are NW Market Street and Ballard Avenue. If you're driving from Downtown, the easiest way to reach Ballard's center is to take Western Avenue and follow it as it turns into Elliott Avenue West and then 15th Avenue NW. Cross the bridge and make a left onto NW Market Street.

By bus, the Rapid Ride D, 15X, 17X, 18X, 29 and 40 will get you from Downtown to NW Market Street. Ballard is connected to Phinney Ridge, Wallingford, and the U-District by the 44 bus, which picks up passengers on NW Market Street and makes its way to the other northern neighborhoods. Bus 28 connects Fremont's center to NW Market Street.

Note that the neighborhood is more spread out than it appears on a map. For example, walking west from the heart of Market Street to the Locks is almost a mile. Golden Gardens Park is best reached by car, bike, or bus.

VIEWFINDER

■ One of the best spots for an evening view sits at North Ballard's aptly named Sunset Hill Park, on 34th Ave NW between NW 75th and NW 77th Streets. Perched atop the bluffs that overlook Shilshole Bay and Golden Gardens, it offers a panorama of the Puget Sound islands and the Olympic Mountains beyond.

PLANNING YOUR TIME

■ Set aside an hour or two to visit the Hiram M. Chittenden Locks. After that, you can spend your afternoon one of three ways before having dinner in the neighborhood: stroll and shop on Ballard Avenue; relax on the sand at Golden Gardens Park; or visit the National Nordic Museum and area art galleries.

Ballard is Seattle's sweetheart. This historically Scandinavian neighborhood doesn't have many sights; but it's got a great little nightlife, shopping, and restaurant scene, and an outstanding farmers' market every Sunday.

Ballard used to be almost exclusively Scandinavian and working-class; it was the logical home for the Swedish and Norwegian immigrants who worked in the area's fishing, shipbuilding, and lumber industries. Reminders of its origins still exist—most literally in the National Nordic Museum—but the neighborhood is undergoing inevitable changes as density increases and young professionals become the majority. Trendy restaurants, upscale furniture stores, and quirky boutiques abound along NW Market Street and Ballard Avenue, the neighborhood's main commercial strips. But no matter how tidy it gets, or how high the condos rise, there's a little bit of fishing village left behind, coursing through the streets of one of the city's hippest neighborhoods.

 Sights

Golden Gardens Park

BEACH | The waters of Puget Sound may be bone-chillingly cold, but that doesn't stop folks from jumping in to cool off. Besides brave swimmers, who congregate on the small strip of sand between the parking lot and the canteen, this Ballard-area park is packed with sunbathers and walkers in summer. In other seasons, beachcombers explore during low tide, and groups gather around bonfires to socialize and watch the glorious Seattle sunsets. The park has drinking water, grills, picnic tables, a playground, restrooms, and a snack shop. It also has two wetlands, a short loop trail, and unbelievable views of the Olympic Mountains. ■ **TIP→ The park has two dedicated parking lots, but they fill up quickly on summer weekends.** ⊠ *8498 Seaview Pl. NW, near NW 85th St., Ballard* ✛ *From Downtown, take Elliott Avenue North, which becomes 15th Avenue West, and cross the Ballard Bridge. Turn left to head west on Market Street and follow signs to the Ballard Locks; continue about another mile via Seaview Avenue NW to the park.* ☎ *206/684–4075* ⊕ *www.seattle.gov/parks/find/parks/golden-gardens-park.*

★ Hiram M. Chittenden Locks

NAUTICAL SIGHT | FAMILY | There's something intriguing and eerie about seeing two bodies of water, right next to each other, at different levels. The Hiram M. Chittenden Locks (also known as "Ballard Locks") are an important passage in the eight-mile Lake Washington Ship Canal that connects Puget Sound to freshwater Lake Washington and Lake Union.

Families picnic beneath oak trees in the adjacent 7-acre Carl S. English Botanical Gardens; various musical performances (from jazz bands to chamber music) serenade visitors on summer weekends; and steel-tinted salmon awe spectators as they climb a 21-step fish ladder en route to their freshwater spawning grounds—a

Golden Gardens Park is one of the best places to see the sun set in Seattle.

heroic journey from the Pacific to the base of the Cascade Mountains.

In the 1850s, when Seattle was founded, Lake Washington and Lake Union were inaccessible from the tantalizingly close Puget Sound. The city's founding fathers—most notably, Thomas Mercer in 1854—dreamt of a canal that would connect the freshwater lakes and the sound. The lure of freshwater moorage and easier transport of timber and coal proved powerful, but it wasn't until 1917 that General Hiram M. Chittenden and the Army Corps of Engineers completed the Lake Washington Ship Canal and the Locks that officially bear his name. More than 100 years later, the locks are still going strong. Tens of thousands of boaters pass through the locks each year, carrying more than a million tons of commercial products—including seafood, fuel, and building materials.

Free guided tours of the locks depart from the visitor center and give you far more information than the plaques by the locks. ⊠ 3015 NW 54th St., Ballard

⊕ From Fremont, head north on Leary Way NW, west on NW Market St., and south on 54th St. ☎ 206/783–7059 ⊕ www.ballardlocks.org ☞ Tour availability varies by season and day.

National Nordic Museum

HISTORY MUSEUM | Celebrating the Nordic cultures of Sweden, Finland, Norway, Iceland, and Denmark (of which there are many descendants in Ballard), this museum opened in its spacious new building in 2018. Exhibits trace Scandinavian art, artifacts, and heritage all the way from Viking times. Galleries give an in-depth look at how immigrants came to America and settled in the Pacific Northwest. There's also a relaxing "Sense of Place" area, where visitors can immerse themselves in the scenery and sounds of the Nordic region while getting comfortable on plush stuffed rocks. Models of boats lead to the back garden, which contains a century-old functional sauna and a Viking ship. ⊠ 2655 NW Market St., Ballard ☎ 206/789–5707 ⊕ www.nordicmuseum.org ☜ $20; Free 1st Thurs. of the month ⊗ Closed Mon.

🍴 Restaurants

Ballard is the north end's answer to Capitol Hill when it comes to edgy, innovative, and delicious dining. Restaurants have taken a cue from the beloved year-round farmers' market, and fresh produce, local ingredients, and top-notch quality are de rigueur. Savor anything from chewy slices at local pizza darling Delancey to pristine Northwest oysters at the Walrus and the Carpenter.

★ Asadero Prime

$$$ | MEXICAN | This steakhouse incorporates high-quality beef into the culinary traditions of northern Mexico. Barley-fed Australian Angus and American, Japanese, and Australian Wagyu hit the grill, while USDA Prime meat goes into tacos and tortas. **Known for:** varied mezcal collection; colorful salsa bar; high-quality beef. [$] *Average main: $25* ✉ *5405 Leary Ave. NW, Ballard* ☎ *206/659–4499* 🌐 *www.asaderoprime.com.*

Brimmer & Heeltap

$$$ | MODERN AMERICAN | This stunning gastropub is the quintessential neighborhood restaurant, built on warm service and great food. Seated in the white wooden chairs or on the bold turquoise benches, to eat here is to be welcomed into the dining room of a long-lost friend. **Known for:** good cocktails; garden patio; well-prepared seafood. [$] *Average main: $25* ✉ *425 NW Market St., Ballard* ☎ *206/420–2534* 🌐 *www.brimmerand-heeltap.com* 🕒 *Closed Mon.–Tues.*

★ Cafe Munir

$$ | LEBANESE | Perhaps the best-kept secret in the city, this neighborhood Lebanese joint is adorable and affordable. Whitewashed walls sparsely populated by old-world art match the white tablecloths, which are topped with intricate metal candleholders. **Known for:** hummus with lamb; beautiful decor; whiskey specials. [$] *Average main: $20* ✉ *2408 NW 80th St., Ballard* ☎ *206/472–4150* 🌐 *www.instagram.com/cafemunirseattle* 🕒 *Closed Mon. No lunch.*

★ Delancey

$$ | PIZZA | Brandon Pettit spent years developing his thin-but-chewy pizza crust, and the final product has made him a contender for the city's best pies. Neighborhood families and far-flung travelers alike line up before opening time for seasonal pizzas topped with anything from fresh sausage and local clams to blistered padrón peppers and cremini mushrooms. **Known for:** welcoming service; quality pizza toppings; wonderful desserts. [$] *Average main: $19* ✉ *1415 NW 70th St., Ballard* ☎ *206/838–1960* 🌐 *www.delanceyseattle.com* 🕒 *Closed Mon. No lunch.*

El Moose

$$ | MEXICAN | Looking like a cross between a truck-stop diner and a Tex-Mex restaurant, this tiny café has outstanding breakfast options—including traditional favorites from every region of Mexico. Wait for a space in the tiny dining room, belly up to the counter, or just watch the frenetic activity as everything from soup to salsa is made from scratch. **Known for:** strong margaritas; excellent breakfasts; house-made salsas and moles. [$] *Average main: $18* ✉ *5242 Leary Ave. NW, Ballard* ☎ *206/784–5568* 🌐 *www.elmoose.com.*

★ The Fat Hen

$$ | CONTEMPORARY | An Instagram-perfect brunch spot, this Ballard charmer deals in trends like thick ricotta toast, and classic comforts like Benedicts and cheesy egg bakes. The light-filled café offers house-made baked goods and coffee from the marble countertop. **Known for:** hearty brunch; comforting egg bakes; stunning ricotta toast. [$] *Average main: $17* ✉ *1418 NW 70th St., Ballard* 🌐 *www.thefathenseattle.com* 🕒 *No dinner.*

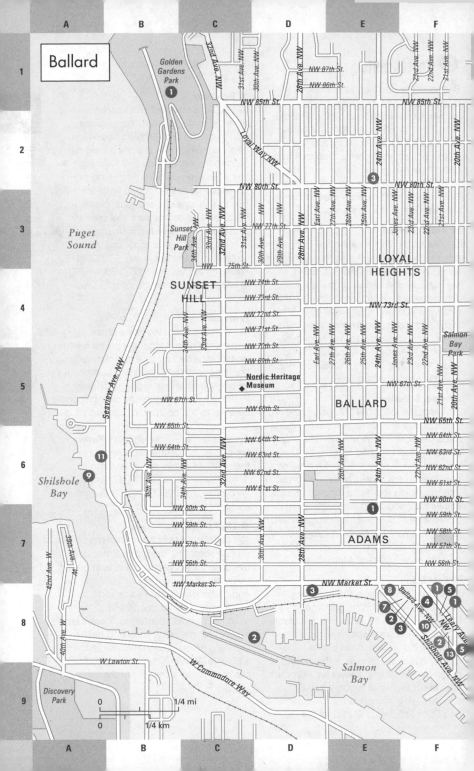

Ballard

Puget Sound

Golden Gardens Park ①

Sunset Hill Park

SUNSET HILL

Nordic Heritage Museum ◆

LOYAL HEIGHTS

Salmon Bay Park

BALLARD

③

⑪

⑨

Shilshole Bay

①

ADAMS

③

②

⑧
⑦
②
③

① ⑤
④ ①
⑩
②
⑬

Salmon Bay

Discovery Park

W Lawton St

W Commodore Way

0 | 1/4 mi

0 | 1/4 km

Sights ▼

1 Golden Gardens Park **B1**
2 Hiram M. Chittenden Locks....... **D8**
3 National Nordic Museum......... **D8**

Restaurants ▼

1 Asadero Prime **F8**
2 Brimmer & Heeltap................ **J8**
3 Cafe Munir........................... **E2**
4 Delancey.............................. **H5**
5 El Moose............................. **F8**
6 The Fat Hen......................... **H4**
7 La Carta de Oaxaca **F8**
8 Pestle Rock.......................... **E8**
9 Ray's Boathouse.................... **A6**
10 San Fermo **F0**
11 Secret Congee **A6**
12 Staple & Fancy...................... **G9**
13 Stoneburner.......................... **F8**
14 The Walrus and
   the Carpenter **G9**
15 Watson's Counter.................. **G6**

Quick Bites ▼

1 Cafe Besalu **E7**
2 Hot Cakes............................ **F8**
3 Miro Tea **F8**
4 Rachel's Bagels & Burritos........ **F8**
5 Valentina's Cafe..................... **F8**

Hotels ▼

1 Ballard Inn........................... **F8**
2 Hotel Ballard **F8**

KEY

1 *Sights*
1 *Restaurants*
1 *Quick Bites*
1 *Hotels*

WHITTIER HEIGHTS

WEST WOODLAND

La Carta de Oaxaca

$$ | **MEXICAN** | True to its name, this low-key, bustling Ballard favorite serves traditional Mexican cooking with Oaxacan accents. The mole negro is a must, served with chicken or pork; another standout is the *albóndigas* (a spicy vegetable soup with meatballs). **Known for:** excellent margaritas; savory albóndigas; house-made mole. [$] *Average main: $19* ✉ *5431 Ballard Ave. NW, Ballard* ☎ *206/782–8722* 🌐 *www.seattlemeetsoaxaca.com* 🕒 *Closed Sun.*

Pestle Rock

$$ | **THAI** | Convincing Seattleites to forgo their pad Thai in favor of the spicy, herb-filled Isan cuisine of northern Thailand was a tough battle, but with a sleek, modern restaurant, skillful cooking, and plenty of peppers, Pestle Rock succeeded handily. Today, the tables are filled with locals knowingly ordering the house-made sausage, the coconut-milk curry noodles called *kao soi,* and pungent papaya salads, all filled with local ingredients such as wild salmon, Dungeness crab, and thoughtfully sourced meats. **Known for:** chicken wings; elegant atmosphere; kao soi. [$] *Average main: $19* ✉ *2305 NW Market St., Ballard* ☎ *206/466-6671* 🌐 *www.pestlerock.com.*

Ray's Boathouse

$$$$ | **SEAFOOD** | The view of Shilshole Bay might be the main draw, but the seafood is also fresh and well prepared. Perennial favorites include grilled salmon, Kasu sake–marinated sablefish, Dungeness crab, and regional oysters on the half shell. **Known for:** classic elegance; local seafood; excellent view of Shilshole Bay. [$] *Average main: $48* ✉ *6049 Seaview Ave. NW, Ballard* ☎ *206/789–3770* 🌐 *www.rays.com.*

San Fermo

$$$ | **ITALIAN** | The charming old house smack in the middle of Ballard's main drag stands out among the shops in much the same way that San Fermo's menu of classic Italian dishes made with seasonal ingredients stands out with its simple, elegant excellence. Appetizers of grilled vegetables and snacky starters pair perfectly with glasses of Prosecco on the porch that wraps the side of the restaurant, while rustic house-made pastas and hearty meat dishes match the Italian red wines and low light of a late dinner in the dining room. **Known for:** regional Italian cuisine; great porch seating; seasonal vegetable starters. [$] *Average main: $29* ✉ *5341 Ballard Ave. NW, Ballard* ☎ *206/342-1530* 🌐 *www.sanfermoseattle.com* 🕒 *No lunch.*

★ **Secret Congee**

$$ | **ASIAN** | Only in Seattle would rice porridge qualify as a beach eat, but like Sam I Am, you should eat this anywhere. In 2022, this congee-only shop moved from a shared space into its own location on Golden Gardens, where it continues to use its single dish as a canvas on which it paints museum-worthy flavors. **Known for:** crispy fried dough; Southeast Asian flavors; creative congee. [$] *Average main: $16* ✉ *6301 Seaview Ave. NW, Ballard* 🌐 *www.secretcongee.com* 🕒 *Closed Mon. No dinner.*

Staple & Fancy

$$$$ | **ITALIAN** | The "Staple" side of this Ethan Stowell restaurant might mean gnocchi with corn and chanterelles or a whole grilled branzino. But visitors to the glam, remodeled, historic brick building are best served by going "fancy," meaning the chef's menu dinner where diners are presented with several courses (technically four, but the appetizer usually consists of a few different plates) of whatever the cooks are playing with on the line that night—cured meats, salads of exotic greens, handmade pastas, seasonal desserts. **Known for:** Northwest and Italian dishes; multicourse menu; pasta. [$] *Average main: $36* ✉ *4739 Ballard Ave. NW, Ballard* ☎ *206/789–1200* 🌐 *www.ethanstowellrestaurants.com* 🕒 *No lunch.*

Continued on page 202

THE BALLARD LOCKS AND SEATTLE'S MANY WATERWAYS

by Nick Horton

DID YOU KNOW?

More than 40,000 commercial vessels, private yachts, sailboats, and even kayaks pass through the Ballard Locks each year.

SEATTLE'S WATERWAYS

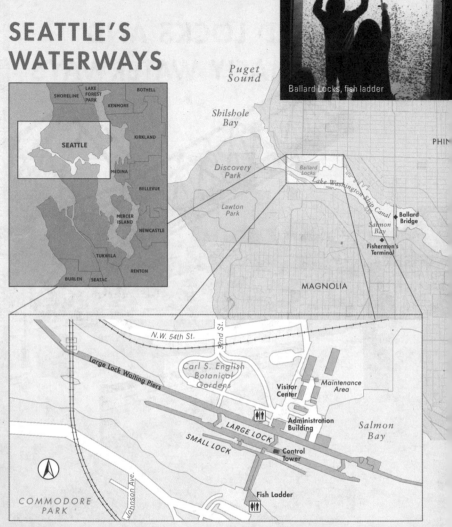

Ballard Locks, fish ladder

From its earliest days as a tribal settlement to its current status as high-tech hub, Seattle has been defined by its lakes, canals, and bays. Everywhere you look there is water: To the west is the deep, chilly saltwater of Puget Sound, and to the east are the welcoming, warmer waters of Lake Washington. Linking the two is the Lake Washington Ship Canal, a bustling marine thoroughfare. This astounding network of waterways plays a vital role in Seattle's daily life, whether it is for livelihood, transport, recreation, or sweet summertime relaxation.

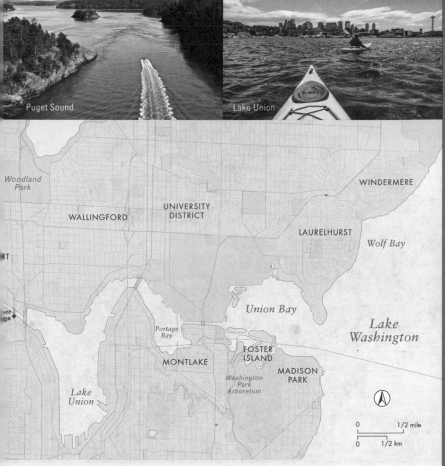

Puget Sound

Lake Union

Woodland Park

WINDERMERE

UNIVERSITY DISTRICT

WALLINGFORD

LAURELHURST

Wolf Bay

Union Bay

Portage Bay

Lake Washington

FOSTER ISLAND

MONTLAKE

MADISON PARK

Washington Park Arboretum

Lake Union

0   1/2 mile
0   1/2 km

Each of Seattle's bodies of water has a unique appeal. At 33 miles in length, **Lake Washington** is the city's largest lake. Come summer, it's a pleasure boater's paradise, often speckled with kayaks, motorboats, sailboats, and multimillion-dollar yachts. Its many beaches become crowded with sunbathers.

From Lake Washington, vessels may travel west via the Lake Washington Ship Canal toward **Lake Union,** a smaller, more urban lake that is the center of the city's maritime industry. The shoreline here is lined by yacht brokerages and ship-yards, but Lake Union isn't all business. It hosts weekly sailing regattas and an annual Fourth of July fireworks show. In addition, its northern shores are rife with houseboats—including the home made famous in the film *Sleepless in Seattle*. These live-aboard communities are the dwellings of well-off yuppies, eccentric sailors, and grizzled fishermen alike.

Traveling farther west, the Ship Canal leads vessels under the Fremont and Ballard bridges toward the bustling docks at **Fishermen's Terminal**, home to the city's vibrant fleet of commercial fishing boats. Finally, the canal leads through the **Ballard Locks**—the final step in a miles-long journey to **Puget Sound**, where oceangoing cargo ships sail in and out of Seattle's booming port.

Hiram M. Chittenden

In the 1850s, when Seattle was founded, Lake Washington and Lake Union were inaccessible from the tantalizingly close Puget Sound. The city's founding fathers—most notably, Thomas Mercer in 1854—began dreaming of a canal that would connect the freshwater lakes and the Sound.

The lure of freshwater moorage and easier transport of timber and coal proved powerful, but it wasn't until 1917 that General Hiram M. Chittenden and the Army Corps of Engineers completed the Lake Washington Ship Canal and the locks that officially bear his name. More than 90 years later, the Ballard Locks, as they are more commonly known, are still going strong. Tens of thousands of boaters pass through the Locks each year, carrying over a million tons of commercial products—including seafood, fuel, and building materials.

THE LOCKS ESSENTIALS

✉ 3015 N.W. 54th St., Seattle, WA 98107

📠 206/783–7059 (visitor center)

🌐 www.ci.seattle.wa.us/tour/locks.htm (City of Seattle)

🕐 Grounds are open 7 AM–9 PM year-round; fish ladder is open 7 AM–8:45 PM year-round; visitor center is open 10 AM–6 PM daily from May 1 through Sept. 30 and Thurs.–Mon. 10 AM–4 PM from Oct. 1 through April 30

The Locks are one of the city's most popular attractions, receiving more than one million visitors annually. Families picnic beneath oak trees in the adjacent 7-acre Carl S. English Botanical Gardens; jazz bands serenade visitors on summer Sundays; and steel-tinted salmon awe spectators as they climb a 21-step fish ladder en route to their freshwater spawning grounds—a heroic journey from the Pacific to the base of the Cascade Mountains. Hummingbirds flit from flower to flower in the nearby gardens, and the occasional sea lion can be spotted to the west of the Locks, snacking on unsuspecting salmon.

Best time to visit: The salmon runs and recreational boat traffic are most active from mid-June through mid-September.

Public transportation from downtown: Metro Route 17 runs from downtown Seattle to Ballard/Sunset Hill, and includes a stop at the Locks. Buses run approximately twice per hour from 5 AM–11 PM. The fare is $2.

Ample public parking ($2/hr) is available at the entrance to the Locks.

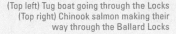

(Top left) Tug boat going through the Locks
(Top right) Chinook salmon making their way through the Ballard Locks

FISH AT THE LOCKS

Chinook (king): Chinook tend to arrive at the locks in July, with late August being the best time to view them.

Coho (silver): Primetime coho viewing occurs in late September.

Sockeye (red): July is the peak time to view these fish, which gradually turn red as they migrate upstream.

Steelhead: Peak steelhead viewing occurs from mid-February through the end of March.

MIGRATING FISH

In a place where engineering has reshaped the natural landscape, it comes as a surprise that the most alluring and electrifying attraction at the Ballard Locks may be nature itself. Every summer, the fish ladder here flashes to life, and Seattle comes to watch.

Thousands upon thousands of migrating salmon pass through the ladder each year, making their way to freshwater spawning grounds in rivers and lakes throughout the region. They traverse the ladder's 21 steps, headed for the streams of their birth and distant gravel beds that will soon be their graves, as well. But their journey isn't in vain: The salmon carry with them the seeds of the next generation. It's a miraculous and mysterious voyage, and the fish ladder at the Locks is a wonderful place to witness it.

BEST BETS ON SEATTLE'S WATERS

LAKE WASHINGTON

BEACHES: The hands-down favorite sun-and-swim spots in Seattle are **Madison Park** (⊠ E. Madison St. and E. Howe St. ☎ 206/684–4075) and **Matthews Beach** (⊠ Sand Point Way NE and NE 93rd St. ☎ 206/684–4075).

BEACHSIDE PARK: Seward Park (⊠ 5895 Lake Washington Blvd. S ☎ 206/684–4075) is a 300-acre piece of woodland along the Lake's western shore, and is a great spot for eagle-watching and trail walking.

CRUISE IT: Argosy Cruises (⊠ 1101 Alaskan Way #201 ☎ 888/623–1445; ⊕ www.argosycruises.com) offers thrice-daily cruises of the lakes, including a peek at the lakeside estate of Microsoft co-founder Bill Gates.

SUMMER FEST: Every summer, Seattleites welcome **Seafair** (⊕ www.seafair.org), a monthlong celebration of the summer, water, and sun. Events include a triathlon, parades, an air show featuring the Blue Angels, and a hydroplane race.

LAKE UNION

LEARN TO PADDLE: South Lake Union's **Center for Wooden Boats** (⊠ 1010 Valley Street ☎ 206/382–2628 ⊕ www.cwb.org) is a wonderful resource for all things maritime, including small-boat rental and tours.

RENT A BOAT: Northwest Outdoor Center (⊠ 2100 Westlake Ave. N, Suite 101, on West Lake Union ☎ 206/281–9694 ⊕ www.nwoc.com) has a large fleet of rentable kayaks, wetsuits, paddleboards, and more.

QUACK: Ride the **Ducks of Seattle** (⊠ 516 Broad St. ☎ 206/441–3825 ⊕ www.ridetheducksofseattle.com) offers 90-minute amphibian-vehicle tours around Seattle; the tour includes a brief cruise in Lake Union.

EAT AND PADDLE: Agua Verde Café and Paddle Club (⊠ 1307 NE Boat St. ☎ 206/545–8570 ⊕ www.aguaverde.com), on Portage Bay, just west of Lake Union, rents kayaks by the hour; the upstairs café serves top-notch Mexican-American fare.

PUGET SOUND

RIDE A FERRY: Washington State Ferries (☎ 888/808–7977 ⊕ www.wsdot.wa.gov/ferries) serves twenty ports of call around Puget Sound. The Seattle to Bainbridge Island round trip is a pleasant jaunt from the Downtown area.

CRUISE IT: Argosy Cruises (⊠ 1101 Alaskan Way ☎ 888/623–1445 ⊕ www.argosycruises.com) offers sightseeing tours of Puget Sound; some include a trip through the Locks.

GO WEST: West Seattle's **Alki Beach** is a great summertime hangout. **Alki Kayak** Tours (⊠ 1660 Harbor Ave SW ☎ 206/953–0237 ⊕ www.kayakalki.com) leads guided sunset tours for beginners and offers rentals to experienced paddlers.

EAT AT RAY'S: At the far western edge of Ballard is **Ray's Boathouse** (⊠ 6049 Seaview Ave NW ☎ 206/789 3770 ⊕ www.rays.com). The food is worth the trip, but it's the waterfront location and incredible sunsets that have made this place an institution.

(left) Areal view of Lake Washington (center) kayaking in Lake Union, (right) Seattle Ferry in Puget Sound.

Stoneburner

$$$ | **ITALIAN** | Stylish and swimming in light, the oak paneling, dark accents, and wide windows onto bustling Ballard Avenue give this quasi-Italian joint an exciting vibe. The menu keeps one foot firmly rooted in Italy, with sections for pizza and pasta on the menu full of Mediterranean sensibilities. **Known for:** family-friendly; Sunday brunch; pizzas. $ *Average main: $29* ✉ *5214 Ballard Ave. NW, Ballard* ☎ *206/695-2051* ⊕ *www.stoneburnerseattle.com* ⊙ *Closed Mon.–Tues.*

The Walrus and the Carpenter

$$$ | **SEAFOOD** | Reneé Erickson was inspired by the casual oyster bars of Paris to open this bustling shoebox of a restaurant. Seats fill fast at the zinc bar and the scattered tall tables where seafood fans slurp on fresh-shucked Olympias, Blue Pools, and other local oysters. **Known for:** variety of oysters; small plates; very popular. $ *Average main: $32* ✉ *4743 Ballard Ave. NW, Ballard* ☎ *206/395–9227* ⊕ *www.thewalrusbar.com* ⊙ *No lunch.*

Watson's Counter

$$ | **CAFÉ** | Watson's Counter keeps things quirky: the Fruity Pebs French Toast tends to go viral on Instagram, but the Korean-style fried chicken (alone, on waffles, or in a sandwich) and assorted eclectic breakfast foods keep this spot from one-hit-wonder status. Friendly service, excellent coffee, and a spare, modern look make it an easy place to love. Just don't fall too hard: the crowds mean they sometimes enforce time limits on tables that linger too long. **Known for:** excellent coffee; Korean fried chicken; fun French toast. $ *Average main: $20* ✉ *6201 15th Ave. NW, Ballard* ⊕ *www.watsonscounter.com* ⊙ *No dinner.*

☕ Coffee and Quick Bites

Cafe Besalu

$ | **BAKERY** | This small, casual bakery gets patrons from across the entire city thanks to its "I *swear* I'm in Paris" croissants with buttery, flaky perfection. Weekend lines are long, but if you score a table, you'll be in heaven. **Known for:** beautiful pastries; flaky croissants; lovely jam. $ *Average main: $6* ✉ *5909 24th Ave. NW, Ballard* ☎ *206/789–1463* ⊕ *www.cafebesalu.com* ⊙ *Closed Mon.*

Hot Cakes

$ | **CAFÉ** | Autumn Martin, formerly head chocolatier at Theo Chocolate, specializes in creative, high-quality desserts (including vegan options) such as a s'mores molten chocolate cake with house-made marshmallows and caramel, and cookies with house-smoked chocolate chips. Thick, rich milkshakes come in gourmet seasonal flavors like Meyer lemon with lavender, or grownup boozy shakes like smoked chocolate and scotch. **Known for:** molten chocolate cakes; take-and-bake desserts; extravagant shakes. $ *Average main: $13* ✉ *5427 Ballard Ave. NW, Ballard* ☎ *206/453–3792* ⊕ *www.getyourhotcakes.com.*

Miro Tea

$ | **CAFÉ** | Modern, hip Miro Tea is the place to go for a wide variety of interesting, high-quality teas, fascinating people-watching, and artisan Japanese pastries. A serious tea shop with well-sourced leaves and informed staff, Miro is also a product of its location—a pleasant seating area looking out on Ballard Avenue makes it a bit of a hipster hang out. **Known for:** Japanese pastries; long list of high-quality loose leaf teas; nice seating area. $ *Average main: $6* ✉ *5405 Ballard Ave. NW, Ballard* ☎ *206/782–6832* ⊕ *www.mirotea.com* ▭ *No credit cards.*

Rachel's Bagels & Burritos

$ | **SANDWICHES** | What began as an effort to clear the fridges during a pandemic shutdown resulted in a new concept for this small Ballard café. Some of the city's best bagels come stacked into towering sandwiches slathered with traditional toppings like cream cheese and lox, and creative originals like scallion cheddar spread with baked egg, kale, and king oyster mushrooms. **Known for:** enormous breakfast burritos; creative sandwiches; Seattle's best bagels. $ *Average main:* *$12* ✉ *5451 Leary Ave. NW, Ballard* ☎ *206/257–5761* ⊕ *www.rachelsbagels.* *com* ⊗ *Closed Tues.*

Valentina's Cafe

$ | **CAFÉ** | A sibling spot to the Mexican steakhouse next door, this ode to Mexican coffee serves a single-origin bean grown by a cooperative in Oaxaca and roasted locally by Fulcrum. Fresh-squeezed orange juice and tres leches cakes complete the feel of a contemporary Mexico City café, but a few touches keep it Seattle, including the assortment of locally baked pastries. **Known for:** fresh-squeezed juice; single-origin Mexican coffee; local pastries. $ *Average main: $5* ✉ *5405 Leary Ave. NW, Ballard* ⊕ *www.* *valentinascafe.com.*

Hotels

Ballard has a real neighborhood vibe, so staying here is a good way to feel like a local. You'll be farther from some of the tourist locations, but public transportation to Downtown is fast and frequent, and the excellent restaurant and nightlife scene make up for the distance. There are only two hotels in the area, but home rentals abound in the neighborhood's old craftsman-style houses. Pay attention to the actual location, though, as Ballard is huge and spots farther north will put you out of walking distance from the fun and buses.

Ballard Inn

$ | **B&B/INN** | Travelers seeking an authentic Seattle neighborhood experience will fall hard for this charming budget-friendly inn right in the heart of Ballard, tucked between coffee shops, trendy boutiques, and restaurants. **Pros:** friendly staff; free Wi-Fi; comfy beds. **Cons:** no elevator (ask for a room on main floor if stairs are an issue); thin walls and street noise; no air-conditioning. $ *Rooms from:* *$169* ✉ *5300 Ballard Ave. NW, Ballard* ☎ *206/789–5011* ⊕ *www.ballardinnseat-* *tle.com* ⇥ *16 rooms* ⊙ *No Meals.*

★ Hotel Ballard

$$$ | **HOTEL** | In the heart of historic Ballard, this chic boutique hotel features a modern take on baroque style, with gilded mirrors and sumptuous carpeting and furnishings in every room. **Pros:** friendly service; close to Ballard attractions; free access to one of the city's best gyms. **Cons:** refrigerators not standard in rooms; some street noise at night, especially on weekends; rooftop event space can be disruptive for guests. $ *Rooms from:* *$319* ✉ *5216 Ballard Ave. NW, Ballard* ☎ *206/789–5012* ⊕ *www.hotelballardse-* *attle.com* ⇥ *29 rooms* ⊙ *No Meals.*

Nightlife

On weekends, Ballard rivals Capitol Hill in popularity. There are at least a dozen bars and restaurants on Ballard Avenue alone. The neighborhood has quickly evolved from a few pubs full of old salts to a bustling nightlife district that has equal parts average-Joe bars, trendy haunts, music spots, wine bars, and lounges.

BARS AND LOUNGES
The Ballard Smoke Shop Restaurant and Lounge

BARS | One of the last of the classic Ballard dives still standing: it used to be that fishermen started drinking here before the day dawned, though now it's just as likely to be hipsters drinking cold cans of Rainier beer and asking for pull tabs. While one side has kept the same servers with studied nonchalance bringing the drinks, a snazzy arcade now fills the other room. ⊠ *5439 Ballard Ave. NW, Ballard* ⊕ *the-ballard-smoke-shop. business.site.*

Barnacle

BARS | Part of the Sea Creatures mini-empire led by chef Renee Erickson, Barnacle is a narrow bar adjacent to the popular restaurant The Walrus and the Carpenter. It invariably collects people waiting for tables, but with a beautiful copper-topped bar, tiled walls, and plates of oysters, cured meats, and fish to go with the aperitivos, it's a great place to drink and snack even if you aren't planning to dine next door. ⊠ *4743 Ballard Ave. NW, Ballard* ☎ *206/706–3379* ⊕ *www.barnacleseattle.com* ⊗ *Closed Tues.*

Essex

COCKTAIL LOUNGES | On a quiet street removed from bustling Ballard, Essex boasts craft cocktails, a handful of which are served on tap. The rotating cocktails often include house-made ingredients or are barrel aged, and all have something of a cocktail-nerd bent. A solid wine list and local beer selections are also available, as is a selection of wood-fired dishes that come out of the pizza oven at next-door sibling shop Delancey. ⊠ *1421 NW 70th St., Ballard* ⊕ *www.essexbarseattle. com* ⊗ *Closed Mon.–Tues.*

King's Hardware

BARS | From the owner of Linda's Tavern in Capitol Hill, King's Hardware has the same ironic rustic decor, great patio space, and cachet with hipsters. It also has great burgers. It gets packed on weekends—if you want the same scene with fewer crowds, go two doors down to Hattie's Hat, which was the reigning spot until King's showed up. ⊠ *5225 Ballard Ave. NW, Ballard* ☎ *206/782–0027* ⊕ *www.kingsballard.com.*

The Noble Fir

BARS | A rotating selection of great beer, cider, and wine and a truly varied crowd are just part of the appeal of this popular bar. The rustic-modern interior includes a library-like seating area stocked with large trail maps and hundreds of travel books. The Noble Fir serves a few simple snacks, like cheese, charcuterie, fish, and vegan and vegetarian options, in case you feel like settling in and planning your next big adventure. ⊠ *5316 Ballard Ave., Ballard* ☎ *206/420–7425* ⊕ *www.thenoblefir. com* ⊗ *Closed Mon.-Tues.*

Ocho

BARS | Blink and you'll miss it, and that would be a shame, because this tiny corner spot crafts some of the finest cocktails in town. Dimly lit and loud, Ocho fills up fast with a mixed crowd that flocks here for the drinks and top-notch Spanish tapas. Come summer, the sidewalk patio is an ideal spot for soaking up the sun and people-watching. ⊠ *2325 NW Market St., Ballard* ☎ *206/784–0699* ⊕ *www.ochoseattle.com.*

Rupee

BARS | A short ride from the heart of Ballard's nightlife, Rupee offers an elegant, upscale experience. Inspired by the owners' travels in Sri Lanka and India, the drinks are spice heavy and employ tropical fruit without cloying sweetness. The food is also excellent. Rich colors and dark wood give the narrow space a transportive feel, but don't take too many people on the journey with you: there's no room for large groups, and waits can get long. ⊠ *6307 24th Ave. NW, Ballard* ☎ *206/397–3263* ⊕ *www.rupeeseattle. com* ⊗ *Closed Mon.–Tues.*

The Splintered Wand

THEMED ENTERTAINMENT | **FAMILY** | Pack your spellbook and leave your cynicism at home: this wizard-themed pub goes all in on magic and imagination. Grab a seat under a sea monster skeleton, order up an elixir or butterbee mead, and dig into tadpole in a hole, storm buffalo

Suds Appeal

Seattle loves its beer, and for good reason. America's ever-burgeoning craft-beer scene owes this city a big debt. In 1981, Redhook Ale Brewery opened in Ballard and became one of the country's first microbreweries, and Seattle's love affair with the good stuff hasn't faltered since.

Craft beer aficionados will find plenty of spots for sampling local brews as well as the best imports from around the country and the world. Nearly every neighborhood worth its weight boasts a great beer bar or two, and brewery taprooms abound, but Ballard has risen to become the indisputable king of brewery neighborhoods. More than a dozen breweries pepper the area, so look around for one that fits your tastes.

bourguignon, and a spitting fizzle nest for dessert. Reservations are recommended, especially for families, but the bar is reserved for walk-ins only. ⊠ *5135 Ballard Ave. NW, Ballard* ☎ *206/739–5960* ✑ *reservations@splinteredwand.com* ⊕ *www.thesplinteredwand.com* ☾ *Closed Mon.*

BREWPUBS

Bale Breaker and Yonder Cider Taproom

BEER GARDENS | The fruits of Yakima's hops and apple crops come to the westside at this sprawling joint facility. One of the state's best breweries brings its vertically integrated beers to the space shared with a creative-minded cidery. Together, they offer 32 drinks on tap, a rotating selection of food trucks, and plenty of seating of various sorts at the kid- and dog-friendly, indoor and gravel-lined outdoor space. ⊠ *826 NW 49th St., Ballard* ☎ *773/998-1464* ⊕ *www.bbycballard.com* ☾ *Closed Mon.*

Fair Isle Brewing

BEER GARDENS | In the land of IPA enthusiasts, Fair Isle bravely brews an assortment of innovative saisons and farmhouse ales, often incorporating local ingredients such as rhubarb and elderberry. Fair Isle lends its kitchen to a wide variety of pop-ups serving everything from Turkish lamb roasts to Taiwanese soups. While the taproom is adults-only, the food is sold from a tent in front, allowing all-ages access (and plenty of nearby breweries will let you bring in food). On Fridays at 5 pm, one of the co-owners guides tours through the brewery that include a tasting of young ales. ⊠ *936 NW 49th St., Ballard* ☎ *206/428–3434* ⊕ *www.fairislebrewing.com* ☾ *Closed Mon.*

Reuben's Brews

BEER GARDENS | One of the pioneers of the current generation of Ballard breweries, Reuben's Brews' warehouse-like taproom and outdoor patios often burst at the seams with excited IPA drinkers. The barebones space offers 24 taps serving the brewery's offerings. Close to half the offerings are usually IPAs, like the World Beer Cup Gold Medal-winning Hazelicious IPA and the popular Crikey, but the rest run the gamut from wild farmhouse pale to the aptly named Robust Porter. ⊠ *5010 14th Ave. NW, Ballard* ⊕ *www.reubensbrews.com.*

★ Stoup

BEER GARDENS | Stoup is a great starting point for exploring Ballard's excellent craft-beer scene. A good-size tap room and patio area are family-friendly, and a rotating roster of food trucks feeds beer enthusiasts as they sip staples like the Citra IPA and Mosaic Pale Ale, as well as new and experimental brews. ⊠ *1108*

NW 52nd St., Ballard ☎ *206/457-5524* ⊕ *www.stoupbrewing.com.*

MUSIC CLUBS

Conor Byrne Pub

LIVE MUSIC | You might actually hear an Irish accent or two at this laid-back pub, along with live folk, roots, alt-country, bluegrass, and traditional Irish music. There's live music almost every night and great beer (including the obligatory Guinness on tap). ✉ *1540 Ballard Ave. NW, Ballard* ☎ *206/784–3640* ⊕ *www. conorbyrnepub.com.*

Egan's Ballard Jam House

LIVE MUSIC | A true neighborhood spot, this small jazz club and restaurant is devoted to music education during the day and performances from local and touring acts in the evenings. ✉ *1707 NW Market St., Ballard* ☎ *206/789–1621* ⊕ *www.ballardjamhouse.com.*

Sunset Tavern

LIVE MUSIC | Sunset Tavern attracts just about everyone: punks, college students, postgrad nomads, neighborhood old-timers. They come for the ever-changing eclectic music acts, but there's also a bar in front, Betty's Room, where you can grab a drink before the show. ✉ *5433 Ballard Ave. NW, Ballard* ☎ *206/784–4880* ⊕ *www.sunsettavern.com.*

Tractor Tavern

LIVE MUSIC | Seattle's top spot for roots music and alt-country has a large, dimly lighted hall with all the right touches— tires as decor, exposed-brick walls, and a cheery staff. The sound system is outstanding. ✉ *5213 Ballard Ave. NW, Ballard* ☎ *206/789–3599* ⊕ *www.tractor-tavern.com.*

🛍 Shopping

Ballard is the shining star of the north end when it comes to shopping. Packed with cute home stores, great clothing boutiques, locally made gifts, and just about every genre of store imaginable, this neighborhood is a must-visit locale. The Sunday Farmers' Market is one of the best in the city, and it operates year-round for a dependably fun outing. Pick up smoked salmon, artisanal cheese, and vegan baked goods, and pop into the shops listed here if the rain starts.

■ **TIP→ Find the best shopping on Ballard Avenue between 22nd Avenue NW and 20th Avenue NW, and on NE Market Street between 20th and 24th Avenues.**

APPAREL

Horseshoe

WOMEN'S CLOTHING | "A little bit country, a little bit rock and roll," Horseshoe offers girlie Western wear and hipster styles. Comfy, sassy shirts and dresses are available from designers like Sanctuary, Lovestitch, and Amuse Society. Premium denim, cowboy boots, and unique jewelry are among the wares. ✉ *5344 Ballard Ave. NW, Ballard* ☎ *206/547–9639* ⊕ *www.shophorseshoe.com.*

KAVU

MIXED CLOTHING | Founded in the Pacific Northwest, KAVU's flagship store in Ballard is an outdoor shopping staple. Loudly printed fleece pullovers, thermal vests, and sturdy duffel bags are just a few items you'll find in this funky shop that feels like REI's cooler kid brother. ✉ *5419 Ballard Ave. NW, Ballard* ☎ *206/783-0060* ⊕ *www.kavu.com.*

Market Street Shoes

SHOES | One of the best shoe stores in town, Market Street stocks so many styles and brands that you're likely to find something. Shoes for men, women, and children prioritize comfort, so you'll see sensible picks from Dansko, Hoka One One, and Blundstone, but there are plenty of fun options by Eric Michael, Pendleton, and Bueno, as well. ✉ *2232 NW Market St., Ballard* ☎ *206/783–1670* ⊕ *www.marketstreetshoes.com.*

The lively Ballard Farmers' Market is held every Sunday.

re-souL

SHOES | Stocking cool but comfortable shoes from Karhu, Clae, Miz Mooz, and the like, this hip space offers a small selection of crazy fashionable boots, shoes, sneaks, and high heels. In keeping with the "little bit of everything" trend so popular with Seattle boutiques, re-souL also sells great jewelry pieces. They carry both men's and women's shoes, some clothes, and accessories. Everything is a bit pricey, but not excessively so, and the service earns the price tag. ✉ 5319 Ballard Ave. NW, Ballard ☎ 206/789–7312 ⊕ www.resoul.com.

Second Ascent

SPORTING GOODS | Outdoorsy types should check out Second Ascent for a range of new and used cycling, climbing, running, and ski gear. The store stocks just about everything you need for wilderness fun, from carabiners to Telemark boots, most at discount prices. And the knowledgeable staff is super friendly. ✉ 5209 Ballard Ave. NW, Ballard ☎ 206/545–8810 ⊕ www.secondascent.com.

BOOKS AND MUSIC

Secret Garden Bookshop

BOOKS | **FAMILY** | Named after the Francis Hodgson Burnett classic, this cozy shop has delighted readers for decades. A favorite of teachers, librarians, and parents, it stocks a wide array of imaginative literature and thoughtful nonfiction for all ages; their children's section is particularly noteworthy. ✉ 2214 NW Market St., Ballard ☎ 206/789–5006 ⊕ www.secretgardenbooks.com.

★ Sonic Boom

MUSIC | An independent record store that is just the kind of place you would want to find on a Seattle street corner: clean, helpful, and organized, but just a little bit time-worn and too cool. You can count on them to have music from the latest indie darlings alongside the classics, on vinyl, CD, or even cassette tape. If they have one of their free in-store events when you're in the neighborhood, stop in for a unique musical experience. ✉ *2209 NW Market St., Ballard* ☎ *206/297–2666* ⊕ *www.sonicboomrecords.com.*

MARKETS
Ballard Farmers' Market
MARKET | FAMILY | Every Sunday, rain or shine, loads of vendors come to Ballard Avenue to set up colorful, welcoming stands to sell produce and all types of local, artisanal foods, as well as gift items like candles and hats. Meanwhile, local buskers entertain foodies and families, and vendors cook up pizzas, crepes, dumplings, and more. ✉ *Ballard Ave., between 20th Ave. NW and 22nd Ave. NW, then continuing up 22nd Ave. NW to Market St., Ballard* ⊕ *www.sfmamarkets. com* ☞ *Sun. only, 9am-2pm.*

TOYS AND GIFTS
★ Baleen
JEWELRY & WATCHES | This independent studio makes some of the most stunning, yet affordable, jewelry you can find. Impressively simple, each design manages to be unique, giving them an elegant and modern edge. While the business has outgrown using the same space as both production and store, you can still stop by to shop all the hand-crafted, locally made necklaces, earrings, and bracelets in the light-filled corner shop. ✉ *6418 20th Ave. NW, Ballard* ⊕ *www. shopbaleen.com.*

Clover Toys
TOYS | FAMILY | What's easily the cutest children's store in town carries wonderful handcrafted wooden toys, European figurines, works by local artists, and a variety of swoon-worthy, perfectly crafted little clothes. Even shoppers without children will be smitten—it's hard to resist the vintage French Tintin posters, knit-wool cow dolls, and classic figurines. ✉ *5333 Ballard Ave. NW, Ballard* ☎ *206/782–0715* ⊕ *www.clovertoys.com.*

Venue
SOUVENIRS | Venue is the chic version of the Made In Washington stores: it stocks only goods made by local artists (some of whom have their studios in the sleek bilevel space), but you won't find any tacky souvenirs here. Watch the designers at work, chat with the staff (most are artists taking shifts), or just browse through artisanal chocolates, custom handbags, handmade soaps, baby wear, and colorful prints and mosaics. ✉ *5408 22nd Ave. NW, Ballard* ☎ *206/789–3335* ⊕ *www.venueballard.com.*

Woodland Mod
HOUSEWARES | Taking cues from the neighborhood's Scandinavian history, this boutique brings the minimalist mindset of modern Scandinavian design back to Ballard's streets. High-quality and timeless home goods, art in mostly neutral tones, and useful gifts fill the shelves in the store, which itself embodies the same principles, making shopping a delightful and calming experience. ✉ *5330 Ballard Ave. NW, Ballard* ⊕ *www.woodlandmod. com* ☾ *Closed Mon.*

🏃 Activities

Ballard's waterfront location makes it a destination for active locals and visitors wanting to soak in the scenery while they play. Though the Burke-Gilman, a popular rail trail for bikes and pedestrians, has a "missing link" from Ballard to the east toward Fremont, the final section to the west runs from the Locks up to Golden Gardens Park. Grabbing one of Seattle's many bike share options, the ride out to the beach is quite pleasant. Folks looking for something more organized will also find plenty of options.

FISHING

Fish Finders Private Charters

FISHING | Fish Finders Private Charters takes small groups of two or more out on Puget Sound for guided salmon and ling cod fishing trips. Morning trips last about six hours; afternoon trips are about four hours. ⊠ *7501 Seaview Ave. NW, Ballard* ☎ *206/632–2611* ⊕ *www.fishingseattle. com* ✉ *$275 (excluding fishing license).*

Seattle Fishing Charters

FISHING | Go out on a six-person trolling boat to fish for salmon, bottom fish, and crab—depending on the season. Guided trips from Shilshole Bay Marina or Edmonds Marina last around six hours. ⊠ *7001 Seaview Ave., Ballard* ☎ *206/316–6561* ⊕ *www.seattlefishing.com* ✉ *$275.*

WATER SPORTS

Ballard Kayak

KAYAKING | Get a new perspective on Seattle by exploring from the water with Ballard Kayak's kayak and paddleboard tours. They'll rent you a board or boat on your own, but it's worth joining one of their tours of Puget Sound, the nearby Locks, or the best bowls of clam chowder in the area for a fun experience. They also offer sea kayak lessons. ⊠ *Shilshole Bay Marina, W-dock, 7901 Seaview Ave. NW, Ballard* ⊹ *Near the Corinthian Yacht Club* ☎ *206/494–3353* ⊕ *www.ballardkay-ak.com* ◌ *Closed Mon.–Tues.* ⬦ *Open Spring to early Fall but tours can be booked by request in off-season.*

Surf Ballard

STAND UP PADDLEBOARDING | While nobody is doing any actual surfing on Shilshole Bay, this quaint surf shack carries everything you might need to surf, and also offers rentals for more appropriate water sports like kayaking and stand-up paddleboarding (SUP). They offer SUP lessons and even have an on-site SUP yoga school. You can (and should) book ahead on their website. ⊠ *6300 Seaview Ave. NW, Ballard* ☎ *206/726–7878* ⊕ *www. surfballard.com* ◌ *Closed Mon.–Tues.*

Chapter 11

WALLINGFORD AND GREEN LAKE

Updated by
Naomi Tomky

◉ Sights	🍴 Restaurants	🛏 Hotels	🛍 Shopping	🍸 Nightlife
★★☆☆☆	★★★☆☆	★☆☆☆☆	★★☆☆☆	★★☆☆☆

NEIGHBORHOOD SNAPSHOT

TOP REASONS TO GO

■ Go souvenir hunting at **Archie McPhee,** a shrine to irreverence. You'll find great Seattle-themed items here, like Tofu Mints and librarian and barista action figures, amid tons of assorted weirdness and fun gifts.

■ Take in the view of Lake Union from the top of Kite Hill at **Gas Works Park** then head to **Westward** for a closer look at the water over a cocktail.

■ Stroll or jog around **Green Lake**'s loop. If your running shoes are a little ragged, stop at Super Jock 'n Jill (⊠ *7210 E. Green Lake Drive N*) for a new pair.

GETTING HERE AND AROUND

Bus 62 connects Downtown to North 45th Street in Wallingford (the neighborhood's main drag) and continues north to the east (and main) entrance of Green Lake Park (get off at NE Ravenna Boulevard and Woodlawn Avenue NE) before continuing on to the Roosevelt light rail station. From Downtown it takes about a half hour to reach the lake by bus or combination of bus and light rail; the trip between the lake and North 45th Street takes about 10 minutes. Route 44 connects Wallingford to the University District to the east and to Ballard to the west. Bus 45 skirts the northeast side of the lake and connects to Greenwood and the Roosevelt light rail stop, while the Rapid Ride E runs on the west side, along Aurora Avenue North.

To reach Green Lake by car, take either Aurora Avenue North (Route 99) to West Green Lake Way or I–5 to 50th Street (go west back over the highway at that exit). There are parking lots at both Green Lake Park and Woodland Park; lots at the latter are generally less full. Wallingford is a five-minute drive from Green Lake—if there's no traffic.

FUN FACT

■ Meeting a friend at Green Lake can be confusing: there's the Boat House on the east side and the Bath House on the west side, which is also a theater. But not the Aqua Theater: you'll find the remnants of that on the southwest edge of the lake, where the rowing clubs house their boats. Only a single section of seats remains of the 1950 stadium that once held more than 5500 people as they watched aquatic performances of all sorts and the occasional concert. In 1969, the Grateful Dead played one of the Aqua Theater's final shows.

PLANNING YOUR TIME

■ Green Lake is adjacent to Woodland Park Zoo. In summer, you could spend an entire day outdoors, touring the zoo, then strolling around the lake—or floating in a rented rowboat or paddleboat. The Tangletown area of Green Lake can be reached on foot (follow North 55th Street east to the "K" streets of Kenwood, Keystone, Kirkwood, and Kensington) and has a few good casual eateries. Some of the city's best chefs have put down roots in Wallingford, making the neighborhood a good place to end the day.

Wallingford and Green Lake are low-profile neighborhoods without much in the way of sights to see, but these are great spots for strolling, especially around the former's Ship Canal shoreline and the latter's eponymous lake.

Wallingford

Sights

The laid-back neighborhood of Wallingford is directly east of Fremont—the boundaries blur quite a bit. There are several lovely parks, and residential streets are brimming with colorful Craftsman houses. The main drag, North 45th Street, has an eclectic group of shops, from a gourmet beer store to a Hawaiian merchant, along with a few nice coffeehouses and notable restaurants.

In the 1920s, Wallingford was one of the city's most important neighborhoods. It went from forest and cow pasture (one of which, incidentally, hosted Seattle's first golf course for a very short time) to a densely populated neighborhood of 50,000 in less than two decades. The game changer was a trolley line from the University District to Fremont—once the tracks were laid, the bungalow-building frenzy started. Although the initial hoopla died down after a major commercial district on Stone Way never materialized, the neighborhood grew steadily, if quietly. It still holds the same sort of off-radar charm, with low-key restaurants from great chefs and an oddly impressive collection of Japanese restaurants. While it isn't on track to be anybody's culinary hot spot, it has plenty of places ready to serve a good meal. That's basically Wallingford in a nutshell: welcoming, wonderful, and humble.

★ **Gas Works Park**

CITY PARK | FAMILY | Far from being an eyesore, the hulking remains of an old 1907 gas plant actually lend quirky character to the otherwise open, hilly, 20-acre park. Get a great view of Downtown Seattle while seaplanes rise up from the south shore of Lake Union; the best vantage point is from the zodiac sculpture at the top of the very steep Kite Hill, so be sure to wear appropriate walking shoes. This is a great spot for couples and families alike; the enormous and modern playground has rope climbing structures, a variety of swings, and a padded floor. Crowds throng to picnic and enjoy outdoor summer concerts, movies, and the July 4th fireworks display over Lake Union. ■ **TIP→ Gas Works can easily be reached on foot from Fremont, via the waterfront Burke-Gilman Trail.** ⊠ *2101 N. Northlake Way, at Meridian Ave. N (the north end of Lake Union), Wallingford* ☎ *206/684-4075* ⊕ *www.seattle.gov/ parks/find/parks/gas-works-park.*

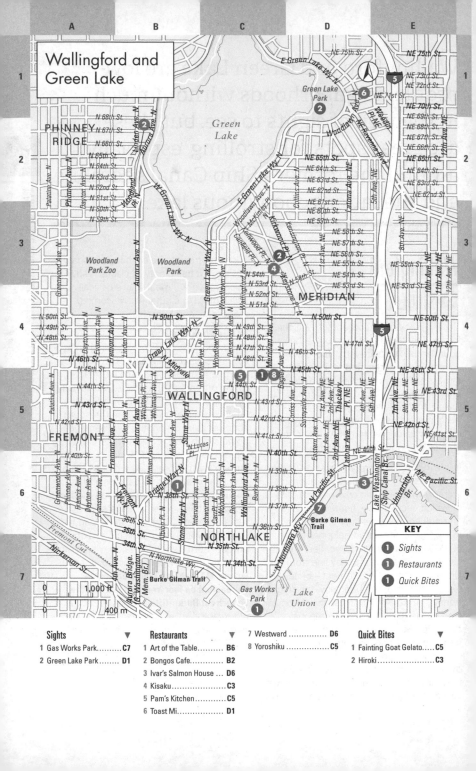

Wallingford and Green Lake

PHINNEY RIDGE

Green Lake

Green Lake Park

Woodland Park Zoo

Woodland Park

MERIDIAN

WALLINGFORD

FREMONT

NORTHLAKE

Burke Gilman Trail

Burke Gilman Trail

Gas Works Park

Lake Union

Ship Canal Br.

KEY

1 *Sights*

1 *Restaurants*

1 *Quick Bites*

0   1,000 ft

0   400 m

Sights ▼	Restaurants ▼	7 Westward **D6**	Quick Bites ▼
1 Gas Works Park.......... **C7**	1 Art of the Table.......... **B6**	8 Yoroshiku **C5**	1 Fainting Goat Gelato..... **C5**
2 Green Lake Park **D1**	2 Bongos Cafe............. **B2**		2 Hiroki...................... **C3**
	3 Ivar's Salmon House ... **D6**		
	4 Kisaku..................... **C3**		
	5 Pam's Kitchen........... **C5**		
	6 Toast Mi.................. **D1**		

Dining with Kids

Seattle is just as serious about its food as it is about ensuring that no visiting parent leaves town without knowing why. Here are some picks you and your kids will enjoy.

Cafe Munir, Ballard. Later, this intimate, gorgeous spot turns romantic, but until about 7:30 pm, kids rule the roost, squealing with joy as they're allowed to eat hummus with their hands.

Delancey, Ballard. What kind of kid could turn down pizza this good? None, and neither can their parents, which is why this place stays packed with families.

Dough Zone Dumpling House, various locations. Consider the in-house dumpling makers live entertainment, and the oodles of noodles the perfect meal to keep kids happy.

Marination Ma Kai, West Seattle. Bright colors, fun food, and endless flavors of Hawaiian shave ice should keep the wee ones grinning.

Uneeda Burger, Fremont. A classic, casual burger joint that has as many options for grown-up tastes as it does for the little ones.

Restaurants

With everything from taco shops to ice cream, Trinidadian cuisine to prix-fixe dining, Wallingford has blossomed into a dining destination. With Kisaku as the anchor, this part of town has become something of a Japanese restaurant row. Look for sushi spots from cheap and decent to spectacular and ramen shops with deep, savory broths.

Art of the Table

$$$$ | AMERICAN | Small, pricey, and utterly unforgettable, Art of the Table is a constantly changing tour de force where you're sure to experience an inspired meal. Fresh farmers' market finds are an absolute obsession here, and, on any given night, diners might enjoy offerings like caramelized Brussels sprouts with pistachios, braised oxtail, rockfish ceviche, manila clams with cauliflower, and rhubarb soup with crème fraîche. **Known for:** unforgettable experience; tasting menu; local ingredients. $ *Average main: $135* ⊠ *3801 Stone Way N, Suite A, Wallingford* ☎ *206/282–0942* ⊕ *www. artofthetable.net* ☉ *Closed Sun.–Tues.*

Ivar's Salmon House

$$$$ | SEAFOOD | FAMILY | This long dining room facing Lake Union has original Northwest Indian artwork collected by the restaurant's namesake founder. It's touristy, often gimmicky, and always packed. **Known for:** epic water views; quirky setting; Seattle institution. $ *Average main: $40* ⊠ *401 NE Northlake Way, Wallingford* ☎ *206/632–0767* ⊕ *www. ivars.com.*

Pam's Kitchen

$$$ | CARIBBEAN | This Seattle classic has been bringing the flavors of the Caribbean to the city for more than two decades, since the owner moved to town and grew frustrated with the lack of dishes like roti, curry, and jerk that she missed from home in Trinidad. Open only a few days each week, and only for a few hours, people clamor to get in and grab Pam's aloo pies, flaky breads, and tender curry goat. **Known for:** flaky flatbreads; coveted few hours; spicy Caribbean cuisine. $ *Average main: $30* ⊠ *1715 N. 45th St., Wallingford* ☎ *206/696-7010* ⊕ *www.pams-kitchen.com* ☉ *Closed Mon.-Thurs. No lunch.*

★ Westward

$$$ | SEAFOOD | Westward singularly nails the dream of Seattle visitors and locals alike: serving high-quality, fresh local seafood from a waterfront location with a view. Lake Union laps at the rocky shore just feet from where diners look out toward Downtown as just-shucked oysters gleam from seafood towers. **Known for:** variety of fresh oysters; waterfront and view tables; elegant shellfish towers. $ *Average main: $30* ✉ *2501 N. Northlake Way, Wallingford* ☎ *206/552-8215* ⊕ *www.westwardseattle.com.*

★ Yoroshiku

$ | JAPANESE | Wallingford's strip of Japanese food holds sushi, grilled meats, and ramen for every budget, with this slip of a spot ranking among the best. Ramen comes in a wide variety, including high-end versions made with Wagyu broth and super traditional shio and shoyu options, plus vegan mushroom and gluten-free versions. **Known for:** deeply flavorful ramen broth; drinking snacks; okonomiyaki (savory pancakes). $ *Average main: $15* ✉ *1911 N. 45th St., Wallingford* ☎ *206/547-4649* ⊕ *www.yoroshikuseattle.com* ⊗ *Closed Mon.*

☕ Coffee and Quick Bites

Fainting Goat Gelato

$ | ICE CREAM | Sample gelato in seasonal flavors like honey lavender and fig vanilla at this small, sweet family-owned shop. Locals in the know skip the big lines at other local chains and come here instead for a quick and delicious frozen treat. **Known for:** house-made gelato; artisan flavors; quick service. $ *Average main: $6* ✉ *1903 N. 45th St., Wallingford* ☎ *206/327-9459* ⊕ *www.faintinggoatseattle.com.*

Hiroki

$ | BAKERY | Hiroki makes wonderful Japanese desserts like soufflé cheesecake and matcha tiramisu along with some standards like gateau Basque and almond custard brioche. There are a few outdoor tables and even more inside, and the Tangletown location makes an easy stop during a stroll around the lake or a quick detour to pick up dessert afterward. **Known for:** light Japanese sweets; easy to get to from Green Lake; colorful cheesecakes. $ *Average main: $6* ✉ *2224 N. 56th St., Seattle* ☎ *206/547-4128* ⊕ *www.instagram.com/hirokidesserts* ⊗ *Closed Mon.-Tues.*

Nightlife

BARS
Korochka Tavern

BARS | This small, sweet bar gives grandpa's basement vibes, if grandpa came from Eastern Europe and alternated his glass of house-infused vodka with the occasional craft cocktail. A few booths surround the live-edge, U-shaped bar, and floral wallpaper completes the feel. The small food menu features Slavic classics, including a variety of dumplings, pickles, and borscht. ✉ *2317 N. 45th St., Wallingford* ⊕ *www.korochkatavern.net* ⊗ *Closed Mon.*

The Octopus Bar

BARS | Though it moved from a tiny hallway of a space to a sprawling building in 2021, this fun and funky bar keeps its small-fish spirit. Quirky art and nautically themed curiosities hang from the ceilings and wall, like a chandelier made from crab traps. House cocktails tend toward the basic side, but that keeps them affordable, and a seasonal slushie rounds out the options. The kitchen serves a selection of nice and creatively named sandwiches and hot dogs. ✉ *2121 N. 45th St., Wallingford* ☎ *206/397-4557* ⊕ *www.theoctopusbar.com.*

MUSIC CLUBS
SeaMonster Lounge

LIVE MUSIC | With its low lighting and cozy seating, SeaMonster makes the tame Wallingford neighborhood just a little bit sexier. The space is small and the stage is sandwiched between the bar and a

Native American Culture and Crafts

Looking at a map of the Seattle area, you'll encounter many Native American names: Enumclaw, Mukilteo, Puyallup, Snohomish, Tukwila. They're legacies of the dozens of tribes and nations that first occupied the region.

Seattle is named after Chief Si'ahl, a leader of the Suquamish and Duwamish tribes. For thousands of years, Native American tribes have called the Pacific Northwest home—from the salmon-packed Skagit River to the high country of the Cascade Mountains. Most of these tribes were subgroups of the Coast Salish peoples, who inhabited the Puget Sound region from Olympia to British Columbia.

Tribes in the Seattle area included Duwamish, Suquamish, Tulalip, Muckleshoot, and Snoqualmie. Each tribe developed complex cultural traditions, and a regional language—Lushootseed—allowed tribes to trade resources. Today, tribe members are keeping their traditions alive; basketry, weaving, and sculpture—including tall carved welcome poles—are traditional artistic media of the Coast Salish that are still thriving. Contemporary Salish artists also work in media like painting, studio glass, and printmaking.

The **Burke Museum of Natural History and Culture** houses thousands of Coast Salish artifacts and artworks. The museum's exhibits also feature artwork from farther-flung tribes, including the Tlingit and Haida of British Columbia and southeast Alaska. The Native-owned cafe, Off the Rez, serves modern and traditional Native cuisine. (⊠ *4300 15th Ave. NE, University District* ☎ *206/543-7907* ⊕ *www.burkemuseum.org.*)

The **Duwamish Longhouse and Cultural Center**, run by the Duwamish Tribe, displays archeological finds, offers tours of the traditional-style building, and runs a small shop of Native crafts and designs, with all proceeds supporting the tribe. (⊠ *4705 W. Marginal Way SW, West Seattle* ☎ *206/431-1582* ⊕ *www.duwamishtribe.org.*)

In Discovery Park, the **Daybreak Star Indian Cultural Center** hosts both a permanent collection of Native art and rotating exhibits in the Sacred Circle Gallery. The building incorporates Northwest Native details into its architecture. (⊠ *5011 Bernie Whitebear Way, Magnolia* ☎ *206/285-4425* ⊕ *www.unitedindians.org/daybreak-star-center.*)

Seattle University's **taqʷšəblu Vi Hilbert Ethnobotanical Garden** displays plants that the local Salish Sea tribes grew for food and traditional medicine. The signs label each plant in both English and Lushootseed. (⊠ *924 E. Cherry St., First Hill.* ☎ *206/296-2235* ⊕ *www.seattleu.edu/indigenous-peoples-institute*)

Coast Salish arts and crafts can be purchased in many galleries around Seattle, including:

Steinbrueck Native Gallery (⊠ *2030 Western Ave., Belltown* ⊕ *www.steinbruecknativegallery.com.*)

Stonington Gallery (⊠ *125 S Jackson St., Pioneer Square* ⊕ *www.stoningtongallery.com.*)

Eighth Generation (⊠ *93 Pike St., #103* ⊕ *www.eighthgeneration.com.*)

few tables—but that just makes it all the more intimate and friendly. The bar presents high-quality local acts, mainly of the jazz, funk, and soul varieties. ✉ *2202 N. 45th St., Wallingford* ☎ *206/355-4247* ⊕ *www.seamonsterlounge.com* ⊘ *Closed Sun.–Mon.*

🛍 Shopping

Wallingford offers a more grown-up selection of shopping than Fremont or Ballard. You won't find trendy clothing boutiques here, but with a great selection of independent shops, specialty bookstores, fabulous gift-buying opportunities, and one of the best beer stores in the city, you're likely to have a fun afternoon poking through this neighborhood.

■ TIP→ **Find the best shopping on 45th Street between Stone Way and Meridian Avenue.**

★ Archie McPhee

SOUVENIRS | FAMILY | If your life is missing a punching-nun puppet, an Edgar Allen Poe action figure, or a bacon-scented air freshener, there's hope. Leave your cares and woes at the door and step into a warehouse of the weird and wonderful. It's nearly impossible to feel bad while perusing stacks of armadillo handbags, demon rubber duckies, handerpants (don't ask), and homicidal unicorn play sets. Grab a cat-in-a-can to keep you company or leave with a dramatic chipmunk oil painting. You'll feel better. Trust us. ✉ *1300 N. 45th St., Wallingford* ☎ *206/297-0240* ⊕ *www.archiemcphee-seattle.com.*

Bottleworks

WINE/SPIRITS | If you love microbrews, then make a pilgrimage to Bottleworks to peruse its massive collection. With 16 taps plus around 950 chilled varieties of malty goodness available, including seasonal varieties, vintage bottles, and global rarities, there's a beer for everyone here—as well as a good sampling of mead and cider. Try a few beers from the

A Good Combo

A trip to Woodland Park Zoo (on the border of Phinney Ridge and Green Lake), a stroll around (or boat ride on) adjacent Green Lake, and then exploring Wallingford's main drag (North 45th Street) is a great way to spend a sunny day. Or instead of Wallingford, you could drive to Ballard and peruse its many shops and restaurants.

taps or bottles (with corkage fee) in their sit-down area, too. ✉ *1710 N. 45th St., #3, Wallingford* ☎ *206/633–2437* ⊕ *www.bottleworks.com.*

Hawaii General Store and Gallery

SOUVENIRS | Outside of San Francisco, Seattle has the largest Hawaiian population on the mainland. Hawaii General Store is a great resource for both those expats and anyone who loves Hawaii (and who doesn't?). With food, music, art, bath products, luau party supplies, and jewelry from the islands, the store is a warm little respite from Seattle's rainy winters. ✉ *258 N. 45th St., Wallingford* ☎ *206/633–5233* ⊕ *www.hawaiigeneralstore.net.*

Green Lake

The neighborhood of Green Lake surrounds the eponymous lake, which is 50,000 years old. It was formed by the Vashon Glacial Ice Sheet, which also gave Seattle, among other things, Puget Sound. Green Lake (the neighborhood) is a pleasant stroll. It has a few shops and eateries along the lake, if you're looking to be far from Downtown's busy streets.

Runners and bikers take in the views along the 2½-mile paved Green Lake Trail.

Sights

Green Lake Park

CITY PARK | FAMILY | This beautiful 342-acre park is a favorite of Seattleites, who jog, bike, and walk their dogs along the 2½-mile paved path that surrounds the lake. Beaches on both the east and west sides (around 72nd Street) have swimming rafts. Canoes, kayaks, and paddleboats can be rented (seasonally) at Green Lake Boat Rental on the eastern side of the lake. There are also basketball and tennis courts and baseball and soccer fields. A first-rate play area includes a giant sandbox, swings, slides, and all the climbing equipment a child could ever dream of—and the wading pool is a perfect spot for tots to cool off (in summer, when the temp is above 70 degrees). The park is generally packed, especially on weekends. And you'd better love dogs: the canine-to-human ratio here is just about even. Surrounding the park are lovely homes, plus a few compact commercial districts where you can grab snacks or dinner after your walk. ✉ *7201 E. Green Lake Dr. N, Green Lake* ☎ *206/684–4075 general info, 206/527–0171 Greenlake Boat Rental* 🌐 *www.seattle.gov/parks/find/parks/green-lake-park.*

Restaurants

Bongos Cafe

$ | CARIBBEAN | FAMILY | Welcome to the year-round beach party at this Caribbean barbecue and sandwich shop located in an old gas station—even though the water is only Green Lake and its across a six-lane highway. The neon-green building with hot pink and blue graffiti sets the tone and the sand-covered floor drives the message home that no matter the weather in Seattle, Bongos brings the island sunshine. **Known for:** great outdoor seating; flavorful sandwiches; beach party vibes. [$] *Average main: $13* ✉ *6501 Aurora Ave. N., Green Lake* ✥ *Enter via Woodland Pl. N. at Linden Ave N.* ☎ *206/420-8548* 🌐 *www.bongosseattle.com* 🕒 *Closed Mon.–Tues.*

Kisaku

$$$$ | JAPANESE | This outstanding sushi restaurant quietly nestled in Green Lake brings diners in droves. Fresh sushi is the mainstay, along with signature rolls such as the Green Lake variety, with salmon, flying fish eggs, asparagus, avocado, and marinated seaweed, or the Wallingford, with yellowtail, green onion, cucumber, radish, sprouts, and flying fish eggs. **Known for:** omakase (chef's menu); family-friendly; signature sushi rolls. $ *Average main: $55* ⊠ *2101 N. 55th St., Green Lake* ☎ *206/545–9050* ⊕ *www. kisaku.com.*

Toast Mi

$ | VIETNAMESE | This Green Lake sandwich shop is as cute and modern as the illustrations on the menu board hanging over its counter. The Vietnamese sandwiches on offer get fun new names like the Mekong (grilled pork) and Sapa (sauteed tofu) but stay true to the flavor of classic banh mi, stacked with jalapenos, pickled carrots and daikon, and basil-cilantro aioli. **Known for:** customizable bubble tea; park adjacent; quick, friendly service. $ *Average main: $10* ⊠ *7130 Woodlawn Ave. NE, Green Lake* ☎ *206/402–5546* ⊕ *www.instagram.com/ toastmiplease.*

Nightlife

MUSIC CLUBS

The Little Red Hen

LIVE MUSIC | Bring your cowboy boots and hats to this honky-tonk, which is inexplicably located in one of Seattle's most gentrified neighborhoods. Live country bands take the stage most nights; there are free line-dancing lessons on Monday nights and two-step lessons on Thursdays. Don't expect anything fancy—this place has not been sanitized for tourists. ⊠ *7115 Woodlawn Ave. NE, Green Lake* ☎ *206/522–1168* ⊕ *www.littleredhen. com* ☞ *Cover charges start at 8pm Thurs.-Sun.*

Performing Arts

★ Seattle Public Theater

THEATER | Beloved by locals for its humorous, ground-breaking, and unique choices, Seattle Public Theater brings five shows a year to an intimate stage. This tiny company puts on performances worth scheduling a day around. ⊠ *7312 West Green Lake Dr. N, Green Lake* ☎ *206/524–1300* ⊕ *www.seattlepublictheater.org.*

Activities

★ Green Lake Boathouse

BOATING | FAMILY | This shop is the source for pedal boats, kayaks, stand-up paddleboards, and rowboats to take out on Green Lake's calm waters. On beautiful summer afternoons, however, be prepared to spend most of your time dealing with traffic: in the parking lot, in line for a boat, and on the water. Fees are $27 an hour for pedal boats, single kayaks, rowboats, and stand-up paddleboards. ■**TIP→ Rent before noon to get the "Happy Hour" rate of $21.** ⊠ *7351 E. Green Lake Dr. N, Green Lake* ☎ *206/527–0171* ⊕ *www.greenlakeboathouse.com* ⊗ *Closed October through March* ☞ *Openings are weather permitting, particularly in spring and fall.*

Chapter 12

UNIVERSITY DISTRICT

12

Updated by
Naomi Tomky

⊙ Sights	🍴 Restaurants	🛏 Hotels	⊖ Shopping	🍸 Nightlife
★★☆☆☆	★★★☆☆	★★★☆☆	★☆☆☆☆	★★☆☆☆

NEIGHBORHOOD SNAPSHOT

TOP REASONS TO GO

■ See the **Red Square,** UW's main plaza, named for its brick paving. Stop here for views of college life and, on sunny days, Mt. Rainier (it's also one of the best places to spot spring's fleeting cherry-blossom bloom). Then check out the well-curated exhibits at the **Henry Art Gallery** or explore the spacious **Burke Museum of Natural History and Culture**.

■ Paddle around **Portage Bay** from Agua Verde Café & Paddle Club. They can set you up with a kayak—and a margarita and Mexican grub when you return.

■ Make a detour to the **Center for Urban Horticulture**, which is across the street from outdoor shopping center **University Village**, on the shores of Lake Washington, for a relaxing stroll, bird-watching, or an evening picnic.

GETTING HERE AND AROUND

A quick light-rail ride takes you from the airport, Downtown, or Capitol Hill to the Link light-rail underground stations next to Husky Stadium (University of Washington Station) or in the heart of the U-District (U District Station). (Note that neither of these is the University Street Station, which is Downtown.) Without traffic, I–5 north to 45th Street takes only 10 minutes by car from Downtown, but that rarely happens.

Bus 43, which you can catch Downtown along Pike Street, takes a pleasant route through Capitol Hill, over the Montlake Bridge, and stops on the western side of the campus in front of the Henry Art Gallery.

Getting around the U-District is fairly easy. The major action happens on "The Ave" (University Way NE), between 42nd and 50th Streets. Getting to the other northern neighborhoods of Wallingford, Fremont, and Ballard is easy, too. The only thing not convenient is the University Village shopping center, which is a long walk.

PAUSE HERE

■ Fritz Hedges Waterway Park opened in 2020, designed to help mitigate the environmental impact of the nearby highway bridges. Bright yellow chairs dot the pier and the big grassy area along the salmon-friendly shoreline, looking out across the Ship Canal.

PLANNING YOUR TIME

■ The few sights the neighborhood has are helpfully grouped close together. The Henry Art Gallery and the Burke Museum are on the lovely UW campus. You can combine a museum stop with a campus stroll and then hit The Ave (the area's main drag) for lunch.

The U-District, as everyone calls it, is the neighborhood surrounding the University of Washington (UW or "U-Dub" to locals). The campus is extraordinarily beautiful (especially in springtime, when the cherry blossoms are flowering), and the Henry Art Gallery is one of the city's best small museums. Beyond that, the appeal of the neighborhood lies in its youthful energy and its variety of cheap, delicious cuisines from around the world.

The U-District isn't everyone's cup of chai. Almost all businesses are geared toward students, and everything flows along the school year calendar. The area often feels like it's separate from the city—and that's no accident. The university was founded in 1861 and was constructed on newly clear-cut land long before there were any convenient ways to get to the city that was growing Downtown. More so than any other northern neighborhood, the U-District had to be self-sufficient, even though the light rail now links the neighborhood with Capitol Hill and Downtown to the south and residential neighborhoods to the north. Residents don't even have to travel to Downtown to get their shopping done: they have their own upscale megamall, University Village ("U Village"), an elegant outdoor shopping center with an Apple store, chain stores (including H&M, Gap, Eddie Bauer, Crate & Barrel, Room & Board, and Banana Republic), as well as restaurants, boutiques, and two large grocery stores. The Burke-Gilman Trail, Magnuson Park, and the UW Botanic Gardens Center for Urban Horticulture offer scenic detours.

Sights

Burke Museum of Natural History and Culture

SCIENCE MUSEUM | FAMILY | Founded in 1885, the Burke is the state's oldest museum with one of the newest buildings, thanks to a 2019 re-opening in a brand new space. It features exhibits that survey the natural history of the Pacific Northwest and a behind-the-scenes look at how museums work, with its open doors and windows. Highlights include artifacts from Washington's 35 Native American tribes, dinosaur skeletons, and dioramas depicting the traditions of Pacific Rim cultures. An adjacent ethnobotanical garden is planted with species

Fascinating exhibits fill the Burke Museum of Natural History and Culture.

that were important to the region's Native American communities, and the Native-owned café serves fry bread and Indigenous foods. Check out the schedule for family events and adult classes. ⊠ *University of Washington Campus, 4300 15th Ave. NE, University District* ☎ *206/543–7907* ⊕ *www.burkemuseum. org* 🎫 *$22, free 1st Thurs. of month* ☉ *Closed Mon.*

Center for Urban Horticulture

GARDEN | Nestled between a residential lakefront neighborhood to the east and the University of Washington campus to the west are the 16-acre landscaped gardens of the Center for Urban Horticulture and the 74-acre Union Bay Natural Area, part of the University of Washington Botanic Gardens. Inside the Center is the Elisabeth C. Miller Library, open to the public and home to 15,000 books and 500 periodicals on gardening techniques. The Union Bay Natural Area serves as an outdoor laboratory for UW research with some of the best bird-watching in the city. With a ¾-mile loop gravel trail,

it's also a terrific place for a walk or a jog, and on a nice day, the views of Mt. Rainier and the surrounding waterfront are simply divine. From the U-District, head east on NE 45th Street and take a right onto Mary Gates Drive. ⊠ *3501 NE 41st St., University District* ☎ *206/543–8616* ⊕ *www.botanicgardens.uw.edu/ center-for-urban-horticulture* ☉ *Library closed Sat.–Sun.*

★ Henry Art Gallery

ART MUSEUM | This large gallery that consistently presents sophisticated and thought-provoking contemporary work is perhaps the best reason to take a trip to the U-District. Exhibits pull from many different genres and include mixed media, photography, and paintings. Richard C. Elliott used more than 21,500 bicycle and truck reflectors of different colors and sizes in his paintings that fit into the sculpture alcoves on the exterior walls of the museum; in another permanent installation, *Light Reign*, a "Skyspace" from artist James Turrell, an elliptical chamber allows visitors to view the sky. More than a few people have used this as a meditation spot; at night the chamber is illuminated by thousands of LED lights. ✉ *University of Washington campus, 15th Ave. NE and NE 41st St., University District* ☎ *206/543–2280* ⊕ *www.henryart.org* ✉ *$1–20 suggested donation* ☽ *Closed Mon.–Wed.*

Northwest Puppet Center

OTHER MUSEUM | FAMILY | In a renovated church in the Maple Leaf neighborhood, the only puppet center in the Northwest highlights the renowned marionettes of the Carter family, professional puppeteers trained by masters from Italy, Romania, and China. For their talent, they have received a Fulbright Award and a UNIMA/USA Citation of Excellence, the highest award in American puppet theater. New museum exhibits are curated each fall and may focus on a particular tradition, technique, or historic period. Past exhibits have included *Puppetry from Around the World* and *Cheering up the Great Depression: Puppetry & the WPA.* ✉ *9123 15th Ave. NE, University District* ✛ *Take I–5 north, Exit 171 to Lake City Way, turn left on 15th Ave. NE and continue to 92nd St.* ⊕ *www.nwpuppet. org* ✉ *Museum is free, performance ticket prices vary; call ahead to reserve* ☽ *Closed Mon.-Fri. and June–Sept.*

★ University District Farmers' Market

MARKET | One of the country's longest-running farmers' markets and Seattle's largest "farmers only" market (no crafts, imports, or flea-market finds) operates year-round on Saturday from 9 am to 2 pm in the heart of the U-District, rain or shine. With more than 50 Washington State farmers and producers participating, you'll find a great selection of produce, baked goods, preserves, flowers, cheese, soups, pies, wines, pasta, and handmade chocolates. ✉ *University Way NE between NE 50th and 52nd Sts., University District* ⊕ *seattlefarmersmarkets.org/udfm.*

A Good Combo

The Henry Art Gallery is well worth the trip. Stroll around the UW campus in the morning, especially if you visit in spring when the school's many cherry blossom trees are blooming. Then pay a visit to the Henry when it opens at 11 am, followed by spicy Xi'an noodles or Thai curry for lunch on The Ave—the U-District's main drag. If you still have energy, stroll from there to the Montlake Bridge; part of your walk can be along the Burke Gilman Trail. The bridge is a fun place to watch passing boats and kayakers in summer.

Warren G. Magnuson Park

CITY PARK | FAMILY | Also called Sand Point–Magnuson Park, this 350-acre park northeast of the University District was once an active naval air base. Evidence of the park's roots are on full display, with barracks and hangars in various stages of use and upkeep. Keep your focus on the areas toward the lake, as the paved trails are wonderful for cycling, jogging, or pushing a stroller. Leashed dogs are welcome on the trails and a gigantic off-leash area includes one of the few public beaches where pooches can swim. Farther south, on the mile-long shore, there's a swimming beach, a seasonal wading pool, and a boat launch. Innovative art is threaded through the grounds, including *Fin Art* (made from submarine fins, on Kite Hill) and *Straight Shot* (which allows visitors to experience what a surveyor does). A fabulous playground engages little ones near the north end.

Various community organizations and non-profits fill the buildings. Arena Sports is an indoor soccer facility which offers an inflatable play area for children, and Sail Sand Point rents sailboats, kayaks, and stand-up paddleboards in summer.

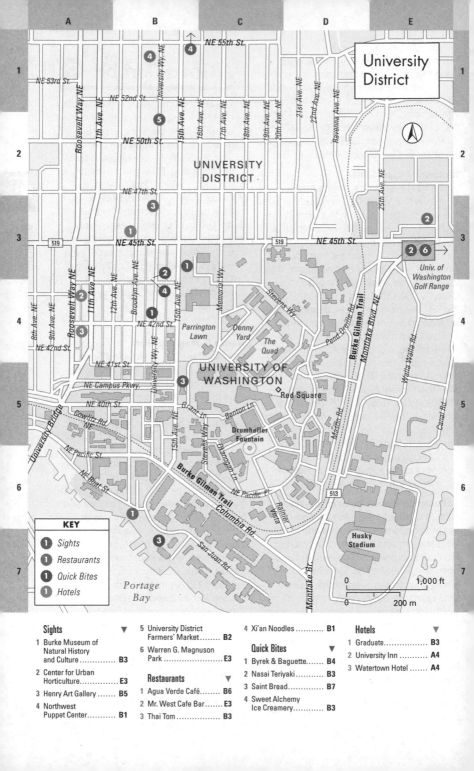

University District

Map Labels

NE 55th St.

NE 53rd St.

NE 52nd St.

NE 50th St.

UNIVERSITY DISTRICT

NE 47th St.

NE 45th St.

NE 45th St.

NE 42nd St.

NE 41st St.

NE Campus Pkwy.

NE 40th St.

NE 42nd St.

Roosevelt Way NE

11th Ave. NE

University Way NE

15th Ave. NE

16th Ave. NE

17th Ave. NE

18th Ave. NE

19th Ave. NE

20th Ave. NE

21st Ave. NE

22nd Ave. NE

Ravenna Ave. NE

25th Ave. NE

8th Ave. NE

9th Ave. NE

Roosevelt Way NE

11th Ave. NE

12th Ave. NE

Brooklyn Ave. NE

University Way NE

15th Ave. NE

Memorial Way

Stevens Wy.

Pend Oreille Rd.

Burke Gilman Trail

Montlake Blvd. NE

Walla Walla Rd.

Canal Rd.

Mason Rd.

UNIVERSITY OF WASHINGTON

Parrington Lawn

Denny Yard

The Quad

Red Square

Grant Ln.

Benton Ln.

Stevens Way

Okanogan Ln.

Drumheller Fountain

NE Pacific Pl.

Rainier Vista

Burke Gilman Trail

Columbia Rd.

San Juan Rd.

NE Pacific St.

Cowlitz Rd. NE

NE Boat St.

University Bridge

Portage Bay

Husky Stadium

Montlake Br.

Univ. of Washington Golf Range

513

519

519

0   1,000 ft

0   200 m

KEY

- **1** Sights
- **1** Restaurants
- **1** Quick Bites
- **1** Hotels

✉ *Park entrance, 6500 Sand Point Way NE, Sand Point* ☎ *206/684–4946* ⊕ *www. seattle.gov/parks/magnuson.*

🍴 Restaurants

The U-District is great for finding a variety of good options on a budget, but falls short on fine dining. It's worth strolling up and down The Ave (University Way NE) to see if anything beckons to you before settling on a spot. Down the hill, University Village offers a few more-up-scale places, but still nothing fancy.

Agua Verde Café

$$ | MEXICAN | Baja California Mexican cuisine and a laid-back vibe define this casual spot that's done up in bright, beachy colors, with a lively deck come summertime. Regulars swear by the fresh fish tacos and *mangodillas* (quesa-dillas with mango and poblano chilies). **Known for:** stellar views of the Ship Canal; Baja-style tacos with wild local fish; prick-ly pear margaritas. $ *Average main: $16* ✉ *1303 NE Boat St., University District* ☎ *206/545–8570* ⊕ *www.aguaverdecafe. com.*

Mr. West Cafe Bar

$ | AMERICAN | This elegant but ultimately casual all-day café suits the needs of upscale U-Village perfectly. Whether you're looking to recharge with a fancy coffee drink, bubbles, or a cocktail, this spot has just the thing. **Known for:** Insta-grammable avocado toast; great happy hour deals; coffee egg cream. $ *Average main: $14* ✉ *2685 NE Village Lane, Uni-versity District* ☎ *206/900–9378* ⊕ *www. mrwestcafebar.com.*

Thai Tom

$ | THAI | This might be the cheapest Thai restaurant in town, but rock-bottom prices aren't the only reason this place is always packed—the food is delicious, authentic, and spicy (two stars is usually pretty hot). Plus, you get dinner and a show as the flames lick up the woks in front of the bar. **Known for:** affordable

prices; quick meals; spicy dishes. $ *Av-erage main: $12* ✉ *4543 University Ave., University District* ☎ *206/548–9548.*

Xi'an Noodles

$ | CHINESE | Diners here sometimes find their meal interrupted by the soft thump-ing noise for which the chewy, ropy noodles the restaurant specializes in are named. Biang biang noodles are made by slapping strands of dough against the hard counter, which elongates them without toughening the dough. **Known for:** fresh hand-pulled noodles; zingy salads; delightfully spicy food. $ *Average main: $14* ✉ *5259 University Way NE, Univer-sity District* ☎ *206/522–8888* ⊕ *www. xiannoodles.com.*

☕ Coffee and Quick Bites

Byrek & Baguette

$ | MEDITERRANEAN | Don't get distracted by the eye-catching decor: as cute as the lemon-patterned chair is and as striking as the plant wall is, the main attraction is the brightness of the flavors. Fresh squeezed orange juice (on its own or in a mimosa) goes well with the breakfast baguettes and flaky stuffed Balkan pas-tries for which the shop is named. **Known for:** fresh Mediterranean breakfasts and salads; delightful decor; Balkan pastries. $ *Average main: $10* ✉ *4209 University Way NE, University District* ☎ *206/632–3864* ⊕ *www.byrekandbaguette.org.*

Nacai Toriyaki

$ | JAPANESE FUSION | Though it shares its name with a half-dozen other teriyaki shops in town, this location on The Ave is the original, and while it shows its age, it also shows why so many tried to emu-late it. Ignore the many options and stick to what they do best: cook up exception-al versions of the classic Seattle-style teriyaki. **Known for:** quick, friendly service; classic local joint; Seattle-style teriyaki. $ *Average main: $13* ✉ *4305 University Way NE, University District* ☎ *206/632–3572* ☽ *Closed Sun.*

★ Saint Bread

$ | **BAKERY** | The stained glass saint, holding wheat in one hand and a Japanese *melonpan* (bun) in the other, summarizes this eccentric but excellent bakery perched on the shore of the Ship Canal. Scandanavian-style cardamom knots, classic French croissants, and fried egg sandwiches with Thai-style turkey sausage exemplify the breakfast selection here. **Known for:** eclectic but interesting menu; innovative breakfast sandwiches; lovely covered outdoor patio. $ *Average main: $7* ⊠ *1421 NE Boat St., University District* ☎ *206/566–5195* ⊕ *www.saintbread.com.*

Sweet Alchemy Ice Creamery

$ | **ICE CREAM** | After working her way through school at a chain ice-cream shop, UW graduate Lois Ko bought the space and opened up an independent local ice creamery, committed to making each ice cream from scratch daily using organic, local ingredients whenever possible. The passion for quality ice cream shows both in standard flavors like sweet cream and salted caramel, and in the originals, like *makgeolli* (Korean rice beer) or kettle corn. **Known for:** made-from-scratch ice creams; innovative flavors; vegan options. $ *Average main: $6* ⊠ *4301 University Way NE, University District* ☎ *206/632–0243* ⊕ *www.sweetalchemyicecreamery.com.*

 # Hotels

Seattleites have a love-hate relationship with the University District. On one hand, you'll find some reasonably priced, decent accommodations here, thanks to the many parents visiting their kids at the University of Washington (UW). On the other hand, the areas closest to the main drag, University Way (The Ave) can feel both college-y and gritty. One plus of staying close to The Ave is the plethora of affordable food of all kinds. You'll also

enjoy access to the city's largest farmers' market on Saturdays as well as the UW's Henry Art Gallery and the Burke Museum. The area on the other side of the campus, closest to the upscale open-air mall University Village, is nicer and more residential but inconvenient to the rest of the city. In terms of location, the U-District hotels listed offer fairly quick commutes to both Downtown and Capitol Hill, via car or light rail.

Graduate

$$ | **HOTEL** | The 1931 building that began as the Edmond Meany Hotel finally got the upgrade it needed, reopening in late 2018 as the Graduate, designed to appeal to friends and family of UW students. **Pros:** modern decor; rooftop bar; large rooms. **Cons:** far from tourist sights; expensive parking; streetside rooms can be noisy. $ *Rooms from: $230* ⊠ *4507 Brooklyn Avenue NE, University District* ☎ *206/634–2000* ⊕ *www.graduateseattle.com* ⤳ *175 rooms* ⦿ *No Meals.*

University Inn

$$ | **HOTEL** | **FAMILY** | This impeccably maintained inn (a sister property to the Watertown Hotel) has earned its popularity by steadfastly offering clean, friendly lodging in a city where the price for a room is liable to cause sticker shock. **Pros:** great value; outdoor pool; friendly staff. **Cons:** not as nice as the Watertown next door; pool is a little cold; not close to many tourist attractions. $ *Rooms from: $238* ⊠ *4140 Roosevelt Way NE, University District* ☎ *206/632–5055, 866/866–7977* ⊕ *www.universityinnseattle.com* ⤳ *102 rooms* ⦿ *No Meals.*

Watertown Hotel

$$ | **HOTEL** | **FAMILY** | Assorted amenities make this University District hotel a great deal, including inexpensive parking ($20), free Wi-Fi, and an afternoon reception with coffee and treats. **Pros:** complimentary bikes; on-site café; pool access. **Cons:** street noise in some rooms; can

get expensive at busy times; not as close to attractions as other hotels. **$** *Rooms from: $249* ✉ *4242 Roosevelt Way NE, University District* ☎ *206/826–4242* ⊕ *www.watertownseattle.com* ⇨ *100 rooms* ⦿ *No Meals.*

⦿ Nightlife

The U-District doesn't offer much nightlife of interest unless you're taking your new fake ID out for a spin. With the exception of the Mountaineering Club at the Graduate Hotel, most haunts fall firmly in the pub category and are filled with students on weekends. If you don't want to drink, you'll have better luck: the neighborhood has a comedy club, a few theater troupes, and several good movie theaters, including beloved art house Grand Illusion Cinema.

BARS AND LOUNGES
Big Time Brewery
BREWPUBS | With its neat brick walls, polished wood floors, and vintage memorabilia, Big Time Brewery is one of the best places in the U-District for a quiet beer away from the frenetic college scene. Opened in 1988, it was one of the first local brewpubs of the craft beer movement. The brewery offers more than a dozen beers on tap, including cask ales. Skip the mediocre pub grub. ✉ *4133 University Way NE, University District* ☎ *206/545–4509* ⊕ *www.bigtimebrewery.com.*

Mountaineering Club
BARS | It's all about the amazing view at this rooftop bar that crowns the art deco Graduate Hotel. Windows that stretch to the ceiling surround the exploration-themed inside, while the patio space extends the view from the 16th floor outside. In a neighborhood with few tall buildings, this spot feels truly on top of the world. The drinks and food menus are concise and locally themed, but the bartenders can mix a good classic cocktail upon request. ✉ *4507 Brooklyn Ave*

NE, University District ☎ *206/634–2000* ⊕ *www.themountaineeringclub.com* ⦿ *Closed Mon.*

Supreme Bar
BARS | This dimly lit pizza joint serves tasty frozen slushies and pizza with a few playful gourmet extras from the founder, a former fine-dining chef. With cocktails a step above dive bar levels, and a much cleaner setting than the classic college pub, this spot is a sort of ironic take on the classic New York pizza joint bar. The pizza and scallion garlic knots are very good and worth ordering, too. ✉ *4529 University Way, University District* ⊕ *www.supreme.bar.*

COMEDY CLUBS
Laughs Comedy Club
COMEDY CLUBS | This small comedy venue attracts well-known national comedians on weekends and keeps a good flow of local talent and up-and-comers on weeknights. Headliners usually play two shows per night, which makes last-minute tickets easy to find. Box office prices are generally reasonable, though the ticket price doesn't include the two-item minimum order for each person. Unfortunately, the food is not anything worth recommending, so grab a few drinks and plan to eat before or after the show. ✉ *5220 Roosevelt Way NE, University District* ☎ *206/526–5653* ⊕ *www.laughscomedyclub.com* ⦿ *Closed Sun.–Tues.*

⦿ Performing Arts

DANCE
Meany Hall for the Performing Arts
MODERN DANCE | National and international companies perform October through May at the University of Washington's Meany Hall. The emphasis is on modern and jazz dance and generally innovative, diverse performance art. ✉ *4040 George Washington Lane NE, University District* ☎ *206/543–4880* ⊕ *www.meanycenter.org.*

FILM
The Grand Illusion Cinema

FILM | Seattle's longest-running independent movie house is an outstanding and unique home for independent and art film that feels as comfortable as a home theater. The non-profit, volunteer-run theater shows independent, classic, and other types of films that otherwise tend to fly under the radar of pop culture. ⊠ *1403 NE 50th St., University District* ☎ *206/523–3935* ⊕ *www.grandillusion-cinema.org.*

THEATER
The Neptune Theatre

MUSIC | A cultural hub for the nearby University of Washington since opening in 1921, this striking Renaissance-revival theater is operated by STG Presents, which also runs the Paramount and Moore. The lineup—featuring mostly music and comedy—includes a mix of emerging and well-established acts. ⊠ *1303 NE 45th St., University District* ☎ *206/682–1414* ⊕ *www.stgpresents. org.*

🛍 Shopping

The U-District is packed with predictably college-friendly shopping—lots of used clothing, books, and coffee. Meander down University Way (known to locals as "The Ave") to find the standout shops listed here, and stop at any of the numerous restaurants serving all kinds of food from around the world at budget-friendly prices to refuel.

■ TIP→ **Find the best shopping on University Way NE between NE 42nd and 47th Streets, and University Village at 25th Avenue NE and NE 45th Street.**

APPAREL
Crossroads Trading Co.

SECOND-HAND | Crossroads Trading Co. carries dependably cute and trendy used clothes, bags, and accessories. Their buyers screen each item, so you won't be stuck poring over a rack of stained T-shirts. It's all clean, bright, and fun. ⊠ *4300 University Way NE, University District* ☎ *206/632–1850* ⊕ *www.cross-roadstrading.com.*

Red Light Vintage and Costume

SECOND-HAND | Nostalgia rules in this cavernous space filled with well-organized, good-quality (and sometimes pricey) vintage and new clothing. Fantasy outfits from decades past—complete with accessories—adorn the dressing rooms. It's a go-to spot for stylists and thrifters. Fun fact: this funky shop was one of the locations in Macklemore's "Thrift Shop" video. ⊠ *4560 University Way NE, University District* ☎ *206/545–4044* ⊕ *www. redlightvintage.com.*

Woolly Mammoth

SHOES | A conservative take on Pacific Northwest footwear, this cozy shop offers brands like Birkenstock, Blundstone, Keens, and Toms. The friendly and knowledgeable staff will happily help customers with hard-to-fit feet and help find the perfect shoe. ⊠ *4303 University Way NE, Seattle* ☎ *206/632–3254* ⊕ *www. woollymammothshoes.com.*

BOOKS, MOVIES, AND MUSIC
Pink Gorilla Games

OTHER SPECIALTY STORE | Primarily a video game store, here you'll find a huge variety of new and used classics and rare games for all consoles, with a focus on imported and retro games going back to Atari times. They also carry toys and their own branded merchandise, which is pretty snazzy. They have a second store in the International District. ⊠ *4341 University Way NE, University District*

Huskies Stadium has been called "the greatest setting in college football."

☎ *206/547–5790* ⊕ *www.pinkgorillag-ames.com.*

★ Scarecrow Video

OTHER SPECIALTY STORE | Forget going obsolete—this shop shows how video stores can keep up with modern viewers. One of the biggest and best independent film shops in the country can be found on Roosevelt Way, where 145,000 rare, out-of-production, foreign, and main-stream films are available to rent and buy. Scarecrow's friendly staff are bona fide film geeks—pick their brains for sugges-tions, or stop by for one of the non-profit shop's many in-store events. ⊠ *5030 Roosevelt Way NE, University District* ☎ *206/524–8554* ⊕ *www.scarecrow.com* ⊗ *Closed Mon.*

University Book Store

BOOKS | Campus bookstores are usually rip-offs to be endured only by students clutching syllabi, but the University of Washington's store is a big exception to that rule. This enormous resource has a well-stocked general book department in addition to the requisite textbooks. Author events are scheduled all year long. Check out the bargain-book tables and the basement crammed with every art supply imaginable. They also carry a good selection of UW Husky gear if you need a souvenir and plenty of local gifts. ⊠ *4326 University Way NE, University District* ⊹ *In order to enter the parking lot, drive down 15th Ave NE and make a turn onto NE 43rd Street* ☎ *206/634–3400* ⊕ *www.ubookstore.com.*

MALLS

University Village

MALL | Make a beeline here for fabulous upscale shopping and good restaurants in a pretty, outdoor, tree- and foun-tain-laden shopping village. You can have your fill of chains like Williams-Sonoma, Banana Republic, L'Occitane, Crate & Barrel, Sephora, Aveda, Warby Parker, H&M, Madewell, Apple, Anthropologie, and Kiehl's. If you get enough of that at home, however, there are a few unique gems among the batch, including the excellent Village Maternity Store, candy wonderland The Confectionery, and local artsy chain Fireworks. Note that parking here can be tough, especially in the holiday season, and the atmosphere is slightly snobby. ■TIP→ **If you're in the mood to walk a bit farther, go immediately to one of the free parking garages.** ✉ *2623 NE University Village St., University District* ☎ *206/523–0622* ⊕ *www.uvillage. com.*

 Activities

SPORTS

As you might imagine, in the University District, the University of Washington Huskies are a big deal. The Huskies are often at the top of the national rankings in football and both men's and women's soccer, basketball, rowing, volleyball, and much more. Other than football and men's basketball, these events are an affordable way to see future professional or Olympic athletes.

UW Huskies Basketball

BASKETBALL | FAMILY | Representing Seattle basketball in the Pac-12 Conference, the UW Huskies have been a consistent force for many years now. Along with several conference titles, the team has advanced to the NCAA tournament four times in a decade. The always-tough women's team—which also enjoys a very loyal (and loud) fan base—has advanced to the NCAA tournament several times in recent years as well. Both the men's and women's basketball teams play at Alaska Airlines Arena at Hec Edmundson Pavilion, known locally as "Hec Ed." ✉ *3870 Montlake Blvd. NE, University District* ☎ *206/543–2200* ⊕ *gohuskies.com.*

UW Huskies Football

FOOTBALL | The UW Huskies are almost as popular as the Seahawks and play in "the greatest setting in college football."

The Dawgs host some of the best teams in the nation at the U-shape Husky Stadium, which overlooks Lake Washington and the snow-capped Cascades mountains beyond it. For all but the biggest events, tickets can be found right up until game time for reasonable prices. ✉ *University of Washington, 3800 Montlake Blvd. NE, University District* ☎ *206/543–2200* ⊕ *gohuskies.com.*

WATER SPORTS

Agua Verde Paddle Club

BOATING | Rent a kayak and paddle along either the Lake Union shoreline, with its hodgepodge of funky-to-fabulous houseboats and dramatic Downtown vistas, or Union Bay on Lake Washington, with its marshes and cattails. Afterward, take in the lakefront as you wash down some Mexican food with a margarita at the neighboring cafe. Kayaks and stand-up paddleboards are available March through October and are rented by the hour—$23 for single kayaks, $30 for doubles, and $25 for SUPs. They also offer tours and classes a few times a week. ✉ *1307 NE Boat St., University District* ☎ *206/632–1862* ⊕ *www.aguaverdepaddleclub.com* ⊘ *Closed Tues.–Weds., and Nov.–Feb.*

★ Waterfront Activities Center

BOATING | FAMILY | This center, located behind UW's Husky Stadium on Union Bay, rents three-person canoes ($14 an hour) and single or double kayaks ($16/$20 an hour) from May through October. You can tour the Lake Washington shoreline or paddle through the lily pads at nearby Foster Island and visit the Washington Park Arboretum. ✉ *3710 Montlake Blvd. NE, University District* ☎ *206/543–9433* ⊕ *washington.edu/ima/ waterfront* ⊘ *Hours change monthly, closed mid-October—April. Closed on Husky Football game days.* ☞ *Opening is weather dependent.*

WEST SEATTLE

Updated by
Naomi Tomky

● Sights	🍴 Restaurants	🛏 Hotels	🛍 Shopping	🍸 Nightlife
★★☆☆☆	★★★☆☆	★☆☆☆☆	★★☆☆☆	★☆☆☆☆

NEIGHBORHOOD SNAPSHOT

TOP REASONS TO GO

■ Any trip to West Seattle should include some time on Alki Beach, but be sure to make it around the western edge of the peninsula to see the **Alki Point** lighthouse and the spot where the first settlers landed.

■ Dine on **California Avenue SW.** The stretch between SW Genesee and SW Edmonds streets has most of West Seattle's notable eateries.

■ Cool off in the saltwater swimming pool at **Lincoln Park**.

■ Catch the ferry to **Vashon Island** where you can visit orchards, farms, and wineries.

■ Climb **Schurman Rock**, an outdoor climbing gym next to the West Seattle Golf Course.

GETTING HERE AND AROUND

Driving north or south on I–5 or south on Highway 99, take the West Seattle Bridge exit. The Harbor Avenue SW exit will take you to Alki Beach; SW Admiral Way will get you to California Avenue. By bus, take RapidRide C or bus 21, 55, 56, or 57 from Downtown; where they run down 3rd Avenue, and then cross the West Seattle Bridge. RapidRide C runs south on California Avenue SW, the 21 on 35th Avenue SW. Bus 55 then goes north to the Admiral District, and buses 56 and 57 continue on to the western edge of Alki Beach.

West Seattle is sprawling, and easiest to traverse by car. However, if you arrived by West Seattle Water Taxi (a passenger- and bicycle-only ferry that travels from Pier 50, along the waterfront Downtown, to Seacrest Park at the peninsula's eastern shore), you have several transit options: two shuttles run from the dock, 773 to the Alaska Junction and 775 to Alki and Admiral; or, you can hop on Bus 128, which travels around the peninsula almost as far as Lincoln Park.

FUN FACT

■ Locals used to jokingly call West Seattle "The Island" for its isolation and because getting to the peninsula took crossing a bridge. Then, in March 2020, the main West Seattle Bridge over the Duwamish River developed structural cracks, closing it for two and a half years, which also limited the older "low bridge" to only bicycle and emergency traffic during daylight hours. But the neighborhood developed a real sense of island community, supporting local businesses and proudly wearing shirts bearing phrases like "Greetings from an accidental island," and "West Seattle: so close, yet so far."

PLANNING YOUR TIME

■ Head to Alki Beach and follow the path around the peninsula, enjoying the shore, Alki Point Lighthouse, and Lincoln Park. This is easiest to do by car. If you arrived by water taxi from Downtown, you can rent a bicycle by the terminal; the trip by bike takes roughly 35 minutes. California Avenue, which is in the center of the peninsula, can be your last stop, for sustenance.

Cross the bridge to West Seattle and it's another world altogether. Jutting out into Elliott Bay and Puget Sound, separated from the city by the Duwamish waterway, this out-of-the-way neighborhood covers most of the city's western peninsula—and it has an identity all its own. In summer, throngs of people hang out at Alki Beach—Seattle's taste of California—while others head for the trails and playgrounds of Lincoln Park to the west.

The first white settlers parked their boat at Alki Point in 1851, planning to build a major city here until they discovered a deeper logging port at today's Pioneer Square. This makes West Seattle technically the city's oldest neighborhood. West Seattle is huge, and within it are more than a dozen neighborhoods. The two most-visited neighborhoods are Alki and West Seattle (or Alaska) Junction. The former includes the shoreline and Alki Point; the Alki Point Lighthouse sits on the peninsula's northwest tip, a place for classic sunset views. The main shopping and dining areas line Alki Avenue, next to the beach, and California Junction. The latter neighborhood, named for a spot where old streetcar lines crisscrossed, is the fastest-growing part of West Seattle and has its own thriving dining scene. It also has most of the area's good shopping and ArtsWest, a community theater and gallery.

The Admiral neighborhood, on the northern bluff, is less vital, but it does have an important old movie house that is one of the venues for the Seattle International Film Festival. Fauntleroy has two main attractions: the lovely Lincoln Park and a ferry terminal with service to Vashon Island and Southworth on the Kitsap Peninsula.

⊙ Sights

★ Alki Point and Beach

BEACH | FAMILY | In summer, this is as close to California as Seattle gets—and some hardy residents even swim in the cold, salty waters of Puget Sound here (water temperature ranges from 46°F to 56°F). This 2½-mile stretch of sand has views of the Seattle skyline and the Olympic Mountains, and the beachfront promenade is especially popular with skaters, joggers, strollers, and cyclists. Year-round, Seattleites come to build

Parks Close to Alki

Lincoln Park. Along the neighborhood's southwest edge, near the Fauntleroy ferry terminal, Lincoln Park sets acres of old forests, rocky beaches, waterfront trails, picnic tables, and a historic saltwater pool against views of Puget Sound. ■TIP➔ **Colman Pool is a Seattle landmark you won't want to miss in summer. The saltwater pool is located on the water toward the north end of the park. Public swims often sell out on nice days, so get there early.** ✉ *8011 Fauntleroy Way SW, West Seattle* ☎ *206/684–4075 park, 206/684–7494*

Colman pool ⊕ *www.seattle.gov/parks* ✉ *$6.25 for pool* ☉ *Pool closed from after Labor Day to mid-June.*

Schmitz Preserve Park. Marvel at the lustrous 53 acres of rugged forest at Schmitz Preserve, about 15 blocks east of Alki Point. The Preserve was donated to the city in pieces between 1908 and 1912, and features one of the remaining stands of old-growth forest in Seattle. ✉ *5551 SW Admiral Way, West Seattle* ⊕ *www.seattle.gov/parks.*

sand castles, beachcomb, and fly kites; in winter, storm-watchers come to see the crashing waves. Facilities include drinking water, grills, picnic tables, phones, and restrooms; restaurants line the street across from the beach.

To get here from Downtown, take either Interstate 5 south or Highway 99 south to the West Seattle Bridge (keep an eye out, as this exit is easy to miss) and exit onto Harbor Avenue SW, turning right at the stoplight. Alki Point is the place where David Denny, John Low, and Lee Terry arrived in September 1851, ready to found a city. The Alki Point Lighthouse dates from 1913. One of 195 Lady Liberty replicas found around the country, Miss Liberty (or Little Liberty) lives near the 2700 block of Alki Avenue SW and is a popular meeting point for beachfront picnics and dates. ✉ *1702 Alki Ave. SW, West Seattle.*

The Museum of Flight

HISTORY MUSEUM | Boeing, the world's largest builder of aircrafts, was founded in Seattle in 1916. This facility at Boeing Field, between Downtown and Sea-Tac airport, houses one of the city's best museums, and it's especially fun for kids, who can climb in many of the aircraft and pretend to fly, make flight-related crafts, or attend special programs. The Red Barn, Boeing's original airplane factory, houses an exhibit on the history of flight. The Great Gallery, a dramatic structure designed by Ibsen Nelson, contains more than three dozen vintage airplanes. The Personal Courage Wing showcases World War I and World War II fighter planes, and the Charles Simonyi Space Gallery is home to the NASA Full Fuselage Space Shuttle Trainer. ✉ *9404 E. Marginal Way S* ✛ *Take I–5 south to Exit 158, turn right on Marginal Way S* ☎ *206/764–5700* ⊕ *www.museumofflight.org* ✉ *$25, free the first Thursday of the month.*

West Seattle Junction Murals

PUBLIC ART | Located in Seattle's business district are 11 murals depicting local history. Some are trompe-l'œils, like the realistic 1918 street scene, *The Junction*, which appears to vanish into the horizon. Another mural is taken from a postcard of 1920s Alki. The most colorful is *The Hi-Yu Parade*, with its rendition of a *Wizard of Oz*–theme float reminding locals of a 1973 summer celebration. In 2019, a new Mural Alley off the 4700 block of California Ave SW added five new murals

"The Junction" depicts Seattle in 1918 and is one of 10 notable murals in the area.

to the collection, and the original 11 underwent restoration between 2018 and 2020. ✉ *Along California Ave. SW and Fauntleroy Way SW, between 44th and 47th Aves., West Seattle.*

🍴 Restaurants

West Seattle is enough of a trek from Seattle's central neighborhoods that some restaurants have, historically, had a hard time filling their seats. Luckily, West Seattleites love to eat out, and a new culinary energy is taking hold, giving even gourmands from Ballard reason to make the trek. The superstar here is Il Nido, but plenty of other neighborhood joints are top-notch and inviting—a walk down California Avenue will offer up plenty of choices.

Harry's Beach House
$$$ | **AMERICAN** | Harry's Beach House, where the breeze is always scented with saltwater, is a casual yet exciting restaurant that opened in an old coffee shop in 2019. Spacious, warmly lit, and friendly, it's the perfect place to enjoy a long brunch or a drink and a snack after a day on the beach. **Known for:** great decor; Harry's burger; excellent cocktails. [$] *Average main: $28* ✉ *2676 Alki Ave. SW, West Seattle* ☎ *206/513–6297* 🌐 *www.harrysbeachhouse.com.*

Il Nido
$$$$ | **ITALIAN** | Housed in a historic log cabin a block from Alki Beach, Il Nido (the nest) takes a playful look at Italian culinary traditions. House-made fresh pasta is the star, joined by creative focaccia breads, chicory salads, and entrées like pork coppa. **Known for:** house-made pasta; seasonal local ingredients; Italian drinks and snacks. [$] *Average main: $50* ✉ *2717 61st Ave. SW, West Seattle* ☎ *206/466–6265* 🌐 *www.ilnidoseattle.com* 🕒 *Closed Sun.-Mon. No lunch.*

★ Marination Ma Kai
$ | **HAWAIIAN** | The best view of Downtown comes at an affordable price: the brightly colored Adirondack chairs outside this Korean-Hawaiian fish shack offer a panoramic view of the entire

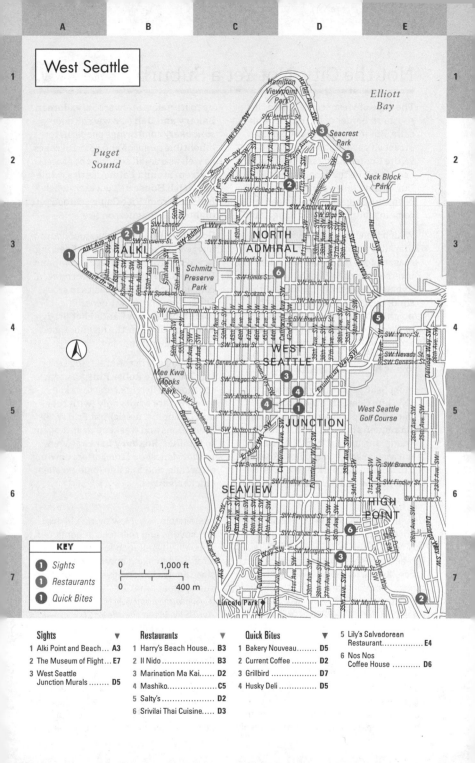

West Seattle

Puget Sound

Elliott Bay

Hamilton Viewpoint Park

Seacrest Park

Jack Block Park

ALKI

NORTH ADMIRAL

Schmitz Preserve Park

WEST SEATTLE

Mee Kwa Mooks Park

West Seattle Golf Course

JUNCTION

SEAVIEW

HIGH POINT

Lincoln Park

KEY

- **1** Sights
- **1** Restaurants
- **1** Quick Bites

| 0 | 1,000 ft |
| 0 | 400 m |

Not the City, Not Yet a Suburb 🍴

The edge of West Seattle is also the southern border of the city, technically. But just across SW Roxbury Street sits a neighborhood called White Center. Addresses read as Seattle, while the schools belong to Burien, and failed annexations by both those adjacent cities mean it remains unincorporated King County.

Which is neither here nor there (quite literally) when it comes to the many reasons for visiting White Center. The intersection of SW Roxbury and 16th Avenue SW anchors the area, with small businesses representing the neighborhood's diverse population packed in along both streets and those around it. It's only about 10 minutes' drive from the Fauntleroy Ferry Dock and 15 from Sea-Tac airport.

Most Seattleites make their way to White Center for the food and imported food shopping. **La Tipica Oaxaqueña** imports food, crafts, home goods, and mezcal from the owners' native Oaxaca, and the **Best Roasted Corn** stand in a parking lot at 15th Avenue SW and SW 98th Street lives up to its name. Stalwart **Salvadorean Bakery and Deli** (🌐 *www.salvadoreanbakery.com*) brings people in for lunchtime *pupusas* and colorful cakes, as well as a small selection of groceries from around Latin America, while **Crawfish House's** (🌐 *www.crawfishhouse206.com*) Viet-Cajun seafood sets nights (and tongues) on fire.

Good Day Donuts (🌐 *www.gooddaydonuts.com*), **Future Primitive Brewing** (🌐 *www.futureprimitivebeer.com*), and **Dubsea Coffee** (*www.dubseacoffee.com*) keep the Seattle basics in stock, while **Tomo** (🌐 *www.tomoseattle.com*), from former Canlis chef Brady Williams, brought the neighborhood its first fine-dining spot.

While you are in the area, stop by the **Southgate Roller Rink** (🌐 *www.southgaterollerrink.com*) for a spin; evenings are adults only (with beer and DJs or live music), but Friday afternoons and weekend days it opens to families. **Roxbury Lanes** (🌐 *www.roxburylanesbowl.com*) offers bowling, an arcade, and a casino (plus excellent chicken wings).

Downtown area. Inside, you'll find tacos filled with Korean beef or "sexy tofu," Spam slider sandwiches, and a classic fish-and-chips—served with kimchi tartar sauce. **Known for:** epic views; Spam sliders; Hawaiian shave ice. [$] *Average main: $12* ✉ *1660 Harbor Ave. SW, West Seattle* ☎ *206/328–8226* 🌐 *www.marinationmobile.com.*

★ Mashiko

$$ | **SUSHI** | Though it opened in 1994 as a typical neighborhood sushi joint, Mashiko quickly gained a reputation as one of the top spots in town for fresh fish, even before the then-owner turned it into the first sushi restaurant to commit to solely sustainable fish. Now owned by his employees and mentees, it continues to uphold its reputation for both quality and a forward-thinking approach to the cuisine. **Known for:** creative spins on classic sushi; great omakase; sustainable sushi. [$] *Average main: $24* ✉ *4725 California Ave. SW, West Seattle* ☎ *206/935–4339* 🌐 *www.mashikorestaurant.com* 🕒 *Closed Tues. No lunch.*

Salty's

$$$$ | **SEAFOOD** | It's undeniably touristy, but the views simply can't be beat on a summer afternoon. Famed for its Sunday and holiday brunches and view of Seattle's skyline across the harbor, Salty's offers more in the way of quantity than quality—and sometimes a bit too much of its namesake ingredient—but it's a couple of steps up from the mainstream seafood chains. **Known for:** patio dining; panoramic views; weekend brunch. $ *Average main: $50 ⊠ 1936 Harbor Ave. SW, just past port complex, West Seattle* ☎ *206/937–1600* ⊕ *www.saltys.com.*

Srivilai Thai Cuisine

$ | **THAI** | One of Seattle's top Thai restaurants (in a crowded field), Srivilai quietly proffers an excellent slate of standards. Friendly, accommodating service in a spare but elegant space combined with a moderately heavy hand with flavors and spices make it a local favorite. **Known for:** good drinks lists; friendly service; flavorful Thai cuisine. $ *Average main: $15* ⊠ *3247 California Ave. SW, West Seattle* ☎ *206/257–5171* ⊕ *www.srivilaithai.com.*

☕ Coffee and Quick Bites

Bakery Nouveau

$ | **CAFÉ** | Widely considered one of the best bakeries in the city, Bakery Nouveau has perfected many things, including cakes, croissants, and tarts. Their chocolate cake, in particular, might make you swoon, though twice-baked almond croissants are so good you might think you're in France when you take a bite—and owner William Leaman did lead a U.S. team to victory in France's Coupe du Monde de la Boulangerie. **Known for:** flaky croissants; delicious chocolate cake; great savory options for lunch. $ *Average main: $7* ⊠ *4737 California Ave. SW, West Seattle* ☎ *206/923–0534* ⊕ *www.bakerynouveau.com* ⊗ *Closed Mon.–Tues.*

Current Coffee

$ | **CAFÉ** | Cheerful two-tone drawings on the walls and blue tile on the counter both evoke the nearby waves that lap at Alki Beach in this multi-roaster cafe, demonstrating its effort to embody the spirit of the neighborhood. Between brewing coffee from local favorites Boon Boona, Dorothea, and Olympia, and serving pastries from Seawolf Bread, this spot brings together some of the city's best, while the view from the dark wood tables in the loft make it a great place to watch the rhythm of life in North Admiral. **Known for:** Seawolf pastries; favorite local coffee beans; subtle nautical ambience. $ *Average main: $6* ⊠ *2206B California Ave. SW, West Seattle* ⊕ *www.current-coffee.cafe* ⊗ *Closed Mon.–Tues.*

Grillbird

$ | **ASIAN** | In a time when many of the corner-store style shops serving Seattle's unique signature teriyaki are fading into the rapidly modernizing city, Grillbird keeps it classic as it hopes to show that the affordable plates of chicken in sauce, rice, and salad, still matter to the city. Stop by for a quick lunch and for a taste of the city's typical workday lunch dish. **Known for:** simple meals; quick lunch; Seattle-style teriyaki. $ *Average main: $14* ⊠ *6501 35th Ave. SW, West Seattle* ☎ *206/402–4388* ⊕ *www.grillbird.com.*

Husky Deli

$ | **ICE CREAM** | Grab a handcrafted ice-cream cone at Husky Deli, a Seattle icon. This grocery store opened in 1932 and retains its old-fashioned feel. **Known for:** family ownership; classic ice-cream shop feel; long list of flavors. $ *Average main: $7* ⊠ *4721 California Ave. SW, West Seattle* ☎ *206/937–2810* ⊕ *www.huskydeli. com* ▭ *No credit cards.*

Lily's Salvadorean Restaurant

$ | **LATIN AMERICAN** | This longtime farmers' market favorite finally settled into a restaurant in 2022, planting roots and putting out pupusas from a large space just under the West Seattle Bridge. The Salvadoran-style griddled corn cakes come stuffed with beans, cheese, pork, peppers, cheese, or some combination of those, and are served from breakfast through dinner. **Known for:** family atmosphere; Salvadorean horchatas; big breakfasts. $ *Average main: $15* ✉ *2940 SW Avalon Way, West Seattle* ☎ *206/397–3429* ⊕ *www.lilyssalvadoreanrestaurant.com* ☞ *Breakfast on weekends only.*

Nos Nos Coffee House

$ | **CAFÉ** | The flavors of Morocco come together with the Seattle coffee scene at this small High Point café. The white walls ringed at the top by a shelf of plants give it a lush, green feeling, shared by the spiced coffees and mint teas (though the menu also includes all the espresso and drip standards). **Known for:** good picnic options; plant-crowned space; Moroccan spiced beverages. $ *Average main: $8* ✉ *6080 35th Ave. SW, West Seattle* ⊕ *www.nosnoscoffee.com.*

Nightlife

Despite the party atmosphere of Alki Beach, the best scene in the evening moves up the hill to various points along California Ave SW. A devotion to local beers, wine, ciders, and spirits runs through the neighborhood's mostly small, independent bars. Removed from the rest of the city by bridge, residents tend to stick close to home, so chat up your neighbor at the bar and you're likely to get an insider's view of the area.

BARS AND LOUNGES

New Luck Toy

BARS | In the skeleton of a classic Chinese-American dive bar, chef Mark Fuller created his own spin on the genre. Under the low lights and a ceiling of red lanterns, bartenders serve pink guava palomas and passion fruit caipirinhas. There's Skee-ball, karaoke, and pinball, and a menu with twists on General Tso's chicken and honey pecan prawns. ✉ *5905 California Ave. SW, West Seattle* ⊕ *www.newlucktoy.bar* ⊘ *Closed Mon.–Tues.*

The Nook

COCKTAIL LOUNGES | This Admiral cocktail bar in a cozy old home leans into that living room feeling with wingback chairs, mid-century couches, and antique lighting. It's a little like drinking in your own house, if you lived in a fancy old mansion with bartenders who turn out intriguing craft cocktails. Not far from Alki, it makes a great post-beach stop if you need to wait out rush hour before heading back Downtown. ✉ *2206 California Ave. SW., West Seattle* ☎ *206/420–7414* ⊕ *www.thenookseattle.com* ⊘ *Closed Mon.*

Ounces Taproom & Beer Garden

BEER GARDENS | **FAMILY** | Though it offers all the trappings of a typical Seattle brewery, in that it's dog-friendly, all ages, and has a rotating selection of food trucks parked in front, this partially covered outdoor beer garden doesn't make its own brews. Instead, the 30 taps at Ounces offer a variety of beers and ciders made by folks all over Washington State, making it an awesome opportunity to try drinks from different regional breweries. ✉ *3809 Delridge Way SW, West Seattle* ⊕ *www.ounceswestseattle.com.*

👜 Shopping

For blocks and blocks along California Avenue SW around the Junction, independent, family-owned shops thrive, and boutiques sell quirky goods. If you're stopping for lunch nearby, definitely plan a postprandial stroll through the business district to do a little window shopping and maybe pick up a souvenir or two.

Alair Gift Shop

SOUVENIRS | Whether you need to bring home an ironic "West Seattle Island" shirt or vintage-style Pacific Northwest hoodie, this cute neighborhood gift shop and boutique has one-of-a-kind clothes to help you remember your visit to Seattle. The rest of the shop is filled with stylish gifts for kids and adults, plenty of cards, and fun locally made products such as bath salts, candles, mugs, and more. ✉ 3270 California Ave. SW, West Seattle ☎ 206/659-7152 For texting, 206/257-1219 For talking ⊕ www.alairseattle.com ⏱ Closed Mon.–Tues.

Alki Surf Shop

SWIMWEAR | Alki Beach gives off SoCal vibes, but the one thing it lacks is surfable waves. Still, that doesn't stop this surf shop from selling everything else you might need for a day on the beaches of L.A. or West Seattle. Beach gear, swimsuits, and sunglasses will keep everyone ready for hanging out in the sand, while the Island-style clothes, accessories, and gifts will make you feel like you might be somewhere warmer or with bigger waves. The merchandise makes a good souvenir (and conversation starter), especially the fleecy sweatshirts for when the sun inevitably goes down and the breeze blows in off the cool water. ✉ 2622 Alki Ave. SW, West Seattle ☎ 206/403–1901 ⊕ www.alkisurfshop. com ⏱ Closed Mon.–Thurs.

Easy Street Records

MUSIC | Opened in 1988 and still thriving, this record store will make you feel cool enough to wander the aisles and browse the new and used vinyl, even if you've never dropped a needle in your life. A staple of Seattle's music scene, it hosts free in-store performances by bands you've probably heard of (Pearl Jam has played here), along with selling records, CDs, cassettes, and DVDs. Listening stations let you preview albums before purchasing, and the attached café offers the kind of breakfast you'd want after a night of rocking out. ✉ 4559 California Ave. SW, West Seattle ☎ 206/938–3279 ⊕ www. easystreetonline.com.

🏃 Activities

GOLF

West Seattle Golf Course

GOLF | This 18-hole course has a reputation for being tough but fair—and for some excellent views of Downtown. Greens fees are around $40 on weekdays and $45 on weekends but are dynamic, depending on demand. The varied course starts out flat but gets into some hills on the back nine, where it rewards players with views of Elliott Bay and the skyline. ✉ 4600 35th Ave. SW, West Seattle ☎ 206/935–5187 ⊕ www. premiergc.com/-west-seattle-golf-course ⛳ From $40; $36 for golf cart; $20 for standard club rentals. 🏌 18 holes, 6805 yards, par /2.

ROCK CLIMBING

Schurman Rock

ROCK CLIMBING | The nation's first man-made climbing rock was designed in the 1930s by local climbing expert Clark Schurman. Generations of climbers have practiced here, from beginners to rescue teams to such legendary mountaineers as Jim Whittaker, the first American to conquer Mt. Everest. Don't expect something grandiose—the rock is only 25 feet high. It's open for climbs Tuesday–Saturday 10–6. Camp Long (where the park is located) also rents cabins March–October. ⊠ *Camp Long, 5200 35th Ave. SW, West Seattle* ☎ *206/684–7434* ⊕ *www.seattle.gov/parks/find/centers/ camp-long/schurman-rock-at-camp-long.*

TOURS

Alki Kayak Tours & Adventure Center

BOATING | For a variety of daylong guided kayak outings—from a Seattle sunset sea kayak tour to an Alki Point lighthouse tour—led by experienced, fun staff, try this great outfitter in West Seattle. In addition to kayaks, you can also rent stand-up paddleboards and longboards, but you need to have your own transportation with straps and vehicle for the first two (reservations required). To rent a kayak without a guide, you must be an experienced kayaker; otherwise, sign up for one of the fascinating guided outings (the popular sunset tour is $89 per person). ⊠ *1660 Harbor Ave. SW, West Seattle* ☎ *206/953–0237* ⊕ *www. kayakalki.com.*

Chapter 14

THE EASTSIDE

Updated by
Naomi Tomky

Sights	Restaurants	Hotels	Shopping	Nightlife
★★☆☆☆	★★★☆☆	★★★☆☆	★★★★☆	★★☆☆☆

NEIGHBORHOOD SNAPSHOT

TOP REASONS TO GO

■ Visit the **Bellevue Botanical Gardens,** a 36-acre park with colorful gardens and trails.

■ Splurge at the **Shops at the Bravern** in Bellevue. The city has many malls, but the Bravern is the ritziest—one-stop shopping for major international labels like Prada, Moncler, and Hermès.

■ Sample Northwest wines in **Woodinville.** The town has more than 130 wineries, wine bars, and tasting rooms, most within easy reach of each other.

■ **Eat your way through the Eastside**: while Bellevue's fine-dining scene falls flat, the suburbs brim with carefully crafted Chinese dumplings and aromatic Indian cuisine.

GETTING HERE AND AROUND

Buses run to the Eastside, and Link light rails should open here in 2024, but if you have more than one stop or want to explore outside the central neighborhoods, drive over one of the bridges. The 520 floating bridge is a toll road and rush-hour traffic is a nightmare, but if you are going anywhere north (such as Kirkland or Woodinville) it is necessary. I–90 tends to be faster otherwise.

Bellevue has a bus hub that's within walking distance of the art museum. The most direct bus route to central Bellevue is route 550. RapidRide B connects Bellevue, Kirkland, and Redmond. Link light rail, scheduled to open in 2024, will serve a number of stops in Bellevue, then continue on to the Microsoft Campus area of Redmond. Downtown Redmond's station is scheduled to open in 2025. (Note that bus routes tend to change drastically when the light rail stations open.)

PAUSE HERE

■ If you hit the "drop" part of shop-'til-you-drop at Bellevue's many malls, find a reprieve in Downtown Park. A walking path rings the twenty acres of green space, which includes a canal leading to a waterfall, a garden, public art, free wi-fi, and more than 140 benches for resting those tired tootsies.

PLANNING YOUR TIME

■ The Eastside doesn't hold enough attractions to be worth planning a full trip around; it's best for targeted excursions, like a shopping and museum visit to Bellevue or a winery or brewery crawl in Woodinville.

■ Hotels in the area generally aren't a great choice for Seattle visitors—the commute into the city is toll and traffic heavy, and the area can be pricey—but there are options if you have reason to be here. Skip the traffic and play in the pool at the Anderson School, or have a romantic night at Willows Lodge after touring Woodinville's wineries.

The suburbs east of Lake Washington can easily supplement any Seattle itinerary. The center of East King County is Bellevue, which has its own downtown core, high-end shopping, and a strong art museum. Kirkland, north of Bellevue, has a few shops and an increasingly notable restaurant scene (including fabulous Café Juanita) plus lakefront promenades.

Kirkland's business district, along the Lake Street waterfront, is lined with shops, restaurants, pubs, and parks. At the height of summer, it's often warm enough to swim in the sheltered waters of Lake Washington; Juanita Beach Park is a popular spot with an enclosed swimming area.

Redmond and Issaquah, to the northeast and southeast respectively, are gateways to greenery. A string of pretty parks makes Redmond an inviting place to experience the outdoors, and the 11-mile Sammamish River Trail is an attraction for locals and tourists alike. The rapidly expanding city is today one of the country's most powerful business capitals, thanks to the presence of such companies as Microsoft, Nintendo, and Eddie Bauer.

Issaquah is experiencing rapid (and not terribly attractive) development, but it's what lies beyond the subdivisions that counts. The surrounding Cougar, Tiger, and Squak mountain foothills—dubbed the Issaquah Alps—are older than the Cascade Range and pocketed with caves, parks, and trails. This area has some of the most accessible hiking and mountain biking in the Seattle area; Seattleites often use these trails to train on in early spring before the more arduous trails in the Cascades and Olympics open for hiking season.

Woodinville, north of Redmond, is the ambassador for Washington State's wine industry, with many wineries and tasting rooms, as well as a growing number of breweries and distilleries. Once the Eastside's most popular day trip, it increasingly offers excellent overnight options, making tasting through the Chateau Ste. Michelle and dozens of other wineries a little more relaxing.

 Sights

Bellevue Arts Museum

ART MUSEUM | A real feather in Bellevue's cap, this museum presents sophisticated exhibits on craft and design, with a focus on regional artists. Past exhibitions have included *High Fiber Diet*—focusing on underexposed media in contemporary art—and *Modern Twist: Contemporary Japanese Bamboo Art*. The dramatic puzzle-piece-looking building, which stands out in Bellevue's somewhat uninspired downtown core, is worth the trip alone.

In late July, the museum hosts the BAM ARTSfair, a prestigious, high-end street festival. Workshops for kids, teens, and adults are also offered regularly. ✉ *510 Bellevue Way NE, Bellevue* ☎ *425/519–0770* ⊕ *www.bellevuearts.org* 🎟 *$15* ⊗ *Closed Mon.–Tues.*

Bellevue Botanical Gardens

GARDEN | This beautiful 53-acre public area just a short drive from downtown Bellevue is encircled by spectacular perennial borders, brilliant rhododendron displays, and patches of alpine and rock gardens. The Ravine Experience encompasses a five-acre area in the heavily forested southwest corner of the gardens with a ⅓-mile nature trail. A 150-foot suspension bridge crosses a deep ravine in one of the most pristine spaces, allowing visitors to observe unique topography and soaring conifers without disturbing the forest floor.

Docents lead tours of the gardens Saturdays and Sundays (April–October), beginning at the visitor center at noon. The Yao Japanese garden is especially beautiful in fall. One of the most interesting features of the park is the Waterwise Garden, which was planted with greenery that needs little water in summer. During the holiday season, the gardens are lit up nightly for Garden d'Lights, one of the area's most popular seasonal attractions. ✉ *12001 Main St., Bellevue* ☎ *425/452–2750* ⊕ *www.bellevuebotanical.org.*

Burke-Gilman/Sammamish River Trail

TRAIL | FAMILY | Approximately 27 miles long, the paved, flat, tree-lined Burke-Gilman Trail runs from Seattle's Gas Works Park, on Lake Union, east along the ship canal, and then north along Lake Washington's eastern shore. At Blyth Park in Bothell, the trail becomes the Sammamish River Trail and continues for 10 miles to Marymoor Park in Redmond. Except for a stretch of the Sammamish River Trail where horses are permitted on a parallel trail, the path is limited to walkers, runners, and bicyclists.

■ TIP→ There are a handful of bike rental shops on Sand Point Way, just north of the University of Washington, an easy access point for the trail. For additional access points, view the map online at ⊕ *www.seattle.gov/transportation/burkegilmantrailmaps.htm.* ✉ *Seattle* ⊕ *www.seattle.gov/parks/find/parks/burke-gilman-trail.*

Houghton Beach Park

BEACH | On hot days, sun worshippers, swimmers, and the beach-volleyball crowd flock to this beach south of downtown Kirkland on the Lake Washington waterfront. The rest of the year, the playground attracts families, and the fishing pier stays busy with anglers. Facilities include drinking water, picnic tables, a beach volleyball court, phones, and restrooms. Perfect Wave offers stand-up paddleboard and kayak rentals at the north end of the park. Park the car and slip on some good walking shoes; it's a lovely stroll along the waterfront to the shops and restaurants of either Carillon Point or downtown Kirkland. ✉ *5811 Lake Washington Blvd., Kirkland* ☎ *425/587–3000* ⊕ *www.kirklandwa.gov/depart/parks.*

Jimi Hendrix Memorial

CEMETERY | Since his death in 1970, the famed guitarist has rested in Greenwood Cemetery, at first with just a simple tombstone. In 2002, the singer's remains moved to this much more elaborate tribute, with domed roof and granite columns. ✉ *350 Monroe Ave. NE, Renton* ⊕ *www.jimihendrixmemorial.com.*

Juanita Bay Park

WILDLIFE REFUGE | FAMILY | A 110-acre urban wildlife habitat, this marshy wetland is the perfect spot to don your binoculars to spot songbirds, shorebirds, turtles, beavers, and other small mammals. Interpretive signs are located throughout the park for self-guided tours along paved trails and boardwalks; or take one of the guided tours conducted by volunteer park rangers from the Eastside Audubon Society on the first Sunday each month.

250

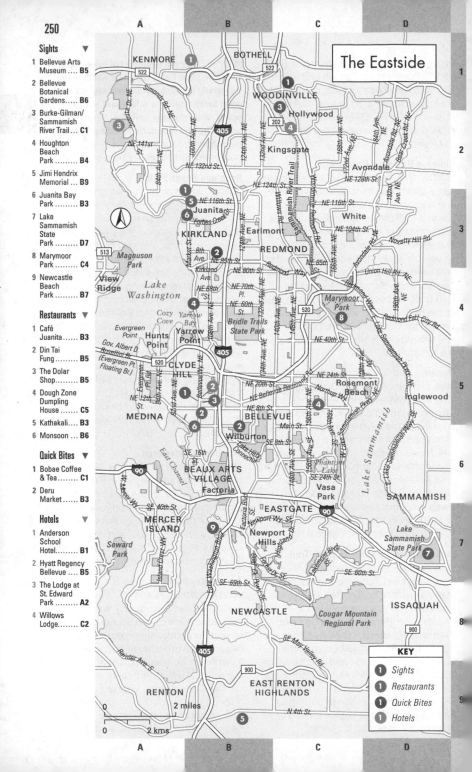

The Eastside

KEY
1 Sights
1 Restaurants
1 Quick Bites
1 Hotels

14

■TIP→ Just to the north of Juanita Bay Park is Juanita Beach Park, a great spot for picnicking, sunbathing, and swimming. On Friday nights, June through September, there's a farmers' market. ⊠ *2201 Market St.* ☎ *425/587–3300* ⊕ *www.kirklandwa. gov/depart/parks.*

Lake Sammamish State Park
STATE/PROVINCIAL PARK | FAMILY | Two sandy beaches anchor this 531-acre park, with plenty of picnic tables (bring your own basket or hit the concession stands), a playground, and seasonal kayak and paddleboard rentals. There are a few shady walking trails, which offer good bird-watching and wildlife viewing. If you head east, you can connect to the Sammamish River Trail and walk or bike all the way to Marymoor Park. ⊠ *2010 NW Sammamish Rd., Issaquah* ✛ *From I–90, drive east to Exit 15 and follow signs* ☎ *425/649–4275* ⊕ *www.lakesa-mmamishfriends.org* ▧ *Discover Pass required ($11.50/day or $35/yr).*

Marymoor Park
CITY PARK | FAMILY | It's not just famous for the Marymoor Velodrome, the Pacific Northwest's sole cycling arena. This 640-acre park also has a 35-foot-high climbing rock, game fields, tennis courts, a model airplane launching area, a huge off-leash dog park, and the Pea Patch community garden. You can row on Lake Sammamish or head straight to the picnic grounds or to the Willowmoor Farm, an estate inside the park. Evenings bring Cirque du Soleil shows, concerts by top bands, and drive-in movies.

Marymoor has some of the best bird-watching in this largely urban area. It's possible to spot some 24 resident species, including great blue herons, belted kingfishers, buffleheads, short-eared and barn owls, and red-tailed hawks. Occasionally, bald eagles soar past the lakefront. The Sammamish River, which flows through the western section of the park, is an important salmon spawning stream.

Ambitious bikers can follow the Burke-Gilman Sammamish River Trail to access the park; Marymoor is just over 20 miles from Seattle, and it's a flat ride most of the way. ⊠ *6046 W. Lake Sammamish Pkwy. NE* ✛ *Take Rte. 520 east to W. Lake Sammamish Pkwy. exit. Turn right (southbound) on W. Lake Sammamish Pkwy. NE. Turn left at traffic light.* ☎ *206/477–7275* ⊕ *www.king-county.gov/recreation/parks/inventory/marymoor.aspx* ☞ *For movie info: www. moviesatmarymoor.com, for concert info: www.marymoorconcerts.com.*

Newcastle Beach Park
BEACH | The biggest and most popular beach park in the Bellevue park system, this large park has a big swimming beach, seasonal lifeguards, a fishing dock, nature trails, restrooms, and a large grassy area with picnic tables. The playground is a favorite, thanks to a train that tots can sit in and older kids can climb on and hop from car to car. ⊠ *4400 Lake Washington Blvd. SE, off 112th SE exit from I–405, Bellevue* ☎ *425/452–6885* ⊕ *bellevuewa.gov/city-government/departments/parks/parks-and-trails/parks/newcastle-beach-park.*

🍴 Restaurants

Bellevue, Kirkland, and Woodinville are theoretically easy to get to from Downtown Seattle: the 520 (toll bridge) and I–90 bridges both are accessible from I–5. However, traffic is always an issue and grinds to a halt during rush hour. Don't plan a culinary expedition unless you already plan to visit this area—unless, of course, you have reservations at Café Juanita, a beloved and critically acclaimed restaurant that is more than worth the trek.

★ Café Juanita
$$$$ | ITALIAN | There are many ways for a pricey "destination restaurant" to go overboard, making itself nothing more than a special-occasion spectacle, but

Woodinville Wineries

The renowned Walla Walla wine country is too far from Seattle if you've only got a few days. Instead, check out Woodinville's excellent wineries, only about 22 miles from Seattle's city center. You'll need a car unless you sign up for a guided tour. Check out ⊕ *www.woodinvillewinecountry.com* for a full list of wineries and touring maps. Consider picking up a Passport to Woodinville Wine Country for $90 or one of the $55 select passes that gets you free tastings at participating wineries and tasting rooms (⊕ *woodinvillewinecountry.com/tasting-passes*). Alternatively, some Eastside hotel packages include wine tastings.

Wineries

There are more than 130 wineries in Woodinville, though not all have public tastings. This list includes some of the best-known, but make sure to seek out some of the smaller boutique wineries that match your personal tastes.

Chateau Ste. Michelle is the grande dame of the Woodinville wine scene. Guided tours of the winery and its historic grounds (which include a chateau) are available daily. Complimentary wine tastings run throughout the day. Specialty tours and tastings start at $15. In summer Chateau Ste. Michelle hosts nationally known performers and arts events in its amphitheater. ⊕ *www.ste-michelle.com*.

DeLille Cellars is on the wine list of nearly every fancy restaurant in Seattle and garners national acclaim for the predominantly Cab-Sauv blend Chaleur Estate. The elegant, modern tasting room is open daily, and in 2021, they opened a restaurant in an adjacent building. ⊕ *www.delillecellars.com*.

Mark Ryan is an indie winery that has earned praise nationwide for its use of mostly Red Mountain AVA grapes—especially for the Dead Horse reds. The winery has a small tasting room open daily. ⊕ *www.markryanwinery.com*.

Novelty Hill-Januik is often described as the most Napa-esque experience in Woodinville. The tasting room is sleek and modern (open daily, by appointment only) and brick-oven pizza is available on weekends. ⊕ *www.noveltyhilljanuik.com*.

Dining and Lodging

One of the swankiest hotels in the Puget Sound region, **Willows Lodge**, is only a few minutes away from the major wineries; the hotel's restaurant, **Barking Frog**, is also well-liked. For a more casual stay, **The Lodge at St. Edward Park** sits in a historic landmark on 326 forested acres and **The Anderson School** brings pools, live music, and fun to an overnight in a 1930s schoolhouse.

Chateau Ste. Michelle winery hosts dinners, tours, tastings, and concerts.

Café Juanita gets everything just right. This Kirkland space is refined without being overly posh, and the food—much of which has a northern Italian influence—is perfectly balanced. **Known for:** excellent use of seasonal ingredients; personal touches; tasting menus. $ *Average main: $190* ⊠ *9702 N.E. 120th Pl., Kirkland* ☎ *425/823–1505* ⊕ *www.cafejuanita.com* ⊘ *Closed Sun., Mon., and Thurs. No lunch.*

Din Tai Fung
$$ | CHINESE | Watch dumplings being pleated by hand through the large glass windows in the waiting area for this restaurant on the second floor of Lincoln Square mall—it's a good thing the sight is so entertaining, because there's often a long wait. The *xiao long bao*, or soup dumplings, are the famous attraction at Din Tai Fung, a U.S. branch of the famed Taipei-based chain. **Known for:** soup dumplings; long waits; visible dumpling-pleating process. $ *Average main: $17* ⊠ *700 Bellevue Way, #280, Bellevue* ⊹ *Inside*

Lincoln Square North ☎ *425/698–1095* ⊕ *www.dintaifungusa.com.*

The Dolar Shop
$$$$ | CHINESE | Luxury touches take the hot pot experience upscale with personal broth bowls, an extensive sauce buffet, and high-end ingredients like A5 Miyazaki beef, live prawns, and house-made noodles. This local outlet of a chain that began in Macau knows that you eat with your eyes first, and everything here comes out looking straight out of a glossy magazine photoshoot. **Known for:** personal broth pots; extensive sauce buffet; luxury ingredients. $ *Average main: $50* ⊠ *The Bravern, 11020 NE 6th St., Suite 90, Fastside* ☎ *425/390–8888* ⊕ *www.dolarshop.com.*

Dough Zone Dumpling House
$ | CHINESE | This home-grown chain that started in Bellevue lives up to its name, serving freshly made carb-filled delights of many types: noodles, flatbreads, crepes, and dumplings. The signature steamed juicy pork dumplings and fried jian buns, both filled with a meat and

soup filling, have earned it a reputation and helped it expand to locations around the city and along the entire West Coast. **Known for:** soup dumplings; quick service; big flavors. $ *Average main: $8* ✉ *10300 Main St., Bellevue* ☎ *425/454–3333* ⊕ *www.doughzonedumplinghouse.com.*

Kathakali

$$ | **INDIAN** | Come for the giant dosas, stay for the sweet service at this delightful South Indian restaurant tucked into a suburban strip mall. Rich colors adorn the walls and the plates, the latter in the form of vibrantly flavored chutneys, masalas, and curries. **Known for:** seafood curries; lots of vegetarian options; Keralan specialties. $ *Average main: $18* ✉ *11451 98th Ave. NE, Eastside* ☎ *425/821–8188* ⊕ *www.kathakali-juanita.com* ⊙ *Closed Mon.*

Monsoon

$$$ | **VIETNAMESE** | The Eastside sibling of Capitol Hill's darling Vietnamese eatery is utterly polished and sleek— much fancier than the original restaurant. But the favorites remain the same: diners love the bo la lot beef, crispy drunken chicken, catfish clay pot, and barbecued hoisin pork ribs, and all go impressively well with the specialty cocktails. **Known for:** upscale Vietnamese cuisine; seafood specials; drunken chicken. $ *Average main: $29* ✉ *10245 Main St., Bellevue* ☎ *425/635–1112* ⊕ *monsoonrestaurants. com/bellevue.*

☕ Coffee and Quick Bites

Bobae Coffee & Tea

$ | **ASIAN** | Bubble tea shops exist around the world, but this just might be the only "farm-to-straw" boba shop. The owners source their tea and the produce to make all their flavors directly from farms, and make all the boba in-house, too. **Known for:** quality tea sourcing; trendy boba drinks; monthly doughnuts specials. $ *Average main: $7* ✉ *14015*

NE Woodinville Duvall Rd, Eastside ☎ *425/818-3228* ⊕ *www.bobaeusa.com.*

★ Deru Market

$$ | **AMERICAN** | An organic café with everything you need for a picnic to-go or a leisurely lunch, Deru Market has something for everything. The bright, modern space starts the day with excellent coffee and pastries, with filling brunches on weekends. **Known for:** beautiful cakes; pretty interior; excellent vegetable dishes. $ *Average main: $18* ✉ *723 9th Ave, Kirkland* ☎ *425/298–0268* ⊕ *www. derumarket.com* ⊙ *Closed Mon.–Tues.* ☞ *The line can get long, but you can join it remotely from the restaurant's website.*

Hotels

Anderson School Hotel

$$ | **HOTEL** | **FAMILY** | A giant indoor pool is a rarity in the Pacific Northwest, making this spot in demand for that reason alone, but the proximity to Woodinville's wine country and location in the sweet lakeside suburb of Bothell are almost as compelling. **Pros:** enormous pool; unique art; multiple food and drink options. **Cons:** dated bathroom fixtures; dark hallways; little signage. $ *Rooms from: $240* ✉ *18607 Bothell Way NE, Eastside* ☎ *425/398–0122* ⊕ *www.mcmenamins. com/anderson-school* ⤸ *72 rooms* ⦿| *No Meals.*

Hyatt Regency Bellevue

$$$ | **HOTEL** | Near Bellevue Square and other downtown Bellevue shopping centers, the Hyatt looks like any other sleek high-rise but its interior is well-maintained and elegant with marble floors and a grand piano. **Pros:** free parking on weekends; great location in the heart of Bellevue; great staff. **Cons:** spotty housekeeping; confusing or missing signage; decor could use an update. $ *Rooms from: $340* ✉ *900 Bellevue Way NE, Bellevue* ☎ *425/462– 1234* ⊕ *www.hyatt.com/en-US/hotel/*

Marymoor Park has an outdoor concert series in the summer.

washington/hyatt-regency-bellevue-on-seattles-eastside/belle 🛏 *732 rooms* 🍴 *No Meals.*

The Lodge at St. Edward Park

$$ | **HOTEL** | This restored historic seminary overlooks 326 acres of beautiful parkland, making it an incredible place to relax and take in the lush greenery of the Pacific Northwest. **Pros:** easy access to hiking, biking, and park; beautiful architectural details with modern amenities; free drinks, snacks, and games. **Cons:** dining options can be slow; sound carries in old building; small rooms. [$] *Rooms from: $246* ✉ *14477 Juanita Dr. NE, Eastside* ☎ *425/470–6500* 🌐 *www.thelodgeatstedward.com* 🛏 *84 rooms* 🍴 *No Meals.*

★ **Willows Lodge**

$$$$ | **HOTEL** | Timbers salvaged from a 19th-century warehouse are rustic counterpoints to sleek, modern design of this elegant spa hotel in the heart of Woodinville wine country. **Pros:** great wine people; lovely spa; impeccable service. **Cons:** not really for families; far from Downtown; rooms a bit dark. [$] *Rooms from: $369* ✉ *14580 NE 145th St.* ☎ *425/424–3900* 🌐 *www.willowslodge.com* 🛏 *84 rooms* 🍴 *No Meals.*

Shopping

The core of Bellevue's growing shopping district is the Bellevue Collection (Bellevue Square Mall, Lincoln Center, and Bellevue Place) and the sparkling upscale mall called the Bravern. The community's retail strip stretches from Bellevue Square between NE 4th and 8th Streets to the community-centered Crossroads Shopping Center several miles to the east.

TIP→ Find the best shopping at Bellevue Square and The Shops at the Bravern.

The Bellevue Collection

MALL | **FAMILY** | In this impressive trifecta of shopping centers, you'll find just about any chain store you've heard of (and some that you haven't). Bellevue Square's wide walkways and benches, its many children's clothing stores, kid's hair salon, and first-floor play area make this a great place for little ones, too. A variety of local restaurant groups and national chains serve quick, good casual food, and you can park for free in the attached garage. Take the sky bridge to Lincoln Center to catch a flick at their 16-screen cinema, organize your life at the Container Store, or sample an assortment of other retail outlets. Eat at one of the several high-end restaurants, the famous Din Tai Fung, or the upscale food court. Bellevue Place, across from Lincoln Center, hosts a variety of stores and a Fonte Coffee Roaster. ⊠ *Bellevue Way, 575 Bellevue Sq., Bellevue* ☎ *425/454–8096* ⊕ *www. bellevuecollection.com.*

The Shops at the Bravern

MALL | If you have some serious cash to burn, the sleek, upscale Bravern might be the Eastside spot for you. With high-end shops like Moncler, Hermès, Prada, Gucci, and Louis Vuitton, it's tempting to empty your wallet—but save room for a spa treatment at the Gene Juarez Salon & Spa or a meal at luxury Chinese hot-pot spot the Dolar Shop. Valet and complimentary parking (with validation) are available. ⊠ *11111 NE 8th St., Bellevue* ☎ *425/456–8780* ⊕ *www.thebravern. com.*

Activities

The Golf Club at Newcastle

GOLF | Probably the best option on the Eastside, this golf complex, which includes a pair of courses and an 18-hole putting green, has views, views, and more views. From the hilly greens you'll see Seattle, the Olympic Mountains, and Lake Washington. The 7,000-yard, par-72 Coal Creek course is the more challenging of the two, though the China Creek course has its challenges and more sections of undisturbed natural areas. This is the Seattle area's most expensive golf club—dynamic greens fees for Coal Creek range from $150 to $215 depending on the season; fees for China Creek range from $115 to $160. Newcastle is about 35 minutes from Downtown—if you don't hit traffic. ⊠ *15500 Six Penny La., Newcastle, Seattle* ☎ *425/793–5566* ⊕ *www.newcastlegolf.com.*

Chapter 15

SIDE TRIPS
FROM SEATTLE

Updated by
AnnaMaria Stephens

👁 Sights	🍴 Restaurants	🛏 Hotels	🛍 Shopping	🍸 Nightlife
★★★★★	★★★★★	★★★☆☆	★★☆☆☆	★★☆☆☆

WELCOME TO SIDE TRIPS FROM SEATTLE

TOP REASONS TO GO

★ **Idyllic surrounds.** Experience peace and quiet for a day or overnight away from the city, and appreciate just how majestic the islands outside Seattle can be.

★ **Incredible seafood.** Top-notch oysters and mussels paired with equally delicious wine make for an unforgettable dining experience.

★ **Outdoor adventure.** From hiking to kayaking to cycling to camping, Washington offers plenty of ways to keep you moving.

From the stunning National Parks to the jaw-dropping islands just a ferry's distance from the city, whichever trip you choose to take from Seattle, you'll be amazed at the scenery and wilderness that are immediately evident upon exiting the city. As you leave the city by ferry, the gorgeous Seattle skyline starts to fade as you get closer to the craggy, forested islands. As you drive toward your destination, whether into the Cascade National Park or toward Mt. Rainier, you'll encounter huge evergreen trees surrounding the road.

1 **Puget Sound Islands.** A highly popular destination for day-trips, the Puget Sound Islands include the well known Bainbridge, Vashon, and Whidbey. All are unique with their own character.

2 **San Juan Islands.** The waters of the Pacific Northwest's Salish Sea, between mainland Washington and Vancouver Island, contain hundreds of islands, some little more than rocky reefs, others rising to nearly 2,500 feet. Among these, the San Juans are considered by many to be the loveliest.

3 **Mt. Rainier National Park.** Mt. Rainier is the mountain scene in the distance of every quintessential Seattle panorama. The mountain holds the largest glacial system in the contiguous United States, with more than two dozen major glaciers.

4 **Olympic National Park.** A spellbinding setting is tucked into the country's far northwestern corner, within the heart-shape Olympic Peninsula.

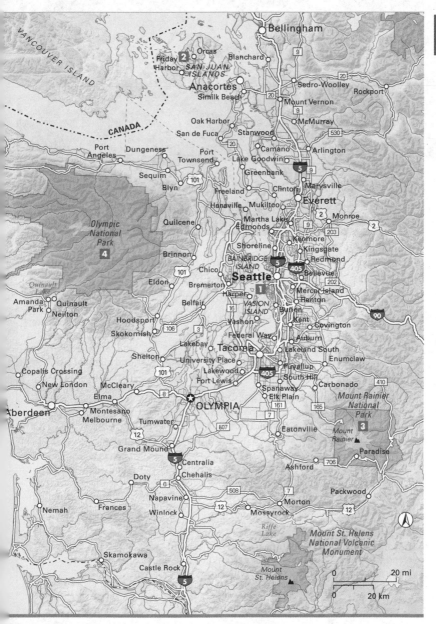

MT. ST. HELENS

One of the most prominent peaks in the Northwest's rugged Cascade Range, Mt. St. Helens National Volcanic Monument affords visitors an up-close look at the site of the most destructive volcanic blast in U.S. history.

Just 55 miles northeast of Portland and 155 miles southeast of Seattle, this once soaring, conical summit stood at 9,667 feet above sea level. Then, on May 18, 1980, a massive eruption launched a 36,000-foot plume of steam and ash into the air and sent nearly 4 million cubic yards of debris through the Toutle and Cowlitz river valleys. The devastating eruption leveled a 230-square-mile area, claiming 57 lives and more than 250 homes. The mountain now stands at 8,365 feet, and a horseshoe-shape crater—most visible from the north—now forms the scarred summit. A modern, scenic highway carries travelers to within about five miles of the summit, and the surrounding region offers thrilling opportunities for climbing, hiking, and learning about volcanology.

BEST TIME TO GO

It's best to visit from mid-May through late October, as the last section of Spirit Lake Highway, Johnston Ridge Observatory, and many of the park's forest roads are closed the rest of the year. The other visitor centers along the lower sections of the highway are open year-round, but overcast skies typically obscure the mountain's summit in winter.

PARK HIGHLIGHTS

Ape Cave. Measuring nearly 2½ miles in mapped length, Ape Cave is the longest continuous lava tube in the continental United States. Two routes traverse the tube: the lower route is an easy hour-long hike, while the upper route is more challenging and takes about three hours. Bring at least two light sources (you can rent lanterns from the headquarters for $5 in summer) and warm clothing. In high season ranger-led walks are sometimes available; inquire at the Apes' Headquarters (☎ 360/449–7800), off Forest Service Road 8303, three miles north of the junction of Forest Roads 83 and 90. Although Ape Cave is open year-round, the headquarters closes November through April. A Northwest Forest Pass ($5 daily) is required for parking (or a Sno-Park permit during winter). ⊠ *Cougar* ☎ *360/449–7800* ⊕ *www. fs.usda.gov/giffordpinchot.*

Johnston Ridge Observatory. The visitor center closest to the summit is named for scientist David Johnston, who died in the mountain's immense lateral blast. Inside are fascinating exhibits on the mountain's geology, instruments measuring volcanic and seismic activity, and a theater that shows a riveting film recounting the 1980 eruption. Several short trails afford spectacular views of the summit. ⊠ *2400 Spirit Lake Hwy., Toutle* ☎ *360/274–2140* ⊕ *www.fs.usda.gov/giffordpinchot* ⊠ *$8 parking* ⊘ *Closed mid-May–early Nov.*

Spirit Lake Highway. Officially known as Highway 504, this winding road rises 4,000 feet from the town of Castle Rock (just off I–5, Exit 49) to within about five miles of the Mt. St. Helens summit. Several visitor centers explain the region's geology and geography, and several turnouts afford views of the destruction wrought upon the Toutle and Cowlitz river valleys. ⊠ *Castle Rock.*

STAY THE NIGHT

The Kelso-Longview area, about 10 to 15 miles south of the start of Spirit Lake Highway, has several chain hotels. You'll also find a wide selection of lodgings in Vancouver.

Fire Mountain Grill. For good burgers, sandwiches, beer, and a memorable setting, drop by this rustic roadhouse with a veranda overlooking the North Fork Toutle River. Save room for the signature mountain berry cobbler. **Known for:** scenic river views; tasty desserts; comfort food. ⊠ 9440 *Spirit Lake Hwy., Toutle* ☎ *360/274–5217* ⊘ *Closed late Nov.–Mar. No dinner.*

McMenamins Kalama Harbor Lodge. This 11-room lodge overlooking the Columbia River is part of the funky McMenamins hotel and tavern chain. **Pros:** good base for Mt. St. Helens; pleasant views of the Columbia River; on-site food and drinks options. **Cons:** noise from passing trains; small bathrooms; food quality is uneven. ⊠ *215 N. Hendrickson Dr.* ☎ *360/673–6970* ⊕ *www. mcmenamins.com/ kalama-harbor-lodge* ⊶ *11 rooms* ⦿ *No Meals.*

The beauty of Seattle is enough to wow most visitors, but it can't compare to the splendor of the state that surrounds it. You simply must put aside a day or two to venture out to one of the islands of Puget Sound or do a hike or scenic drive in one of the spectacular mountain ranges a few hours outside the city.

If you head west to Olympic National Park, north to North Cascades National Park, or east to the Cascade Range, you can hike, bike, or ski. Two and a half hours southeast of Seattle is majestic Mt. Rainier, the fifth-highest mountain in the contiguous United States. Two hours beyond Rainier, close to the Oregon border, is the Mt. St. Helens National Volcanic Monument. The state-of-the-art visitor centers here show breathtaking views of the crater and lava dome and the spectacular recovery of the areas surrounding the 1980 blast.

You can get a taste of island life on Bainbridge, Whidbey, or Vashon—all easily accessible for day trips—or settle in for a few days on one of the San Juan Islands, where you can hike, kayak, or spot migrating whales and resident sea lions or otters.

The Puget Sound Islands

The islands of Puget Sound—particularly Bainbridge, Vashon, and Whidbey—are easy and popular day trips for Seattle visitors, and riding the Washington State ferries is half the fun. There are a few classic inns and B&Bs in the historic towns of Langley and Coupeville if you

want to spend the night. It's definitely worth planning your trip around meal-times because the islands of Puget Sound have top-notch restaurants serving local foods—including locally grown produce, seafood, and even island-raised beef. On Vashon Island, Earthen is at the top of the locavore pack; Bainbridge, Whidbey, and the San Juans also have a myriad of small farms and charming restaurants worth a visit. Seafood, of course, is a big draw. Local crab, salmon, and shellfish should be on your not-to-miss list, including the world-renowned Penn Cove mussels from Whidbey Island.

Whidbey Island has the most spectacular natural attractions, but it requires the biggest time commitment to get to (it's 30 miles northwest of Seattle). Bainbridge is the most developed island—it's something of a moneyed bedroom community—with higher-end restaurants and shops supplementing its natural attractions. It's also the easiest to get to—just hop on a ferry from Pier 52 on the Downtown Seattle waterfront. Vashon is the most pastoral of the islands—if you don't like leisurely strolls, beachcombing, or bike rides, you might get bored there quickly. Bainbridge and Whidbey get tons of visitors in summer. Though you'll be able to snag a walk-on spot

Where to See Whales

The Salish Sea—which includes the Puget Sound and Straits of Georgia and Juan de Fuca—is teeming with incredibly diverse marine life. The area has even been called the American Serengeti. Seeing whales up close makes for a spectacular, memorable experience, from the huge migrating humpbacks with their powerful blows and tail slaps to the area's playful resident orca pods. The orcas, which face critical challenges from climate change, have an important role in the Pacific Northwest identity; many coastal Indigenous people consider them the guardians of the sea and honor them in their culture and artwork.

With a good pair of binoculars, you can see whales from the shore in a few spots, including Lime Kiln Park on San Juan Island, but your best bet is to get out on the water. You'll find many tour options throughout the Puget Sound and San Juan Islands; most start at around $100 and they typically offer guarantees—if you don't see any whales, you can return for free. If you don't have enough time to explore the islands during your visit to Seattle, consider taking a half-day tour out of Edmonds—just north of Seattle—on the Puget Sound Express, which zips over to prime whale-watching spots near the San Juan Islands on a boat.

on the ferry, spaces for cars can fill up, so arrive early. Whidbey is big, so you'll most likely want to tour by car (you can actually drive there, too, as the north end of the island is accessible via Deception Pass), and a car is handy on Bainbridge as well, especially if you want to tour the entire island or visit spectacular Bloedel Reserve. Otherwise, Bainbridge is your best bet if you want to walk on the ferry and tour by foot.

Bainbridge Island

35 mins west of Seattle by ferry.

Of the three main islands in Puget Sound, Bainbridge has by far the largest population of Seattle commuters. Certain parts of the island are dense enough to have rush-hour traffic problems, while other areas retain a semirural, small-town vibe. Longtime residents work hard to keep parks and protected areas out of the hands of condominium builders, and despite the increasing number of stressed-out commuters, the island

still has resident artists, craftspeople, and old-timers who can't be bothered to venture into the big city. Though not as dramatic as Whidbey or as idyllic as Vashon, Bainbridge always makes for a pleasant day trip.

The ferry, which departs from the Downtown terminal at Pier 52, drops you off in the charming village of Winslow. Along its compact main street, Winslow Way, it's easy to while away an afternoon among the antiques shops, art galleries, bookstores, and cafés. There are two bike-rental shops in Winslow, too, if you plan on touring the island on two wheels. Getting out of town on a bike can be a bit nerve-racking, as the traffic to and from the ferry terminal is thick, and there aren't a lot of dedicated bike lanes, but you'll soon be on quieter country roads. Be sure to ask for maps at the rental shop, and if you want to avoid the worst of the island's hills, ask the staff to go over your options with you before you set out. (The rental shops have a selection of e-bikes but those go fast so book in advance.)

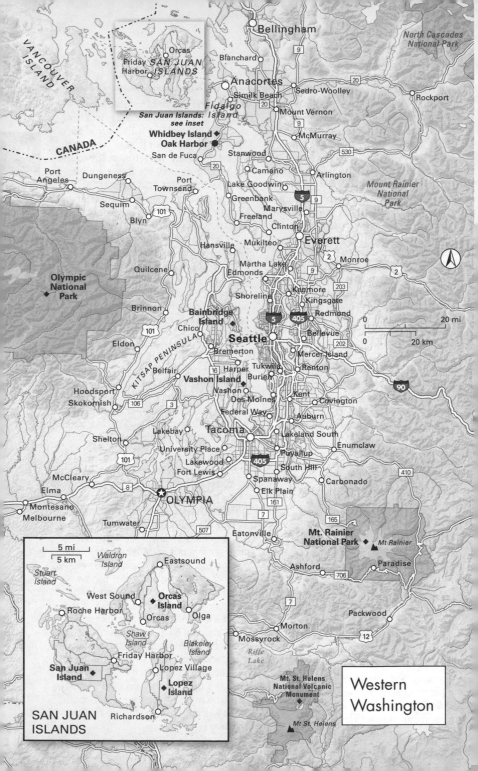

Many of the island's most reliable dining options are in Winslow—or close to it. You'll also find the delightful Town & Country supermarket on the main stretch if you want to pick up some provisions for a picnic, though you can also easily do that in Seattle at the Pike Place Market before you get on the ferry.

GETTING HERE AND AROUND

Unless you're coming from Tacoma or points farther south, or from the Olympic Peninsula, the only way to get to Bainbridge is via the ferry from Pier 52 Downtown. Round-trip fares start at $9.25 per person; round-trip fare for a car and driver is $20.90. Crossing time is 35 minutes. If you confine your visit to the village of Winslow, as many visitors do, then you won't need anything other than a pair of walking shoes.

Out on the island, besides driving or biking, the only way to get around is on public transit. While routed buses do traverse the island, the easiest way for on-foot visitors to get around is BI Ride, an on-demand ride-share service that runs weekdays from 8:45 am to 3:45 pm and Saturdays from 9 am to 6 pm. BI Ride can be taken just about anywhere on the island, including the Bloedel Reserve; book through the downloadable "Ride Pingo" app or call ☎ 844/424–7433. The fee, payable through the app or on an ORCA card, is $2.

CONTACTS Bainbridge Chamber of Commerce. ☎ 206/842–3700 ⊕ www. bainbridgechamber.com. **Kitsap Transit.** ☎ 800/501–7433 ⊕ www.kitsaptransit. com.

Sights

Bainbridge Island Studio Tour

ART GALLERY | Twice a year (the second weekend in August and the first weekend in December), the island's artists and craftspeople put their best pieces on display for these three-day events, and you can buy anything from watercolors to furniture directly from the artists. Even if you can't make the official studio tours, check out the website, which has maps and information on studios and shops throughout the island, as well as links to artists' websites. Many of the shops have regular hours, and you can easily put together your own tour. ⊠ *Bainbridge Island* ⊕ *www.bistudiotour.com.*

Bainbridge Vineyards

WINERY | Under cooperative ownership and led by women, this longtime certified-organic winery five miles from the ferry landing produces around 1,200 bottles a year from entirely island-grown varietals that thrive in the Puget Sound region. The winemakers compare their offerings to those that come from the Alsace or Loire Valley in France—on the light and fruity side—and you can enjoy a tasting of five pours for $8 on the winery's lovely sun-dappled patio. Kids will want to say hi to the draft horses that help till the fields. The tasting room is open Thursday to Sunday from 12 to 5 pm. ⊠ *8989 Day Rd. E, Bainbridge Island* ☎ *206/842–9463* ⊕ *www.bainbridgevine-yards.com* ⊙ *Closed Mon.–Wed.*

★ Bloedel Reserve

GARDEN | This 150-acre internationally recognized preserve is a stunning mix of natural woodlands and beautifully landscaped gardens—including a moss garden, a Japanese garden, a reflection pool, and the impressive former Bloedel estate home. Dazzling rhododendrons and azaleas bloom in spring, and Japanese maples colorfully signal autumn's arrival. Picnicking is not permitted, and you'll need to leave the pooch behind—pets are not allowed on the property, even if they stay in the car. Check the website for special events, lectures, and exhibits. Timed tickets can be reserved in advance. ⊠ *7571 NE Dolphin Dr., 6 miles west of Winslow, via Hwy. 305* ☎ *206/842–7631* ⊕ *www.bloedelreserve. org* ⊠ *$20* ⊙ *Closed Mon.*

Bloedel Reserve is 150 acres of gardens and woodlands.

Fletcher Bay Winery

WINERY | A boutique winery with stylish coastal decor, Fletcher Bay focuses on Bordeaux grapes along with Tempranillo and Sangiovese sourced from Washington State's Yakima and Walla Walla valleys. The casual, dog-friendly winery, set in the Coppertop Business Park (next door to Bainbridge Island Brewery), has a kids' play area with a DVD player, an enclosed patio with a fireplace and heat lamps, and live music every Wednesday from 6 to 8 pm. There's also a tasting room right in town (✉ *500 Winslow Way E*). ✉ *9415 Coppertop Loop NE, Bainbridge Island* ☎ *206/780–9463* 🌐 *www.fletcherbaywinery.com* ⏲ *Closed Mon.*

Fort Ward Park

STATE/PROVINCIAL PARK | On the southwest side of the island is this lovely and tranquil 137-acre park. There are two miles of hiking trails through forest, a long stretch of (sometimes) sun-drenched rocky beach, several picnic tables, a boat launch, and even an underwater park for scuba diving. Along with views of the water and the Olympic Mountains, you might be lucky and get a peek of Mt. Rainier—or of the massive sea lions that frequent the near-shore waters. A loop trail through the park is suitable for all ability levels, and will take you past vestiges of the park's previous life as a military installation. ✉ *Fort Ward Hill Rd. NE, Bainbridge Island* ✣ *Take Hwy. 305 out of Winslow; turn west on High School Rd. and follow signs to park* ☎ *206/842–3931* 🌐 *www.biparks.org/parksandfacilities/pkftward.html.*

Restaurants

Harbour Public House

$ | **SEAFOOD** | An 1881 estate home overlooking Eagle Harbor was renovated to create this casual pub and restaurant at Winslow's Harbor Marina, where a complimentary boat tie-up is available for pub patrons. Local seafood—including steamed mussels, clams, and oyster sliders—plus burgers, fish-and-chips, and poutine are typical fare, and there are 12 beers on tap. **Known for:** destination for kayakers; harbor views; an "honest" pint. $ *Average main: $16 ⊠ 231 Parfitt Way SW, Winslow ☎ 206/842–0969 ⊕ www. harbourpub.com.*

Streamliner Diner

$ | **DINER** | **FAMILY** | It may be a no-frills diner, but Streamliner is a local institution on Bainbridge Island thanks to its hearty breakfasts and vegetarian options. Many travelers grab a quick bite here when they hop off the ferry, though you'll see just as many locals lining up for breakfast and lunch. **Known for:** family-friendly casual spot; vegan menu selections; quick and friendly service. $ *Average main: $10 ⊠ 397 Winslow Way E, Bainbridge Island.*

☕ Coffee and Quick Bites

Blackbird Bakery

$ | **BAKERY** | A great place to grab a cup of coffee and a snack before exploring the island, Blackbird serves rich pastries and cakes along with quiche, soups, and a good selection of teas and espresso drinks. Though there is some nice window seating that allows you to watch the human parade on Winslow Way, the place gets very crowded, especially when the ferries come in, so you might want to take your order to go. **Known for:** close to ferry; variety of tea and espresso; delicious pastries. $ *Average main: $7 ⊠ 210 Winslow Way E, Winslow ☎ 206/780–1322 ⊕ www.blackbirdbakery. com ⊟ No credit cards ☽ No dinner.*

Pegasus Coffee

$ | **CAFÉ** | Pegasus is a Bainbridge Island fixture with all the best coffeehouse characteristics: a crackling fire, cozy seating, fresh java, and a clientele of artsy locals. The charming ivy-covered brick building is the original location for longtime roaster Pegasus, which is sold all over the region. **Known for:** local coffee roaster; gallery art by locals; live music. $ *Average main: $6 ⊠ 131 Parfitt Way SW, Winslow ☎ 206/317-6914.*

Vashon Island

20 minutes by ferry from West Seattle.

Vashon is the most peaceful and rural of the islands easily reached from the city, home to fruit growers, commune dwellers, and Seattle commuters.

Biking, beachcombing, picnicking, and kayaking are the main activities here. A tour of the 13-mile-long island will take you down country lanes and past orchards and lavender farms. There are several artists' studios and galleries on the island, as well as a small commercial district in the center of the island, where a farmers' market is a highlight every Saturday from April to October (and Wednesday afternoons, as well, from June to September). The popular Strawberry Festival takes place every July. The Vashon Ciderfest takes place in early October.

GETTING HERE

Washington State Ferries leave from Fauntleroy in West Seattle (about nine miles southwest of Downtown) for the 20-minute ride to Vashon Island. The ferry docks at the northern tip of the island. Round-trip fares are $6.10 per person or $26.55 for a car and driver. A water taxi also goes to Vashon from Pier 50 on the Seattle waterfront, but it's primarily for commuters, operating only on weekdays during commuter hours (no holiday service). One-way fares are $6.75. There's limited bus service on the island; the best way to get around is by car or by bicycle (bring your own or rent in Seattle). Note that there's a huge hill as you immediately disembark the ferry dock and head up to town.

VISITOR INFORMATION

Vashon-Maury Island Chamber of Commerce The office is open Monday to Friday 10 to 3. ⊠ 17141 Vashon Hwy. SW, Vashon ☎ 206/463–6217 ⊕ www.vashonchamber.com.

[👁] Sights

Jensen Point and Burton Acres Park

FOREST | Vashon has many parks and protected areas. This park, on the lush Burton Peninsula overlooking Quartermaster Harbor, is home to 64 acres of secluded hiking and horseback-riding trails. The adjacent Jensen Point, a four-acre shoreline park, has picnic tables, a swimming beach, and kayak and paddleboard rentals (May through September). ✉ *8900 SW Harbor Dr., Vashon* ✥ *From ferry terminal, take Vashon Hwy. SW to SW Burton Dr. and turn left. Turn left on 97 Ave. SW and follow it around as it becomes SW Harbor Dr.* 🌐 *www.vashonparks.org.*

Point Robinson Park

LIGHTHOUSE | You can stroll along the beach, which is very picturesque thanks to Point Robinson Lighthouse. The lighthouse is typically open to the public from noon to four on Sunday during the summer; call to arrange a tour or rent out one of the historic beachfront Keepers' Quarters (two multibedroom houses) by the week. If you're lucky, you might even see an orca swim surprisingly close to the shore. ✉ *3705 SW Pt. Robinson Rd., Vashon* ☎ *206/463–9602* 🌐 *www.vashonparks.org.*

Vashon Center for the Arts

ARTS CENTER | The best representative of the island's diverse arts community presents monthly exhibits and events that span all mediums, including dance, chamber music, and art lectures. The VCA gallery's exhibits rotate monthly, featuring local and Northwest artists. ✉ *19600 Vashon Hwy., Vashon* ☎ *206/463–5131* 🌐 *www.vashonalliedarts.org.*

🍴 Restaurants

The Hardware Store

$$ | **AMERICAN** | This all-day restaurant's unusual name comes from its former life as a mom-and-pop hardware shop—it occupies the oldest commercial building on Vashon, and certainly looks like a relic from the outside. Inside, you'll find a bistro-meets-upscale-diner serving "Northwest Americana" cuisine, with classic dishes ranging from rustic French toast for breakfast to buttermilk-fried chicken and meatloaf for dinner. **Known for:** iconic Vashon Island building; refined takes on diner favorites; decent wine list with Northwest options. [$] *Average main: $21* ✉ *17601 Vashon Hwy. SW, Vashon* ☎ *206/463–1800* 🌐 *www.thsrestaurant.com* 🕒 *Closed Mon.–Tues.*

★ May Kitchen + Bar

$$ | **THAI** | This is where sophisticated foodies swoon over delectable and highly authentic Thai dishes. The ambience is scene-y (atypical for Vashon): dark with fully paneled walls in mahogany and teak—wood that owner May Chaleoy had shipped from Thailand, where it previously lived in the interior of a 150-year-old home. **Known for:** real-deal Thai food that goes way beyond pad Thai; vibrant atmosphere; unique cocktails. [$] *Average main: $20* ✉ *17614 Vashon Hwy. SW, Vashon* ☎ *206/408–7196* 🌐 *www.maykitchen.com* 🕒 *Closed Mon.–Tue. No lunch.*

Whidbey Island

20 minutes by ferry from Mukilteo (20 miles north of Seattle) to Clinton, at the southern end of Whidbey Island, or drive north 87 miles to Deception Pass at the north end of the island.

Whidbey is a blend of low pastoral hills, evergreen and oak forests, meadows of wildflowers (including some endemic species), sandy beaches, and dramatic bluffs with a few pockets of unfortunate suburban sprawl. It's a great place for a scenic drive, viewing sunsets over the water, taking ridge hikes that give you uninterrupted views of the Strait of Juan de Fuca, walking along miles of rugged seaweed-strewn beaches, and boating or

kayaking along the protected shorelines of Saratoga Passage, Holmes Harbor, Penn Cove, and Skagit Bay.

The best beaches are on the west side, where wooded and wildflower-bedecked bluffs drop steeply to sand or surf, which can cover the beaches at high tide and can be unexpectedly rough on this exposed shore. Both beaches and bluffs have great views of the shipping lanes and the Olympic Mountains. Maxwelton Beach, with its sand, driftwood, and amazing sunsets, is popular with the locals. Possession Point includes a park and a beach, but it's best known for its boat launch. West of Coupeville, Ft. Ebey State Park has a sandy spread and an incredible bluff trail; West Beach is a stormy patch north of the fort with mounds of driftwood. At 35 miles long, Whidbey's island vibe is split between north and south; the historic southern and central towns of Langley and Coupeville are quaint and offer the most to do; Clinton (near the ferry terminal) isn't much of a destination, nor is the sprawling Navy town of Oak Harbor farther north. Yet Deception Pass at the island's northern tip offers the most jaw-dropping splendor, so plan enough time to visit both ends of the island. One fun way to see it all is to arrive via the Clinton ferry and drive back to Seattle via Deception Pass, or vice versa.

GETTING HERE

You can reach Whidbey Island by heading north from Seattle on I–5, west on Route 20 onto Fidalgo Island, and south across Deception Pass Bridge. The Deception Pass Bridge links Whidbey to Fidalgo Island. From the bridge it's a short drive to Anacortes, Fidalgo's main town and the terminus for ferries to the San Juan Islands. It's easier—and more pleasant—to take the 20-minute ferry trip from Mukilteo (30 miles northwest of Seattle) to Clinton, on Whidbey's south end, as

long as you don't time your trip on a Friday evening, which could leave you waiting in the car line for hours. Fares are $5.65 per person for walk-ons (round-trip) and $12.50 per car and driver (round-trip). Be sure to look at a map before choosing your point of entry; the ferry ride may not make sense if your main destination is Deception Pass State Park. Buses on Whidbey Island, provided by Island Transit, are free. Routes are fairly comprehensive, but keep in mind that Whidbey is big—it takes at least 35 minutes just to drive from the southern ferry terminal to the midway point at Coupeville—and if your itinerary is far-reaching, a car is your best bet.

CONTACT Island Transit. ☎ *800/240–8747* ⊕ *www.islandtransit.org.*

VISITOR INFORMATION
Langley Chamber of Commerce
Start off the "Langley Loop"—an 8-mile scenic driving or biking tour—at the Chamber offices, which will point you in the right direction for South Whidbey's eclectic mix of restaurants, galleries, wineries, and markets. ✉ *208 Anthes Ave., Langley* ☎ *360/221–6765* ⊕ *www.visitlangley.com.*

Langley

The historic village of Langley, seven miles north of Clinton on Whidbey Island, is above a 50-foot-high bluff overlooking Saratoga Passage, which separates Whidbey from Camano Island. A grassy terrace just above the beach is a great place for viewing birds on the water or in the air. On a clear day you can see Mt. Baker in the distance. Upscale boutiques selling art, glass, jewelry, books, and clothing line 1st and 2nd Streets in the heart of town.

🍴 Restaurants

Prima Bistro

$$ | **BISTRO** | Langley's most popular gathering spot occupies a second-story space on 1st Street, right above the Star Store Grocery. Northwest-inspired French cuisine is the headliner here; classic bistro dishes like steak frites, salade nicoise, and confit of duck leg are favorites. **Known for:** Penn Cove mussels and oysters; patio views of Saratoga Passage and Camano Island; live music on Thursday nights. [$] *Average main: $24* ✉ *201½ 1st St., Langley* ☎ *360/221–4060* 🌐 *www.primabistro.com.*

🛏 Hotels

★ Inn at Langley

$$$$ | **B&B/INN** | Perched on a bluff above the beach, this concrete-and-wood Frank Lloyd Wright–inspired structure is just steps from the center of town and features elegant, contemporary guest rooms, all with soaking tubs, wood-burning fireplaces, balconies, and dramatic marine and mountain views. **Pros:** no children under 12; stunning views of the Saratoga Passage; destination restaurant (with priority seating for inn guests). **Cons:** some rooms can be on the small side; expensive for the area; not family-friendly for young kids. [$] *Rooms from: $500* ✉ *400 1st St., Langley* ☎ *360/221–3033* 🌐 *www.innatlangley.com* 🔑 *28 rooms* 🍽 *Free Breakfast.*

Saratoga Inn

$$$ | **B&B/INN** | At the edge of Langley, this cedar-shake, Nantucket-style inn features cozy decor and fireplaces in every room and is just a short walk from the town's shops and restaurants. **Pros:** wraparound porches with rocking chairs; some rooms have water and mountain views; afternoon tea. **Cons:** a bit rustic; some small bathrooms; no on-site restaurant. [$] *Rooms from: $309* ✉ *201 Cascade Ave., Langley* ☎ *360/221–5801, 800/698–2910* 🌐 *www.saratogainnw-hidbeyisland.com* 🔑 *16 rooms* 🍽 *Free Breakfast.*

🛍 Shopping

Moonraker Books

BOOKS | Langley's independent bookshop, an institution since 1972, stocks a wonderful and eclectic array of fiction, nonfiction, cookbooks—and, according to the owners, "books you didn't even know you wanted until you stepped inside." ✉ *209 1st St., Langley* ☎ *360/221–6962.*

Museo

ART GALLERIES | This contemporary fine art gallery focused on Northwest and regional artists is known for its glass art, sculpture, and handcrafted jewelry. Artist receptions are held on the first Saturday of each month from 5 to 7 pm, part of Langley's First Saturday Art Walk. ✉ *215 1st St., Langley* ☎ *360/221–7737* 🌐 *www.museo.cc.*

Greenbank

About halfway up Whidbey Island, 14 miles northwest of Langley, is the hamlet of Greenbank, home to a former farm turned multiuse attraction encircled by views of the Olympic and Cascade ranges.

👁 Sights

Greenbank Farm

FARM/RANCH | **FAMILY** | You can't miss the huge, chestnut-color, two-story barn out front—the centerpiece to this picturesque, 150-acre property, a former working farm that now houses two art galleries, a café, and several shops. Greenbank's grounds include a demonstration garden and lovely walking trails, many of which are dog-friendly. ✉ *765 Wonn Rd., Greenbank* ☎ *360/678–7700* 🌐 *www.greenbankfarm.com* 🎟 *Free.*

This Historic Ferry House is part of Ebey's Landing National Historic Reserve on Whidbey Island.

Meerkerk Gardens

GARDEN | The 53-acre Meerkerk Rhododendron Gardens contain 1,500 native and hybrid species of rhododendrons and more than 100,000 spring bulbs on 10 acres of display gardens with more than four miles of nature trails. The flowers are in full bloom in April and May; summer flowers and fall color provide interest later in the year. The 43 remaining acres are kept wild as a nature preserve. Leashed pets are permitted on the gravel paths. ⊠ *Hwy. 525 and Resort Rd., Greenbank* ☎ *360/678–1912* ⊕ *www.meerkerkgardens.org* ⤳ *$5.*

Coupeville

Restored Victorian houses grace many of the streets in quiet Coupeville, Washington's second-oldest city, on the south shore of Penn Cove, 12 miles north of Greenbank. It also has one of the largest national historic districts in the state and has been used for filming movies depicting 19th-century New England villages. Stores above the waterfront have maintained their old-fashioned character. Captain Thomas Coupe founded the town in 1852. His house was built the following year, and other houses and commercial buildings were built in the late 1800s. Even though Coupeville is the island county seat, the town has a laid-back, almost 19th-century air.

 Sights

★ **Ebey's Landing National Historic Reserve**
BEACH | **FAMILY** | The reserve encompasses a sand-and-cobble beach, bluffs with dramatic views down the Strait of Juan de Fuca, two state parks (Ft. Casey and Ft. Ebey; see separate listings), and several privately held pioneer farms homesteaded in the early 1850s. The first and largest reserve of its kind holds nearly 400 nationally registered historic structures (including those located within the town of Coupeville), most of them from the 19th century. Miles of trails lead along the beach and through the woods. Cedar Gulch, south of the main

entrance to Ft. Ebey, has a lovely picnic area in a wooded ravine above the beach. ✉ *Coupeville* ✥ *From Hwy. 20, turn south on Main St. in Coupeville. This road turns into Engles Rd. as you head out of town. Turn right on Hill Rd. and follow it to reserve* 🌐 *www.nps.gov/ebla.*

Ft. Casey and Keystone State Park
STATE/PROVINCIAL PARK | FAMILY | The 467-acre Ft. Casey State Park, on a bluff overlooking sweeping views of Strait of Juan de Fuca and the Port Townsend ferry landing, was one of three forts (the "Triangle of Death") built after 1890 to protect the entrance to Admiralty Inlet from naval invasion. Look for the concrete gun emplacement and a couple of eight-inch "disappearing" guns. The charming Admiralty Head Lighthouse Interpretive Center is north of the gunnery emplacements. There are also grassy picnic sites, rocky fishing spots, waterfront campsites, and a boat launch. A Washington State Discover Pass is required ($30/year or $10/day; see 🌐 *www.discoverpass.wa.gov*). Once you're done exploring the park, take the ferry to Port Townsend for a quick side trip or a long lunch. ✉ *2 miles west of Rte. 20, Coupeville* ☎ *360/678–4519* 🌐 *www.parks.wa.gov/parks* 🎫 *Discover Pass required; $30/year or $10/day.*

Ft. Ebey State Park
STATE/PROVINCIAL PARK | FAMILY | In late May and early June, Ft. Ebey State Park blazes with native rhododendrons. West of Coupeville on Point Partridge, it has three miles of shoreline, campsites in the woods, trails to the headlands, a freshwater lake for fishing, World War II gun emplacements, wildflower meadows, spectacular views down the Strait of Juan de Fuca, and miles of hiking and biking trails. A Washington State Discover Pass is required. ✉ *3 miles west of Rte. 20, Coupeville* ☎ *360/678–4636* 🌐 *www.parks.wa.gov* 🎫 *Washington State Discover Pass required ($30/year or $10/day).*

Island County Historical Museum
HISTORY MUSEUM | FAMILY | Collections include Ice Age relics, mammoth remains, and a strong Native American collection, including three rare cedar dugout canoes. The square-timber Alexander Blockhouse outside dates from 1855. Note the squared logs and dovetail joints of the corners—no overlapping log ends. This construction technique was favored by many western Washington pioneers. ✉ *908 NW Alexander St., Coupeville* ☎ *360/678–3310* 🎫 *Free (donations welcomed).*

🍴 Restaurants

Front Street Grill
$$ | SEAFOOD | Many regulars skip right past the rest of the menu to get to the restaurant's selection of local Penn Cove mussels. They're served eight different ways, from a traditional white wine sauce to the signature coconut green curry. **Known for:** picturesque views; big bowls of local mussels; a long wait during peak season. [$] *Average main: $25* ✉ *20 Front St. NW, Coupeville* ☎ *206/682–2551* 🌐 *www.fsgcoupeville.com.*

🛏 Hotels

Captain Whidbey Inn
$$ | B&B/INN | Steps from the shorefront of Penn Cove, this venerable historic lodge surrounded by old-growth firs was recently refreshed with more of a hip boutique hotel vibe (think Ace Hotel) while maintaining the rustic charm that's made it a favorite for decades. **Pros:** a few lodging options, including private cabins with hot tubs; secluded "upscale summer camp" vibe; pedestal sinks in rooms. **Cons:** shared bathrooms; poor soundproofing in the main motel; spotty cell phone coverage. [$] *Rooms from: $255* ✉ *2072 Captain Whidbey Inn Rd., off Madrona Way, Coupeville* ☎ *360/678–4097, 800/366–4097* 🌐 *www.*

captainwhidbey.com ⮡ *29 rooms, 2 suites, 4 cabins* ⦿ *Free Breakfast.*

Compass Rose Bed and Breakfast
$ | **B&B/INN** | Inside this stately 1890 Queen Anne Victorian on the National Register of Historic Places, a veritable museum of art, artifacts, and antiques awaits you. **Pros:** wonderful, interesting hosts; elegant breakfast with china, silver, linen, and lace; lots of eye candy for antiques lovers. **Cons:** only two rooms, so it gets booked up fast; too old-fashioned for some travelers; not kid-friendly (too many things to break). Ⓢ *Rooms from: $140* ✉ *508 S Main St., Coupeville* ☎ *360/678–5318, 800/237–3881* ⊕ *www.compassrosebandb.com* ▭ *No credit cards* ⮡ *2 rooms* ⦿ *Free Breakfast.*

Oak Harbor

Oak Harbor, about 10 miles north of Coupeville, is the least attractive and least interesting part of Whidbey—it mainly exists to serve the Whidbey Island Naval Air Station, and has none of the historic or pastoral charm of the rest of the island. It is, however, the largest town on the island and the one closest to Deception Pass State Park. If you need to stock up on provisions, you'll find all the big-box stores here, in addition to major supermarkets. In town, the marina, at the east side of the bay, has a picnic area with views of Saratoga Passage and the entrance of Penn Cove.

Sights

Deception Pass State Park
STATE/PROVINCIAL PARK | FAMILY | The biggest draw of the park is the historic two-lane Deception Pass Bridge connecting Whidbey Island to Fidalgo Island, about nine miles north of Oak Harbor. Park the car and walk across in order to get the best views of the dramatic saltwater gorges and churning whirlpools below. Then spend a few hours walking the 19 miles of rocky shore and beaches, exploring three freshwater lakes, or walking along the many forest and meadow trails. ✉ *Rte. 20, 9 miles north of Oak Harbor, Whidbey Island* ☎ *360/675–2417* ⊕ *www.parks.wa.gov* ✉ *Daily Discover pass $10 per vehicle; annual $30 (valid at all state parks); campsite fees vary.*

The San Juan Islands

About 100 miles northwest of Seattle, these romantic islands abound with breathtaking rolling pastures, rocky shorelines, and thickly forested ridges, and their quaint villages draw art lovers, foodies, and city folk seeking serenity. Inns are easygoing and well appointed, and many restaurants are helmed by highly talented chefs emphasizing local ingredients.

Each of the San Juans maintains a distinct character, though all share in the archipelago's blessings of serene farmlands, unspoiled coves, blue-green or gray tidal waters, and radiant light. Offshore, seals haul out on sandbanks and orcas patrol the deep channels. You may see the occasional minke whale frolicking in the kelp, and humpback whales have become increasingly visible around the islands. You'll very rarely spy gray whales, which stay closer to Washington's mainland.

There are 172 named islands in the archipelago. Sixty are populated (though most have only a house or two), and 10 are state marine parks, some of which are accessible only to nonmotorized craft—kayakers, canoes, small sailboats—navigating the Cascadia Marine Trail.

The San Juan Islands have valleys and mountains where eagles soar and forests and leafy glens where the small island deer browse. Even a species of prickly pear cactus (*Opuntia fragilis*) grows here. Beaches can be of sand or shingle (covered in small pebbles). The islands are home to ducks and swans, herons and hawks, otters and whales. The main draw is the great outdoors, but there's plenty to do once you've seen the whales or hiked. Each island, even tiny Lopez, has at least one commercial center, where you'll find shops, restaurants, and history museums. Not surprisingly, many artists take inspiration from the dramatic surroundings, and each island has a collection of galleries; Friday Harbor even has an impressive sculpture park and art museum. Lavender and alpaca farms, spas and yoga studios, a whale museum and lighthouse tours—the San Juans have a little bit of everything.

WHEN TO GO

This part of Washington has a mild, maritime climate. Winter temperatures average in the low 40s, while summer temps hover in the mid 70s. July and August are by far the most popular months to visit the three main islands—they can get busy during this time, with resorts, boating tours, and ferries often at capacity. To beat the crowds and avoid the worst of the wet weather, visit in late spring or early fall—September and early October can be fair and stunningly gorgeous, as can May and early June. Hotel rates are generally lower everywhere during these shoulder seasons, and even lower once often drizzly winter starts.

Orcas, Lopez, and San Juan islands are extremely popular in high season; securing hotel reservations in advance is essential. If you're bringing a car to the islands, be sure to book a ferry reservation well in advance. Or if you're traveling light and plan to stay put in one place in the islands, consider walking or biking. Lot parking at Anacortes is $13 per day and $60 per week in summer and half that October–April.

■TIP→ **Though a few places close or have limited hours and the incredible views are frequently obscured by drizzle during the winter, the San Juan Islands are still worth a visit in the off-season, except in January, when many spots shutter for the entire month.**

FESTIVALS
Orcas Island Chamber Music Festival
FESTIVALS | Around for more than two decades, this music festival comprises more than two weeks of "classical music with a view" in August. These concerts are immensely popular with chamber-music fans around the Pacific Northwest. ⊠ *Orcas Island* ☎ *866/492–0003* ⊕ *www. oicmf.org.*

Savor the San Juans
FESTIVALS | Autumn has become increasingly popular thanks to the growth of this culinary festival, which runs about six weeks. It consists of an islands-wide series of events celebrating local foods and beverages, including farm tours, film screenings, and harvest dinners. ⊠ *San Juan Island* ☎ *360/378–3277* ⊕ *www. visitsanjuans.com/savor.*

GETTING HERE AND AROUND
Port of Friday Harbor is the main San Juan Islands airport, but there are also small airports on Lopez, Shaw, and Orcas Islands. Seaplanes land on the waterfront at Friday Harbor and Roche Harbor on San Juan Island; Rosario Resort, Deer Harbor, and West Sound on Orcas Island; and Fisherman Bay on Lopez Island. Daily scheduled flights link the San Juan Islands with mainland airports at Anacortes, Bellingham, Lake Washington, Renton, and Boeing Field near Seattle. Some airlines also offer charter services.

If traffic and ferry lines really aren't your thing, consider hopping aboard a seaplane for the quick flight from Seattle. Kenmore Air offers several daily departures from Lake Union, Lake Washington, and Boeing Field. Flights on San Juan Airlines from Bellingham and Anacortes run about $120 each way.

AIR CONTACTS Kenmore Air. ⊠ *Kenmore* ☎ *425/486–1257, 866/435–9524* ⊕ *www. kenmoreair.com.* **San Juan Airlines.** ⊠ *Bellingham* ☎ *800/874–4434* ⊕ *www. sanjuanairlines.com.*

Most visitors arrive by car, which is the best way to explore these mostly rural islands comprehensively, especially if you plan on visiting for more than a couple of days. You can also park your car at the Anacortes ferry terminal ($10 per day or $40 per week high season, and half that fall through spring), as fares are cheaper and lines much shorter for passengers without cars. B&B owners can often pick guests up at the ferry terminal by prior arrangement, and you can rely on bikes and occasional taxis or on-island car or moped rentals (on San Juan and Orcas) for getting around. Also, in summer, a shuttle bus makes its way daily around San Juan Island and on weekends on Orcas and Lopez islands. From Seattle, it's a 90-minute drive via Interstate 5 north and Highway 20 west to reach Anacortes.

Island roads are narrow and often windy, with one or two lanes. Slow down and hug the shoulder when passing another car on a one-lane road. Expect rough patches, some unpaved lanes, deer and rabbits, bicyclists, and other hazards—plus the distractions of sweeping water views. There are a few car-rental agencies on San Juan and Orcas, with daily rates running about $60 to $100 in summer, and as much as 25% less off-season. You'll likely save money renting a car on the mainland, even factoring in the cost of ferry transport (which in high season is about $45 to $65 for a standard vehicle including driver, plus around $14 per passenger, depending on which island you're headed to).

RENTAL CAR CONTACTS M and W Rental Cars. ⊠ 725 Spring St., Friday Harbor ☎ 360/376–5266 Orcas, 360/378–2794 San Juan ⊕ www.sanjuanauto.com. **Orcas Island Rental Cars.** ⊠ Friday Harbor ☎ 360/376–7433 ⊕ www.orcasislandshuttle.com. **Susie's Mopeds.** ⊠ 125 Nichols St., Friday Harbor ☎ 360/378–5244, 800/532–0087 ⊕ www.susiesmopeds.com.

The Washington State Ferries system can become overloaded during peak travel times. Thankfully, a reservations system makes it far easier to plan trips and avoid lines. Reservations are highly recommended, especially in summer and on weekends, although a small number of spaces on every sailing are always reserved for standby. Always arrive at least 45 minutes ahead of your departure, and as much as two hours ahead at busy times if you don't have a reservation. You'll find information on the Washington State Ferries website on up-to-the-minute wait times as well as tips on which ferries tend to be the most crowded. It's rarely a problem to get a walk-on spot, although arriving a bit early to ensure you get a ticket is wise.

■ TIP→ **Avoid returning to Anacortes on the daily ferries that originate in Sidney, BC; though they're more direct routes, domestic passengers have to wait in the Customs and Border Protection line to exit along with Canadian passengers, which can take a very long time.**

FERRY CONTACT Washington State Ferries. ⊠ 2100 Ferry Terminal Rd., Anacortes ☎ 206/464–6400, 888/808–7977 ⊕ www.wsdot.wa.gov/ferries.

RESTAURANTS
The San Juans have myriad small farms and restaurants serving local foods and fresh-harvested seafood, and culinary agritourism—visiting local farmers, growers, and chefs at their places of business—is on the rise.

Restaurant reviews have been shortened. For full information, visit Fodors.com.

HOTELS
With the exception of Lopez Island, which has just a handful of inns, accommodations in the San Juans are quite varied and tend be plush, if also expensive during the high summer season. Rosario Resort & Spa on Orcas Island and Roche Harbor Resort on San Juan Island are

favorite spots for special-occasion splurges, and both islands have seen an influx of either new or luxuriously updated inns in recent years. These places often have perks like lavish breakfasts and on-site outfitters and tour operators.

Hotel reviews have been shortened. For full information, visit Fodors.com.

VISITOR INFORMATION

Look to the San Juan Islands Visitors Bureau for general information on all the islands—the website is very useful.

CONTACT San Juan Islands Visitors Bureau. ⊠ *The Technology Center, 640 Mullis St., Suites 210–211, Friday Harbor* ☎ *360/378–3277, 888/468–3701* ⊕ *www. visitsanjuans.com.*

Lopez Island

45 minutes by ferry from Anacortes.

Known affectionately as "Slow-pez," the closest significantly populated island to the mainland is a broad, bay-encircled bit of terrain set amid sparkling blue seas, a place where cabinlike homes are tucked into the woods, and boats are moored in lonely coves.

Of the three San Juan Islands with facilities to accommodate overnight visitors, Lopez has the smallest population (approximately 2,200), and with its old orchards, weathered barns, and rolling green pastures, it's the most rustic and least crowded in the archipelago. Gently sloping roads cut wide curves through golden farmlands and trace the edges of pebbly beaches, while peaceful trails wind through thick patches of forest. Sweeping country views make Lopez a favorite year-round biking locale, and except for the long hill up from the ferry docks, most roads and designated bike paths are easy for novices to negotiate.

The only settlement is Lopez Village, really just a cluster of cafés and boutiques, as well as a summer market and

outdoor theater, an upscale inn, a visitor information center, and a grocery store. Other attractions—such as seasonal berry-picking farms, small wineries, kitschy galleries, intimate restaurants, and one secluded bed-and-breakfast—are scattered around the island.

GETTING HERE AND AROUND

The Washington State Ferries crossing from Anacortes take about 45 minutes; round-trip peak-season fares are $14.85 per person, $51.15 for a car and driver. One-hour flights from Seattle cost about $160 to $210 each way. You can get around the island by car (bring your own—there are no rentals) or bike; there are bike-rental facilities by the ferry terminal.

ESSENTIALS

VISITOR INFORMATION Lopez Island Chamber of Commerce. ⊠ *Lopez Rd., at Tower Rd., Lopez* ☎ *360/468–4664* ⊕ *www.lopezisland.com.*

 Sights

Lopez Island Historical Museum

HISTORY MUSEUM | Artifacts from the region's Native American tribes and early settlers include some impressive ship and small-boat models and maps of local landmarks. You can also listen to fascinating digital recordings of early settlers discussing life on Lopez Island. ⊠ *Weeks Rd. and Washburn Pl., Lopez* ☎ *360/468–2049* ⊕ *www.lopezmuseum.org* ⊠ *Free* ⊗ *Closed Mon.–Tues. and Oct.–Apr.*

★ Shark Reef Sanctuary

TRAIL | A quiet forest trail along beautiful Shark Reef leads to an isolated headland jutting out above the bay. The sounds of raucous barks and squeals mean you're nearly there, and eventually you may see throngs of seals and seagulls on the rocky islets across from the point. Bring binoculars to spot bald eagles in the trees as you walk and to view sea otters frolicking in the waves near the shore. The trail starts at the Shark Reef Road parking lot south of the airport, and it's a 15-minute walk to the headland. ✉ *Shark Reef Rd., Lopez* ✣ *2 miles south of Lopez Island Airport* 🎫 *Free.*

Spencer Spit State Park
STATE/PROVINCIAL PARK | Set on a spit along the Cascadia Marine Trail for kayakers, this popular spot for summer camping is on former Native American clamming, crabbing, and fishing grounds. A variety of campsites is available, from primitive tent sites to full hookups. This is one of the few Washington beaches where cars are permitted. ✉ *521 A Bakerview Rd., Lopez* ☎ *360/468–2251* 🌐 *www.parks.wa.gov/parks* 🎫 *$10.*

🍴 Restaurants

Haven Kitchen & Bar
$$ | AMERICAN | You'll find something for everyone at this Lopez eatery, which seems to have picked favorite dishes from various cuisines and created solid versions of them, sometimes with inventive twists (tater tots in a burrito, for example); they've got everything from Thai fresh rolls to gamberoni linguine with fresh, locally made pasta. **Known for:** eclectic menu; expansive flower-lined outdoor deck; well-crafted artisanal cocktails. [$] *Average main: $24* ✉ *9 Old Post Rd., Lopez* ☎ *360/468–3272* 🌐 *www.lopezhaven.com* 🕒 *Closed Sun.–Weds.*

Ursa Minor
$$$$ | PACIFIC NORTHWEST | One of the latest upscale farm-to-table restaurants to put the San Juan Islands on the culinary map (reservations strongly recommended), Ursa Minor is helmed by Nick Coffey, formerly of the now-closed Sitka & Spruce in Seattle. He celebrates the Islands' incredible bounty with a creative seasonal menu featuring seafood, foraged mushrooms, and produce from island farms. **Known for:** airy, serene organic-modern space; island-sourced ingredients; unique Northwest fare. [$] *Average main: $45* ✉ *210 Lopez Rd., Lopez* ☎ *360/622–2730* 🌐 *www.ursaminorlopez.com* 🕒 *Closed Mon.–Thu. and Jan.*

☕ Coffee and Quick Bites

Holly B's Bakery
$ | BAKERY | Tucked into a small, cabinlike strip of businesses set back from the water, this cozy, wood-paneled bakery has been a source of delicious fresh ham-and-Gruyère croissants, marionberry scones, slices of pizza, and other savory and sweet treats since 1977. Sunny summer mornings bring diners out onto the patio, where kids play and parents relax. **Known for:** ginormous, decadent cinnamon rolls; pizza by the slice; scones flavored with seasonal fruit. [$] *Average main: $8* ✉ *Lopez Plaza, 211 Lopez Rd., Lopez* ☎ *360/468–2133* 🌐 *www.hollybsbakery.com* 💳 *No credit cards* 🕒 *Closed Dec.–Mar. No dinner.*

Isabel's Espresso
$ | CAFÉ | A favorite of Lopez locals, Isabel's sources its coffee from fair trade suppliers and its creamy dairy from the mainland's small Fresh Breeze Organic Dairy Farm. Housed in a charming rustic building in Lopez's tiny "downtown," the café also serves light fare like pastries and sandwiches. **Known for:** good coffee; fresh regional dairy; outdoor seating with views. [$] *Average main: $6* ✉ *308 Lopez Rd., Lopez* ☎ *360/468–4114* 🌐 *www.isabelsespresso.com.*

Vita's Wildly Delicious
$ | CAFÉ | At this gourmet market and wine shop (open primarily during the daytime but until 8 pm on Friday), the proprietors create a daily-changing assortment of prepared foods and some made-to-order items, such as Reuben panini sandwiches. Other favorites include Dungeness crab cakes, hearty meat loaf, lobster mac-and-cheese, and an assortment of tempting desserts. **Known for:** Dungeness crab cakes; pretty garden-dining area; gourmet picnic supplies. [$] *Average main: $11* ✉ *77 Village*

Rd., Lopez ☎ 360/468–4268 🌐 www.vitasonlopez.com 🕒 Closed Sun., Mon., and late fall–late spring. No dinner.

Hotels

Edenwild Boutique Inn
$$$$ | B&B/INN | Thoughtful and friendly owners Anthony and Crystal Rovente operate this large Victorian-style farmhouse surrounded by gardens and framed by Fisherman Bay, where spacious rooms are each painted or papered in different pastel shades and furnished with simple antiques; some have claw-foot tubs and brick fireplaces. **Pros:** lovely outdoor spaces, including an outdoor veranda; nice breakfast buffet using local produce and homemade baked goods; handy location close to village restaurants. **Cons:** no TVs in rooms; decor is a bit plain; two-night minimum. *$ Rooms from: $400 ✉ 132 Lopez Rd., Lopez ☎ 360/468–3238 🌐 www.edenwildinn.com 🛏 9 rooms 🍴 Free Breakfast.*

★ MacKaye Harbor Inn
$$ | B&B/INN | This former sea captain's house, built in 1904, rises two stories above the beach at the southern end of the island and accommodates guests in cheerfully furnished rooms with golden-oak and brass details and wicker furniture; three have views of MacKaye Harbor. **Pros:** fantastic water views; mountain bikes (free) and kayaks (reasonable daily fee) available; friendly and attentive hosts. **Cons:** on far end of the island; several miles from the ferry terminal and airport; some bathrooms are across the hall from rooms. *$ Rooms from: $275 ✉ 949 MacKaye Harbor Rd., Lopez ☎ 360/468–2253, 888/314–6140 🌐 www.mackayeharborinn.com 🛏 5 rooms 🍴 Free Breakfast.*

Activities

BIKING

Bike rental rates start at around $10 an hour and $40 a day. Reservations are recommended, particularly in summer.

Lopez Kayaks and Bicycle Works
BIKING | At the marina 4 miles from the ferry, this full-service operation can bring bicycles right to you. In addition to cruisers and mountain bikes, the shop also rents tandem and recumbent bikes, along with kayaks. *✉ 2847 Fisherman Bay Rd., Lopez ☎ 360/468–2847 🌐 www.lopezbicycleworks.com.*

Village Cycles
BIKING | This aptly named full-service rental and repair shop is in the heart of Lopez Village. Rental options include e-bikes. *✉ 214 Lopez Rd., Lopez ☎ 360/468–4013 🌐 www.villagecycles.net.*

SEA KAYAKING

Edenwild Island Adventures
KAYAKING | In addition to being a lovely inn, Edenwild is also one of the island's outfitters, offering half-day kayak rentals ($30 per person) as well as kayak crabbing gear ($70 per person). Kayakers can drop in a protected bay just steps from the property that's teeming with local sea life. *✉ 132 Lopez Rd, Apt 2, Lopez ☎ 360/468–3238 🌐 www.theedenwild.com/explore.*

Shopping

Chimera Gallery
ART GALLERIES | This local artists' cooperative exhibits and sells crafts, jewelry, and fine art. *✉ Lopez Plaza, 211 Lopez Rd., Lopez ☎ 360/468–3265 🌐 www.chimera-gallery.com.*

Lopez Bookshop
BOOKS | This longtime bookseller is stocked with publications on San Juan Islands history and activities, as well as tomes about the Pacific Northwest. There's also a good selection of

mysteries, literary novels, children's books, and craft kits, plus greeting cards, art prints, and maps. Many of the items sold here are the works of local writers, artists, and photographers. ⊠ *Lopez Plaza, 211 Lopez Rd., Lopez* ☎ *360/468–2132* ⊕ *www.lopezbookshop.com.*

Orcas Island

75 minutes by ferry from Anacortes.

Orcas Island, the largest of the San Juans, is blessed with wide, pastoral valleys and scenic ridges that rise high above the neighboring waters—at 2,409 feet, Orcas's Mt. Constitution is the highest peak in the San Juans. Spanish explorers set foot here in 1791, and the island is actually named for one of these early visitors, Juan Vicente de Güemes Padilla Horcasitas y Aguayo—not for the black-and-white whales that frolic in the surrounding waters. The island was also the home of Native American tribes, whose history is reflected in such places as Pole Pass, where the Lummi people used kelp and cedar-bark nets to catch ducks, and Massacre Bay, where in 1858 a tribe from southeast Alaska attacked a Lummi fishing village.

Today farmers, fishermen, artists, retirees, and summer-home owners make up the population of about 4,500. Houses are spaced far apart, and the island's few hamlets typically have just one major road running through them.

Low-key resorts dotting the island's edges are evidence of the thriving local tourism industry, as is the gradual but steady influx of urbane restaurants, boutiques, and even a trendy late-night bar in the main village of Eastsound. The beauty of this island is beyond compare; Orcas is a favorite place for weekend getaways from Seattle any time of the year, as well as one of the state's top settings for summer weddings.

The main town on Orcas Island lies at the head of the East Sound channel, which nearly divides the island in two. More than 20 small shops and boutiques here sell jewelry, pottery, and crafts by local artisans, as well as gourmet edibles, from baked goods to chocolates.

GETTING HERE AND AROUND

The Washington State Ferries crossing from Anacortes to Orcas Village, in the island's Westsound area, takes about 75 minutes; peak-season round-trip fares are about $15 per person, $62 for a car and driver. One-hour flights from Seattle cost about $160 to $200 each way. Planes land at Deer Harbor, Eastsound, Westsound, and at the Rosario Resort and Spa.

The best way to get around the island is by car—bikes will do in a pinch, but the hilly, curvy roads that generally lack shoulders make cycling a bit risky. Most resorts and inns offer transfers from the ferry terminal.

ESSENTIALS
VISITOR INFORMATION Orcas Island Chamber of Commerce & Visitor Center. ⊠ *65 N. Beach Rd., Orcas Island* ☎ *360/376–2273* ⊕ *www.orcasislandchamber.com.*

 Sights

Moran Museum at Rosario
HOTEL | This 1909 mansion that forms the centerpiece of Rosario Resort was constructed as the vacation home of Seattle shipping magnate and mayor Robert Moran. On the second floor is this fascinating museum that spans several former guest rooms and includes old photos, furniture, and memorabilia related to the Moran family, the resort's history, and the handsome ships built by Moran and his brothers. A highlight is the music room, which contains an incredible two-story 1913 aeolian pipe organ and an ornate, original Tiffany chandelier. The surrounding grounds make for a lovely stroll, which you might combine with lunch or a

The view from Mt. Constitution on Orcas Island, the highest point in the San Juans

cocktail in one of the resort's water-view restaurants. ⊠ *1400 Rosario Rd., Orcas Island* ☎ *360/376–2222* ⊕ *www.rosarioresort.com/museum* ☒ *Free.*

★ Moran State Park

STATE/PROVINCIAL PARK | FAMILY | This pristine patch of wilderness comprises 5,252 acres of hilly, old-growth forests dotted with sparkling lakes, in the middle of which rises the island's highest point, 2,409-foot Mt. Constitution. A drive to the summit affords exhilarating views of the islands, the Cascades, the Olympics, and Vancouver Island, and avid hikers enjoy the strenuous but stunning seven-mile round-trip trek from rippling Mountain Lake to the summit (some 38 miles of trails traverse the entire park). The observation tower on the summit was built by the Civilian Conservation Corps in the 1930s. In summer, you can rent boats to paddle around beautiful Cascade Lake. ⊠ *Mt. Constitution Rd., Orcas Island* ☎ *360/376–2326* ⊕ *www. parks.wa.gov/parks* ☒ *Discover Pass (annual $30/day pass $10).*

Orcas Island Historical Museum

HISTORY MUSEUM | Surrounded by Eastsound's lively shops and cafés, this museum comprises several reassembled and relocated late-19th-century pioneer cabins. An impressive collection of more than 6,000 photographs, documents, and artifacts tells the story of the island's Native American and Anglo history, and in an oral-history exhibit longtime residents of the island talk about how the community has evolved over the decades. The museum also operates the 1888 Crow Valley Schoolhouse, which is available for private tours from Memorial Day to Labor Day ($10 per person; minimum two people); call the museum for hours and directions. ⊠ *181 N. Beach Rd., Orcas Island* ☎ *360/376–4849* ⊕ *www. orcasmuseum.org* ☒ *$5* ⏲ *Closed Oct.– May, Sun.–Tues.*

Orcas Island Winery

WINERY | FAMILY | This lovely boutique winery in a pastoral setting features a modern farmhouse-chic gathering space with picnic-table outdoor seating and a garden. The only winery on Orcas, it's perfect for a sunny afternoon spent sipping wine and listening to concerts. ✉ *2371 Crow Valley Rd., Orcas Island* ☎ *360/797–5062* 🌐 *www.orcasislandwinery.com* 🕒 *Closed Mon.–Tue. and Jan.*

★ Turtleback Mountain Preserve

NATURE PRESERVE | A more peaceful, less crowded hiking and wildlife-watching alternative to Moran State Park, this 1,576-acre expanse of rugged ridges, wildflower-strewn meadows, temperate rain forest, and lush wetlands is one of the natural wonders of the archipelago. Because the San Juan County Land Bank purchased this land in 2006, it will be preserved forever for the public to enjoy. There are eight miles of well-groomed trails, including a steep trek up to 1,519-foot-elevation Raven Ridge and a windy hike to Turtlehead Point, a soaring bluff with spectacular views west of San Juan Island and Vancouver Island beyond that—it's an amazing place to watch the sunset. You can access the preserve either from the North Trailhead, which is just 3 miles southwest of Eastsound on Crow Valley Road, or the South Trailhead, which is three miles northeast of Deer Harbor off Wild Rose Lane—check the website for a trail map and detailed directions. ✉ *North Trailhead parking, Crow Valley Rd., just south of Crow Valley Schoolhouse, Orcas Island* ☎ *360/378–4402* 🌐 *www.sjclandbank.org/turtle_back.html* 🎟 *Free.*

🍴 Restaurants

★ Doe Bay Cafe

$$$ | **AMERICAN** | Most of the tables in this warmly rustic dining room at Doe Bay Resort overlook the tranquil body of water for which the café is named. This is a popular stop for brunch or dinner before or after hiking or biking in nearby Moran State Park—starting your day off with a smoked-salmon Benedict with Calabrian-chili hollandaise will provide you with plenty of fuel for recreation. **Known for:** locally sourced and foraged ingredients; smoked-salmon Benedict; funky, rustic vibe. [$] *Average main: $25* ✉ *107 Doe Bay Rd., Orcas Island* ☎ *360/376–8059* 🌐 *www.doebay.com* 🕒 *Closed Tues.–Thurs. Limited hrs Oct.–May; call ahead.*

Inn at Ship Bay

$$$ | **PACIFIC NORTHWEST** | The restaurant at this stylish, contemporary inn just a mile from Eastsound offers among the most memorable dining experiences on the island. Tucked into a renovated 1869 farmhouse, the dining room and bar serve food that emphasizes local, seasonal ingredients. **Known for:** outstanding wine list; house-made sourdough bread made from a century-old starter yeast; ingredients from on-site garden and orchard. [$] *Average main: $26* ✉ *326 Olga Rd., Orcas Island* ☎ *360/376–5886* 🌐 *www.innatshipbay.com* 🕒 *Closed Sun.–Mon. and mid-Dec.–mid-Mar. No lunch.*

Madrona Bar & Grill

$$ | **PACIFIC NORTHWEST** | Situated on the Eastsound waterfront, this pub-style eatery serves classic Northwest cuisine: pan-fried local oysters, Dungeness crab cakes, Angus beef burgers, and grilled wild Coho salmon. But what really stands out here is the atmosphere. **Known for:** rotating microbrew beer menu; some of the best water views in Eastsound; classic local seafood dishes. [$] *Average main: $23* ✉ *Porter Building, 310 Main St., Orcas Island* ☎ *360/376–7171* 🌐 *www.madronabarandgrill.com.*

Mansion Restaurant

$$$$ | **PACIFIC NORTHWEST** | For a special-occasion dinner, it's worth the drive to this grandly romantic dining room inside the historic main inn at Rosario Resort, known for polished service, sweeping bay views, and Northwest cuisine. The dishes are more classic than creative, like king salmon with risotto and a seared strip steak with potatoes au gratin, but made with high-quality ingredients (some sources are listed on the menu). **Known for:** lovely views of Cascade Bay; dinner service in the mahogany-clad fireside Moran Lounge; small portions for the price. $ *Average main: $45* ⊠ *1400 Rosario Rd., Orcas Island* ☎ *360/376–2222* ⊕ *www.rosarioresort.com.*

Matia
$$$ | **PACIFIC NORTHWEST** | A recent Orcas Island addition, Matia has already garnered national accolades for its outstanding seasonal cuisine that focuses on local ingredients, creative flavor combinations, and artistic presentation. Many of the dishes are vegetable-focused, such as an ancient grain panisse with mushrooms and carrot dumplings with pumpkin-seed pesto, but you'll also find options like a lamb pancake with gochujang creamed cabbage and king salmon with apricot confit and Szechuan chili crisp. **Known for:** local ingredients; small portions; creative vegetarian-friendly fare. $ *Average main: $45* ⊠ *123 N. Beach Rd., Eastsound* ☎ *206/622–2674* ⊕ *www.matiarestaurant.com.*

Mijitas
$$ | **MEXICAN** | **FAMILY** | A bustling family-friendly Mexican restaurant with a cozy dining room and a sprawling shaded garden patio is helmed by Raul Rios, who learned to cook during his years growing up outside Mexico City. The flavorful food here isn't entirely authentic—expect a mix of Mexican and Mexican-American dishes, many featuring local ingredients. **Known for:** sweet, tangy margaritas; expansive garden patio; braised short ribs with blackberry mole sauce. $ *Average main: $23* ⊠ *310 A St., Orcas Island* ☎ *360/376–6722* ⊙ *Closed Sun.-Mon.*

Monti
$$$ | **ITALIAN** | Inspired by the owners' culinary dream visit to Rome, Monti stands out for its authentic homemade pastas made with primo ingredients. The menu also features a small handful of main dishes like whole trout and a pork chop. **Known for:** on the pricey side; perfectly made pastas; a taste of Rome on Orcas. $ *Average main: $35* ⊠ *382 Prune Alley, Eastsound* ⊕ *www.montimontimonti.com.*

☕ Coffee and Quick Bites

Brown Bear Baking
$ | **BAKERY** | You might make it a point to get to this wildly popular village bakery by late morning—come midafternoon, many of the best treats are sold out. Delectables here include flaky almond-coated bear paw pastries, rich croque monsieur sandwiches, hubcap-size "Sasquatch" cookies, Tuscan olive bread, and moist blueberry muffins. **Known for:** almond-coated bear paw; French pastries; alfresco dining on the patio. $ *Average main: $8* ⊠ *29 N. Beach Rd., Eastsound* ☎ *360/855–7456* ⊕ *www.facebook.com/brownbearbaking.*

Olga Rising
$ | **CAFÉ** | A charming small café with bountiful planters of flowers and artsy touches like a gorgeous forest-scene stained glass window, the relatively new Olga Rising has become a neighborhood fixture quickly. (Note: Despite the name, it's in Eastbound, not the tiny hamlet of Olga.) **Known for:** house-made baked goods; friendly service; tasty coffee. $ *Average main: $7* ⊠ *172 N. Beach Rd., Eastsound* ☎ *360/376–3035.*

🛏 Hotels

Doe Bay Resort + Retreat
$$$ | **RESORT** | **FAMILY** | The family-friendly Doe Bay Resort has definite hippie roots, and some of that vibe remains intact—its large communal hot tubs overlooking a lovely little bay are still clothing optional—but the current owners have restored the charming rustic cabins that dot the 38-acre waterfront resort, all of which are clean and comfortable. **Pros:** some cabins have bathrooms, kitchens, and great views; home to the popular grassroots Doe Bay Fest; kayaks available for rent. **Cons:** many cabins have shared bathroom

facilities; farther from Eastsound than most lodging; two-night minimum stay. [$] *Rooms from: $285* ✉ *107 Doe Bay Rd, Orcas Island* ☎ *206/376–2291* 🌐 *www.doebay.com* 🛏 *26 cabins* 🍴 *No Meals.*

Kangaroo House

$$ | B&B/INN | Set back from the road behind a large garden overlooked by a lovely covered porch, this B&B in a local landmark Craftsman features nicely appointed rooms with en suite bathrooms and has an interesting history: it's named for a Depression-era resident kangaroo that provided entertainment for islanders (ask the friendly, knowledgeable hosts for the story), though these days the busy bird feeders and deer wandering through the brush are the main animal attractions. **Pros:** garden hot tub with a sign-up sheet for privacy; 5-minute walk to beach and Eastsound; fabulous multicourse organic breakfast. **Cons:** 3-night minimum for summer visits that include Sat.; kids must be 12 to stay here; 8-step stoop and only one downstairs room. [$] *Rooms from: $204* ✉ *1459 N. Beach Rd, Orcas Island* ☎ *360/376–2175* 🌐 *www.kangaroohouse.com* 🛏 *5 rooms* 🍴 *Free Breakfast.*

Kingfish at West Sound

$$$ | B&B/INN | Spacious units in this atmospheric 1902 house are equipped with a king or queen bed, private bath, and all the serenity a guest could ever want. **Pros:** decor is tasteful and contemporary; good café; water views (two suites have decks). **Cons:** small bathrooms in some rooms; some noise from road and busy marina; two-night minimum. [$] *Rooms from: $250* ✉ *Crow Valley Rd., at Deer Harbor Rd., Orcas Island* ☎ *360/376–2500* 🌐 *www.kingfishinn.com* 🕒 *Closed Jan.* 🛏 *4 rooms* 🍴 *Free Breakfast.*

★ Outlook Inn

$$$ | HOTEL | Outlook Inn caters to a range of budgets with its attractively appointed offerings, including basic options with twin beds and shared bathrooms, mid-range rooms with double or queen beds, and rambling bay-view suites with gas fireplaces, kitchenettes, and two-person Jacuzzi tubs. **Pros:** steps from Eastsound restaurants and shops; friendly and helpful staff; on-site New Leaf Cafe with water-view patio dining. **Cons:** in-town location can be a little noisy; only some rooms have water view; least expensive rooms have shared bath. [$] *Rooms from: $269* ✉ *171 Main St., Eastsound* ☎ *360/376–2200, 888/688–5665* 🌐 *www.outlookinn.com* 🛏 *54 rooms* 🍴 *No Meals.*

★ Rosario Resort and Spa

$$ | RESORT | FAMILY | Shipbuilding magnate Robert Moran built this Arts and Crafts–style waterfront mansion in 1909, and it's now the centerpiece of a gorgeous 40-acre resort that comprises several buildings with sweeping views of Cascade Bay and Rosario Point. **Pros:** water views from all buildings and many rooms; management continues to make improvements; first-rate spa and adults-only pool. **Cons:** often busy with weddings and special events; some rooms/common spaces need updating; 15-minute drive to Eastsound. [$] *Rooms from: $185* ✉ *1400 Rosario Rd., Orcas Island* ☎ *360/376–2222, 800/562–8820* 🌐 *www.rosarioresort.com* 🛏 *67 rooms* 🍴 *No Meals.*

Nightlife

★ The Barnacle

BARS | This quirky hole-in-the-wall bar with a speakeasy vibe has developed a cult following for its sophisticated, well-made craft cocktails—many infused with house-made bitters and local herbs and berries—and interesting wines. On this quiet, early-to-bed island, it's a nice late-night option. Light tapas are served, too. ✉ *249 Prune Alley, Eastsound* ☎ *206/679–5683* 🕒 *Closed Mon.-Tues.*

Island Hoppin' Brewery

BREWPUBS | Set in an otherwise inauspicious industrial area near the airport, this craft brewery and taproom has earned a reputation throughout the archipelago—and even on the mainland in Seattle—for well-made beers, including the faintly citrusy Elwha Rock IPA and the silky Old Salts Brown Ale. Smoked salmon, cheese and crackers, and a few other snacks are sold in the homey taproom. While it's not a late-night haunt, it does stay open two hours later until 9 pm on Thursday through Saturday. ⊠ 33 Hope Lane, Eastsound ☎ 360/376–6079 ⊕ www.islandhoppinbrewery.com.

 ## Activities

BIKING

With hilly terrain and narrow roads, biking on Orcas is not for the faint of heart, though a sturdy e-bike rental and a pre-planned route make the experience approachable for most riders. Consider booking in advance, as e-bikes tend to go fast. Road bikes start at around $30 while e-bikes begin at around $40 for a half-day rental.

Orcas Bikes

BIKING | Orcas carries a fleet of electric bikes by Seattle-based Rad Power Bikes, which feature several levels of pedal assist and big tires, making tooling around the hilly island more doable for leisure bikers. The shop offers a couple of different guided tours, including a beginner-friendly ride that stops at farms and shops, and a much harder haul to Buck Bay. ⊠ 414 N. Beach Rd., Eastsound ☎ 360/820–8282 ⊕ www.orcasbikes.com ◷ Seasonal hours vary.

Wildlife Cycles

BIKING | This trusty shop rents bikes, including road bikes, BMX, and electric models, and can recommend great routes all over the island. ⊠ 350 N. Beach Rd., Eastsound ☎ 360/376–4708 ⊕ www.wildlifecycles.com.

BOATING AND SAILING

Northwest Classic Daysailing

SAILING | It's all hands on deck when you take a private tour of the San Juan Islands aboard the classic 1948 wooden sloop "Aura"—though only if you want to steer and work sails, as the captain will cater the trip to your liking, including instructions for total newbies. Three-hour tours depart from Deer Harbor May through October, cost $300, and can accommodate up to six guests. ⊠ 5164 Deer Harbor Rd., Deer Harbor ☎ 360/376–5581 ⊕ www.classicdaysails.com.

Orcas Boat Rentals

BOATING | You can rent a variety of sailboats, outboards, and skiffs for full- and half-day trips, or book custom charter cruises, with this company. All boats are equipped with GPS systems, and sturdy RIB fishing boats come with a depth finder, GPS, and fish-finder unit. ⊠ 5164 Deer Harbor Rd., Orcas Island ☎ 360/376–7616 ⊕ www.orcasboatrentals.com.

West Beach Resort Marina

BOATING | This is a good option for renting motorized boats, kayaks and canoes, and fishing gear on the island's northwest shore. The resort is also a popular spot for divers, who can fill their tanks here. ⊠ 190 Waterfront Way, Orcas Island ☎ 360/376–2240, 877/937–8224 ⊕ www.westbeachresort.com.

SEA KAYAKING

All equipment is usually included in a rental package or tour. Three-hour trips start at around $75; day tours, around $150.

Orcas Outdoors Sea Kayak Tours

KAYAKING | This outfitter offers one-, two-, and three-hour journeys, as well as day trips, overnight tours, and rentals. ⊠ Orcas Ferry Landing, Orcas Island ☎ 360/376–4611 ⊕ www.orcasoutdoors.com.

Shearwater Kayak Tours

KAYAKING | This established company holds kayaking classes and runs three-hour, day, and overnight tours from Rosario, Deer Harbor, West Beach, and Doe Bay resorts. ⊠ *138 N. Beach Rd., Eastsound* ☎ *360/376–4699* ⊕ *www.shearwaterkayaks.com.*

WHALE-WATCHING

Cruises, which run about four hours, are scheduled daily in summer and once or twice weekly at other times. The cost is around $110 to $130 per person, and boats hold 20 to 40 people. Wear warm clothing and bring a snack.

Deer Harbor Charters

BOATING | This eco-friendly tour company (the first in the San Juans to use biodiesel) offers whale-watching cruises around the island straits, with departures from both Deer Harbor Marina and Rosario Resort. Outboards and skiffs are also available, as is fishing gear. ⊠ *5164 Deer Harbor Rd., Deer Harbor* ☎ *360/376–5989, 800/544–5758* ⊕ *www.deerharborcharters.com.*

Orcas Island Eclipse Charters

BOATING | In addition to tours that search around Orcas Island for whale pods and other sea life, this charter company offers lighthouse tours. ⊠ *Orcas Island Ferry Landing, Orcas Island* ☎ *360/376–6566* ⊕ *www.orcasislandwhales.com.*

Shopping

Darvill's Bookstore

BOOKS | This island favorite, with a coffee bar and a couple of cozy seats with panoramic views of the water, specializes in literary fiction and nautical literature. ⊠ *296 Main St., Eastsound* ☎ *360/376–2135* ⊕ *www.darvillsbookstore.com.*

★ Doe Bay Wine Co.

WINE/SPIRITS | Owned by an Orcas Island-born sommelier who worked at restaurants in Vail and Vegas before returning home, this cheerful little bottle shop and tasting room in Eastsound has a great selection of wine, beer, and cider from around the world, including a wine series, the Orcas Project, that is produced in collaboration with Pacific Northwest winemakers and artists. ⊠ *109 N. Beach Rd., Eastsound* ☎ *360/376–7467* ⊕ *www.doebaywinecompany.com.*

Girl Meets Dirt

FOOD | According to Girl Meets Dirt founder Audra Lawlor, fruit is affected by terroir, just like wine, and the salty San Juan Islands breezes certainly seem to work magic on locally grown stone fruit and pomes. Lawlor's small-batch jams made in a collection of heavy copper pots are the perfect addition to a charcuterie board, with complex flavors like Cherry Fig Leaf, Island Plum, and Orange Peppered Peach. The shop also carries housemade shrubs and bitters. ⊠ *208 Enchanted Forest Rd., Eastsound* ☎ *360/375–6269* ⊕ *www.girlmeetsdirt.com* ⊙ *Closed Sun.*

Island Thyme

SKINCARE | Some of the ingredients used in the small-batch soaps and skincare products sold at this lovely-smelling Eastsound boutique are grown on the local Island Thyme farm. Founded in 1996 on Orcas, the aromatherapy-focused line is now carried across the state and beyond. ⊠ *296 Main St., Orcas Island* ☎ *360/376–4260* ⊕ *www.crowvalley.com.*

★ Orcas Island Artworks Gallery

ART GALLERIES | Stop by this cooperative gallery to see impressive displays of pottery, sculpture, jewelry, art glass, paintings, and quilts by resident artists, including an upstairs gallery devoted to original paintings by well-known Northwest landscape artist James Hardman. You'll find gifts in a wide price range at this wonderful space. ⊠ *11 Point Lawrence Rd., Olga* ☎ *360/376–4408* ⊕ *www.orcasartworks.com.*

★ Orcas Island Pottery

ART GALLERIES | A stroll through the historic house, outbuildings, and gardens of this enchanting arts complex on a bluff overlooking President Channel and Waldron Island is more than just a chance to browse beautiful pottery—it's a great spot simply to relax and soak up the views. More than a dozen regular and guest potters exhibit and sell their wares here, everything from functional dinnerware and mugs to fanciful vases and wall hangings. ■**TIP→ Pottery isn't always the most kid-friendly but this place has playful outdoor pieces and a very cool treehouse to check out.** ⊠ *338 Old Pottery Rd., Orcas Island* ☏ *360/376‑2813* ⊕ *www.orcasislandpottery.com.*

San Juan Island

45 minutes by ferry from Orcas Island, 75–90 mins by ferry from Anacortes or Sidney, BC (near Victoria).

San Juan is the cultural and commercial hub of the archipelago that shares its name. Friday Harbor, the county seat, is larger, more vibrant, and more crowded than any of the towns on Orcas or Lopez, yet San Juan still has miles of rural roads, uncrowded beaches, and rolling woodlands. It's easy to get here, too, making San Juan the preferred destination for travelers who have time to visit only one island.

Several different Coast Salish tribes first settled on San Juan, establishing encampments along the north end of the island. North-end beaches were especially busy during the annual salmon migration, when hundreds of tribal members would gather along the shoreline to fish, cook, and exchange news. Many of the indigenous early inhabitants were killed by smallpox and other imported diseases in the 18th and 19th centuries. Smallpox Bay was where tribal members plunged into the icy water to cool the fevers that came with the disease.

The 18th century brought explorers from England and Spain, but the island remained sparsely populated until the mid-1800s. From the 1880s, Roche Harbor and its newspaper were controlled by lime-company owner and Republican bigwig John S. McMillin, who virtually ran this part of the island as a personal fiefdom from 1886 until his death in 1936. Friday Harbor ultimately emerged as the island's largest community. The town's main street, rising from the harbor and ferry landing up the slopes of a modest hill, hasn't changed much in the past few decades, though the island population has grown along with the rest of the region and the cafés, inns, and shops have become increasingly urbane.

GETTING HERE AND AROUND

With ferry connections from both Anacortes and Sidney, BC (on Vancouver Island, near Victoria), San Juan is the most convenient of the islands to reach, and the island is easily explored by car; public transportation and bicycles also work but require a bit more effort. However, if you're staying in Friday Harbor, you can get from the ferry terminal to your hotel as well as to area shops and restaurants easily on foot.

One-hour flights from Seattle to San Juan Airport, Friday Harbor, or Roche Harbor cost about $180 to $220 each way.

San Juan Transit & Tours operates shuttle buses daily from mid-May to mid-September. Hop on at Friday Harbor to get to all the island's significant points and parks, including the San Juan Vineyards, Krystal Acres Alpaca Farm, Lime Kiln Point State Park, and Snug Harbor and Roche Harbor resorts. Different buses call on different stops, so be sure to check the schedule before you plan your day. Tickets are $5 one-way or $15 for a day pass. From mid-June through mid-September, the Friday Harbor Jolly Trolley offers trips around the island—also stopping at all of the key attractions—in an old-fashioned trolley-style bus; tickets cost $25 and are good for the entire day.

CONTACTS Friday Harbor Jolly Trolley. ✉ *Friday Harbor* ☎ *360/298–8873* ⊕ *www.fridayharborjollytrolley.com.* **San Juan Transit & Tours.** ✉ *Cannery Landing, Friday Harbor* ☎ *360/378–8887* ⊕ *sanjuantransit.com.*

The Washington State Ferries crossings from Anacortes to Friday Harbor takes about 75 to 90 minutes; round-trip fares in high season are about $15 per person or $73 for a car and driver. It's about the same distance from Sidney, BC, on Vancouver Island—this service is available twice daily in summer and once daily spring and fall (there's no BC service in winter). Round-trip fares are about $25 per person, $85 for car and driver. Clipper Navigation operates the passenger-only *San Juan Clipper* jet catamaran service between Pier 69 in Seattle and Friday Harbor. Boats leave Seattle at 8:15 am and return from Friday Harbor at 5 pm. They operate daily mid-June–early September; Thursday–Monday mid-May–mid-June; and weekends only early September–early October—reservations are strongly recommended. During peak season, fares start at $160 for a round-trip ticket, depending on the day (advance tickets are also cheaper). Clipper also offers optional whale-watching excursions, which can be combined with ferry passage.

■**TIP**→ **Some points on the west end of San Juan Island are so close to BC, Canada (which is visible across the Haro Straight), that cell phones may switch to roaming; it's a good idea to turn roaming off while touring the island to avoid unexpected charges.**

CONTACT Clipper Navigation. ✉ *Seattle* ☎ *206/448–5000, 800/888–2535* ⊕ *www. clippervacations.com.*

ESSENTIALS
The San Juan Island Chamber of Commerce has a visitor center (open daily 10 to 4) in Friday Harbor where you can grab brochures and ask for advice.

VISITOR INFORMATION San Juan Island Chamber of Commerce. ✉ *165 1st St., San Juan Island* ☎ *360/378–5240* ⊕ *www. sanjuanisland.org.*

Sights

The Farm at Krystal Acres
FARM/RANCH | FAMILY | Kids and adults love admiring the more than 70 alpacas from South America at this sprawling 80-acre ranch on the west side of the island. The shop in the big barn displays beautiful, high-quality clothing and crafts, all handmade from alpaca hair. ✉ *152 Blazing Tree Rd., San Juan Island* ☎ *360/378–6125* ⊕ *www.krystalacres.com* ✉ *Free* ⊘ *Closed Tues. and Sun.*

★ Lime Kiln Point State Park
STATE/PROVINCIAL PARK | FAMILY | To watch whales cavorting in Haro Strait, head to these 36 acres on San Juan's western side just nine miles from Friday Harbor. A rocky coastal trail leads to lookout points and a little 1919 lighthouse. The best time to spot whales is from the end of April through September, but resident pods of orcas regularly cruise past the point. This park is also a beautiful spot to soak in a summer sunset, with expansive views of Vancouver Island and beyond. ✉ *1567 Westside Rd., San Juan Island* ☎ *360/378–2044* ⊕ *www.parks.wa.gov/ parks* ✉ *$10* ⊘ *Interpretive center closed mid-Sept.–late May.*

Pelindaba Lavender Farm
FARM/RANCH | FAMILY | Wander a spectacular 20-acre valley smothered with endless rows of fragrant purple-and-gold lavender blossoms. The oils are distilled for use in therapeutic, botanical, and household products, all created on-site. The farm hosts the very popular San Juan Island Lavender Festival the third weekend

of July. If you can't make it to the farm, stop at the outlet in the Friday Harbor Center at 150 1st Street, where you can buy their products and sample delicious lavender-infused baked goods, ice cream, and beverages. ⊠ *33 Hawthorne La., Friday Harbor* ☎ *360/378–4248, 866/819–1911* ⊕ *www.pelindabalavender.com* ⊠ *Free* ⊙ *Closed Nov.–Apr.*

★ Roche Harbor

TOWN | FAMILY | It's hard to believe that fashionable Roche Harbor at the northern end of San Juan Island was once the most important producer of builder's lime on the West Coast. In 1882, John S. McMillin gained control of the lime company and expanded production. But even in its heyday as a limestone quarrying village, Roche Harbor was known for abundant flowers and welcoming accommodations. McMillin transformed a bunkhouse into private lodgings for his invited guests, including such notables as Teddy Roosevelt. The guesthouse is now the Hotel de Haro, which displays period photographs and artifacts in its lobby. The staff has maps of the old quarry, kilns, and the Mausoleum, an eerie Greek-inspired memorial to McMillin.

McMillin's heirs operated the quarries and plant until 1956, when they sold the company to the Tarte family, who developed it into an upscale resort (but no longer own it)—the old lime kilns still stand below the bluff. Locals say it took two years for the limestone dust to wash off the trees around the harbor. McMillin's former home is now a restaurant, and workers' cottages have been transformed into comfortable visitors' lodgings. With its rose gardens, cobblestone waterfront, and well-manicured lawns, Roche Harbor retains the flavor of its days as a hangout for McMillin's powerful friends—especially since the sheltered harbor is very popular with well-to-do pleasure boaters. ⊠ *Roche Harbor Rd., San Juan Island* ⊕ *www.rocheharbor.com.*

San Juan Historical Museum

HISTORY MUSEUM | This museum in an old farmhouse presents island life at the turn of the 20th century through historic photography, documents, and buildings. ⊠ *405 Price St., Friday Harbor* ☎ *360/378–3949* ⊕ *www.sjmuseum.org* ⊠ *$8* ⊙ *Closed Nov.–Mar. except by appointment.*

★ San Juan Island National Historical Park

HISTORIC SIGHT | FAMILY | Fortifications and other 19th-century military installments commemorate the Pig War, in which the United States and Great Britain nearly went into battle over their respective claims on the San Juan Islands. The dispute began in 1859 when an American settler killed a British settler's pig and escalated until roughly 500 American soldiers and 2,200 British soldiers with five warships were poised for battle. Fortunately, no blood (other than the pig's) was spilled, and the disagreement was finally settled in 1872 in the Americans' favor, with Kaiser Wilhelm I of Germany as arbitrator.

The park comprises two separate areas on opposite sides of the island. English Camp, in a sheltered cove of Garrison Bay on the northern end, includes a blockhouse, a commissary, and barracks. A popular (though steep) hike is to the top of Young Hill, from which you can get a great view of the northwest side of the island. American Camp, on the southern end, has a visitor center and the remains of fortifications; it stretches along driftwood-strewn beaches. Many of the American Camp's walking trails are through prairie; in the evening, dozens of rabbits emerge from their warrens to nibble in the fields. Great views greet you from the top of the Mt. Finlayson Trail—if you're lucky, you might be able to see Mt. Baker and Mt. Rainier along with the Olympics. From June to August you can take guided hikes and see reenacts of 1860s-era military life. ⊠ *Park headquarters, 125 Spring St., American Camp,*

6 miles southeast of Friday Harbor; English Camp, 9 miles northwest of Friday Harbor, Friday Harbor ☎ 360/378–2240 🌐 www.nps.gov/sajh 🎫 Free ⏲ American Camp visitor center closed mid-Dec.–Feb. English Camp visitor center closed early Sept.–late May.

San Juan Islands Museum of Art

ART MUSEUM | Housed in a sleek, contemporary building, SJIMA presents rotating art shows and exhibits with an emphasis on island and Northwest artists, including the highly touted Artists' Registry Show in winter, which features works by nearly 100 San Juan Islands artists. ✉ *540 Spring St., Friday Harbor* ☎ *360/370–5050* 🌐 *www.sjima.org* 🎫 *$10; Mon. "Pay What You Can"* ⏲ *Closed Tue.–Wed. in summer, Tue.–Thu. off season.*

San Juan Islands Sculpture Park

PUBLIC ART | **FAMILY** | At this serene 20-acre park near Roche Harbor, you can stroll along five winding trails to view more than 150 colorful—and in many cases, large-scale—sculptures spread amid freshwater and saltwater wetlands, open woods, blossoming fields, and rugged terrain. The park is also a haven for birds; more than 120 species nest and breed here. It's a great spot for picnicking, and dogs are welcome. ✉ *Roche Harbor Rd., just before entrance to Roche Harbor Resort, Roche Harbor* 🌐 *www.sjisculpturepark.com* 🎫 *$5 donation recommended.*

San Juan Vineyard

WINERY | A remodeled 1895 schoolhouse serving estate-grown wines, this picturesque winery is worth a visit for the scenery and its award-winning Siegerrebe and Madeleine Angevine varietals (the winery belongs to the Puget Sound AVA, the coolest-climate growing region in Washington). The vineyard's wines show up on many local menus. ✉ *3136 Roche Harbor Rd., San Juan Island* ☎ *360/378–9463* 🌐 *www.sanjuanvineyard.com.*

Whale Museum

SCIENCE MUSEUM | **FAMILY** | A dramatic exterior mural depicting several types of whales welcomes you into a world that is all about these behemoth beauties. Visitors will find models of whales and large whale skeletons, recordings of whale sounds, videos of whales, and information about the plight of the three local orca pods. Head around to the back of the first-floor gift shop to view maps of the latest orca trackings in the area. ✉ *62 1st St. N, Friday Harbor* ☎ *360/378–4710* 🌐 *www.whalemuseum.org* 🎫 *$10.*

🍴 Restaurants

Downriggers

$$$ | **PACIFIC NORTHWEST** | This snazzy, contemporary, seafood-driven restaurant overlooking the harbor has a light-filled dining room that makes a terrific spot to watch boats and ferries come and go while sampling such tempting fare as Penn Cove mussels, pan-seared sockeye salmon with seasonal veggies, and a seafood Cobb salad piled high with Dungeness crab and whole shrimp. **Known for:** pub fare with creative twists; extensive list of craft cocktails; seafood salads. [$] *Average main: $23* ✉ *10 Front St., Friday Harbor* ☎ *360/378–2700* 🌐 *www.downriggerssanjuan.com.*

Ernie's Aviation Cafe

$ | **ECLECTIC** | Ask a local for the best lunch recommendation in town, and you may be surprised by the answer—plenty of folks will send you to this casual diner at the airport, where you can watch planes take off while you eat. You'll find a few Asian-fusion dishes on the menu, including Korean-style *bulgogi* (grilled marinated beef) and hearty noodle bowls, plus diner classics like hefty cheeseburgers, breakfast sandwiches, and flaky popovers. **Known for:** popovers at breakfast; several Korean-inspired dishes; watching airplanes. [$] *Average main: $13* ✉ *744 Airport Circle Dr., Friday Harbor* ☎ *360/378–6605* ⏲ *Closed Thurs.*

★ Restaurant at Friday Harbor House
$$$ | PACIFIC NORTHWEST | Ingenuity and dedication to local ingredients are hallmarks of this stylish, contemporary restaurant, where locals and tourists alike come for dishes such as baked oysters, mushroom panzanella, San Juan Island–raised lamb shoulder cooked in fig leaves, and a popular house burger; during the summer, the hotel's outdoor Raw Bar serves seafood and frozen cocktails. The restaurant's daily breakfast is popular with islanders and convenient for hotel guests: the brunch burger, topped with a fried egg and green-tomato-and-bacon jam, and breakfast poutine with duck confit and cheese curds make for decadent starts to your day. **Known for:** excellent cocktails and an expansive wine list; a popular daily breakfast (until noon on the weekend); panoramic views of Friday Harbor. [$] *Average main: $34* ✉ *Friday Harbor House, 130 West St., Friday Harbor* ☎ *360/378–8455* 🌐 *www.fridayharborhouse.com* ⏲ *No dinner Tues.–Wed.*

San Juan Island Brewing
$ | AMERICAN | The island's local brewery, just a few short blocks from the ferry landing, has a nice selection of suds brewed on-site, along with standard brew-pub fare (pretzels, cheese curds, chicken wings) and surprisingly good individual pizzas. **Known for:** craft beer made on-site; fast service; light eats and pizza. [$] *Average main: $13* ✉ *110 A St., Friday Harbor* ☎ *360/378–2017* 🌐 *www.sanjuanbrew.com* ⏲ *Closed Tues.*

Coffee and Quick Bites

Bakery San Juan
$ | BAKERY | The fabulous aroma lets you know you're in for a treat at this popular island bakery, which makes fresh bread, cakes and pastries, sandwiches, and pizza. **Known for:** wild-yeasted baked goods; fresh sandwiches and pizza; nice place for morning coffee. [$] *Average main: $7* ✉ *775 Mullis St., San Juan Island* ☎ *360/378–5810.*

The Bean Cafe
$ | CAFÉ | This friendly coffee shop has a ferry cam so you can keep track of your ride back to the mainland while enjoying espresso drinks, baked goods, and a selection of breakfast and lunch items. **Known for:** voted best latte on the island; handmade caramels; wine and beer options. [$] *Average main: $6* ✉ *150 B 1st Street, San Juan Island* ☎ *360/370–5858* 🌐 *www.thebeancafe.com* ⏲ *Closed Sat.–Sun.*

The Market Chef
$ | CAFÉ | Only 50 yards from the ferry holding area (though that includes a lot of stairs), this pleasant little café and specialty grocery store makes fantastic sandwiches (try the roast-beef-and-rocket, which is served on a house-baked roll with spicy chili aioli). The soups and deli items—including a decadent macaroni and cheese—are also top-notch. **Known for:** strong coffee; picnic and to-go lunches; gourmet locally made goods. [$] *Average main: $12* ✉ *225 A St., Friday Harbor* ☎ *360/378–4546* ⏲ *Closed Sat.–Mon. No dinner.*

Hotels

Bird Rock Hotel
$$$ | HOTEL | The charming lodging options here range from affordable, compact rooms with private baths down the hall, to downright cushy two-bedroom suites with gas fireplaces, spacious sitting rooms, pitched ceilings, and terrific harbor views. **Pros:** handy downtown Friday Harbor location; tasteful, unfussy furnishings; continental breakfast and fresh-baked afternoon cookies. **Cons:** central location means some street noise and crowds; some rooms are small; no on-site restaurant. [$] *Rooms from: $231* ✉ *35 1st St., Friday Harbor* ☎ *360/378–5848, 800/352–2632* 🌐 *www.*

birdrockhotel.com 🛏 *10 rooms, 5 suites* 🍴 *Free Breakfast.*

★ Friday Harbor House

$$$$ | HOTEL | At this bluff-top getaway floor-to-ceiling windows; sleek, modern wood furnishings; and fabrics in serene hues fill the rooms—all of which have gas fireplaces, deep jetted tubs, Chemex pour-over coffee carafes, and at least partial views of the marina, ferry landing, and San Juan Channel below. **Pros:** some room views are breathtaking (request at booking); excellent restaurant and bar with views; free parking and just steps from downtown shopping and dining. **Cons:** two-night minimum at peak season; among the priciest hotels in the San Juan Islands; some early-morning noise from the ferry landing. [$] *Rooms from: $409* ✉ *130 West St., Friday Harbor* ☎ *360/378–8455, 866/722–7356* 🌐 *www.fridayharborhouse.com* 🛏 *23 rooms* 🍴 *Free Breakfast.*

★ Island Inn at 123 West

$$$ | HOTEL | There's a pretty striking contrast of accommodation styles at this cosmopolitan complex that tumbles down a hillside overlooking Friday Harbor, from intimate Euro-style rooms that lack exterior windows to expansive suites with water views to ginormous bilevel penthouses with two bedrooms, private decks, gorgeous full kitchens, and astounding views. **Pros:** penthouse suites are great for luxurious family getaways; Euro-style standard rooms are a good deal; handy in-town location. **Cons:** suites are quite spendy; standard rooms have no views; no on-site dining. [$] *Rooms from: $300* ✉ *123 West St., Friday Harbor* ☎ *360/378–4400, 877/512–9262* 🌐 *www.123west.com* 🛏 *16 rooms* 🍴 *No Meals.*

Kirk House Bed & Breakfast

$$$ | B&B/INN | Rooms are all differently decorated in this 1907 Craftsman bungalow, the one-time summer home of steel magnate Peter Kirk: the Garden Room has a botanical motif, the sunny Trellis Room is done in soft shades of yellow and green, and the Arbor Room has French doors leading out to the garden. **Pros:** gorgeous house full of stained glass and other lovely details; within walking distance of town; nice breakfast in the parlor or in bed. **Cons:** occasional noise from nearby airport; a couple of the rooms are on the small side; with only four rooms, inn itself may feel too cozy for some. [$] *Rooms from: $245* ✉ *595 Park St., Friday Harbor* ☎ *360/378–3757, 800/639–2762* 🌐 *www.kirkhouse.net* 🛏 *4 rooms* 🍴 *Free Breakfast.*

★ Lakedale

$$$ | RESORT | FAMILY | This 82-acre property may not have invented glamping, but it was one of the first to nail the travel trend, and the resort's hip 450-square-foot yurts—which share a private lakefront beach and fire pit—are as luxurious as they come, with fireplaces, kitchenettes, spacious bathrooms, and private decks with hot tubs. **Pros:** pretty grounds and fun amenities; close to Friday Harbor but feels secluded; serene hotel rooms at the lakefront lodge (16 and up only) were just renovated. **Cons:** some noise from nearby Roche Harbor Road; the grounds include a lot of camping spots, so the resort can feel crowded; books up a year in advance. [$] *Rooms from: $299* ✉ *4313 Roche Harbor Rd., San Juan Island* ☎ *360/378–2350* 🌐 *www.lakedale.com* 🛏 *10 rooms, 7 yurts, 6 cabins* 🍴 *Free Breakfast.*

★ Roche Harbor Resort

$$$ | RESORT | This sprawling resort, with several types of accommodations ranging from historic hotel rooms to luxurious contemporary waterfront suites, occupies the site of the lime works that made John S. McMillin his fortune in the late 19th century. **Pros:** lots of options for families and groups; several on-site restaurants; gorgeous full-service spa. **Cons:** condos have less character and are away from the waterfront; isolated from the rest of the island; the least expensive rooms in Hotel de Haro have shared baths. 💲 *Rooms from: $290* ✉ *248 Reuben Memorial Dr., Roche Harbor* 🕾 *360/378–2155, 800/451–8910* 🌐 *www.rocheharbor.com* 🛏 *53 units* 🍴 *No Meals.*

Snug Harbor Resort

$$$$ | RESORT | FAMILY | At this popular cottage resort and marina on the northwest side of the island, all of the units feature tall windows overlooking the water, high ceilings, well-equipped kitchens, knotty-pine wood paneling, gas fireplaces, and private decks. **Pros:** beautiful, contemporary decor; quiet location with a coffeehouse and small camp store; nice views of the harbor. **Cons:** no pets; 20-minute drive from Friday Harbor; expensive and two-night minimum required. 💲 *Rooms from: $549* ✉ *1997 Mitchell Bay Rd., Friday Harbor* 🕾 *360/378–4762* 🌐 *www.snugresort.com* 🛏 *17 cottages* 🍴 *No Meals.*

Activities

BEACHES

San Juan County Park

BEACH | You'll find a wide gravel beachfront at this park 10 miles west of Friday Harbor, overlooking waters where orcas often frolic in summer, plus grassy lawns with picnic tables and a small campground. **Amenities:** parking (free); toilets. **Best for:** walking. ✉ *380 Westside Rd., San Juan Island* 🕾 *360/378–8420* 🌐 *www.co.san-juan.wa.us.*

South Beach at American Camp

BEACH | This two-mile public beach on the southern end of the island is part of San Juan Island National Historical Park. **Amenities:** parking (free); toilets. **Best for:** solitude; walking. ✉ *Off Cattle Point Rd., San Juan Island* 🌐 *www.nps.gov/sajh.*

BIKING

There are some big hills and narrow shoulders on San Juan Island, but it's a popular place to bike, especially the 35-mile loop out of Friday Harbor that offers gorgeous scenery and no repeat views. You can rent standard, mountain, and BMX bikes for $40 to $50 per day or about $200 to $240 per week. Tandem, recumbent, and electric-assist bikes rent for about $65 to $85 per day.

Download an island bike map of San Juan Island at 🌐 *www.visitsanjuans.com/san-juan-island-bike-map-pdf.pdf.*

Discovery Adventure Tours

BIKING | The island's longest-running brick-and-mortar outfitter rents by bikes by the hour, day, or week. E-bikes tend to go quickly since they make conquering hills a breeze for more novice riders. Guided tours are a great option, as well; Discovery Adventure offers several destinations during summer. ✉ *260 Spring St., Friday Harbor* 🕾 *360/378–2559, 866/461–2559* 🌐 *www.discoveryadventuretours.com.*

BOATING AND SAILING

Port of Friday Harbor

BOATING | The marina at the island's main port offers guest moorage, vessel assistance and repair, bareboat and skippered charters, overnight accommodations, and wildlife- and whale-watching cruises. ✉ *204 Front St., Friday Harbor* 🕾 *360/378–2688* 🌐 *www.portfridayharbor.org.*

Roche Harbor Marina

BOATING | The marina at Roche Harbor Resort has a fuel dock, pool, grocery, and other guest services. ✉ *248 Reuben Memorial Dr., Roche Harbor* 🕾 *360/378–2155* 🌐 *www.rocheharbor.com.*

Snug Harbor Resort Marina

BOATING | This well-located marina adjoins a popular, upscale small resort. It provides van service to and from Friday Harbor and rents small powerboats. ✉ *1997 Mitchell Bay Rd., San Juan Island* 🕾 *360/378–4762* 🌐 *www.snugresort.com.*

SEA KAYAKING

Crystal Seas Kayaking

KAYAKING | Sunset trips and multisport tours that might include a combination of biking, kayaking, yoga, and camping are among the options with this respected guide company. ✉ *40 Spring St., Friday Harbor* ☎ *360/378–4223, 877/732–7877* ⊕ *www.crystalseas.com.*

Discovery Sea Kayaks
KAYAKING | This outfitter offers both sea-kayaking adventures, including sunset trips and multiday excursions and whale-watching paddles. ✉ *260 Spring St., Friday Harbor* ☎ *360/378–2559, 866/461–2559* ⊕ *www.discoveryseakayak.com.*

San Juan Kayak Expeditions
KAYAKING | This reputable company has been running kayaking and camping tours in two-person kayaks since 1980. ✉ *85 Front St., Friday Harbor* ☎ *360/378–4436* ⊕ *www.sanjuankayak.com.*

Sea Quest Expeditions
KAYAKING | Kayak eco-tours with guides who are trained naturalists, biologists, and environmental scientists are available through this popular outfitter. ✉ *Friday Harbor* ☎ *360/378–5767, 888/589–4253* ⊕ *www.sea-quest-kayak.com.*

WHALE-WATCHING
Whale-watching expeditions usually run three to four hours and cost around $125–$150 per person. Note that tours departing from San Juan Island typically get you to the best whale-watching waters faster than those departing from the mainland. Bring warm clothing even if it's a warm day.

■ **TIP→ For the best experience, look for tour companies with small boats that carry under 30 people.**

★ Maya's Legacy Whale Watching
WILDLIFE-WATCHING | These informative tours on small, modern, and speedy boats ensure great views for every passengers; departures are from Friday Harbor and Snug Harbor Marina. ✉ *14 Cannery Landing* ☎ *360/378–7996* ⊕ *www.sanjuanislandwhalewatch.com.*

San Juan Excursions
WILDLIFE-WATCHING | Whale-watching cruises are offered aboard a converted 1941 U.S. Navy research vessel. ✉ *40 Spring St., Friday Harbor* ☎ *360/378–6636, 800/809–4253* ⊕ *www.watch-whales.com.*

San Juan Island Whale & Wildlife Tours
WILDLIFE-WATCHING | Tours from Friday Harbor leave daily at noon and are led by highly knowledgeable marine experts. ✉ *1 Front St., Friday Harbor* ☎ *360/298–0012* ⊕ *www.sanjuanislandwhales.com.*

Western Prince Whale & Wildlife Tours
WILDLIFE-WATCHING | Narrated whale-watching tours last three to four hours. ✉ *1 Spring St., Friday Harbor* ☎ *360/378–5315, 800/757–6722* ⊕ *www.orcawhalewatch.com.*

🛍 Shopping

Friday Harbor is the main shopping area, with dozens of shops selling a variety of art, crafts, and clothing created by residents, as well as a bounty of island-grown produce.

Arctic Raven Gallery
ART GALLERIES | The specialty here is Northwest native art, including scrimshaw and wood carvings. ✉ *130 S. 1st St., Friday Harbor* ☎ *360/378–3433* ⊕ *www.arcticravengalleryfridayharbor.com.*

Cin Cin Goods
CHOCOLATE | The artisan chocolates at this friendly little shop come from all over the Pacific Northwest, including a nice assortment of confections sold by the piece, and the proprietors also stock a selection of ports and natural wines. ✉ *255 Spring St., Friday Harbor* ☎ *360/530–9463* ⊕ *www.fridayharborchocolates.com.*

San Juan Island Farmers Market
MARKET | From April through October, this open-air market with more than 30 vendors selling local produce and crafts

takes place at Friday Harbor Brickworks on Saturdays from 9:30 to 1. The market is also open once or twice a month on Saturdays in winter; check the website for the schedule. ⊠ *150 Nichols St., Friday Harbor* ⊕ *www.sjifarmersmarket. com.*

Waterworks Gallery

ART GALLERIES | This respected gallery represents about 30 eclectic, contemporary artists, from painters to jewelers. ⊠ *315 Argyle Ave., Friday Harbor* ☎ *360/378– 3060* ⊕ *www.waterworksgallery.com* ⊘ *Closed Sun.-Tues.*

Westcott Bay Shellfish Co.

FOOD | This rustic oyster farm is tucked into a small bay two miles south of Roche Harbor; the best time to buy oysters is November through April, and you can buy, shuck, and eat them on-site; the farm sells local bakery bread, cheese, charcuterie, salads, and wine if you want to make a meal of it. ⊠ *904 Westcott Dr., off Roche Harbor Rd.* ☎ *360/378–2489* ⊕ *www.westcottbayshellfish.com* ⊘ *Closed Mon.–Thu.*

Mt. Rainier National Park

The impressive volcanic peak of Mt. Rainier stands at an elevation of 14,411 feet, making it the fifth-highest peak in the lower 48 states. More than two million visitors a year enjoy spectacular views of the mountain and return home with a lifelong memory of its image.

On the lower slopes you find silent forests made up of cathedral-like groves of Douglas fir, western hemlock, and western red cedar, some more than 1,000 years old. Water and lush greenery are everywhere in the park, and dozens of thundering waterfalls, accessible from the road or by a short hike, fill the air with mist.

Established in 1899, it's the fifth-oldest national park in the U.S., created to preserve opportunities for generations to experience nature's beauty and outdoor recreation. Conservationists including John Muir lobbied for its protection as wilderness, saving its flora and fauna from the ravages of logging and mining. You can explore the park's early history in the Longmire Historic District— the location of its original headquarters— which includes a museum in one of the original early 1900 buildings and an inn in another. Farther up the mountain, the historic national park lodge architecture style is on full display in the iconic Paradise Inn, built in 1917. It's definitely worth a visit even if you're not spending the night, though an overnight stay will let you enjoy the park more without worries of traffic or parking. The Paradise area is the park's most visited and parking lots often fill up early on weekends and in the summer.

As the fifth highest mountain in the contiguous U.S., Mt. Rainier is renowned as a premier climbing destination—more than 10,000 people attempt to reach the summit every year. Climbers are strongly encouraged to go with a guide service for at least their first climb, and mountain safety practices are important for all visitors to follow when exploring the park. And there is a lot to explore—369 square miles with 97% designated as wilderness, 275 trails, and 120 miles of roads. Stopping at a visitor center is highly recommended, both to learn more about the park and also to get helpful advice and information on current road and trail conditions. Guided ranger programs and self-guided "Citizen Ranger Quests" are fun ways to make the most of your visit. Scenic drives are fabulous for photography, for spur-of-the-moment stops at intriguing spots, and for taking in the vastness of this stunning park.

WHEN TO GO

Rainier is the Puget Sound's weather vane: if you can see it, skies will be clear. Visitors are most likely to see the summit

Mount Rainier, Looking North

MOUNT RAINIER

Little Tahoma Peak 11,138 ft
Disappointment Cleaver
Ingraham Glacier
CATHEDRAL ROCKS
Anvil Rock 9,584 ft
Paradise Glaciers
McClure Rock 7,385 ft
Unicorn Peak 6917 ft
Muir Snowfield
Camp Muir 10,188 ft
Louise Lake
Panorama Point 6,800 ft
Columbia Crest 14,411 ft
Gibraltar Rock 12,660 ft
Nisqually Glacier
Skyline Trail
Alta Vista
Paradise
The Castle
Reflection Lakes
Liberty Cap 14,122 ft
Point Success 14,153 ft
Wilson Glacier
Pinnacle Peak 6,562 ft
Henry M. Jackson Memorial Visitor Center
SUNSET AMPHITHEATER
St. Andrews Rock 10,992 ft
SUCCESS CLEAVER
Van Trump Glaciers
Plummer Peak 6,370 ft
TATOOSH RANGE
Success Glacier
GLACIER CLEAVER
KAUTZ
WAPOWETY CLEAVER
Lane Peak 6,012 ft
CUSHMAN CREST
Tahoma Glacier
Success Glaciers
South Tahoma Glaciers
Mildred Point
VAN TRUMP PARK
Chutla Peak
Wahpenayo Peak 6,231 ft
PUYALLUP CLEAVER
Tahoma Glacier
GLACIER ISLAND
South Tahoma
SOUTH DIVIDE
Pyramid Glaciers
SUCCESS
PYRAMID PARK
Eagle Peak 5,958 ft
Tokaloo Rock 7684 ft
Pyramid Peak 6,937 ft
RIDGE
Cougar Rock
EMERALD RIDGE
Iron Mountain 6,283 ft
Rampart Ridge Trail
RAMPART
THE RAMPARTS
Pyramid Creek
Longmire

KEY
—— Paved Roads
– – – Hiking Trails
· · · · Climbing Routes

July through September. Crowds are heaviest in summer, too, meaning the parking lots at Paradise and Sunrise often fill before noon, campsites are reserved months in advance, and other lodgings are reserved as much as a year ahead.

True to its name, Paradise is often sunny during periods when the lowlands are under a cloud layer. The rest of the year, Rainier's summit gathers flying-saucer-like lenticular clouds whenever a Pacific storm approaches; once the peak vanishes from view, it's time to haul out rain gear. The rare periods of clear winter weather bring residents up to Paradise for cross-country skiing.

GETTING HERE AND AROUND
Seattle–Tacoma International Airport, 15 miles south of downtown Seattle, is the nearest airport to the national park.

The Nisqually entrance is on Highway 706, 14 miles east of Route 7; the Ohanapecosh entrance is on Route 123, five miles north of U.S. 12; and the White River entrance is on Route 410, three miles north of the Chinook and Cayuse passes. These highways become mountain roads as they reach Rainier, winding up and down many steep slopes, so cautious driving is essential: use a lower gear, especially on downhill sections, and take care not to overheat brakes by constant use. These roads are subject to storms any time of year and are repaired in the summer from winter damage and washouts.

Side roads into the park's western slope are narrower, unpaved, and subject to flooding and washouts. All are closed by snow in winter except Highway 706 to Paradise and Carbon River Road, though the latter tends to flood near the park boundary. (Route 410 is open to the Crystal Mountain access road entrance.)

Park roads have a maximum speed of 35 mph in most places, and you have to watch for pedestrians, cyclists, and wildlife. Parking can be difficult during peak summer season, especially at Paradise, Sunrise, Grove of the Patriarchs, and at the trailheads between Longmire and Paradise; arrive early if you plan to visit these sites. All off-road-vehicle use—4X4 vehicles, ATVs, motorcycles, snowmobiles—is prohibited in Mt. Rainier National Park.

INSPIRATION
The Ledge: An Adventure Story of Friendship and Survival on Mt. Rainier, by Jim Davidson, details the ill-fated trip of two friends.

Road to Rainier Scenic Byway, by Donald M. Johnstone and the South Pierce County Historical Society and part of the Images of America Series, documents how a Native American trail became a modern scenic route.

The Road to Paradise, by Karen Barnett, is a romance novel set in 1927 that tells the tale of a young woman who follows her naturalist inclinations to start a new life in Mt. Rainier during the early days of the National Park Service.

Tahoma and Its People: A Natural History of Mount Rainier National Park, by Jeff Antonelis-Lapp, focuses on the park's nature and environment from the perspectives of Native Americans, park rangers, archaeologists, and others.

PARK ESSENTIALS
ACCESSIBILITY
The only trail in the park that is fully accessible to those with impaired mobility is Kautz Creek Trail, a half-mile boardwalk that leads to a splendid view of the mountain. Parts of the Trail of the Shadows at Longmire and the Grove of the Patriarchs at Ohanapecosh are also accessible. Campgrounds at Cougar Rock and Ohanapecosh have several accessible sites. All main visitor centers, as well as National Park Inn at Longmire, are accessible. Wheelchairs are available at the Jackson Visitor Center for guests to use in the center.

Mt. Rainier in One Day (or Two)

The best way to get a complete overview of Mt. Rainier in a day is to enter via Nisqually and begin your tour by browsing in **Longmire Museum**. When you're done, get to know the environment in and around Longmire Meadow and the overgrown ruins of Longmire Springs Hotel on the half-mile **Trail of the Shadows** nature loop.

From Longmire, Highway 706 East (Paradise Valley Road) climbs northeast into the mountains toward Paradise. Take a moment to explore two-tiered **Christine Falls**, just north of the road 1½ miles past Cougar Rock Campground, and the cascading **Narada Falls**, three miles farther on; both are spanned by graceful stone footbridges. Fantastic mountain views, alpine meadows crosshatched with nature trails, a welcoming lodge and restaurant, and the excellent **Jackson Memorial Visitor Center** combine to make lofty Paradise the primary goal of most park visitors.

One outstanding (but challenging) way to explore the high country is to hike the five-mile round-trip **Skyline Trail** to Panorama Point, which rewards you with stunning 360-degree views.

Because one of the park's main roads, Stevens Canyon, is currently frequently closed for repairs, it may be difficult to see the entire park in a day. If the mountains are calling, make the time to return the next morning to the highest point in the park, the **Sunrise Visitor Center**, where you can watch the alpenglow fade from Mt. Rainier's domed summit. During July and August, the surrounding hills are blanketed with colorful native wildflowers. Finish with a picnic at **Tipsoo Lake** by driving east for 12 miles on SR 410. The crystal-clear lake offers views of Mt. Rainier in the distance, and you'll also find picnic tables as well as marked trails if you still feel like exploring.

PARK FEES AND PERMITS

The entrance fee of $30 per vehicle, $25 per motorcycle, and $15 for those on foot or bicycle is good for seven days. Annual passes are $55. Climbing permits are $53 per person per climb or glacier trek. Wilderness camping permits must be obtained for all backcountry trips, and advance reservations are highly recommended.

PARK HOURS

Mt. Rainier National Park is open 24/7 year-round, but with limited access in winter. Gates at Nisqually (Longmire) are staffed year-round during the day; facilities at Paradise are open daily from late May to mid-October; and Sunrise is open daily July to early September. During off-hours you can buy passes at the gates from machines that accept credit and debit cards. Winter access to the park is limited to the Nisqually entrance, and the Jackson Memorial Visitor Center at Paradise is open on weekends and holidays in winter. The Paradise snowplay area is open when there is sufficient snow.

CELL PHONE RECEPTION

Cell phone reception is unreliable throughout much of the park, although access is clear at Paradise, Sunrise, and Crystal Mountain. Public telephones are at all park visitor centers, at the National Park Inn at Longmire, and at Paradise Inn at Paradise.

SHOP AND GROCER CONTACTS General Store at Longmire's National Park Inn.
✉ *Longmire Visitor Complex, Ashford* ☎ *360/569–2411* ⊕ *www.mtrainierguest-services.com.* **Morton Country Market.**
✉ *461 2nd St., Mt. Rainier National Park* ☎ *360/496-5021.* **Plaza Market.** ✉ *201 Center St. E, Mt. Rainier National Park* ☎ *360/832–6151.*

HOTELS

The Mt. Rainier area is remarkably bereft of quality lodging. Rainier's two national park lodges, at Longmire and Paradise, are attractive and well maintained. They exude considerable history and charm, especially Paradise Inn, but unless you've made summer reservations a year in advance, getting a room can be a challenge. Dozens of motels, cabin complexes, and private vacation-home rentals are near the park entrances; while they can be pricey, the latter are convenient for longer stays.

Hotel and restaurant reviews have been shortened. For full information visit Fodors.com. Hotel prices are the lowest cost of a standard double room in high season. Restaurant prices are the average cost of a main course at dinner, or if dinner is not served, at lunch.

What It Costs in U.S. Dollars			
$	**$$**	**$$$**	**$$$$**
RESTAURANTS			
under $16	$16–$22	$23–$30	over $30
HOTELS			
under $150	$150–$200	$201–$250	over $250

RESTAURANTS

A limited number of restaurants are inside the park, and a few worth checking out lie beyond its borders. Mt. Rainier's picnic areas are justly famous, especially in summer, when wildflowers fill the meadows. Resist the urge to feed the yellow pine chipmunks darting about.

Park picnic areas are usually open only from late May through September.

VISITOR INFORMATION
PARK CONTACT INFORMATION Mt. Rainier National Park. ✉ *55210 238th Ave. East, Ashford* ☎ *360/569–2211* ⊕ *www. nps.gov/mora.*

Sights

Chinook Pass Road
SCENIC DRIVE | Route 410, the highway to Yakima, follows the eastern edge of the park to Chinook Pass, where it climbs the steep 5,432-foot pass via a series of switchbacks. At its top, take in broad views of Rainier and the east slope of the Cascades. The pass usually closes for the winter in November and reopens by late May. During that time, it's not possible to drive a loop around the park. ✉ *Mt. Rainier National Park* ⊕ *www.wsdot.wa.gov/traffic/passes/chinook-cayuse.*

Christine Falls
WATERFALL | These two-tiered falls were named in honor of Christine Louise Van Trump, who climbed to the 10,000-foot level on Mt. Rainier in 1889 at the age of nine, despite having a disabling nervous-system disorder. ✉ *Mt. Rainier National Park* ✛ *4 miles north of Longmire via Paradise Valley Road, about 2½ miles east of Cougar Rock Campground* ⊕ *www.nps.gov/mora/learn/nature/water-falls.htm.*

Mowich Lake Road
SCENIC DRIVE | In the northwest corner of the park, this 24-mile mountain road begins in Wilkeson and heads up the Rainier foothills to Mowich Lake, traversing beautiful mountain meadows along the way. Mowich Lake is a pleasant spot for a picnic. The road is open mid-July to mid-October. ✉ *Mt. Rainier National Park* ⊕ *www.nps.gov/mora/planyourvisit/carbon-river-and-mowich.htm* ⊗ *Closed mid-Oct.–mid-July.*

Narada Falls

WATERFALL | A steep but short trail leads to the viewing area for these spectacular 168-foot falls, which expand to a width of 75 feet during peak flow times. In winter the frozen falls are popular with ice climbers. ✉ *Paradise Valley Rd., Mt. Rainier National Park* ✥ *1 mile west of turnoff for Paradise, 6 miles east of Cougar Rock Campground* 🌐 *www.nps.gov/mora/planyourvisit/longmire.htm.*

Paradise Road

SCENIC DRIVE | This nine-mile stretch of Highway 706 winds its way up the mountain's southwest flank from Longmire to Paradise, taking you from lowland forest to the ever-expanding vistas of the mountain above. Visit early on a weekday if possible, especially in peak summer months, when the road is packed with cars. The route is open year-round, though there may be some weekday closures in winter. From November through April, all vehicles must carry chains. ✉ *Mt. Rainier National Park* 🌐 *www.nps.gov/mora/planyourvisit/paradise.htm.*

Route 123 and Stevens Canyon Road

SCENIC DRIVE | At Chinook Pass you can pick up Route 123 and head south to its junction with Stevens Canyon Road. Take this road west to its junction with the Paradise–Nisqually entrance road, which runs west through Longmire and exits the park at Nisqually. The route winds among valley-floor rain forest and uphill slopes; vistas of Puget Sound and the Cascade Range appear at numerous points along the way. ✉ *Mt. Rainier National Park.*

Sunrise Road

SCENIC DRIVE | This popular (and often crowded) scenic road to the highest drivable point at Mt. Rainier carves its way 11 miles up Sunrise Ridge from the White River Valley on the northeast side of the park. As you top the ridge, there are sweeping views of the surrounding lowlands. The road is usually open July through September. ✉ *Mt. Rainier National Park* 🌐 *www.nps.gov/mora/planyourvisit/sunrise.htm* ⏲ *Usually closed Oct.–June.*

Tipsoo Lake

BODY OF WATER | **FAMILY** | The short, pleasant trail that circles the lake—ideal for families—provides breathtaking views. Enjoy the subalpine wildflower meadows during the summer months; in late summer to early fall there is an abundant supply of huckleberries. ✉ *Mt. Rainier National Park* ✥ *Off Cayuse Pass east on Hwy. 410* 🌐 *www.nps.gov/mora/planyourvisit/sunrise.htm.*

🍴 Restaurants

National Park Inn Dining Room

$$$ | **AMERICAN** | Meals are simple but tasty in this inn's large dining room: flat iron steak, bison meat loaf, rosemary grilled salmon, and blackberry cobbler à la mode. Photos of Mt. Rainier taken by top photographers adorn the walls—a bonus on the many days the mountain refuses to show itself. **Known for:** only restaurant open year-round in the park; hearty breakfast options; nice dessert choices. [$] *Average main: $28* ✉ *Hwy. 706, Ashford* ☎ *360/569–2411* 🌐 *www.mtrainierguestservices.com.*

Paradise Inn Dining Room

$$$ | **AMERICAN** | Tall windows in this historic timber lodge provide terrific views of Rainier, and the warm glow of native wood permeates the large dining room, where hearty Pacific Northwest fare is served. Sunday brunch is legendary and served during the summer months; on other days and during the shoulder season there's a breakfast buffet. **Known for:** locally sourced ingredients; warm liquor drinks; great Sunday brunch. [$] *Average main: $27* ✉ *E. Paradise Rd., near Jackson Visitor Center, Ashford* ☎ *360/569–2275, 855/755–2275* 🌐 *www.mtrainierguestservices.com* ⏲ *Closed Oct.–mid-May.*

Summit House
$$ | **PACIFIC NORTHWEST** | On top of Crystal Mountain at 6,872 feet is Washington's highest-elevation restaurant with stunning views of the northeastern face of Mt. Rainier. The Summit House is a popular stop for skiers, hikers, and summer tourists, with a menu featuring Northwest cuisine, including wild Pacific cod fish-and-chips in summer (halibut in winter), elk and bison chili, burgers, and huckleberry ice cream. **Known for:** mountain views; leisurely dining experience; accessible only by gondola (tickets sold separately). [$] *Average main: $22* ✉ *33914 Crystal Mountain Blvd., Mt. Rainier National Park* ☎ *360/663–3050* 🌐 *crystalmountainresort.com* 🕒 *Open seasonally during summer and ski season; check website or call for current hrs.*

Coffee and Quick Bites

Paradise Camp Deli
$ | **AMERICAN** | Grilled meats, sandwiches, salads, and soft drinks are served daily from May through early October and on weekends and holidays the rest of the year. **Known for:** a quick bite to eat; family-friendly cuisine; mountain-size deli sandwiches. [$] *Average main: $10* ✉ *Jackson Visitor Center, Paradise Rd. E, Paradise* ☎ *360/569–6571 visitor center, 855/755–2275 guest services* 🌐 *www.mtrainierguestservices.com* 🕒 *Closed weekdays early Oct.–Apr.*

Scaleburgers
$ | **BURGER** | **FAMILY** | Once a 1939 logging-truck weigh station, the building is now a popular summer-season restaurant serving homemade hamburgers, fries, and shakes. Eat outside on tables overlooking the hills. **Known for:** handy location on the way to Mt. Rainier; homemade burgers; luscious milkshakes. [$] *Average main: $10* ✉ *54109 Mountain Hwy. E, Elbe* ✣ *11 miles west of Ashford* ☎ *360/569–2247* 💳 *No credit cards* 🕒 *Closed from Oct.–May.*

Sunrise Day Lodge Food Service
$ | **AMERICAN** | **FAMILY** | A cafeteria and grill serve tasty hamburgers, chili, hot dogs, and soft-serve ice cream from July through September. **Known for:** grill favorites; only food service in this part of the park; often busy. [$] *Average main: $11* ✉ *Sunrise Rd., Ashford* ✣ *15 miles from White River park entrance* ☎ *360/663–2425 visitor center, 855/755–2275 guest services* 🌐 *www.mtrainierguestservices.com* 🕒 *Closed Oct.–June.*

Hotels

National Park Inn
$$$ | **B&B/INN** | A large stone fireplace warms the common room while wrought-iron lamps and antique bentwood headboards adorn the small bedrooms of this country inn, the only one of the park's two inns that's open year-round. **Pros:** classic national park lodge ambience; on-site restaurant with simple American fare; winter packages with perks like breakfast and free snowshoe use. **Cons:** jam-packed in summer; must book far in advance; some rooms have a shared bath. [$] *Rooms from: $270* ✉ *Longmire Visitor Complex, Hwy. 706, Ashford* ✣ *6 miles east of Nisqually entrance* ☎ *360/569–2275, 855/755–2275* 🌐 *www.mtrainierguestservices.com* 🛏 *43 rooms* 🍴 *No Meals.*

★ **Paradise Inn**
$$$ | **HOTEL** | With its hand-carved Alaskan cedar logs, burnished parquet floors, stone fireplaces, and glorious mountain views, this 1917 inn is a classic example of a national park lodge. **Pros:** central to trails; pristine vistas; nature-inspired details. **Cons:** rooms are small and basic; many rooms have shared bathrooms; no elevators, air-conditioning, cell service, TV, or Wi-Fi. [$] *Rooms from: $272* ✉ *E. Paradise Rd., near Jackson Visitor Center, Paradise* ☎ *360/569–2275, 855/755–2275* 🌐 *www.mtrainierguestservices.com* 🕒 *Closed mid-Oct.–mid-May* 🛏 *121 rooms* 🍴 *No Meals.*

Best Campgrounds in Mt. Rainier

Three drive-in campgrounds are in the park—Cougar Rock, Ohanapecosh, and White River—with almost 500 sites for tents and RVs. None has hot water or RV hookups. The nightly fee is $20. The more primitive Mowich Lake Campground has 10 walk-in sites for tents only; no fee is charged. For backcountry camping, get a free wilderness permit at a visitor center on a first-come, first-served basis. Primitive sites are spaced at seven- to eight-mile intervals along the Wonderland Trail.

Cougar Rock Campground. A secluded, heavily wooded campground with an amphitheater, Cougar Rock is one of the first to fill up. Reservations are accepted for summer only. ✉ *2½ miles north of Longmire* ☎ *877/444–6777* 🌐 *www.recreation.gov* for reservations.

Mowich Lake Campground. This is Rainier's only lakeside campground and has just 10 primitive campsites. At 4,959 feet, it's also peaceful and secluded. ✉ *Mowich Lake Rd., 6 miles east of park boundary* ☎ *360/569–2211.*

Ohanapecosh Campground. This lush, green campground in the park's southeast corner has an amphitheater and self-guided trail. It's one of the first campgrounds to open for the season. ✉ *Rte. 123, 1½ miles north of park boundary* ☎ *877/444–6777* 🌐 *www.recreation.gov* for reservations.

White River Campground. At an elevation of 4,400 feet, White River is one of the park's highest and least wooded campgrounds. Here you can enjoy campfire programs, self-guided trails, and partial views of Mt. Rainier's summit. ✉ *5 miles west of White River entrance* ☎ *360/569–2211.*

Outside the Park

Alexander's Lodge

$$ | B&B/INN | A mile from Mt. Rainier's Nisqually entrance, this ideally located lodging's vintage furnishings lend romance to rooms in the main building, which dates back to 1912; there are also two adjacent guesthouses at the charming property. **Pros:** plenty of historical character; in-room spa services available; some rooms are pet-friendly. **Cons:** steep stairs to some units; decor is a bit old-fashioned; some rooms are quite small. [$] *Rooms from: $229* ✉ *37515 Hwy. 706, Ashford* ☎ *360/569–2300* 🌐 *www.alexanderslodge.com* 🛏 *21 rooms* 🍴 *Free Breakfast.*

Alta Crystal Resort

$$$$ | B&B/INN | FAMILY | This small resort with family-friendly amenities feels remote yet is very close to Mt. Rainier's Sunrise entrance and Crystal Mountain Ski Resort; suites feature fireplaces and full kitchens, and the property has a year-round outdoor pool and hot tub, sports field, and a recreation center. **Pros:** fun, nightly activities; mini-grocery store and movie library; several standalone cabins for added privacy. **Cons:** expensive and not close to restaurants or provisions; cell phone and Internet can be spotty; pool area gets noisy, especially for first-floor units. [$] *Rooms from: $349* ✉ *68317 SR 410 E* ☎ *800/277–6475* 🌐 *www.altacrystalresort.com* 🛏 *27 rooms* 🍴 *No Meals.*

Nisqually Lodge

$$$ | **HOTEL** | Crackling flames from the massive stone fireplace lend warmth and cheer to the great room of this hotel, a few miles west of Mt. Rainier National Park. **Pros:** breakfast included; central to mountain activities; some rooms are pet-friendly (call first). **Cons:** no frills; no elevator; service can be inconsistent. ⓢ *Rooms from: $210* ⊠ *31609 Hwy. 706 E, Ashford* ☎ *360/569–8804, 888/674–3554* ⊕ *www.whitepasstravel.com/nisqually* ↝ *24 rooms* ⦿ *Free Breakfast.*

Silver Skis Condominiums

$$$$ | **APARTMENT** | With rooms overlooking Crystal Mountain Resort, Silver Skis Condominiums provide convenient slopeside family-friendly lodging, with well-equipped one- and two-bedroom condos featuring kitchens or kitchenettes, Wi-Fi, DVD players, and satellite TV (some have fireplaces, too). **Pros:** each unit uniquely decorated by its owner; lots of amenities for families including a heated pool; off-season rates make this a good base for summer recreation, too. **Cons:** many of the condos have loft or bunk beds and may not be accessible for all; condos fill up quickly during the ski season; older property. ⓢ *Rooms from: $289* ⊠ *33000 Crystal Mountain Blvd., Mt. Rainier National Park* ☎ *888/668–4368, 360/663–2558* ⊕ *silverskischalet. com* ↝ *60 condos* ⦿ *No Meals.*

★ Stormking Spa and Cabins

$$$ | **B&B/INN** | In a forest setting a mile from the Nisqually entrance of Mt. Rainier National Park, Stormking features four luxury cabins for adults; all are shaped like yurts and have cozy gas fireplaces, hot tubs, private outdoor seating areas, and natural finishes of wood and stone. **Pros:** very romantic and secluded; reasonably priced for special occasion getaways; deer and other wildlife frequent the property. **Cons:** no check-ins on Sunday; Wi-Fi available at spa but not in cabins; three-night minimum stay. ⓢ *Rooms from: $240* ⊠ *37311 SR 706*

Plants and Wildlife

Wildflower season in the meadows at and above timberline is mid-July through August. Large mammals like deer, elk, black bears, and cougars tend to occupy the less accessible wilderness areas of the park and thus elude the average visitor. The best times to see wildlife are at dawn and dusk at the forest's edge, though you'll occasionally see bears ambling through meadows in the distance during the day. Fawns are born in May, and the bugling of bull elk on the high ridges can be heard in late September and October.

E, Mt. Rainier National Park ☎ *360/569–2964* ⊕ *www.stormkingspa.com* ↝ *4 cabins* ⦿ *No Meals.*

🏃 Activities

MULTISPORT OUTFITTERS

RMI Expeditions

MOUNTAIN CLIMBING | Reserve a private hiking guide through this highly regarded outfitter, or take part in its one-day mountaineering classes (mid-May through late September), where participants are evaluated on their fitness for the climb and must be able to withstand a 16-mile round-trip hike with a 9,000-foot gain in elevation. The company also arranges private cross-country skiing and snowshoeing guides. ⊠ *30027 SR 706 E, Ashford* ☎ *888/892–5462, 360/569–2227* ⊕ *www. rmiguides.com* ⓢ *From $1222 for 4-day package.*

Whittaker Mountaineering

MOUNTAIN CLIMBING | You can rent hiking and climbing gear, cross-country skis, snowshoes, and other outdoor equipment at this all-purpose Rainier Base

Camp outfitter, which also arranges for private cross-country skiing and hiking guides. If you forget to bring tire chains (which all vehicles are required to carry in the national park in winter), they rent those, too. ✉ *30027 SR 706 E, Ashford* ☎ *800/238–5756, 360/569–2982* ⊕ *www. whittakermountaineering.com.*

BIRD-WATCHING

Be alert for kestrels, red-tailed hawks, and, occasionally, golden eagles on snags in the lowland forests. Also present at Rainier, but rarely seen, are great horned owls, spotted owls, and screech owls. Iridescent rufous hummingbirds flit from blossom to blossom in the drowsy summer lowlands, and sprightly water ouzels flutter in the many forest creeks. Raucous Steller's jays and gray jays scold passersby from trees, often darting boldly down to steal morsels from unguarded picnic tables. At higher elevations, look for the pure white plumage of the white-tailed ptarmigan as it hunts for seeds and insects in winter. Waxwings, vireos, nuthatches, sapsuckers, warblers, flycatchers, larks, thrushes, siskins, tanagers, and finches are common throughout the park.

BOATING

Nonmotorized boating is permitted on all lakes inside the park except Frozen, Ghost, Reflection, Shadow, and Tipsoo lakes. Mowich Lake, in the northwest corner of the park, is the only lake easily accessible to canoes and kayaks. There are no boat rentals inside the park.

HIKING

Although the mountain can seem remarkably benign on calm summer days, hiking Rainier is not a city-park stroll. Dozens of hikers and trekkers annually lose their way and must be rescued—and lives are lost on the mountain each year. Weather that approaches cyclonic levels can appear quite suddenly, any month of the year. All visitors venturing far from vehicle access points, with the possible exception of the short loop hikes listed

here, should carry day packs with warm clothing, food, and other emergency supplies.

Burroughs Mountain Trail

TRAIL | Starting at the south side of the Sunrise parking area, this 2½-hour, 4¾-mile round-trip hike offers spectacular views of the peak named in honor of naturalist and essayist John Burroughs. The challenging trail passes Shadow Lake before climbing to an overlook of the White River and Emmon's Glacier. Continue on and you reach First Burroughs Mountain and Second Burroughs Mountain. This area on the northeast slope of Mt. Rainier has some of the most accessible tundra in the Cascades, and you can observe the delicate slow-growing plants that survive in this harsh environment. Early season hiking on this trail can be particularly hazardous due to snow and ice on the steep mountain slopes; check conditions before starting out. *Difficult.* ⊹ *Trailhead: at south side of Sunrise parking area* ⊕ *www.nps.gov/mora/plan-yourvisit/burroughs-mountain.htm.*

Nisqually Vista Trail

TRAIL | Equally popular in summer and winter, this trail is a 1¼-mile round-trip through subalpine meadows to an overlook point for Nisqually Glacier. The gradually sloping path is a favorite venue for cross-country skiers in winter; in summer, listen for the shrill alarm calls of the area's marmots. *Easy.* ⊹ *Trailhead: At Jackson Memorial Visitor Center, Rte. 123, 1 mile north of Ohanapecosh, at high point of Hwy. 706* ⊕ *www.nps.gov/ mora/planyourvisit/day-hiking-at-mount-rainier.htm.*

Mt. Si

HIKING & WALKING | This thigh-buster is where mountaineers train to climb grueling Mt. Rainier. Mt. Si offers a challenging hike with views of a valley (slightly marred by the suburbs) and the Olympic Mountains in the distance. The main trail to Haystack Basin, eight miles round-trip, climbs some 4,000 vertical feet, but there are several obvious places to rest or turn around if you'd like to keep the hike to three or four miles. Note that solitude is in short supply here—this is an extremely popular trail thanks to its proximity to Seattle. On the bright side, it's one of the best places to witness the local hikers and trail runners in all their weird and wonderful splendor. ✢ *Take I–90 E to Exit 31 (toward North Bend). Turn onto North Bend Way and then make left onto Mt. Si Rd. and follow that road to trailhead parking lot.*

★ Skyline Trail

TRAIL | This five-mile loop, one of the highest trails in the park, beckons day-trippers with a vista of alpine ridges and, in summer, meadows filled with brilliant flowers and birds. At 6,800 feet, Panorama Point, the spine of the Cascade Range, spreads away to the east, and Nisqually Glacier tumbles downslope. *Moderate.* ✢ *Trailhead: Jackson Memorial Visitor Center, Rte. 123, 1 mile north of Ohanapecosh at high point of Hwy. 706 ⊕ www.nps.gov/mora/planyourvisit/skyline-trail.htm.*

Sunrise Nature Trail

TRAIL | The 1½-mile-long loop of this self-guided trail takes you through the delicate subalpine meadows near the Sunrise Visitor Center. A gradual climb to the ridgetop yields magnificent views of Mt. Rainier and the more distant volcanic cones of Mt. Baker, Mt. Adams, and Glacier Peak. *Easy.* ✢ *Trailhead: At Sunrise Visitor Center, Sunrise Rd., 15 miles from White River park entrance ⊕ www.nps.gov/mora/planyourvisit/sunrise.htm.*

Trail of the Shadows

TRAIL | This ¾-mile loop is notable for its glimpses of meadowland ecology, its colorful soda springs (don't drink the water), James Longmire's old homestead cabin, and the foundation of the old Longmire Springs Hotel, which was destroyed by fire around 1900. *Easy.* ✢ *Trailhead: At Hwy. 706, 10 miles east of Nisqually entrance ⊕ www.nps.gov/mora/planyourvisit/day-hiking-at-mount-rainier.htm.*

Van Trump Park Trail

TRAIL | You gain an exhilarating 2,200 feet on this route while hiking through a vast expanse of meadow with views of the southern Puget Sound and Mt. Adams and Mt. St. Helens. On the way up is one of the highest waterfalls in the park, Comet Falls. The 5¾-mile track provides good footing, and the average hiker can make it up and back in five hours. *Moderate.* ✢ *Trailhead: Hwy. 706 at Christine Falls, 4½ miles east of Longmire ⊕ www.nps.gov/mora/planyourvisit/comet-falls-van-trump-park-trail.htm.*

★ Wonderland Trail

TRAIL | All other Mt. Rainier hikes pale in comparison to this stunning 93-mile trek, which completely encircles the mountain. The trail passes through all the major life zones of the park, from the old-growth forests of the lowlands to the alpine meadows and goat-haunted glaciers of the highlands—pick up a mountain-goat sighting card from a ranger station or visitor center if you want to help in the park's effort to learn more about these elusive animals. Wonderland is a rugged trail; elevation gains and losses totaling 3,500 feet are common in a day's hike, which averages eight miles. Most hikers start out from Longmire or Sunrise and take 10–14 days to cover the 93-mile route. Snow lingers on the high passes well into June (sometimes July); count on rain any time of the year. Campsites are wilderness areas with pit toilets and water that must be purified before drinking. Only hardy, well-equipped, and experienced wilderness trekkers should attempt this trip, but those who do will be amply rewarded. Wilderness permits are required and the campsite reservations are highly competitive; you can enter an optional lottery for early access to the reservations system. *Difficult.* ✢ *Trailheads: Longmire Visitor Center, Hwy. 706, 17 miles east of Ashford; Sunrise Visitor Center, Sunrise Rd., 15 miles west of White River park entrance*

Did You Know?

Named after British admiral Peter Rainier in the late 18th century, Mt. Rainier had an earlier name. Tahoma (also Takhoma), its American Indian name, means "the mountain that was God." Various unsuccessful attempts have been made to restore the aboriginal name to the peak. Of course, to most Puget Sound residents, Rainier is simply "the mountain."

⊕ *www.nps.gov/mora/planyourvisit/ the-wonderland-trail.htm.*

MOUNTAIN CLIMBING

Climbing Mt. Rainier is not for amateurs; each year adventurers die on the mountain, and many get lost and must be rescued. Near-catastrophic weather can appear quite suddenly any month of the year. If you're experienced in technical, high-elevation snow, rock, and ice-field adventuring, Mt. Rainier can be a memorable adventure. Climbers can fill out a climbing card at the Paradise, White River, or Carbon River ranger station and lead their own groups of two or more. Climbers must register with a ranger before leaving and check out on return. A $53 annual climbing fee applies to anyone heading above 10,000 feet or onto one of Rainier's glaciers. During peak season it is recommended that climbers make their camping reservations ($20 per site) in advance; reservations are taken by fax and mail beginning in mid-March on a first-come, first-served basis (find the reservation form at ⊕ *www.nps.gov/ mora/planyourvisit/climbing.htm*).

SKIING AND SNOWSHOEING

Mt. Rainier is a major Nordic ski center for cross-country and telemark skiing. Although trails are not groomed, those around Paradise are extremely popular; it's also a great place for snowshoeing.

If you want to ski with fewer people, try the trails in and around the Ohanapecosh–Stevens Canyon area, which are just as beautiful and, because of their more easterly exposure, slightly less subject to the rains that can douse the Longmire side, even in the dead of winter. Never ski on plowed main roads, especially around Paradise—the snowplow operator can't see you. Rentals aren't available on the eastern side of the park. Deep snows make Mt. Rainier a snowshoeing pleasure. The Paradise area, with its network of trails, is the best choice. The park's east-side roads, Routes 123 and 410, are unplowed and

provide other good snowshoeing venues, although you must share the main routes with snowmobilers.

Paradise Snowplay Area and Nordic Ski Route

SKIING & SNOWBOARDING | Sledding on flexible sleds (no toboggans or runners), inner tubes, and plastic saucers is allowed only in the Paradise snowplay area adjacent to the Jackson Visitor Center. The area is open when there is sufficient snow, usually from late December through mid-March. The easy 3½-mile Paradise Valley Road Nordic ski route begins at the Paradise parking lot and follows Paradise Valley/Stevens Canyon Road to Reflection Lakes. Equipment rentals are available at Whittaker Mountaineering in Ashford or at the National Park Inn's General Store in Longmire. ⊠ *Adjacent to Jackson Visitor Center at Paradise* ☎ *360/569–2211* ⊕ *www.nps. gov/mora/planyourvisit/winter-recreation. htm.*

General Store at the National Park Inn

SKIING & SNOWBOARDING | The store at the National Park Inn in Longmire rents cross-country ski equipment and snowshoes. It's open daily in winter, depending on snow conditions. ⊠ *National Park Inn* ☎ *360/569–2411* ⊕ *www.mtrainierguestservices.com/activities-and-events/ winter-activities/cross-country-skiing.*

PICNIC AREAS

Park picnic areas are usually open only from late May through September.

Paradise Picnic Area

CAMPGROUND | This site has great views on clear days. After picnicking at Paradise, you can take an easy hike to one of the many waterfalls in the area—Sluiskin, Myrtle, or Narada, to name a few. ⊠ *Hwy. 706* ✛ *11 miles east of Longmire* ⊕ *www.nps.gov/mora.*

Sunrise Picnic Area

CAMPGROUND | Set in an alpine meadow that's filled with wildflowers in July and August, this picnic area provides expansive views of the mountain and surrounding ranges in good weather. ⊠ *Sunrise Rd.* ✛ *11 miles west of White River entrance* ⊕ *www.nps.gov/mora/ planyourvisit/sunrise.htm* ⊗ *Road to Sunrise usually closed Oct.–June.*

WHAT'S NEARBY

Ashford sits astride an ancient trail across the Cascades used by the Yakama tribe to trade with the coastal tribes of western Washington. The town began as a logging railway terminal; today it's the main gateway to Mt. Rainier—and the only year-round access point to the park—with lodges, restaurants, grocery stores, and gift shops. Surrounded by Cascade peaks, Packwood is a pretty mountain village on U.S. 12, below White Pass and less than 12 miles from the Ohanapecosh area of the national park. It's a perfect jumping-off point for exploring local wilderness areas. Near the Sunrise entrance on the northeast side of the park, the Crystal Mountain area provides lodging, dining, and year-round outdoor recreation options, including a popular resort for snow sports.

 Sights

Goat Rocks Wilderness

FOREST | The crags in Gifford Pinchot National Forest, south of Mt. Rainier, are aptly named. You often see mountain goats here in this vast and unspoiled 108,000-acre wilderness, especially when you hike into the backcountry. Goat Lake is a particularly good spot for viewing these elusive creatures. See the goats without backpacking by taking Forest Road 21 to Forest Road 2140, south from U.S. 12. The goats will be on Stonewall Ridge looming up ahead of you. ⊠ *NF-21 and NF-2140* ☎ *360/891–5000* ⊕ *www.fs.usda.gov/giffordpinchot.*

Northwest Trek Wildlife Park

WILDLIFE REFUGE | **FAMILY** | This spectacular, 723-acre wildlife park 30 miles southeast of Tacoma is devoted to native creatures of the Pacific Northwest. Walking paths wind through natural surroundings—so natural that a cougar once entered the park and started snacking on the deer (it was finally trapped and relocated to the North Cascades). See beavers, otters, and wolverines; get close to wolves, foxes, coyotes; and observe several species of big cats and bears in wild environments. You can also book the separate Wild Drive Premier Tour, which lets you slowly explore park grounds from your own car, near free-roaming bison, elk, mountain goats, caribou, and a female moose named Aspen. Tickets for the drive tour are $90 and include general park admission. ⊠ *11610 Trek Dr. E* ✛ *23 miles northwest of Ashford via Hwy. 706 and 161* ☎ *360/832–6117* ⊕ *www.nwtrek. org* 🖲 *$22 online/$25 at park entry* ⊗ *Closed Mon.–Thurs. in Oct.–mid-Mar.*

🏃 Activities

SKIING

Crystal Mountain Ski Area

SKIING & SNOWBOARDING | Washington State's biggest and best-known ski area has nine lifts (plus a children's lift and a gondola) and 57 runs. In summer, it's open for hiking, rides on the Mt. Rainier Gondola, and meals at the Summit House, all providing sensational views of Rainier and the Cascades. The resort is included in the multi-resort IKON pass. **Facilities:** 57 trails; 2,600 acres; 3,100-foot vertical drop; 11 lifts. ■**TIP➔ Because of chronic overcrowding at the ski resort, during which many people were turned away, Crystal no longer sells day-of tickets during peak winter season.** ⊠ *33914 Crystal Mountain Blvd., off Rte. 410* ☎ *360/663–2265* ⊕ *www.crystalmountainresort.com* 🖲 *From $25 (gondola), $80 (day ski ticket).*

Olympic National Park

Edged on all sides by water, the forested landscape is remote and pristine, and works its way around the sharpened ridges of the snowcapped Olympic Mountains. Big lakes cut pockets of blue in the rugged blanket of pine forests. From towering trees in mossy green rain forests to sea stacks jutting from ocean shores, nature puts the awe in awesome here.

The region has been described as magical by many a visitor for more than a century, and appreciated by the Native Americans that lived here for centuries before. In the late 1800s efforts began to preserve this unique area of mountains, rain forest, coast, and the diverse flora and fauna that thrive in its environment. Responding to conservationist John Muir's encouragement to save the old growth forests, President Grover Cleveland created the Olympic Forest Reserve in his final days in office in 1897. In 1909 President Theodore Roosevelt designated the area as the Mount Olympus National Monument, in part to protect the native elk that were later renamed in his honor and still roam in the Hoh Rain Forest.

The park gets more than 3 million visitors annually and covers a lot of area—nearly 1,500 square miles. There are more than 600 miles of trails, 168 miles of roads, 73 miles of shoreline … in other words, a lot to see and do! Most of the park's attractions are found either off U.S. Highway 101 or down trails that require hikes of 15 minutes or longer. The coastal beaches are linked to the highway by downhill tracks; the number of cars parked alongside the road at the start of the paths indicates how crowded the beach will be.

Five in-park lodging options—including two historic lodges on sparkling lakes and one perched above the Pacific Ocean—make it possible to take your time and really immerse yourself in this wondrous place, while gazing out at the same views that have been inspiring awe for generations. It can be an exercise in patience to try and book a room during the high season at these very popular lodges, where some families return every year. Plan ahead, visit midweek, or consider a spring or fall stay (especially fun if you like storm-watching).

WHEN TO GO

Summer, with its long stretches of sun-filled days, is prime touring time for Olympic National Park. June through September are the peak months; Hurricane Ridge, the Hoh Rain Forest, Lake Crescent, and Ruby Beach are bustling by 10 am.

Late spring and early autumn are also good bets for clear weather; anytime between April and October, you'll have a good chance of fair skies. Between Thanksgiving and Easter, it's a toss-up as to which days will turn out fair; prepare for heavy clouds, rain showers, and chilly temperatures, then hope for the best.

Winter is a great time to visit if you enjoy isolation. Locals are usually the only hardy souls here during this time, except for weekend skiers heading to the snowfields around Hurricane Ridge. Many visitor facilities have limited hours or are closed from October to April, and some of the park lodgings close for the winter, too.

GETTING HERE AND AROUND

You can enter the park at a number of points, but because the park is mostly wilderness, access roads do not penetrate far. The best way to get around and to see many of the park's top sights is on foot.

Seattle–Tacoma International Airport is the nearest airport to Olympic National Park. It's roughly a two-hour drive from the park.

Ferries provide another unique (though indirect) link to the Olympic area from

Seattle; contact Washington State Ferries (☎ 888/808–7977, 206/464–6400) for information.

Grays Harbor Transit runs buses Monday through Saturday from Aberdeen and Hoquiam to Amanda Park, on the west end of Lake Quinault. Jefferson Transit operates a Forks–Amanda Park route Monday through Saturday.

BUS CONTACTS Grays Harbor Transit. ☎ 360/532–2770, 800/562–9730 ⊕ www.ghtransit.com. **Jefferson Transit.** ☎ 800/371–0497, 360/385–4777 ⊕ www.jeffersontransit.com.

U.S. 101 essentially encircles the main section of Olympic National Park, and a number of roads lead from the highway into the park's mountains and toward its beaches. You can reach U.S. 101 via Interstate 5 at Olympia, via Route 12 at Aberdeen, or via Route 104 from the Washington state ferry terminals at Bainbridge or Kingston.

INSPIRATION

Robert L. Wood's *Olympic Mountains Trail Guide* is a great resource for both day hikers and those planning longer excursions.

Craig Romano's *Day Hiking Olympic Peninsula: National Park/Coastal Beaches/Southwest Washington* is a detailed guide to day hikes in and around the national park.

Rob Sandelin and Stephen Whitney's *A Field Guide to the Cascades and Olympics* is an excellent trailside reference, covering more than 500 plant and animal species found in the park.

The park's newspaper, the *Olympic Bugler*, is a seasonal guide for activities and opportunities in the park. You can pick it up at the visitor centers.

A handy online catalog of books, maps, and passes for northwest parks is available from Discover Your Northwest (⊕ www.discovernw.org).

PARK ESSENTIALS
ACCESSIBILITY

There are wheelchair-accessible facilities—including trails, campgrounds, and visitor centers—throughout the park; contact visitor centers for information.

PARK FEES AND PERMITS

Seven-day vehicle admission is $30; an annual pass is $50. Individuals arriving on foot, bike, or motorcycle pay $15. An overnight wilderness permit, available at visitor centers and ranger stations, is $8 per person per night plus a $6 per night reservation fee. An annual wilderness camping permit costs $45. Fishing in freshwater streams and lakes within Olympic National Park does not require a Washington state fishing license; however, anglers must acquire a salmon-steelhead catch record card when fishing for those species. Ocean fishing and harvesting shellfish require licenses, which are available at sporting-goods and outdoor-supply stores.

PARK HOURS

Six park entrances are open 24/7; gate kiosk hours (for buying passes) vary according to season and location, but most are staffed during daylight hours. Olympic National Park is in the Pacific time zone.

CELL PHONE RECEPTION

Note that cell reception is sketchy in wilderness areas. There are public telephones at the Olympic National Park Visitor Center, Hoh Rain Forest Visitor Center, and lodging properties within the park—Lake Crescent, Kalaloch, and Sol Duc Hot Springs. Fairholme General Store also has a phone.

HOTELS

Major park resorts run from good to terrific, with generally comfortable rooms, excellent facilities, and easy access to trails, beaches, and activity centers. Midsize accommodations, like Sol Duc Hot Springs Resort, are often shockingly rustic—but remember, you're here for the park, not for the rooms.

The towns around the park have motels, hotels, and resorts for every budget. For a full beach-town vacation experience, base yourself in a home or cottage in the coastal community of Seabrook (near Pacific Beach). Sequim, Port Angeles, and Port Townsend have many attractive, friendly B&Bs, plus lots of inexpensive chain hotels and motels. Forks has mostly motels, with a few guesthouses on the fringes of town.

Hotel and restaurant reviews have been shortened. For full information visit Fodors.com. Hotel prices are the lowest cost of a standard double room in high season. Restaurant prices are the average cost of a main course at dinner, or if dinner is not served, at lunch.

What It Costs in U.S. Dollars

	$	$$	$$$	$$$$
RESTAURANTS				
	under $16	$16–$22	$23–$30	over $30
HOTELS				
	under $150	$150–$200	$201–$250	over $250

RESTAURANTS

The major resorts are your best bets for eating out in the park. Each has a main restaurant, café, and/or kiosk, as well as casually upscale dinner service, with regional seafood, meat, and produce complemented by a range of microbrews and good Washington and international wines. Reservations are either recommended or required.

All Olympic National Park campgrounds have adjacent picnic areas with tables, some shelters, and restrooms, but no cooking facilities. The same is true for major visitor centers, such as Hoh Rain Forest. Drinking water is available at ranger stations, interpretive centers, and inside campgrounds.

Outside the park, small, easygoing cafés and bistros line the main thoroughfares in Sequim, Port Angeles, Port Townsend, and Forks, offering cuisine that ranges from hearty American-style fare to more eclectic local flavor.

VISITOR INFORMATION
PARK CONTACT INFORMATION Olympic National Park. ✉ *Olympic National Park Visitor Center, 3002 Mt. Angeles Rd., Port Angeles* 📞 *360/565–3130* 🌐 *www. nps.gov/olym.*

 Sights

★ Hoh Rain Forest
FOREST | South of Forks, an 18-mile spur road links Highway 101 with this unique temperate rain forest, where spruce and hemlock trees soar to heights of more than 200 feet. Alders and big-leaf maples are so densely covered with mosses they look more like shaggy prehistoric animals than trees, and elk browse in shaded glens. Be prepared for precipitation: the region receives 140 inches or more each year. ✉ *Upper Hoh Rd., Olympic National Park* 📞 *360/374–6925* 🌐 *www.nps.gov/ olym/planyourvisit/visiting-the-hoh.htm.*

★ Hurricane Ridge
MOUNTAIN | The panoramic view from this 5,200-foot-high ridge encompasses the Olympic range, the Strait of Juan de Fuca, and Vancouver Island. Guided tours from the visitor center are given in summer along the many paved and unpaved trails, where wildflowers and wildlife such as deer and marmots flourish. ✉ *Hurricane Ridge Rd., Olympic National Park* ✛ *17 miles south of Port Angeles* 📞 *360/565–3130* 🌐 *www.nps.gov/olym/ planyourvisit/visiting-hurricane-ridge.htm* ☾ *Closed when road is closed.*

Kalaloch
BEACH | With a lodge and restaurant, a huge campground, miles of coastline,

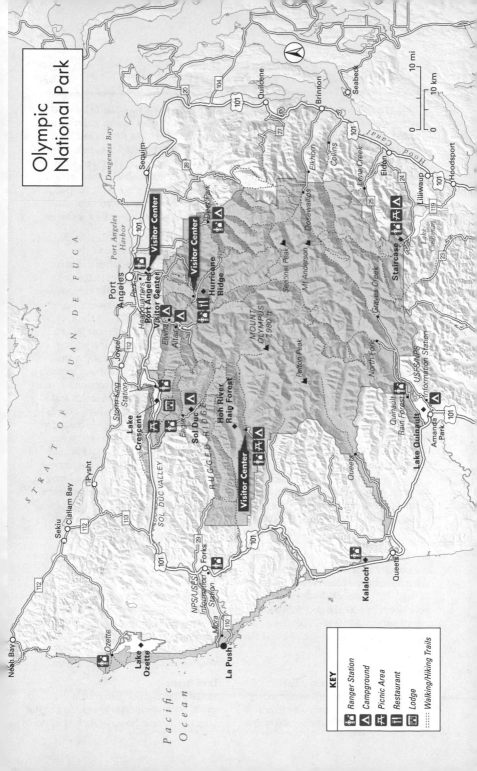

Plants and Wildlife in the Park

Along the high mountain slopes, hardy cedar, fir, and hemlock trees stand tough on the rugged land; the lower montane forests are filled with thickets of silver firs; and valleys stream with Douglas firs and western hemlock. The park's famous temperate rain forests are on the peninsula's western side, marked by broad western red cedars, towering red spruces, and ferns festooned with strands of mosses and patchwork lichens. This lower landscape is also home to some of the Northwest's largest trees: massive cedar and Sitka spruce near Lake Quinault can measure more than 700 inches around, and Douglas firs near the Queets and Hoh rivers are nearly as wide.

These landscapes are home to a variety of wildlife, including many large mammals and 15 creatures found nowhere else in the world. Hikers often come across Roosevelt elk, black-tailed deer, mountain goats, beavers, raccoons, skunks, opossums, and foxes; Douglas squirrels and flying squirrels populate the heights of the forest. Less common are black bears (most prevalent from May through August); wolves, bobcats, and cougars are rarely seen. Birdlife includes bald eagles, red-tailed hawks, osprey, and great horned owls. Rivers and lakes are filled with freshwater fish, while beaches hold crabs, sea stars, anemones, and other shelled creatures. Get out in a boat on the Pacific to spot seals, sea lions, and sea otters—and perhaps a pod of porpoises, orcas, or gray whales.

Beware of jellyfish around the shores—beached jellyfish can still sting. In the woods, check for ticks after every hike and after each shower. Biting nasties include black flies, horseflies, sand fleas, and the ever-present mosquitoes. Yellow jacket nests populate tree hollows along many trails; signs throughout the Hoh Rain Forest warn hikers to move quickly through these sections. If one or two chase you, remain calm and keep walking; these are just "guards" making sure you're keeping away from the hive. Poison oak is common, so familiarize yourself with its appearance. Bug repellent, sunscreen, and long pants and sleeves will go a long way toward making your experience more comfortable.

and easy access from the highway, this is a popular spot. Keen-eyed beachcombers may spot sea otters just offshore. ✉ *Hwy. 101, Kalaloch ✛ 43 miles southwest of Forks* ☎ *360/565–3130 visitor center, 360/962–2283* ⊕ *www. nps.gov/olym/planyourvisit/visiting-kalaloch-and-ruby-beach.htm.*

Lake Crescent
BODY OF WATER | Visitors see Lake Crescent as Highway 101 winds along its southern shore, giving way to gorgeous views of teal waters rippling in a basin formed by Tuscan-like hills. In the evening, low bands of clouds caught between the surrounding mountains often linger over its reflective surface. ✉ *Hwy. 101, Olympic National Park ✛ 16 miles west of Port Angeles and 28 miles northeast of Forks* ☎ *360/565–3130 visitor center* ⊕ *www.nps.gov/olym/planyourvisit/visiting-lake-crescent.htm.*

Lake Ozette
BEACH | The third-largest glacial impoundment in Washington anchors the coastal strip of Olympic National Park at its north

end. The small town of Ozette, home to a coastal tribe, is the trailhead for two of the park's better one-day hikes. Both three-mile trails lead over boardwalks through swampy wetland and coastal old-growth forest to the ocean shore and uncrowded beaches. ⊠ *Ozette ⚓ At end of Hoko-Ozette Rd., 26 miles southwest of Hwy. 112 near Sekiu* ☎ *360/565–3130* ⊕ *www.nps.gov/olym/planyourvisit/visiting-ozette.htm.*

Lake Quinault

FOREST | This glimmering lake, 4½ miles long and 300 feet deep, is the first landmark you'll reach when driving the westside loop of U.S. 101. The rain forest is thickest here, with moss-draped maples and alders, and towering spruce, fir, and hemlock. Enchanted Valley, high up near the Quinault River's source, is a deeply glaciated valley that's closer to the Hood Canal than to the Pacific Ocean. A scenic loop drive circles the lake and travels around a section of the Quinault River. ⊠ *Hwy. 101, Olympic National Park ⚓ 38 miles north of Hoquiam* ☎ *360/565–3131 Quinault Rain Forest ranger station* ⊕ *www.nps.gov/olym/planyourvisit/visiting-quinault.htm.*

La Push

BEACH | At the mouth of Quileute River, La Push is the tribal center of the Quileute people. In fact, the town's name is a variation on the French *la bouche*, which means "the mouth." Offshore rock spires known as sea stacks dot the coast here, and you may catch a glimpse of bald eagles nesting in the nearby cliffs. ⊠ *Rte. 110, La Push ⚓ 14 miles west of Forks* ⊕ *www.nps.gov/olym/planyourvisit/upload/mora.pdf.*

Second and Third Beaches

BEACH | During low tide these flat, driftwood-strewn expanses are perfect for long afternoon strolls. Second Beach, accessed via an easy forest trail through Quileute lands, opens to a vista of the Pacific Ocean and sea stacks. Third Beach offers a 1¼-mile forest hike for a warm-up before reaching the sands. ⊠ *Hwy. 101, Olympic National Park ⚓ 14 miles west of Forks* ☎ *360/565–3130* ⊕ *www.nps.gov/olym.*

Sol Duc Valley

NATURE SIGHT | Sol Duc Valley is one of those magical places where all the Northwest's virtues seem at hand: lush lowland forests, sparkling river scenes, salmon runs, and serene hiking trails. Here, the popular Sol Duc Hot Springs area includes three attractive sulfuric pools ranging in temperature from 98°F to 104°F. ⊠ *Sol Duc Rd., Olympic National Park ⚓ South of U.S. 101, 12 miles past west end of Lake Crescent* ☎ *360/565–3130* ⊕ *www.nps.gov/olym/planyourvisit/visiting-the-sol-duc-valley.htm* ⛱ *Sulfuric pools $18.*

Staircase

TRAIL | Unlike the forests of the park's south and west sides, Douglas fir is the dominant tree on the east slope of the Olympic Mountains. Fire has played an important role in creating the majestic forest here, as the Staircase Ranger Station explains in interpretive exhibits. ⊠ *Olympic National Park ⚓ At end of Rte. 119, 15 miles from U.S. 101 at Hoodsport* ☎ *360/565–3130* ⊕ *www.nps.gov/olym/planyourvisit/visiting-staircase.htm.*

Hotels

★ Kalaloch Lodge

$$$$ | **HOTEL** | **FAMILY** | Overlooking the Pacific, Kalaloch has cozy lodge rooms with sea views and separate cabins along the bluff. **Pros:** ranger tours; clam digging; supreme storm-watching in winter. **Cons:** no Wi-Fi and most units don't have TVs; some rooms are two blocks from main lodge; limited cell phone service. $ *Rooms from: $319* ⊠ *157151 U.S. 101, Kalaloch* ☎ *360/962–2271, 866/662–9928* ⊕ *www.thekalalochlodge.com* ⤴ *64 rooms* ⫱ *No Meals.*

Best Campgrounds in Olympic

Note that only a few places take reservations; if you can't book in advance, you'll have to arrive early to get a place. Each site usually has a picnic table and grill or fire pit, and most campgrounds have water, toilets, and garbage containers; for hookups, showers, and laundry facilities, you'll have to head into the towns or stay at a privately owned campground. Firewood is available from camp concessions, but if there's no store you can collect dead wood within a mile of your campsite. Dogs are allowed in campgrounds, but not on most trails or in the backcountry. Trailers should be 21 feet long or less (15 feet or less at Queets Campground), though a few campgrounds can accommodate up to 35 feet. There's a camping limit of two weeks. Nightly rates run $15–$22 per site.

If you have a backcountry pass, you can camp virtually anywhere throughout the park's forests and shores. Overnight wilderness permits are $8 per person per night and are available at visitor centers and ranger stations. Note that when you camp in the backcountry, you must choose a site at least a half mile inside the park boundary.

Fairholme Campground. One of just three lakeside campgrounds in the park, Fairholme is near the Lake Crescent Resort. ⊠ *U.S. 101, 28 miles west of Port Angeles, on west end of Lake Crescent, Olympic National Park.*

Kalaloch Campground. Kalaloch is the biggest and most popular Olympic campground, and it's open all year. Its vantage of the Pacific is unmatched on the park's coastal stretch. ⊠ *U.S. 101, ½ mile north of Kalaloch Information Station, Olympic National*

Park ☎ *877/444–6777* or ⊕ *www.recreation.gov* for reservations.

Lake Quinault Rain Forest Resort Village Campground. Stretching along the south shore of Lake Quinault, this RV campground has many recreation facilities, including beaches, canoes, ball fields, and horseshoe pits. The 31 RV sites, which rent for $36 per night, are open year-round, but bathrooms are closed in winter. ⊠ *3½ miles east of U.S. 101, South Shore Rd., Lake Quinault* ☎ *360/288–2535, 800/255–6936* ⊕ *www.rainforestresort.com.*

Mora Campground. Along the Quillayute estuary, this campground doubles as a popular staging point for hikes northward along the coast's wilderness stretch. ⊠ *Rte. 110, 13 miles west of Forks.*

Ozette Campground. Hikers heading to Cape Alava, a scenic promontory that is the westernmost point in the lower 48 states, use this lakeshore campground as a jumping-off point. ⊠ *Hoko-Ozette Rd., 26 miles south of Hwy. 112.*

Sol Duc Campground. Sol Duc resembles virtually all Olympic campgrounds save one distinguishing feature—the famed hot springs are a short walk away. ⊠ *Sol Duc Rd., 11 miles south of U.S. 101* ☎ *877/444–6777* or ⊕ *www.recreation.gov* for reservations.

Staircase Campground. In deep woods away from the river, this campground is a popular jumping-off point for hikes into the Skokomish River Valley and the Olympic high country. ⊠ *Rte. 119, 16 miles northwest of U.S. 101.*

Lake Crescent Lodge

$$$ | HOTEL | Deep in the forest at the foot of Mt. Storm King, this 1916 lodge has a variety of comfortable accommodations, from basic rooms with shared baths to spacious two-bedroom fireplace cottages. **Pros:** gorgeous setting; free wireless access in the lobby; lots of opportunities for off-the-grid fun outdoors. **Cons:** no laundry, a few rooms with shared baths; Roosevelt Cottages often are booked a year in advance for summer stays; crowded with nonguest visitors. $ *Rooms from: $230* ⊠ *416 Lake Crescent Rd., Olympic National Park* ☎ *360/928–3211, 888/896–3818* ⊕ *www. olympicnationalparks.com/lodging/ lake-crescent-lodge* ⊗ *Closed Jan.–Apr., except Roosevelt fireplace cabins open weekends* ⤵ 52 rooms ⦿ *No Meals.*

Lake Quinault Lodge

$$$$ | HOTEL | On a lovely glacial lake in Olympic National Forest, this beautiful early-20th-century lodge complex is within walking distance of the lakeshore and hiking trails in the spectacular old-growth forest. **Pros:** boat tours of the lake are interesting; family-friendly ambience; year-round pool and sauna. **Cons:** no TV in some rooms; some units are noisy and not very private; Wi-Fi is expensive after first 30 minutes free. $ *Rooms from: $325* ⊠ *345 S. Shore Rd., Quinault* ☎ *360/288–2900, 888/896–3818* ⊕ *www. olympicnationalparks.com/lodging/lake-quinault-lodge* ⤵ 92 rooms ⦿ *No Meals.*

Log Cabin Resort

$$$ | HOTEL | FAMILY | This rustic resort has an idyllic setting at the northeast end of Lake Crescent with lodging choices that include A-frame chalet units, standard cabins, small camper cabins, motel units, and RV sites with full hookups. **Pros:** boat rentals available on-site; convenient general store; pets allowed in some cabins. **Cons:** cabins are extremely rustic; no plumbing in the camper cabins; no TVs. $ *Rooms from: $186* ⊠ *3183 E. Beach Rd., Port Angeles* ☎ *888/896–3818,*

360/928–3325 ⊕ *www.olympicnational-parks.com* ⊗ *Closed Oct.–late May* ⤵ 24 rooms ⦿ *No Meals.*

Sol Duc Hot Springs Resort

$$$ | HOTEL | Deep in the brooding forest along the Sol Duc River and surrounded by 5,000-foot-tall mountains, the main draw of this remote 1910 resort is the pool area, with soothing mineral baths and a freshwater swimming pool. **Pros:** nearby trails; peaceful setting; some units are pet-friendly. **Cons:** units are dated and very basic; no air-conditioning, TV, or Wi-Fi; pools get crowded. $ *Rooms from: $244* ⊠ *12076 Sol Duc Hot Springs Rd., Olympic National Park* ☎ *888/896–3818, 360/327–3583* ⊕ *www. olympicnationalparks.com/lodging/sol-duc-hot-springs-resort* ⊗ *Closed Oct.–late May* ⤵ 33 rooms ⦿ *No Meals.*

🍴 Restaurants

Creekside Restaurant

$$$ | AMERICAN | A tranquil country setting and ocean views at Kalaloch Lodge's restaurant create the perfect backdrop for savoring Pacific Northwest dinner specialties like grilled salmon, fresh shellfish, and elk burgers. Tempting seasonal desserts include local fruit tarts and cobblers in summer and organic winter-squash bread pudding in winter; flourless chocolate torte is enjoyed year-round. **Known for:** locally sourced food; Washington wines; stunning setting. $ *Average main: $30* ⊠ *157151 Hwy. 101, Kalaloch* ☎ *866/662–9928, 360/962–2271* ⊕ *www.thekalalochlodge. com/dine-and-shop/creekside-restaurant* ⤳ *No cash accepted.*

Lake Crescent Lodge

$$$ | AMERICAN | Part of the original 1916 lodge, the fir-paneled dining room overlooks the lake; you won't find a better spot for sunset views. Dinner entrées include wild salmon, brown butter–basted halibut, grilled steak, and roasted chicken breast; the lunch menu features elk cheeseburgers, inventive salads, and a variety of sandwiches. **Known for:** award-winning Pacific Northwest wine list; house-made lavender lemonade; lovely setting. [$] *Average main: $29* ✉ *416 Lake Crescent Rd., Port Angeles* ☎ *360/928–3211* 🌐 *www.olympicnationalparks.com/lodging/dining/lake-crescent-lodge* 🕒 *Closed Jan.–Apr.*

The Springs Restaurant

$$$ | **AMERICAN** | The main Sol Duc Hot Springs Resort restaurant is a rustic, fir-and-cedar-paneled dining room surrounded by trees. In summer big breakfasts are turned out daily—hikers can fill up on biscuits and sage-pork-sausage gravy, bananas foster French toast, and omelets before hitting the trails; for lighter fare, there's steel cut oatmeal and yogurt and granola parfaits. **Known for:** classic comfort foods; three breakfast mimosa choices; boxed lunches. [$] *Average main: $26* ✉ *Sol Duc Hot Springs Resort, 12076 Sol Duc Rd., at U.S. 101, Port Angeles* ☎ *360/327–3583* 🌐 *www.olympicnationalparks.com/dining/sol-duc-hot-springs-resort* 🕒 *Closed Nov.–late Mar.*

Activities

BICYCLING

Sound Bike & Kayak

BIKING | This sports outfitter rents and sells bikes, and sells kayaks, climbing gear, and related equipment. They offer several guided mountain climbs, day hikes, and custom trips, and a climbing wall to practice skills. ✉ *120 E. Front St.* ☎ *360/457–1240* 🌐 *www.soundbikeskayaks.com.*

Elwha eBike Adventures

BIKING | This Port Angeles-based outfitters, part of a family-owned campground and RV park, rents a variety of Pedego Electric Bikes, some of which can accommodate child passengers. They offer pre-scheduled bike drop-offs and pick-ups at trailheads (from $50) and you can also book premium guided tours around Port Angeles, the Olympic Hot Springs, or Lake Crescent. E-bike rentals start at two hours for $65. ✉ *47 Lower Dam Rd., Port Angeles* ☎ *360/457–9024* 🌐 *www.elwhaebikeadventures.com.*

CLIMBING

At 7,980 feet, Mt. Olympus is the highest peak in the park and the most popular climb in the region. To attempt the summit, climbers must register at the Glacier Meadows Ranger Station. Mt. Constance, the third-highest Olympic peak at 7,743 feet, has a well-traversed climbing route that requires technical experience; reservations are recommended for the Lake Constance stop, which is limited to 20 campers. Mt. Deception is another possibility, though tricky snows have caused fatalities and injuries in the last decade.

Climbing season runs from late June through September. Note that crevasse skills and self-rescue experience are highly recommended. Climbers must register with park officials and purchase wilderness permits before setting out. The best resource for climbing advice is the Wilderness Information Center in Port Angeles.

TOURS AND OUTFITTERS

Mountain Madness

MOUNTAIN CLIMBING | Adventure through the rain forest to the glaciated summit of Mt. Olympus on a five-day trip, offered several times per year by Mountain Madness. ☎ *800/328–5925, 206/937–8389* 🌐 *www.mountainmadness.com* 🎟 *From $1,390 for 5-day climb.*

FISHING

There are numerous fishing possibilities throughout the park. Lake Crescent is home to cutthroat and rainbow trout, as well as petite kokanee salmon; lakes Cushman, Quinault, and Ozette have trout, salmon, and steelhead. As for rivers, the Bogachiel and Queets have steelhead salmon in season. The glacier-fed Hoh River is home to Chinook

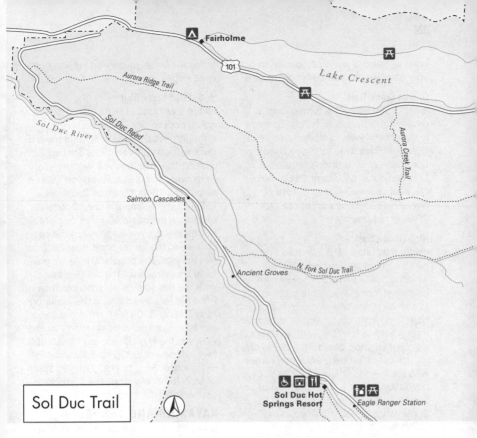

Sol Duc Trail

salmon April to November, and coho salmon from August through November; the Sol Duc River offers all five species of salmon. The Elwha River has been undergoing restoration since two dams were removed; strong salmon and steelhead runs have returned, although a fishing moratorium has been in place for several years. Other places to go after salmon and trout include the Dosewallips, Duckabush, Quillayute, Quinault, Salmon, and Skokomish rivers. A Washington state punch card is required during salmon-spawning months; fishing regulations vary throughout the park, and some areas are for catch and release only. Punch cards are available from sporting-goods and outdoor-supply stores.

Piscatorial Pursuits

FISHING | This company, based in Forks, offers salmon and steelhead fishing trips around the Olympic Peninsula from October through mid-May. ☎ 866/347–4232 ⊕ www.piscatorialpursuits.com ✉ From $225 (rate per person for parties of 2 or more).

HIKING

Know your tides, or you might be trapped by high water. Pick up tide tables at a visitor center or ranger stations. Remember: wilderness permits are required for overnight backcountry visits.

Cape Alava Trail

HIKING & WALKING | Beginning at Ozette, this three-mile boardwalk trail leads from the forest to wave-tossed headlands. *Moderate.* ⊹ *Trailhead: End of Hoko-Ozette Rd., 26 miles south of Hwy. 112,* west of Sekiu ⊕ www.nps.gov/olym/plan-yourvisit/lake-ozette-area-brochure.htm.

Graves Creek Trail

HIKING & WALKING | This 6-mile-long moderately strenuous trail climbs from lowland rain forest to alpine territory at Sundown Pass. Due to spring floods, a fjord halfway up is often impassable in May and June. *Moderate.* ⊠ *Olympic National Park* ✛ *Trailhead: End of S. Shore Rd., 23 miles east of U.S. 101* ⊕ *www.nps.gov/olym.*

High Divide Trail

HIKING & WALKING | A 9-mile hike in the park's high country defines this trail, which includes some strenuous climbing on its last four miles before topping out at a small alpine lake. A return loop along High Divide wends its way an extra mile through alpine territory, with sensational views of Olympic peaks. This trail is only for dedicated, properly equipped hikers who are in good shape. *Difficult.* ⊠ *Olympic National Park* ✛ *Trailhead: End of Sol Duc River Rd., 13 miles south of U.S. 101* ⊕ *www.nps.gov/olym/planyourvisit/high-divide-loop.htm.*

★ Hoh River Trail

HIKING & WALKING | **FAMILY** | From the Hoh Visitor Center, this rain-forest jaunt takes you into the Hoh Valley, wending its way for 17½ miles alongside the river, through moss-draped maple and alder trees and past open meadows where elk roam in winter. *Easy.* ⊠ *Olympic National Park* ✛ *Trailhead: Hoh Visitor Center, 18 miles east of U.S. 101* ⊕ *www.nps.gov/olym/planyourvisit/hoh-river-trail.htm.*

Hurricane Ridge Meadow Trail

HIKING & WALKING | A quarter-mile alpine loop, most of it wheelchair accessible, leads through wildflower meadows overlooking numerous vistas of the interior Olympic peaks to the south and a panorama of the Strait of Juan de Fuca to the north. *Easy.* ⊠ *Olympic National Park* ✛ *Trailhead: Hurricane Ridge Rd., 17 miles south of Port Angeles* ⊕ *www.*

nps.gov/olym/planyourvisit/visiting-hurri-cane-ridge.htm.

★ Sol Duc River Trail

HIKING & WALKING | **FAMILY** | The 1½-mile gravel path off Sol Duc Road winds through thick Douglas fir forests toward the thundering, three-chute Sol Duc Falls. Just off the road, below a wooden platform over the Sol Duc River, you'll come across the 70-foot Salmon Cascades. In late summer and autumn, thousands of salmon negotiate 50 miles or more of treacherous waters to reach the cascades and the tamer pools near Sol Duc Hot Springs. The popular 6-mile Lovers Lane Loop Trail links the Sol Duc falls with the hot springs. You can continue up from the falls five miles to the Appleton Pass Trail, at 3,100 feet. From there you can hike on to the 8½-mile mark, where views at the High Divide are from 5,050 feet. *Moderate.* ⊠ *Olympic National Park* ✛ *Trailhead: Sol Duc Rd., 12 miles south of U.S. 101* ⊕ *www.nps.gov/olym/planyourvisit/sol-duc-river-trail.htm.*

KAYAKING AND CANOEING

Lake Crescent, a serene expanse of teal-color waters surrounded by deep-green pine forests, is one of the park's best boating areas. Note that the west end is for swimming only; no speedboats are allowed here.

Lake Quinault has boating access from a gravel ramp on the north shore. From U.S. 101, take a right on North Shore Road, another right on Hemlock Way, and a left on Lakeview Drive. There are plank ramps at Falls Creek and Willoughby campgrounds on South Shore Drive, just past the Quinault Ranger Station.

Lake Ozette, with just one access road, is a good place for overnight trips. Only experienced canoe and kayak handlers should travel far from the put-in, since fierce storms occasionally strike—even in summer.

Fairholme General Store

CANOEING & ROWING | Kayaks and canoes on Lake Crescent are available to rent from $20 per hour to $60 for eight hours. The store is at the lake's west end, 27 miles west of Port Angeles. ✉ *221121 U.S. 101, Olympic National Park* ☏ *360/928–3020* ⊕ *www.olympicnationalparks.com* ⊙ *Closed after Labor Day until Memorial Day weekend.*

Lake Crescent Lodge

CANOEING & ROWING | You can rent kayaks, canoes, and paddleboards here for $45 for four hours. ✉ *416 Lake Crescent Rd., Olympic National Park* ☏ *360/928–3211* ⊕ *www.olympicnationalparks.com* ⊙ *Closed Oct.-May.*

Log Cabin Resort

CANOEING & ROWING | This resort, 17 miles west of Port Angeles, offers full-day rentals of kayaks ($23 per day) and canoes ($29 per day). The dock provides easy access to Lake Crescent's northeast section. ✉ *3183 E. Beach Rd.* ☏ *360/928–3325* ⊕ *www.olympicnationalparks.com* ⊙ *Closed Oct.–mid-May.*

PICNIC AREAS

All Olympic National Park campgrounds have adjacent picnic areas with tables, some shelters, and restrooms, but no cooking facilities. The same is true for major visitor centers, such as Hoh Rain Forest. Drinking water is available at ranger stations, interpretive centers, and inside campgrounds.

East Beach Picnic Area

CAMPGROUND | Set on a grassy meadow overlooking Lake Crescent, this popular swimming spot has six picnic tables and vault toilets. ✉ *E. Beach Rd.* ✛ *At far east end of Lake Crescent, off Hwy. 101, 17 miles west of Port Angeles.*

La Poel Picnic Area

CAMPGROUND | Tall firs lean over a tiny gravel beach at this small picnic area, which has several picnic tables and a splendid view of Pyramid Mountain across Lake Crescent. It's closed

October to April. ✉ *Olympic National Park* ✛ *Off Hwy. 101, 22 miles west of Port Angeles.*

North Shore Picnic Area

CAMPGROUND | This site lies beneath Pyramid Mountain along the north shore of Lake Crescent; a steep trail leads from the eight-table picnic ground to the mountaintop. ✛ *3 miles east of Fairholm.*

Rialto Beach Picnic Area

CAMPGROUND | Relatively secluded at the end of the road from Forks, this is one of the premier day-use areas in the park's Pacific coast segment. This site has 12 picnic tables, fire grills, and vault toilets. ✉ *Rte. 110* ✛ *14 miles west of Forks.*

RAFTING

Olympic has excellent rafting rivers, with Class II to Class V rapids. The Elwha River is a popular place to paddle, with some exciting turns. The Hoh is better for those who like a smooth, easy float.

Hoh River Rafters

RAFTING | Wilderness enthusiast and fishing/rafting guide Pat Neal and his staff take guests on rafting tours of the Hoh River, passing through the temperate rain forest filled with towering trees and wildlife on easy Class II rapids. ✉ *4883 Upper Hoh Rd., Forks* ☏ *360/683–9867* ⊕ *www.hohriverrafters.com* ⊠ *$85 for three-hour tour.*

WINTER SPORTS

Hurricane Ridge Visitor Center

SNOW SPORTS | Rent snowshoes and ski equipment here December through March. There's also a small restaurant, an interpretive center, and restrooms. ✉ *Hurricane Ridge Rd.* ☏ *360/565–3131 road condition information* ⊕ *www.nps.gov/olym/planyourvisit/hurricane-ridge-in-winter.htm* ⊙ *Closed Mon.–Thurs.*

Hurricane Ridge Ski and Snowboard Area

SKIING & SNOWBOARDING | The cross-country trails here begin at the lodge and have great views of Mt. Olympus. A small

Did You Know?

Encompassing more than
70 miles of beachfront,
Olympic is one of the
few national parks of
the West with an ocean
beach (Redwood, Channel
Islands, and some of
the Alaskan parks are
the others). The park is
therefore home to many
marine animals, includ-
ing sea otters, whales, sea
lions, and seals.

downhill ski and snowboarding area is open weekends and holidays; lift tickets are $17–$40. There's also a tubing/sledding hill. Admission to the park is $30 per vehicle. Call ahead for road conditions before taking the three-hour drive from Seattle. ⊠ *Olympic National Park, 17 miles south of Port Angeles, Seattle* ☎ *360/565–3100, 360/565–3131 for road reports* ⊕ *www.hurricaneridge.com.*

Nearby Olympic National Park

Although most Olympic Peninsula towns have evolved from their exclusive reliance on timber, Forks, outside the national park's northwest tip, remains one of the region's logging capitals. Washington state's wettest town (100 inches or more of rain a year), it's a small, friendly place with just over 3,800 residents and a modicum of visitor facilities. South of Forks and Lake Quinault, Washington's newest beach community, Seabrook, near the tiny village of Pacific Beach, is 25 miles from the southwest corner of the national park via the Moclips Highway. Created as a planned community mainly for vacationers, it's convenient for visiting both the park and the state's ocean beaches to the south. Port Angeles, a city of around 20,000, focuses on its status as the main gateway to Olympic National Park and Victoria, British Columbia. Set below the Strait of Juan de Fuca and looking north to Vancouver Island, it's an enviably scenic settlement filled with attractive, Craftsman-style homes.

The Pacific Northwest has its very own "Banana Belt" in the waterfront community of Sequim, 17 miles east of Port Angeles along U.S. 101. The town of 7,500 is in the rain shadow of the Olympics and receives only 16 inches of rain per year (compared with the 140 to 170 inches that drench the Hoh Rain Forest just 40 miles away). The Victorian-era town of ⸱⸱

Port Towsend, in the northeast corner of the Olympic Peninsula, has around 9,700 residents. It's a popular destination for day trips, romantic getaways to the many historic B&Bs, families exploring the old military forts and aquatic learning centers, and anyone looking for an interesting detour before or after a trip to the national park.

Sights

★ Dungeness Spit

NAUTICAL SIGHT | FAMILY | Curving nearly six miles into the Strait of Juan de Fuca, the longest natural sand spit in the United States is a wild, beautiful section of shoreline. More than 30,000 migratory waterfowl stop here each spring and fall, but you'll see plenty of birdlife any time of year. The entire spit is part of the Dungeness National Wildlife Refuge (⊕ *www.fws.gov/refuge/dungeness*). You can access it from the trail that begins in the 216-acre Dungeness Recreation Area, which serves as a portal to the shoreline. At the end of the spit is the towering white 1857 New Dungeness Lighthouse (⊕ *www.newdungenesslighthouse.com*). Tours, including a 74-step climb to the top, are available, though access is limited to those who can hike 5½ miles or paddle about 3½ miles out to the end of the spit—the closest launch is from Cline Spit County Park. You can also enroll to serve a one-week stint as a lighthouse keeper. If you'd prefer not to make the long trek all the way out to the lighthouse, an endeavor you should only attempt at low tide to avoid having to climb over massive driftwood logs, you can still take in plenty of beautiful scenery and spot myriad wildlife by hiking just a mile or so out along the spit and back. ⊠ *554 Voice of America Rd. W* ☎ *360/683–5847* ⊕ *www.clallam.net/Parks/Dungeness.html.*

Feiro Marine Life Center

AQUARIUM | FAMILY | Beside a small beach, this modest but nicely designed sea-life center has a perfect location right along the Port Angeles waterfront near the ferry terminal. Murals of historic Port Angeles scenes decorate the outside; inside are plenty of touch tanks where kids can say hello to sea creatures. ✉ *Port Angeles City Pier, 315 N. Lincoln St., Port Angeles* ☎ *360/417–6254* ⊕ *www. feiromarinelifecenter.org* ⛵ *$6.*

Jamestown S'Klallam Tribe

INDIGENOUS SIGHT | This village on the beach near the mouth of the Dungeness River has been occupied by the James-town S'Klallam tribe for thousands of years. The tribe, whose name means "strong people," was driven to the Skokomish Reservation on Hood Canal after the signing of the Treaty of Point No Point in 1855. However, in 1874, tribal leader James Balch and some 130 S'Klallam collectively purchased 210 acres where the community is today, and S'Klallam members have lived here ever since. An excellent gallery, Northwest Native Expressions, sells tribal artwork, including baskets, jewelry, textiles, and totems. Less than a mile away on U.S. 101, the tribe operates 7 Cedars Casino along with a market and deli. The tribe opened a 100-room hotel adjacent to the casino in late 2020. ✉ *Old Blyn Hwy. at U.S. 101* ⊕ *www.jamestowntribe.org.*

Olympic Discovery Trail

TRAIL | Eventually, 140 miles of nonmotorized trail will lead from Port Townsend west to the Pacific Coast. As of this writing, 80 miles of the paved trail are complete and available for use by hikers, bikers, equestrians, and disabled users. The trail has been conceived as the northern portion of a route that will eventually encircle the entire Olympic Peninsula. ⊕ *www.olympicdiscoverytrail. org.*

Port Angeles Fine Arts Center

ART MUSEUM | With modern, funky, and intriguing exhibits by new and emerging artists, this small, beautifully designed modern museum is inside the former

home of the late artist and publisher Esther Barrows Webster, one of Port Angeles's most energetic and cultured citizens. Outside, Webster's Woods Sculpture Park—open daily dawn to dusk—is dotted with oversize art installations set against a backdrop of the city and harbor. ✉ *1203 E. Lauridsen Blvd., Port Angeles* ☎ *360/457–3532* ⊕ *www.pafac.org* ☾ *Closed Mon.–Wed. in Oct.–Mar.*

Seiku to Neah Bay

SCENIC DRIVE | Few travelers make it out to the far northwestern tip of the continental United States, but the drive is well worth the time. From Seiku, Highway 112 meanders west along the coastline in roller-coaster dips, rises, and curves, which make the two-lane route seem all too narrow. Right-side passengers have the best views heading toward Neah Bay, as the road hugs the rocky coastline and its frothing, salty bays; the forest is thick and towering on the other side. The drive is best made in the late afternoon, when summer sunlight brings out the colors of the water and trees, or when winter clouds show just how foreboding this edge of the country can be.

Sequim Bay State Park

BEACH | Protected by a sand spit four miles southeast of Sequim on Sequim Bay, this 92-acre woodsy inlet park has picnic tables, campsites, hiking trails, tennis courts, and a boat ramp. ✉ *269035 U.S. 101* ☎ *360/683–4235* ⊕ *www.parks. state.wa.us/582/Sequim-Bay* ⛵ *Parking $10.*

Timber Museum

OTHER MUSEUM | This museum highlights Forks's logging history since the 1870s; a garden and fire tower are also on the grounds. ✉ *1421 S. Forks Ave., Forks* ☎ *360/374–9663* ⊕ *www.forkstimbermuseum.org* ⛵ *$3.*

🍴 Restaurants

★ Alder Wood Bistro

$$$ | **PACIFIC NORTHWEST** | Look to this easygoing, art-filled restaurant for inventive, locally sourced, and mostly organic dishes, including pizzas from the wood-fired oven with creative toppings like pesto, truffled goat cheese, and pickled onions. The menu's sustainably harvested seafood selections highlight whatever is in season and also get the wood-fire treatment. **Known for:** alfresco dining in a garden courtyard; local craft beer and cider; crème brûlée with local lavender. [$] *Average main: $25* ✉ *139 W Alder St., Sequim* ☎ *360/683–4321* 🌐 *www.alderwoodbistro.com* 🕑 *Closed Sun.–Tues.*

Dockside Grill

$$$ | **SEAFOOD** | With memorable views of John Wayne Marina and Sequim Bay, this is a fun place to watch boats placidly sail by while nibbling on Dungeness crab fritters, steamed clams, bouillabaisse, cioppino, and seafood pastas. The kitchen also serves an excellent cedar-plank rib-eye steak, coffee-rubbed and served with jalapeño-garlic butter. **Known for:** outdoor deck overlooking the water; oyster po'boys and crab melt sandwiches at lunch; espresso brownie à la mode. [$] *Average main: $29* ✉ *2577 W. Sequim Bay Rd., Sequim* ☎ *360/683–7510* 🌐 *www.docksidegrill-sequim.com* 🕑 *Closed Mon.–Tues.*

★ Fountain Café

$$ | **MEDITERRANEAN** | Local artwork lines the walls of this cozy, eclectic bistro tucked inside a historic clapboard building a block off the main drag, near the foot of the Taylor Street staircase. The delicious seafood- and pasta-intensive menu reveals Mediterranean and Pacific Northwest influences—think cioppino with local shellfish in a tomato-saffron broth, and roasted walnut and gorgonzola penne with wild boar. **Known for:** friendly, unpretentious service; fresh-baked baguette with herbed butter; warm gingerbread with vanilla custard. [$] *Average main: $22* ✉ *920 Washington St., Port Townsend* ☎ *360/385–1364* 🌐 *www.fountaincafept.com.*

Oak Table Cafe

$ | **AMERICAN** | Carefully crafted breakfasts and lunches are the focus of this well-run, family-friendly eatery, a Sequim institution since 1981. Breakfast is served throughout the day, and on Sunday morning the large, well-lit dining room is especially bustling. **Known for:** Eggs Nicole with veggies and hollandaise sauce on a croissant; huge soufflé-style apple-cinnamon pancakes; char-broiled burgers at lunch. [$] *Average main: $15* ✉ *292 W. Bell St., Sequim* ☎ *360/683–2179* 🌐 *www.oaktablecafe.com* 🕑 *No dinner.*

Toga's Soup House Deli & Gourmet

$ | **ECLECTIC** | Toga's serves an eclectic menu of casual fare, ranging from housemade soups and fresh salads to hearty sandwiches. The many windows provide views of the Olympic Mountains, and there's also an open-air patio. **Known for:** pork schnitzel sandwich; variety of soups, chili, and chowders; decadent desserts. [$] *Average main: $15* ✉ *122 W. Lauridsen Blvd., Port Angeles* ☎ *360/452–1952* 🌐 *www.togassouphouse.com* 🕑 *Closed weekends.*

🛏 Hotels

★ Colette's Bed & Breakfast

$$$$ | **B&B/INN** | This contemporary oceanfront mansion set on a 10-acre sanctuary of gorgeous gardens offers a level of service and luxury that's unmatched in the area, with water-view suites that have fireplaces, patios, and two-person spa tubs, and multicourse breakfasts featuring organic fresh local produce, decadent baked goods, and house specialties like Dungeness crab hash, smoked salmon frittata, and dill crepes. **Pros:** sweeping water views; highly professional staff; lush gardens and grounds. **Cons:** not suitable for kids; 15-minute drive from

town; a bit pricy for the area. $ *Rooms from: $525* ⊠ *339 Finn Hall Rd., Port Angeles* ☎ *360/457–9197, 888/457–9777* ⊕ *www.colettes.com* ⇗ *5 suites* ‖○‖ *Free Breakfast.*

Domaine Madeleine

$$$$ | **B&B/INN** | Perched on a bluff above the Strait of Juan de Fuca, these opulent suites and cottages have updated contemporary decor, colorful murals, fireplaces, and water, mountain, and garden views. **Pros:** gorgeous gardens and water views; abundant wildlife viewing; large private decks or patios. **Cons:** no children under 10; breakfast costs extra; 15-minute drive from downtown. $ *Rooms from: $520* ⊠ *146 Wildflower La., Port Angeles* ☎ *360/457–4174* ⊕ *www.domainemadeleine.com* ⇗ *6 suites* ‖○‖ *No Meals.*

Fort Worden State Park Conference Center

$$$$ | **HOUSE** | **FAMILY** | The 330-acre Fort Worden, built as a late-19th-century gun emplacement to guard the mouth of Puget Sound, gained a new purpose when enterprising souls turned the spacious Victorian homes on Officers Row into some of the more memorable lodgings on the Olympic Peninsula. **Pros:** myriad activities; acres of waterfront for play; historic ambience. **Cons:** books up fast for summer dates; no TV or air-conditioning in the houses; only some rentals are pet-friendly. $ *Rooms from: $311* ⊠ *200 Battery Way, Port Townsend* ⊹ *1 mile north of Port Townsend* ☎ *360/344–4400* ⊕ *www.fortworden.org* ⇗ *38 rental homes* ‖○‖ *No Meals.*

★ Miller Tree Inn Bed and Breakfast

$$ | **B&B/INN** | With country antiques, fluffy quilts, and big windows overlooking peaceful pastures, this 1916 farmhouse on the east side of downtown Forks is nicknamed the "Cullen House" for its resemblance to the description in Stephenie Meyer's Twilight books. **Pros:** some rooms have whirlpool tubs and gas fireplaces; nearby rivers offer prime salmon and steelhead fishing; children are welcome in some rooms. **Cons:** lots of Twilight-related tchotchkes; some rooms require climbing stairs; pricey in summer. $ *Rooms from: $190* ⊠ *654 E. Division St.* ☎ *360/374–6806, 800/943–6563* ⊕ *www.millertreeinn.com* ⇗ *8 rooms* ‖○‖ *Free Breakfast.*

🏃 Activities

GOLF

Gold Mountain Golf Complex

GOLF | Most people make the trek to Bremerton to play the Olympic Course, a beautiful and challenging par 72 that is widely considered the best public course in Washington. The older, less-sculpted Cascade Course is also popular, and better suited to beginners. There are four putting greens, a driving range, and a striking clubhouse with views of the Belfair Valley. Rates vary but start as low as $23 for midweek, off-season tee times booked online. You can drive all the way to Bremerton via Interstate 5, or you can take the car ferry to Bremerton from Pier 52. The trip will take roughly 1½ hours no matter which way you do it, but the ferry ride might be a more pleasant way to spend a large part of the journey. Note, however, that the earliest departure time for the ferry is 6 am, so this option won't work for very early tee times. ⊠ *7263 W. Belfair Valley Rd., Bremerton* ☎ *360/415–5433* ⊕ *www.goldmt.com.*

Index

Photo Credits

Front Cover: PhotoBliss / Alamy Stock Photo [**Description:** Gas Works Park in Seattle, Washington state, USA]. **Back cover, from left to right:** Neelsky/shutterstock. Jerryway/Dreamstime. Osaka.Perkins/Shutterstock. **Spine:** Fotoguy22/iStockphoto. **Interior, from left to right:** David7/Shutterstock (1). NatChittamai/iStockphoto (2-3). Marina Poushkina/Shutterstock (5). **Chapter 1: Experience Seattle:** UlrichBeinert/iStockphoto (6-7). Trong Nguyen/Shutterstock (8-9). Eakkarat Rangram/Shutterstock (9). Burke Museum/Visit Seattle (9). Seattle Children's Museum/Visit Seattle (10). Happycreator/Shutterstock (10). Mike Reid/Sky View Observatory (10). Checubus/Shutterstock (10). Juntinglin/Dreamstime (11). DeymosHR/Shutterstock (11). ScottWalmsley/Shutterstock (12). Splank/Dreamstime (12). Deborah Bernard/The Seattle Public Library (12). Zack Frank/Shutterstock (12). Alabastro Photography/Visit Seattle (13). Checubus/Shutterstock (14). Cdrin/Shutterstock (14). July7th/iStockphoto (14). Ryan Hawk/Visit Seattle (14). Oksana.perkins/Shutterstock (15). Elena_Suvorova/Shutterstock (15). Gary Ives (Gnives50)/Dreamstime (18). Laith Higazin/Shutterstock (18). David7/Shutterstock (18). Mint Images Limited/Alamy Stock Photo (19). Tory Kallman/Shutterstock (19). TomSparks/Flickr (20). Andrew Mwangi/West Cafe Bar (21). Brent Hofacker/Shutterstock (22). Svlvsl/Dreamstime (23). Denise Lett/Shutterstock (24). Ian Dewar Photography/Shutterstock (24). Cpaulfell/Shutterstock (24). Curtis Cronn/Flickr (24). Jon Bilous/Shutterstock (25). **Chapter 3: Downtown and Belltown:** Uladzik Kryhin/ Shutterstock (53). Andriy Blokhin/Shutterstock (59). Gexydaf/Flickr (61). Jordan Petram/Flickr (72). Mark B. Bauschke/Shutterstock (74-75). Charles Amundson/Shutterstock (74). The Tasting Room (76). piroshky bakery (76). Courtesy of Beecheris Handmade Cheese (76). Public Domain (77). Photo courtesy of Nick Jurich of flashpd.com (77). eng1ne/Flickr (77). Liem Bahneman/Shutterstock (78). Pike Place Market PDA (78). World Pictures/Phot / agefotostock (78). Rootology/wikipedia.org (79). Stephen Power / Alamy (79). Mariusz S. Jurgielewicz/ Shutterstock (82). **Chapter 4: South Lake Union and Queen Anne:** Seattle Parks and Recreation (89). Alex Cimbal/Shutterstock (92). Darryl Brooks/Shutterstock (98). Emerald Umbrella Studio/Dreamstime (100). Andrei Medvedev/Shutterstock (103). **Chapter 5: Pioneer Square:** Deymos/Dreamstime (107). Courtesy of Foster/White Gallery (111). MPH Photos/Shutterstock (113). Greg Vaughn (116) Kevin Cruff (119) Public Domain (119) Charles Finkel (119) Victrola Coffee/Kent Colony (120) Victrola Coffee/Kent Colony (120) Victrola Coffee/Kent Colony (120) Victrola Coffee/Kent Colony (120) Victrola Coffee/Kent Colony (120) LWY/Flickr (121) mtcarlson/Flickr (121) Victrola Coffee/Kent Colony (121) Elysian Brewing Company (122) Laurence Vincent/Flickr (122) Patrick Wright Photography (123) Flickr/Travis (123) Charles Finkel (123) Chateau Ste. Michelle (124) Greg Vaughn (124) Chateau Ste. Michelle (125) Kevin Cruff (125). **Chapter 6: The Chinatown–International District:** F11photo/ Dreamstime (127). David Tonelson/Shutterstock (130). Nomadic Lana/Flickr (135). **Chapter 7: First Hill and the Central District:** VDB Photos/Shutterstock (137). A.Davey/Flickr (140). Seattle Parks/Flickr (147). **Chapter 8: Capitol Hill and Madison Park:** Bon Koo/Dreamstime (149). Paul Gordon/Alamy Stock Photo (152). Ctj71081/Flickr (162). Graham Cornall/ Shutterstock (168). **Chapter 9: Fremont, Phinney Ridge, and Greenwood:** Chamomile Alyia/Shutterstock (171). David Tonelson/Shutterstock (174). Kirsten Ann Robertson/ Shutterstock (182). **Chapter 10: Ballard:** David6135/Dreamstime (187). Bon9/Shutterstock (190). cpaulfell/Shutterstock (195). Katie Barnes Photography/Shutterstock (196). Marina Poushkina/Shutterstock (197). oksana.perkins/Shutterstock (197). vewfinder/Shutterstock (198-199). Public Domain (198). vladdon/Shutterstock (199). Public Domain (200). Public Domain (200). Public Domain (200). Public Domain (200). Danita Delimont/Shutterstock (201). oksana.perkins/Shutterstock (201). Chad Davis (201). CL Shebley/Shutterstock (207). **Chapter 11: Wallingford and Green Lake:** Steve Estvanik/Shutterstock (211). Srd. Sirada/Shutterstock (219). **Chapter 12: University District:** cpaulfell/Shutterstock (221). Andrew Waits/Burke Museum (224) Kristi Dosh/Shutterstock (231). **Chapter 13: West Seattle:** SeastockiStockphoto (233). Tammy Wolfe/iStockphoto (236). Sean O'Neill/Flickr (238). **Chapter 14: The Eastside:** Jkasher/Shutterstock (245). Joyfuldesigns/Dreamstime (248). Courtesy of Chateau Ste. Michelle (253). Courtesy of Marymoor Park Concerts (255). **Chapter 15: Side Trips from Seattle:** YinYang/iStockphoto (257). Tusharkoley/Dreamstime (260). Bpperry/Dreamstime (261). Bjulien03/Dreamstime (261). LegalAdmin/Flickr (266). Tim Ventura/Shutterstock (269). Zack Frank/Shutterstock (272). Jdanne/Dreamstime (281). YinYang/iStockphoto (306-307). Antony spencer/iStockphoto (320-321). **About Our Writers:** All photos are courtesy of the writers except for the following: Naomi Tomky Courtesy of Claire van der Lee.

*Every effort has been made to trace the copyright holders, and we apologize in advance for any accidental errors. We would be happy to apply the corrections in the following edition of this publication.

Fodor's SEATTLE

Publisher: Stephen Horowitz, *General Manager*

Editorial: Douglas Stallings, *Editorial Director;* Jill Fergus, Amanda Sadlowski, *Senior Editors;* Brian Eschrich, Alexis Kelly, *Editors;* Angelique Kennedy-Chavannes, *Assistant Editor*

Design: Tina Malaney, *Director of Design and Production;* Jessica Gonzalez, *Senior Designer;* Erin Caceres, *Graphic Design Associate*

Production: Jennifer DePrima, *Editorial Production Manager;* Elyse Rozelle, *Senior Production Editor;* Monica White, *Production Editor*

Maps: Rebecca Baer, *Senior Map Editor;* Mark Stroud (Moon Street Cartography) and David Lindroth, *Cartographers*

Photography: Viviane Teles, *Senior Photo Editor;* Namrata Aggarwal, Neha Gupta, Payal Gupta, Ashok Kumar, *Photo Editors;* Eddie Aldrete, *Photo Production Intern;* Kadeem McPherson, *Photo Production Associate Intern*

Business and Operations: Chuck Hoover, *Chief Marketing Officer;* Robert Ames, *Group General Manager*

Public Relations and Marketing: Joe Ewaskiw, *Senior Director of Communications and Public Relations*

Fodors.com: Jeremy Tarr, *Editorial Director;* Rachael Levitt, *Managing Editor*

Technology: Jon Atkinson, *Director of Technology;* Rudresh Teotia, *Associate Director of Technology;* Alison Lieu, *Project Manager*

Writers: AnnaMaria Stephens, Naomi Tomky

Editor: Brian Eschrich

Production Editor: Monica White

8th Edition

ISBN 978-1-64097-571-2

ISSN 1531-3417

SPECIAL SALES

This book is available at special discounts for bulk purchases for sales promotions or premiums. For more information, e-mail SpecialMarkets@fodors.com.

PRINTED IN CANADA

10 9 8 7 6 5 4 3 2 1

About Our Writers

 AnnaMaria Stephens is a Seattle-based freelance writer who covers travel, design, food, and more. She's a fan of everything her city has to offer, from the coffee and culture to the countless views of mountains and water. She also firmly believes that Seattle's spectacular summers are worth a few months of drizzle.

 Seattle-based writer **Naomi Tomky** explores the world with a hungry eye, digging into the intersection of food, culture, and travel for publications such as *Saveur*, the *New York Times*, and *Travel + Leisure*. She is an Association of Food Journalists and Lowell Thomas award-winner, and her cookbook, *The Pacific Northwest Seafood Cookbook*, was declared one of 2019's best by the *San Francisco Chronicle*. Follow her culinary travels and hunger-inducing ramblings on Twitter @Gastrognome and Instagram @the_gastrognome.